New Perspectives on Information Systems Modeling and Design

António Miguel Rosado da Cruz
Polytechnic Institute of Viana do Castelo, Portugal

Maria Estrela Ferreira da Cruz
Polytechnic Institute of Viana do Castelo, Portugal

A volume in the Advances in Computer and
Electrical Engineering (ACEE) Book Series

Published in the United States of America by
    IGI Global
    Engineering Science Reference (an imprint of IGI Global)
    701 E. Chocolate Avenue
    Hershey PA, USA 17033
    Tel: 717-533-8845
    Fax: 717-533-8661
    E-mail: cust@igi-global.com
    Web site: http://www.igi-global.com

                    Library of Congress Cataloging-in-Publication Data

Names: Cruz, Antonio Miguel Rosado da, 1970- editor. | Cruz, Maria Estrela
    Ferreira da, 1969- editor.
Title: New perspectives on information systems modeling and design / Antonio
    Miguel Rosado da Cruz and Maria Estrela Ferreira da Cruz, editors.
Description: Hershey, PA : Engineering Science Reference, an imprint of IGI
    Global, [2019] | Includes bibliographical references and index.
Identifiers: LCCN 2018022051| ISBN 9781522572718 (hardcover) | ISBN
    9781522572725 (ebook)
Subjects: LCSH: Database design. | Information storage and retrieval
    systems--Business.
Classification: LCC QA76.9.D26 N484 2019 | DDC 005.74/3--dc23 LC record available at https://lccn.loc.gov/2018022051

This book is published in the IGI Global book series Advances in Computer and Electrical Engineering (ACEE) (ISSN: 2327-039X; eISSN: 2327-0403)

British Cataloguing in Publication Data
A Cataloguing in Publication record for this book is available from the British Library.

The views expressed in this book are those of the authors, but not necessarily of the publisher.

For electronic access to this publication, please contact: eresources@igi-global.com.

Advances in Computer and Electrical Engineering (ACEE) Book Series

Srikanta Patnaik
SOA University, India

ISSN:2327-039X
EISSN:2327-0403

MISSION

The fields of computer engineering and electrical engineering encompass a broad range of interdisciplinary topics allowing for expansive research developments across multiple fields. Research in these areas continues to develop and become increasingly important as computer and electrical systems have become an integral part of everyday life.

The **Advances in Computer and Electrical Engineering (ACEE) Book Series** aims to publish research on diverse topics pertaining to computer engineering and electrical engineering. **ACEE** encourages scholarly discourse on the latest applications, tools, and methodologies being implemented in the field for the design and development of computer and electrical systems.

COVERAGE

- Sensor Technologies
- Algorithms
- Chip Design
- Computer Hardware
- Microprocessor Design
- VLSI Design
- Computer science
- Electrical Power Conversion
- Qualitative Methods
- Digital Electronics

IGI Global is currently accepting manuscripts for publication within this series. To submit a proposal for a volume in this series, please contact our Acquisition Editors at Acquisitions@igi-global.com or visit: http://www.igi-global.com/publish/.

Titles in this Series

For a list of additional titles in this series, please visit: www.igi-global.com/book-series

Exploring Critical Approaches of Evolutionary Computation
Muhammad Sarfraz (Kuwait University, Kuwait)
Engineering Science Reference • copyright 2019 • 390pp • H/C (ISBN: 9781522558323) • US $215.00 (our price)

Applications of Security, Mobile, Analytic, and Cloud (SMAC) Technologies for Effective Information Processing and Management
P. Karthikeyan (Thiagarajar College of Engineering, India) and M. Thangavel (Thiagarajar College of Engineering, India)
Engineering Science Reference • copyright 2018 • 300pp • H/C (ISBN: 9781522540441) • US $215.00 (our price)

Smart Grid Analytics for Sustainability and Urbanization
Zbigniew H. Gontar (SGH Warsaw School of Economics, Poland)
Engineering Science Reference • copyright 2018 • 306pp • H/C (ISBN: 9781522539964) • US $215.00 (our price)

Vehicular Cloud Computing for Traffic Management and Systems
Jyoti Grover (Manipal University Jaipur, India) P. Vinod (SCMS School of Engineering and Technology, India) and Chhagan Lal (Manipal University Jaipur, India)
Engineering Science Reference • copyright 2018 • 281pp • H/C (ISBN: 9781522539810) • US $235.00 (our price)

Multidisciplinary Approaches to Service-Oriented Engineering
Mehdi Khosrow-Pour, D.B.A. (Information Resources Management Association, USA)
Engineering Science Reference • copyright 2018 • 389pp • H/C (ISBN: 9781522559511) • US $245.00 (our price)

Cyber-Physical Systems for Next-Generation Networks
Joel J. P. C. Rodrigues (National Institute of Telecommunications (Inatel), Brazil & Instituto de Telecomunicações, Portugal & University of Fortaleza (UNIFOR), Brazil) and Amjad Gawanmeh (Khalifa University, UAE)
Engineering Science Reference • copyright 2018 • 293pp • H/C (ISBN: 9781522555100) • US $210.00 (our price)

Augmented Reality for Enhanced Learning Environments
Gerardo Reyes Ruiz (Universidad Autónoma del Estado de México, Mexico) and Marisol Hernández Hernández (Universidad Autónoma del Estado de México, Mexico)
Information Science Reference • copyright 2018 • 322pp • H/C (ISBN: 9781522552437) • US $195.00 (our price)

701 East Chocolate Avenue, Hershey, PA 17033, USA
Tel: 717-533-8845 x100 • Fax: 717-533-8661
E-Mail: cust@igi-global.com • www.igi-global.com

Table of Contents

Section 2
Social Media in Organizational Transformation

Section 3
Models and Technology Issues in Business Applications

Chapter 12

Detailed Table of Contents

Section 1
Coping With Organizational Change

Organizations are constantly changing to improve their efficiency, to embrace innovative actions, and to improve their profits. This section provides insight on how to cope with and manage that change. The first chapter discusses models as a fundamental aspect of enterprise architecture and presents a catalog of operations to support enterprise architecture model migration through meta-model transformations. The second chapter deals with business process agility and examines the CMMN standard for the design and modeling of human-centric processes. The third chapter discusses practices for managing change in information systems' environments and how information systems' changes affect organizational personnel. And, Chapter 4 presents functional method engineering.

    Nuno Silva, University of Lisbon, Portugal & INOV INESC Inovação, Portugal
    Pedro Sousa, University of Lisbon, Portugal & Link Consulting SA, Portugal
    Miguel Mira da Silva, University of Lisbon, Portugal & INOV INESC Inovação, Portugal

Models are a fundamental aspect of enterprise architecture, as they capture the concepts and relationships that describe the essentials of the different enterprise domains. These models are tightly coupled to an enterprise architecture modeling language that defines the rules for creating and updating such models. In the model-driven engineering field, these languages are formalized as meta-models. Over time, to keep up with the need to capture a more complex reality in their enterprise architecture models, organizations need to enrich the meta-model and, consequently, migrate the existing models. Model migration poses a strenuous modeling effort with the gathering of enterprise data and model redesign, leading to an error-prone and time-consuming task. In this chapter, the authors present a catalog of co-evolution operations for enabling automation of ArchiMate model migration based on a set of meta-model changes.

    Ioannis Routis, Harokopio University of Athens, Greece
    Mara Nikolaidou, Harokopio University of Athens, Greece
    Nancy Alexopoulou, Harokopio University of Athens, Greece

Business process agility remains an intriguing issue for business process management (BPM) when it comes to modeling human-centric processes. Several attempts were made from academia to find alternative approaches, with the reputable adaptive case management to be introduced recently as an alternative to BPM methodology and case management modeling and notation (CMMN) standard, as an alternative language of business process management notation (BPMN), targeting the modeling of human-centric processes characterized by agility. This chapter identifies the nature of human-centric processes, as its main objective is to examine whether using CMMN for the design and modeling of such processes could cover their agility requirements.

    Jeffrey S. Zanzig, Jacksonville State University, USA
    Guillermo A. Francia III, Jacksonville State University, USA
    Xavier P. Francia, Jacksonville State University, USA

Situations such as improvements in business transaction processing and various security issues keep today's information systems in a constant state of change. Serious disruption of company operations can occur when changes are improperly planned and/or carried out. In addition to technological issues, an equally important consideration is in regard to how information system changes will affect organizational personnel. The Institute of Internal Auditors has identified seven steps that can be used to effectively implement change in an information system environment. This along with a discussion of significant issues in managing system patches provides an appropriate background to consider a model for evaluating the maturity of an organization's change management process in an information system environment. The highly respected COBIT guidance from the ISACA is included throughout much of the discussion to provide support for many of the suggested change management practices.

    S. B. Goyal, City University, Malaysia

In situational method engineering (SME), there are two core intentions that method engineers look for: 1) a set method engineering goal that is the kind of method needed and 2) a method allowing him to satisfy this goal. This chapter can capture method engineering's goal using a generic process model (GPM) that guides the method engineering in the definition of his project method engineering goal and in the selection approach that best allows him to achieve it. The authors wish to move to functional method engineering so as to explore the context of method engineering/situational method engineering more fully based on functional and non-functional method situation. The implications of the approach on CAME tool design are considered and illustrated through a running example.

Section 2
Social Media in Organizational Transformation

Social media are changing the way we communicate, shop, entertain, work, and consequently, the way we live. This section looks to the effect of social media in organizations and how social media may be used and integrated in the organizations' business processes. The first chapter points out advantages of adoption of social media by organizations and provides a view of a new context of labor faced within digital transformation of organizations. The second chapter ponders about the participation in online social networks and about the technologies that support and promote these as a fundamental role in organizations.

Enterprise 4.0 is already referred to as the next stage of the evolution of global business and the global economy. This wave is achieved by technology enablers often referred as digital transformation (DT). Social media represent a subset of these technologies which contribute to organizational transformation. However, the adoption of social media does not imply such a transformation; changes in the organization's culture and behavior are also needed. While the technology enablers allow the production, sharing, and management of information and knowledge within the organization they also require the updating of the supporting information systems (IS). Thus, using technologies in organizations requires an exercise in understanding how to demonstrate their usefulness in relation to the creation, access, and sharing of contents and IS improvements in a safe way. To this end, this chapter envisages a new context of labor faced within DT of organizations, largely boosted by the organizational adoption of social media, and which the authors propose to be implemented through the m_CSDIT framework.

Social networking systems can be considered one of the most important social phenomena because they succeeded in involving billions of people all around the world and in attracting users from several social groups, regardless of age, gender, education, or nationality. Social networking systems blur the distinction between the private and working spheres, and users are known to use such systems both at home and at the work place both professionally and with recreational goals. Social networking systems can be equally used to organize a work meeting, a dinner with the colleagues, or a birthday party with friends. In the vast majority of cases, social networking platforms are still used without corporate blessing. However, several traditional information systems, such as CRMs and ERPs, have also been modified in order to include social aspects. This chapter discusses the participation in online social networking activities and, in particular, the technologies that support and promote the participation in online social network.

Section 3
Models and Technology Issues in Business Applications

Organizational information systems support organizations' business processes. This section covers models and technology issues in business supporting applications. The first chapter proposes an approach to enable the robust handling of single process activities on mobile devices based on a mobile process model. The second chapter builds on the idea that business process models already include much of the organization's knowledge or information needed to build the business processes' supporting software systems and proposes two approaches that use that information to derive a set of integrated software models, although it focuses on generating a data model. The SOA and REST application integration approaches are used in this section's third chapter as a starting point for conceiving a new architectural style, structural services, which allows to tune applications' integration between pure service-based and pure resource-based, or an intermediate mix. The fourth chapter provides a comparative review of reference schemes in different modeling languages. The fifth chapter addresses data warehouse support for policy enforcement rule formulation. The last chapter presents a variability management workflow aimed at supporting different developer roles in an ecosystem context. Two kinds of variability are addressed: in-system operation and associated with quality of service.

Chapter 7

Process technology constitutes a crucial component of information systems. In this context, high flexibility is required as business functions must be quickly adaptable to cope with dynamic business changes. As recent developments allow for the use of mobile devices in knowledge-intensive areas, it is often demanded to enhance process-aware information systems with mobile activity support. In general, the technical integration of this activity type with existing process management technology is challenging. For example, protocols governing the communication between mobile devices and process management systems must be adapted. If a mobile context shall be additionally considered, the integration gets even more complex. However, the use of a mobile context offers advantages. For example, the mobile activity execution time may be decreased if mobile activities are only assigned to those users whose location is beneficial. This chapter proposes an approach to enable the robust handling of single process activities on mobile devices based on a mobile process model.

Chapter 8

  Maria Estrela Ferreira da Cruz, Polytechnic Institute of Viana do Castelo, Portugal
  Ricardo J. Machado, Universidade do Minho, Portugal
  Maribel Yasmina Santos, Universidade do Minho, Portugal

The constant change and rising complexity of organizations, mainly due to the transforming nature of their business processes, has driven the increase of interest in business process management by organizations. It is recognized that knowing business processes can help to ensure that the software under development will meet the business needs. Some of software development processes (like unified process) already refer to business process modeling as a first effort in the software development process. A business process model usually is created under the supervision, clarification, approval, and validation of the business stakeholders. Thus, a business process model is a proper representation of the reality (as is or to be), having lots of useful information that can be used in the development of the software system that will support the business. The chapter uses the information existing in business process models to derive software models specially focused in generating a data model.

Chapter 9

  José Carlos Martins Delgado, University of Lisbon, Portugal

The main application integration approaches, the service-oriented architecture (SOA) and representational state transfer (REST) architectural styles, are rather different in their modeling paradigm, forcing application developers to choose between one and the other. In addition, both introduce more application coupling than required, since data schemas need to be common, even if not all instantiations of those schemas are used. This chapter contends that it is possible to improve this scenario by conceiving a new architectural style, structural services, which combines services and resources to reduce the semantic gap with the applications, allowing to tune the application integration between pure service-based and pure resource-based, or an intermediate mix. Unlike REST, resources are not constrained to offer a fixed set of operations, and unlike SOA, services are allowed to have structure. In addition, compliance is used to reduce coupling to the bare minimum required by the actually used application features.

Chapter 10

  Terry Halpin, INTI International University, Malaysia

In natural language, individual things are typically referenced by proper names or definite descriptions. Data modeling languages differ considerably in their support for such linguistic reference schemes. Understanding these differences is important both for modeling reference schemes within such languages and for transforming models from one language to another. This chapter provides a comparative review of reference scheme modeling within the Unified Modeling Language (version 2.5.1), the Barker dialect of entity relationship modeling, Object-Role Modeling (version 2), relational database modeling, the Web Ontology Language (version 2.0), and LogiQL (an extended form of datalog). The authors identify which kinds of reference schemes can be captured within these languages as well as those reference schemes that cannot be captured. The analysis covers simple reference schemes, compound reference schemes, disjunctive reference, and context-dependent reference schemes.

It is believed that a data warehouse is for operational decision making. Recently, a proposal was made to support decision making for formulating policy enforcement rules that enforce policies. These rules are expressed in the WHEN-IF-THEN form. Guidelines are proposed to elicit two types of actions, triggering actions that cause the policy violation and the corresponding correcting actions. The decision-making problem is that of selecting the most appropriate correcting action in the event of a policy violation. This selection requires information. The elicited information is unstructured and is "early." This work is extended by proposing a method to directly convert early information into its multi-dimensional form. For this, an early information mode is proposed. The proposed conversion process is a fully automated one. Further, the tool support is extended to accommodate the conversion process. The authors also apply the method to a health domain.

Complex systems usually have to deal with a huge number of potential situations and contingencies. Therefore, a mechanism is required that enables the expression of variability at design-time so that it can be efficiently resolved at run-time. As composability plays an increasingly relevant role in building systems in an economic way, variability management should also contribute to and be taken into account in terms of composability. This chapter presents a variability management workflow aimed at supporting different developer roles in an ecosystem context. Two kinds of variability are addressed: in system operation and associated with quality of service. The former provides robustness to contingencies, while the latter focuses on the quality of the application (in terms of non-functional properties) under changing situations and limited resources. The concepts introduced in this chapter conform to the structures and principles of the H2020 European Project RobMoSys, which consolidates composability in the robotics domain.

Preface

Models, and their views, play an important role in every level of the enterprise information systems' architecture. Models help top managers define strategy, operational managers outline tactics to reach strategic objectives, and system and software engineers and practitioners to understand organizational needs and design information systems that are aligned with the tactics and strategy defined.

In their efforts to become more efficient, organizations adapt by changing their organizational architecture, their business processes, the way they communicate with stakeholders, and many other aspects. Organizational architecture change shall be planned over time and may be the result of projected architectural future states, programmed to face strategy, or may be driven by IT projects, which may provide viewpoints for road mapping the development of the architecture over time (Buckl et al., 2009). Business processes' change may involve the reorganization of activities or their total or partial automation, either by developing new information systems (Valente & Sampaio, 2012) or by integrating new technologies into existing processes and underlying supporting applications. New technologies, such as cloud computing, mobile devices and social networks also currently play an important role in optimizing organizations' business processes.

Nowadays people perform many of their daily activities online, on their personal or working computers, but also on their smartphones, and so, organizations need to adapt and expose their business processes on the Web, either as services to integrate with business partners' processes, or in social networks to better interact with customers, employees and other stakeholders. This social extension of a business process can be viewed as a process optimization phase, where the organization seeks efficiency by extending the reach of a business process to a broader class of stakeholders (Brambilla et al., 2012).

Today's business supporting information systems are process aware, and are typically software-intensive systems integrating heterogeneous, distributed components, large-scale software applications, legacy systems and COTS. This setting demands rigorous approaches for designing, building and maintaining adaptable and configurable information systems that can easily evolve in order to reach business objectives according to defined strategies and rules (Verjus et al., 2012). Process-aware information systems and the variability of the business processes they support, result in process models with large collections of process variants, known as process families. Process variants in the same process family chase the same business objective. These process variants demand variability management approaches addressing their modeling and configuration, their run- time dynamic configuration as well as the evolution of process variants themselves over time (Ayora et al., 2013; La Rosa et al., 2017).

Model-driven engineering separates systems' specification and design from their implementation in a specific technology platform. This allows sharing a common vision and knowledge among technical and non-technical stakeholders, has proven to increase effectiveness and efficiency in project planning and development, and facilitates systems' engineering and evolution through transformation processes between platform independent systems' specification and different implementations (Silva, 2015).

The main goal of this book on *New Perspectives on Information System Modeling and Design* is to publish enhanced versions of the best articles published in the *International Journal of Information System Modeling and Design* (IJISMD) between 2013 and 2016. Additionally, new articles have been accepted for publication as they contribute for the discussion and analysis of current and emerging methodologies, techniques, and practical solutions and trends related to Information Systems' modeling in a comprehensive way. The overall objectives comprise:

- To discuss the importance and the challenges associated to system modeling and design;
- To analyze the state-of-the-art of existing system modeling and design methods and techniques;
- To propose emerging technological developments and practical solutions for system modeling and design;
- To present case studies of application of system modeling and design methods and techniques.

The target audience of this book are professionals and researchers working in the field of systems' modeling and design and systems' engineering, architecting and development. Moreover, the book provides insights and supports decision makers, practitioners, team members, and students on advances in these fields.

The main topics covered in this book are:

- Alignment of business processes with IT operations
- Business Process Modeling
- Component-oriented system design
- Conceptual Modeling
- Data integrity
- Domain-Specific Languages
- Enterprise interoperability
- Enterprise modeling and integration
- Information systems' architecture
- Information systems' methodologies
- Information systems' security
- Knowledge Representation
- Methods of system analysis and design
- Model-based verification and validation
- Model-driven systems' development
- Object-oriented methods
- Ontologies and semantic web services
- Pragmatic aspects of system design

- Quality of design
- Semantic integrity of business process and data
- Separation of concerns in system design
- Service-oriented modeling
- System requirements engineering
- View integration and evolution

ORGANIZATION OF THE BOOK

The book is organized into 12 chapters. A brief description of each of the chapters follows:

Chapter 1 discusses models as a fundamental aspect of enterprise architecture. At this level, models capture the concepts and relationships that describe the essentials of the different enterprise domains and are tightly coupled to an enterprise architecture modeling language. This language defines the rules for creating and updating such models and may be formalized as a meta-model. Over time, to keep up with the need to capture a more complex reality in their enterprise architecture models, organizations need to enrich the meta-model and, consequently, migrate the existing models. Model migration poses a strenuous modeling effort with the gathering of enterprise data and model re-design, leading to an error-prone and time-consuming task. In this chapter, the authors present a catalog of co-evolution operations for enabling automation of ArchiMate model migration based on a set of meta-model changes.

Chapter 2 considers that Business Process agility remains an intriguing issue for Business Process Management (BPM) when it comes to modeling human-centric processes. Several attempts have been made by the academia to find alternative approaches, with the reputable Adaptive Case Management to be introduced recently as an alternative to BPM methodology and Case Management Model and Notation (CMMN) standard, as an alternative language of Business Process Model and Notation (BPMN), targeting the modeling of human-centric processes characterized by agility. This chapter identifies the nature of human-centric processes, and its main objective is to examine whether using CMMN for the design and modeling of such processes could cover their agility requirements.

Chapter 3 considers that situations such as improvements in business transaction processing and various security issues keep today's information systems in a constant state of change. Serious disruption of company operations can occur when changes are improperly planned and/or carried out. In addition to technological issues, an equally important consideration is in regard to how information systems' changes will affect organizational personnel. The Institute of Internal Auditors has identified seven steps that can be used to effectively implement change in an information system environment. This, along with a discussion of significant issues in managing system patches, provides an appropriate background to consider a model for evaluating the maturity of an organization's change management process in an information system environment. The highly respected COBIT guidance from the ISACA is included throughout much of the discussion to provide support for many of the suggested change management practices.

Chapter 4 ponders on Situational Method Engineering, SME, and considers that there are two core intentions that a method engineer looks for a) set method engineering goal, that is the kind of method needed and b) construct a method allowing him to satisfy this goal. The method presented in this chapter can capture method engineering goal using a Generic Process Model, GPM which guides the method engineer in the definition of his project method engineering goal and in the selection approach which best allow him to achieve it. The authors move to functional method engineering to explore the context of method engineering/ situational method engineering more fully based on functional and non-functional method situation. The implications of the approach on CAME tool design are considered and illustrated through a running example.

Chapter 5 reflects on Enterprise 4.0 as the next stage of the evolution of global business and the global economy. The chapter believes that this is achieved by technology enablers often referred to as digital transformation (DT). Social media represent a subset of these technologies which contribute to organizational transformation. However, the adoption of social media does not imply such a transformation; changes in the organization's culture and behavior are also needed. While the technology enablers allow the production, sharing and management of information and knowledge within the organization, they also require the updating of the supporting Information Systems (IS). Thus, using technologies in organizations requires an exercise in understanding how to demonstrate their usefulness in relation to the creation, access and sharing of contents and IS improvements in a safe way. To this end, this chapter envisages a new context of labor faced within DT of organizations, largely boosted by the organizational adoption of social media, and which is proposed to be implemented through the m_CSDIT framework.

Chapter 6 looks at social networking systems as one of nowadays' most important social phenomena, because they succeeded in involving billions of people all around the world and in attracting users from several social groups, regardless of age, gender, education, or nationality. Social networking systems blur the distinction between the private and working spheres, and users are known to use such systems both at home and on the work place for both professional and recreational goals. Social networking systems can be equally used to organize a work meeting, a dinner with colleagues or a birthday party with friends. In the vast majority of cases, social networking platforms are still used without corporate blessing. However, several traditional information systems, such as CRMs and ERPs, have also been modified in order to include social aspects. This chapter ponders over the participation in online social networking activities and, in particular, about the technologies that support and promote the participation in online social networks.

Chapter 7 reflects on Process technology as a crucial component of information systems. In this context, the chapter addresses the high flexibility requirement for business functions, as these need to be quickly adaptable to cope with dynamic business changes. As recent developments allow for the use of mobile devices in knowledge-intensive areas, it is often demanded to enhance process-aware information systems with mobile activity support. In general, the technical integration of this activity type with existing process management technology is challenging. For example, protocols governing the communication between mobile devices and process management systems must be adapted. If a mobile context shall be additionally considered, the integration gets even more complex. However, the use of a mobile context offers advantages. For example, the mobile activity execution time may be decreased if mobile activities are only assigned to those users whose location is beneficial. This chapter proposes an approach to enable the robust handling of single process activities on mobile devices based on a mobile process model.

Chapter 8 considers that the constant change and rising complexity of organizations, mainly due to the transforming nature of their business processes, has driven the increase of interest in Business Process Management. The chapter defends that knowing business processes can help to ensure that the software under development will meet the business needs, and this is already followed by some software development processes (like Unified Process), which refers to business process modeling as a first effort in the software development process. A business process model is usually created under the supervision, clarification, approval and validation of the business stakeholders. Thus, a business process model is a proper representation of the reality (as is or to be), having lots of useful information that can be used in the development of the software system that will support the business. The chapter proposes two approaches that use the information existing in business process models to derive software models specially focused in generating a data model.

Chapter 9 mulls over the main application integration approaches, namely the Service-Oriented Architecture (SOA) and Representational State Transfer (REST) architectural styles. These are rather different in their modeling paradigm, forcing application developers to choose between one and the other. Additionally, the authors consider that both introduce more application coupling than required, since data schemas need to be common, even if not all instantiations of those schemas are used. This chapter contends that it is possible to improve this scenario by conceiving a new architectural style, Structural Services, which combines services and resources to reduce the semantic gap with the applications, allowing to tune the application integration between pure service-based and pure resource-based, or an intermediate mix. Unlike REST, resources are not constrained to offer a fixed set of operations and, unlike SOA, services are allowed to have structure. Moreover, compliance is used to reduce coupling to the bare minimum required by the actually used application features.

Chapter 10 discusses reference schemes in modeling languages. In natural language, individual things are typically referenced by proper names or definite descriptions. Data modeling languages differ considerably in their support for such linguistic reference schemes. Understanding these differences is important both for modeling reference schemes within such languages and for transforming models from one language to another. This chapter provides a comparative review of reference scheme modeling within the Unified Modeling Language (version 2.5.1), the Barker dialect of Entity Relationship modeling, Object-Role Modeling (version 2), relational database modeling, the Web Ontology Language (version 2.0), and LogiQL (an extended form of datalog). The authors identify which kinds of reference schemes can be captured within these languages as well as those reference schemes that cannot be captured. The analysis covers simple reference schemes, compound reference schemes, disjunctive reference and context-dependent reference schemes.

Chapter 11 addresses data warehouse support for policy enforcement rule formulation. It is believed that a data warehouse is for operational decision-making. Recently, a proposal has been made to support decision making for formulating policy enforcement rules. These rules are expressed in the WHEN-IF-THEN form. The chapter presents guidelines to elicit two types of actions, triggering actions that cause the policy violation, and the corresponding correcting actions. The decision-making problem is that of selecting the most appropriate correcting action in the event of a policy violation. This selection requires information. The elicited information is unstructured and is 'early'. This work is extended by proposing a method to directly convert early information into its multi-dimensional form. For this, an early information mode is proposed. The proposed conversion process is a fully automated one. Further, the tool support is extended to accommodate the conversion process. The authors apply the method to the health domain.

Chapter 12 considers that complex systems usually have to deal with a huge number of potential situations and contingencies. Therefore, a mechanism is required to enable to express variability at design-time so that it can be efficiently resolved at run-time. Besides, as composability plays an increasingly relevant role in building systems, in an economic way, variability management should also contribute to and be taken into account in terms of composability. This chapter presents a variability management workflow aimed at supporting different developer roles in an ecosystem context. Two kinds of variability are addressed: in system operation, and associated with quality of service. The former provides robustness to contingencies, while the latter focuses on the quality of the application (in terms of non-functional properties) under changing situations and limited resources. The concepts introduced in this chapter conform to the structures and principles of the H2020 European Project RobMoSys, which consolidates composability in the robotics domain.

António Miguel Rosado da Cruz
Polytechnic Institute of Viana do Castelo, Portugal

Maria Estrela Ferreira da Cruz
Polytechnic Institute of Viana do Castelo, Portugal

REFERENCES

Ayora, C., Torres, V., Reichert, M., Weber, B., & Pelechano, V. (2013). Towards run-time flexibility for process families: open issues and research challenges. In Business Process Management Workshops (pp. 477-488). Springer. doi:10.1007/978-3-642-36285-9_49

Brambilla, M., Fraternali, P., & Vaca Ruiz, C. K. (2012). Combining social web and BPM for improving enterprise performances: the BPM4People approach to social BPM. In *Proceedings of the 21st international conference companion on World Wide Web*. ACM. 10.1145/2187980.2188014

Buckl, S., Ernst, A. M., Matthes, F., & Schweda, C. M. (2009). Visual Roadmaps for Managed Enterprise Architecture Evolution. *10th ACIS International Conference on Software Engineering, Artificial Intelligences, Networking and Parallel/Distributed Computing*, 352-357. 10.1109/SNPD.2009.99

La Rosa, M., van der Aalst, W.M.P., Dumas, M. & Milani, F.P. (2017). Business Process Variability Modeling: A survey. *ACM Computing Surveys, 50*(1), 2:1-2:45. DOI: doi:10.1145/3041957

Silva, A. R. (2015). Model-driven engineering: A survey supported by the unified conceptual model. *Computer Languages, Systems & Structures, 43*(October), 139–155. doi:10.1016/j.cl.2015.06.001

Valente, P., & Sampaio, P. N. M. (2012). Analysis of Interactive Information Systems Using Goals. In Innovative Information Systems Modelling Techniques. InTechOpen. doi:10.5772/36389

Verjus, H., Cîmpan, S., & Alloui, I. (2012). An Architecture-Centric Approach for Information System Architecture Modeling, Enactement and Evolution. In Innovative Information Systems Modelling Techniques. InTechOpen. DOI: doi:10.5772/36808

Section 1
Coping With Organizational Change

Organizations are constantly changing to improve their efficiency, to embrace innovative actions, and to improve their profits. This section provides insight on how to cope with and manage that change. The first chapter discusses models as a fundamental aspect of enterprise architecture and presents a catalog of operations to support enterprise architecture model migration through meta-model transformations. The second chapter deals with business process agility and examines the CMMN standard for the design and modeling of human-centric processes. The third chapter discusses practices for managing change in information systems' environments and how information systems' changes affect organizational personnel. And, Chapter 4 presents functional method engineering.

Chapter 1

Evolution of ArchiMate and ArchiMate Models:
An Operations Catalogue for Automating the Migration of ArchiMate Models

Nuno Silva
University of Lisbon, Portugal & INOV INESC Inovação, Portugal

Pedro Sousa
University of Lisbon, Portugal & Link Consulting SA, Portugal

Miguel Mira da Silva
University of Lisbon, Portugal & INOV INESC Inovação, Portugal

ABSTRACT

Models are a fundamental aspect of enterprise architecture, as they capture the concepts and relationships that describe the essentials of the different enterprise domains. These models are tightly coupled to an enterprise architecture modeling language that defines the rules for creating and updating such models. In the model-driven engineering field, these languages are formalized as meta-models. Over time, to keep up with the need to capture a more complex reality in their enterprise architecture models, organizations need to enrich the meta-model and, consequently, migrate the existing models. Model migration poses a strenuous modeling effort with the gathering of enterprise data and model redesign, leading to an error-prone and time-consuming task. In this chapter, the authors present a catalog of co-evolution operations for enabling automation of ArchiMate model migration based on a set of meta-model changes.

DOI: 10.4018/978-1-5225-7271-8.ch001

INTRODUCTION

Enterprise Architecture (EA) models are fundamental tools of every EA initiative used to design and disseminate the enterprise's organizational structure, business processes, information systems, and IT infrastructure (M. Lankhorst et al., 2013). In general, a particular domain is analyzed and engineered by means of a domain-specific modeling language, also named meta-model by the model-driven engineering community (Cicchetti, Di Ruscio, Eramo, & Pierantonio, 2008b; Herrmannsdoerfer, Vermolen, & Wachsmuth, 2011; Wachsmuth, 2007). Since the EA meta-model is typically defined at the very first steps of EA initiatives, it is likely to evolve in subsequent stages of EA initiatives. There are several causes for an EA meta-model to evolve. Internal causes, when the needs of expressiveness increase along with the evolution and scope of the EA initiatives, and external causes, when the standards or compliance rules change. Take the example of ArchiMate (The Open Group, 2013). The ArchiMate language has seen significant changes since its conception in 2010 up to its current 3.0.1 version (The Open Group, 2013). New domains, concepts, and relationships were added while others were updated or removed from the language. This holds true to other EA meta-models, either proprietary or open.

The real challenge of evolving an EA meta-model is the co-evolution of the models that might no longer conform to the new version of the meta-model. A model is said to conform to a meta-model when such model is expressed by the concepts encoded in the meta-model (Cicchetti, Di Ruscio, Eramo, & Pierantonio, 2008a). The need to adapt the EA model combined with its inherent complexity puts a strenuous effort in organizations that seek to evolve and maintain their existing EA, leading ultimately to an ineffective EA process within organizations.

Taking into account the numerous changes a meta-model can have, one comes to the conclusion that not all the meta-model changes are problematic. In fact, a significant part of the meta-model evolution is just the addition of new concepts, and therefore have no implications for the existing EA models. Another part, however, is the redefinition of concepts in the meta-model, which typically happens when organizations need to increase the expressiveness of their EA models. In spite of being a limited part of the meta-model changes, these last changes are usually responsible for most of the effort implied in the evolution of the meta-model, because they also force changes to the existing models to conform to the new meta-model (Cicchetti et al., 2008a).

The pertinence of this research is justified, in practice, by the pace in which standards themselves change compared to the most of the organization's ability to implement EA initiatives, thus forcing transformations to the initial models. Therefore, the organizations only choice is to spend more effort in evolving their EA meta-model and update their models accordingly. Moreover, with the increase of manual modeling effort comes the error-proneness of performing the model migration task, due to human error. Consequently, EA model migration poses resistance to the incremental approach of EA practice within organizations. As a result, the research problem can be identified as follows: *The process of manually migrating EA models using stepwise EA meta-model evolution is error-prone and time-consuming.*

This paper presents a catalog composed of nine co-evolution operation specifications as an innovative, purposeful IS artifact for automating the migration task of ArchiMate models when stepwise evolution of the ArchiMate language takes place. The remainder of the paper is presented as follows: first, in "RESEARCH PROBLEM", the authors present the problem of model co-evolution from the model-driven engineering field. Then, an overview on the state-of-the-art is presented in "RELATED WORK". In "RESEARCH PROPOSAL", a description of each co-evolution operation specification is made. Then, a stepwise evolution scenario is given in "DEMONSTRATION", showing the application of the proposed migration rules using the fictitious ArchiSurance case study and the EA tool in which the migration rules were implemented. Finally, the research conclusions and themes for future work are presented in "CONCLUSION".

RESEARCH PROBLEM

In EA context, both meta-models and models are targets of the evolutionary pressure with meta-model changes often occurring due to the iterative nature of the meta-model and model construction process (Florez, Sánchez, Villalobos, & Vega, 2012). Changes to the meta-model have a high probability of impacting all models that conform to it. Co-evolution is required when an element from the meta-model changes and the model no longer conforms to the new meta-model, as Figure 1 illustrates. After performing an evolution Δ of a meta-model MM into MM', the goal is to co-evolve model m that conforms to MM, to m' that conforms to MM', by applying a set of model transformations T that are aligned with evolution Δ (Cicchetti et al., 2008a; Florez et al., 2012).

Co-evolution of models is strictly related to the notion of information preservation from which the possible meta-model changes can be distinguished into additive, subtractive, and refactoring (Wachsmuth, 2007). Therefore, changes that occur on a meta-model may have different effects on the related models.

These changes are classified as follows (Cicchetti et al., 2008a, 2008b):

- **Non-Breaking Changes:** Model conformance to a meta-model is preserved when changes are made to the meta-model;
- **Breaking and Resolvable Changes:** Model conformance to a meta-model is broken when changes are made to the meta-model, however, they can be automatically resolved;

Figure 1. The Co-evolution problem

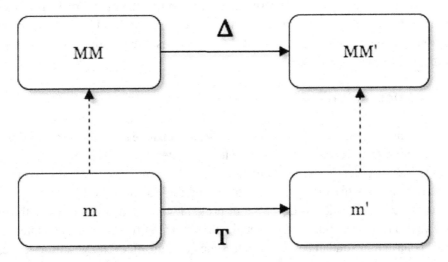

- **Breaking and Unresolvable Changes:** Model conformance to a meta-model is broken when changes are made to the meta-model and cannot be automatically resolved, therefore human intervention is required.

Non-breaking changes consist of additions of new meta-model elements in a meta-model MM, which result in MM' without compromising MM conforming models, which in turn conform to MM'. For example, take the addition of a new element called Facility to meta-model MM depicted in Figure 1. After such a modification to MM, models conforming to MM still conform to MM', thus no co-evolution is necessary.

This does not hold true always since general changes break models, even though automatic resolution can sometimes be performed in case of breaking and resolvable changes. For instance, metamodel MM had an element called Device with two sub-elements: PC and Mainframe. The meta-model change consisted of flattening the element hierarchy, meaning eliminating the Device element and the relation with its sub-elements, i.e., PC and Mainframe. Such a modification breaks the models that conform to MM since according to the new meta-model MM', the Device element can no longer be related. However, adding to each model element that is an instance of PC or Mainframe the shared properties from the Device element can automatically solve such breaking change, thus becoming compliant with MM'.

Regarding the solving of breaking and unresolvable changes, manual intervention is mandatory. This is so because certain changes over the meta-model require the introduction of additional information into the conformant models, the reorganization of the information already present, or even the deletion of some parts that cannot be automatically inferred. Take as an example the addition of a new non-null attribute to a particular element of MM' which was not previously specified in MM. The models cannot co-evolve automatically since the modeler or architect (the person that owns, builds, understands, and uses the models and its information) must take proper decisions regarding this specific change. In this example, either introduce the missing information related to the attribute or otherwise define default values.

RELATED WORK

This section covers existing work on enterprise transformation and on meta-model and model co-evolution. Despite the scarcity of the second topic concerning the EA context, the model-driven engineering community has thoroughly addressed this subject. Furthermore, research has been done with reference to EA evolution from a visual perspective. In the next sub-sections, the authors revisit these publications and highlight the main aspects of each one.

Enterprise Transformation

Enterprise transformation comprises of a set of initiatives that change the organization's domain, i.e., its structure and dynamics, from its current as-is state to a predetermined to-be state (Sousa, Lima, Sampaio, & Pereira, 2009; Tribolet, Sousa, & Caetano, 2014). Keeping EA views up-to-date and aligned with the organizations' goals has brought issues regarding the execution of EA projects (Sousa et al., 2009; Tribolet et al., 2014). To address this, a set of principles were proposed towards the evolution of architecture views (Sousa et al., 2009; Tribolet et al., 2014). One of those principles states that all organizational artifacts have four fundamental invariant states in their lifecycle: gestating, alive, dead, and retired. If one considers ArchiMate, the language makes a distinction between two domains: structure and behavior (The Open Group, 2013). However, there is no reference to time dependencies that allow the models to express the creation, updates, and deletion of EA artifacts. The rationale behind the lifecycle principle presented above brings to the EA domain an important concept neglected in the current EA modeling practice: the concept of time.

Buckl (Buckl, Ernst, Matthes, & Schweda, 2009) presented a viewpoint for road mapping the development of EA over time complementing it with a conceptual model explaining the information demands for such roadmap plans. Both artifacts were drawn from a pattern-based approach for EA management, meaning both can be integrated into a multitude of organization-specific EA management approaches. This approach, however, does not cover how both the EA meta-model and its respective model instances co-evolve throughout the execution of such EA roadmaps.

Buschle (Buschle et al., 2012) identified the challenges of documenting EAs as being a manual, time-consuming and costly task. Hence, he reverse-engineered a vendor-specific Enterprise Service Bus (ESB) to understand the degree of coverage to which the data of a productive system could be used for EA documentation. From there he derived a set of model transformations for automating EA documentation.

Roth (Roth & Matthes, 2014) presented a four-layered conceptual design of an interactive visualization to drill down and analyze model differences in EA meta-models and their respective models. Roth advocated that EA models shared many similarities with software models with respect to complexity, the number of instances, etc. Therefore, one can perceive an EA model as a software model, thus suggesting the possibility of adapting model-driven research in a straightforward manner.

Meta-Model and Model Co-Evolution

In the topic of meta-model and model co-evolution, when approaching model migration, the following requirements must be considered (Mantz, Taentzer, Lamo, & Wolter, 2015):

1. Migrated models must belong to the evolved modeling language;
2. All models of the original modeling language can be migrated to the evolved language.
3. Model migration should be automatically deduced from its meta-model evolution or specified using a high-level language.
4. The specification of model migrations is reusable.
5. General strategies for model co-evolution are formulated independently of a specific meta-modeling approach.

Existing approaches that solve this problem focus on two strategies: identifying the differences between the baseline and the target meta-models and applying a set of transformations on the model in order to be conformant to the new meta-model (Cicchetti et al., 2008b). The first approach uses a declarative evolution specification to define a difference meta-model, which can be calculated from identified changes in the meta-model (Cicchetti et al., 2008b) whereas the second approach specifies meta-model evolution and model co-evolution through a sequence of operations in which each operation is then applied on meta-model and model level (Cicchetti et al., 2008a; Herrmannsdoerfer, Benz, & Juergens, 2009).

This research aims at solving the co-evolution problem in the EA context by giving focus to the second strategy. Hence, the authors aim at compiling into a catalog a set of operations, categorized as breaking and resolvable changes, which can be used in the EA context to automatically modify the existing models, thus achieving meta-model conformance. Other approaches have addressed the co-evolution problem by proposing different frameworks for model transformation.

One approach to model co-evolution classifies the changes in atomic changes and define the process of co-evolution (Cicchetti et al., 2008b). Then, creates a differential meta-model with the identified changes, and it is classified in two new meta-models, the ones that are breaking and resolvable and the ones that are breaking and unresolvable. If there are no relations between the two meta-models, each one is executed independently. If relations between the two meta-models do exist, the co-evolution is done stepwise using user intervention.

COPE is a language used to satisfy two requirements: 1) reuse of recurring migration knowledge and 2) expressiveness to support domain-specific migrations. COPE allows creating coupled transactions that are a combination of meta-model adaptation and model migration (Herrmannsdoerfer et al., 2009). COPE solves the co-evolution problem by executing those coupled transactions and its execution does not require user intervention.

Another approach addressed the co-evolution problem by applying a set of automatic transformations thus solving the problem in one of three categories: addition, delete or rename (Gruschko, Kolovos, & Paige, 2007). When a breaking and unresolvable change is found, the user should specify the way that the elements are going to change by creating a set of transformation rules using ETL.

Mantz (Mantz et al., 2015) proposed a formal approach based on graph transformations to formally model co-evolution of meta-models and models. In his approach, meta-model evolutions and migrations of their instance models are specified by coupled graph transformations. Furthermore, in order to specify model migrations on a high abstraction level and with the possibility of reusing them, Mantz also introduced model migration schemes. These schemes increase the level of automation during a migration step and are derived from given meta-model evolution rules by the identification of model patterns matching meta-model evolution steps. Once a model migration scheme is specified, it can then be applied automatically to instance models yielding well-typed migrated results.

Wachsmuth (Wachsmuth, 2007) proposed a transformational setting for stepwise meta-model adaptation, where each meta-model transformation implements a typical adaptation step performed manually. Then, each transformation is classified according to specific preservation properties. Finally, for each transformation, corresponding instant co-transformations (co-adaptations) of the meta-model instances are provided. At each adaptation step, each model conforms to the actual meta-model version.

In the EA context a platform capable of addressing breaking and unresolvable changes in model co-evolution was proposed that is based on two hypothesis: i) a meta-modeler knowing the rationale behind meta-model changes and capable of providing guidelines for model co-evolution, ii) the modeler being the only one in grade of making the final decisions about his models (Florez et al., 2012). Their proposed languages for meta-modelers allows to specify changes in the meta-models and to propose corresponding changes in the models, which in turn are executed by an engine that automatically solves the changes in models that can be automatically solved.

RESEARCH PROPOSAL

The EA model co-evolution catalog presented in this section is a catalog of operations from the field of model-driven engineering adapted and applied to the EA domain with the purpose of automating the evolution of EA models when changes to the EA modeling language, i.e., the EA meta-model, occurs.

The foundation of each operation is grounded on the specificities of the ArchiMate modeling language. The goal of ArchiMate is to provide an EA meta-model that fully enables integrated, cross-domain, enterprise modeling (M. M. Lankhorst, 2004). For that purpose, ArchiMate serves as a domain-independent ontology for ensuring level coherence and supporting model and cross-model verification, which in turn concerns the evaluation of the conformance of EA models to the rules specified in the respective EA meta-models (Antunes, Bakhshandeh, Mayer, Borbinha, & Caetano, 2013).

As ArchiMate (The Open Group, 2013) states, "a key challenge in the development of a general meta-model for enterprise architecture is to strike a balance between the specificity of languages for individual architecture domains, and a very general set of architecture concepts, which reflects a view of systems as a mere set of inter-related entities". ArchiMate took the effort of minimizing the number of design restrictions so that the language could be used for most EA modeling tasks. As such, ArchiMate modeling the proverbial 80% of practical cases has been limited to the concepts that suffice for (The Open Group, 2013).

ArchiMate Core Concepts

ArchiMate's generic meta-model, illustrated in Figure 2, is built upon three core concepts: active elements (that perform), behavior elements (that describes the behavior of active elements) and passive elements (that hold the information implied in the behavior). Active and Behavior concepts have and hidden (internal) and exposed (external) counterparts.

Definition 1: "An active structure element is defined as an entity that is capable of performing behavior" (The Open Group, 2013).

Figure 2. Generic meta-model: the core concepts of ArchiMate (adapted from (The Open Group, 2013))

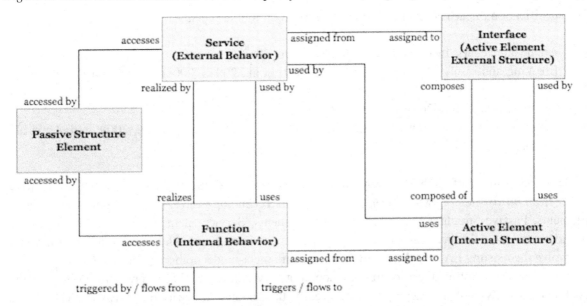

Actors at the business level, Applications at the system level, and Devices at the technological level are examples of active elements. They are assigned to behavioral concepts that define the behavior to be performed.

Definition 2: "A behavior element is defined as a unit of activity performed by one or more active structure elements" (The Open Group, 2013).

Definition 3: "A passive structure element is defined as an object on which behavior is performed" (The Open Group, 2013).

Passive structure elements are usually information or data objects, but they may also be used to represent physical concepts. ArchiMate also distinguishes between external an internal view of systems. When looking at the behavioral aspect, these views reflect the principles of service orientation.

Definition 4: "A service is defined as a unit of functionality that a system exposes to its environment, while hiding internal operations, which provides a certain value (monetary or otherwise)" (The Open Group, 2013).

External users, only perceive the service´s exposed functionality and value, together with non-functional aspects such as the quality of service, costs, etc. Services are accessible through interfaces, which constitute the external view on the active structural aspect.

Definition 5. "An interface is defined as a point of access where one or more services are made available to the environment" (The Open Group, 2013).

An interface provides an external view of the service provider while hiding its internal structure.

Co-Evolution Operations

The specification of each co-evolution operation relies on four aspects:

- ArchiMate generic meta-model (The Open Group, 2013) (Figure 2);
- Breaking and resolvable changes from (Cicchetti et al., 2008a, 2008b; Herrmannsdoerfer et al., 2011);
- Heuristic rules from (De Boer et al., 2005); and
- Lifecycle Principle (gestating, alive, dead, and retired) from (Sousa et al., 2009; Tribolet et al., 2014).

Take the example of ArchiMate version 3.0 that has renamed all the elements in the Technology Layer from *infrastructure <x>* to *technology <x>*. All Technology Layer elements defined as Active Elements, Passive Structure Elements, Function Elements, Service Elements, or Interface Elements would be subject to the breaking and resolvable operation – *rename meta-element* – which in turn would co-evolve the existing EA models accordingly to ensure meta-model conformance.

However, execution of these operations does not solve the co-evolution problem entirely in the context of EA. By applying such operations directly, the semantic integrity of the EA models may be compromised. This is caused by the ripple effect of performing a specific change that may violate the semantics of the relation connecting two or more EA model elements (De Boer et al., 2005). The ripple effect of a meta-model change into the model is the core subject of change´s impact analysis. The goal of such analysis is to take preemptive actions by observing the chain of events that might occur once a change to the model happens before the change really takes place (De Boer et al., 2005). This information can then be used to help in making a decision regarding the application of a change. Therefore, before committing a co-evolution operation, one must verify the model integrity every time a change to the meta-model occurs.

Finally, the four invariant states - *gestating*, *alive*, *dead*, and *retired* - that represent an organizational artifact's lifecycle must also be considered. Hence, it is important to take into consideration not only the structure and behavior of model elements but also the timeline concerning each of those elements expressed by their lifecycle. This time dependency is what enables to express a model element X being created by another model element Y, or an element V deleted by its dependency to W. This approach also synergizes with the heuristic rules presented by (De Boer et al., 2005).

Thus, three aspects must be taken considered to effectively automate model migration when a meta-model change occurs: (i) the type of change, (ii) the semantics of the relation connecting two or more elements, and (iii) the lifecycle state concerning each element.

The type of change is given by the operations identified in (Cicchetti et al., 2008a, 2008b; Herrmannsdoerfer et al., 2011) whereas the relation semantics were compiled into a set of heuristic rules defined in (De Boer et al., 2005) and presented in Table 1. Finally, the invariant states are defined in (Sousa et al., 2009; Tribolet et al., 2014). Taking these factors into consideration, a meta-model change can be applied to existing models if and only if the semantic integrity is preserved after executing the implied operations and if the lifecycle state is coherent with the change. For example, deleting a passive structure element that is accessed by a behavior element implies human intervention to deal with dangling reference left in the behavior element (service or function). Furthermore, the lifecycle state must allow the execution of a specific change, otherwise automation is not possible; in this case the passive structure element should be in the *alive* state. If the result of deleting or modifying a core concept has no impact whatsoever on the related elements and the lifecycle state is consistent with the meta-model change, then the corresponding coevolution operation can be automated and directly applied to the EA model elements. Note that re-factoring co-evolution operations that cause no impact to the structure and semantics of the elements, such as rename meta-element, can also be directly applied to the EA model elements if the lifecycle state of such elements allows.

Table 2 presents the catalog of EA model co-evolution operations (column 2) and the correlation between each operation and its dual model-driven engineering operation. The *Eliminate Class* deletes the class passed on as an argument, which model-wise implies deleting all instances of the specified class. In the EA domain, the behavior of this operation is applied to each ArchiMate core concept (Active Element, Function Element, Passive Structure Element, Service, Interface). The *Flatten Hierarchy* co-evolution consists of deleting the element from which its sub-elements were specialized. For example, flatten-passive-element-hierarchy(el)deletes a specific element and all the specialization relations connecting it to its sub-elements.

The renaming of EA elements – rename-active-structure-element(el, new) – is a direct application of the rename meta-element operation. Such operation is also valid for ArchiMate relations. The extract operation – extract-behavior-element(el1, el2, rel) – involves creating a new element from an existing one and relating both elements by means of one of the relationships presented in Table 1, whereas the

Table 1. Heuristic rules capturing change in EA (De Boer et al., 2005)

Relation X	Concept A <X> Concept B	Relation X	Concept A <X> Concept B
accesses	*Delete(A) -> NOTHING* *Modify(A) -> Modify(B)* *Delete(B) -> Dangle(A)* *Modify(B) -> Modify(A)*	*realizes*	*Delete(A) -> Delete(B)* *Modify(A) -> Modify(B)* *Delete(B) -> NOTHING* *Modify(B) -> Modify(A)*
assignedTo	*Delete(A) -> Dangle(B)* *Modify(A) -> Dangle(B)* *Delete(B) -> NOTHING* *Modify(B) -> Modify(A)*	*triggers*	*Delete(A) -> DANGLE (B)* *Modify(A) -> NOTHING* *Delete(B) -> NOTHING* *Modify(B) -> NOTHING*
usedBy	*Delete(A) -> Dangle(B)* *Modify(A) -> Modify(B)* *Delete(B) -> NOTHING* *Modify(B) -> Modify(A)*	*composedOf*	*Delete(A) -> Delete (B)* *Modify(A) -> Modify (B)* *Delete(B) -> Modify (A)* *Modify(B) -> Modify (A)*

inline operation – inline-behavior-element(el1, el2, rel) – has an opposite behavior, i.e., deleting an element connected to another by one of Table 1 relations.

Merge class merges a number of sibling classes, i.e., classes sharing a common superclass. In the EA domain a prerequisite for merging two or more elements is that every element shares the same meta-type, i.e., every ArchiMate element must be either an Active Element, a Function Element, a Passive Structure Element, a Service, or an Interface. For example, in order to the *Merge Services* operation to be executed, the elements to be merged passed as arguments must be of the Service meta-type, otherwise, the operation returns an error. The *Split class* operation is the safe inverse of merge and splits a class into a number of classes, also passed on as arguments.

Reference to Class makes the reference composite and creates the reference class as its new type. Single-valued references are created in the reference class to target the source and target class of the original reference. In a model, links conforming to the reference are replaced by objects of the reference class, setting source and target reference appropriately. In the EA domain, this relates to *Relation to Active Element, Relation to Function Element, Relation to Passive Structure Element, Relation to Service,* and *Relation to Interface* respectively. *Class to Reference* does the inverse and replaces the class by a reference. In the EA context, this means replacing a particular element for a particular relation.

The authors reduced the meta-property to the relationships between elements since in ArchiMate models consist mainly of elements and relations between elements. *Eliminate Relation* deletes a relation between two elements. *Move Relation* moves a relation from an element e1 to an element e2 – move-relation(el1, el2, rel) – in a straightforward manner without loss of information. Push Relation pushes a relation of a super-element and then clones in all the sub-elements – push-relation(rel, el).

Each of these operations is in turn classified into two types:

- **Heuristic-Dependent:** A heuristic is required as an argument to execute the operation.
- **Heuristic-Independent:** No heuristic is required to execute the operation.

Heuristic-Independent operations[1] are transparent to the modeler, i.e., no decision needs to be computed and passed on as an argument to the operation for it to be executed.

Table 2. Correlation between model-driven operations and EA model co-evolution operations

Model-Driven Engineering Co-Evolution Operations (Cicchetti et al., 2008a, 2008b; Herrmannsdoerfer et al., 2011)	EA Model Co-Evolution Operations Catalog
Eliminate meta-class	Eliminate Active Element Eliminate Function Element Eliminate Passive Structure Element Eliminate Service Eliminate Interface
Flatten Hierarchy	Flatten Active Element Hierarchy Flatten Function Element Hierarchy Flatten Passive Structure Element Hierarchy Flatten Service Hierarchy Flatten Interface Hierarchy
Rename meta-element	Rename Active Element Rename Function Element Rename Passive Structure Element Rename Service Rename Interface Rename Relation
Extract meta-class	Extract Active Element Extract Function Element Extract Passive Structure Element Extract Service Extract Interface
Inline meta-class	Inline Active Element Inline Function Element Inline Passive Structure Element Inline Service Inline Interface
Merge class	Merge Active Elements Merge Function Elements Merge Passive Structure Elements Merge Services Merge Interface
Split class	Split Active Element Split Function Element Split Passive Structure Element Split Service Split Interface
Class to Reference	Active Element to Relation Function Element to Relation Passive Structure Element to Relation Service to Relation Interface to Relation
Reference to Class	Relation to Active Element Relation to Function Element Relation to Passive Structure Element Relation to Service Relation to Interface
Eliminate meta-property	Eliminate Relation
Move meta-property	Move Relation
Push meta-property	Push Relation

As for Heuristic-Dependent operations[2] the modeler needs to provide input *a priori* regarding how the operation should behave. Take for example the *Merge Active Element* operation. If one wants to execute the *Merge Active Element* operation without providing a heuristic rule on how the merge should behave, would render any possible automation impossible of being performed correctly. That would be so because the merging of elements in an ad-hoc manner, even though they share the same meta-type, could potentially render the EA models inconsistent due to behavior issues. Take the example of merging both the Application Component and Actor elements. Despite both being Active Structure Elements, merging both elements would naturally turn every EA model into an incorrect state (since both concepts despite sharing the same meta-type have distinct semantics).

So, if a modeler or architect wanted to merge a System Software and a Device, for instance, he/she could provide as a heuristic: ∀ *System Software & Device: System Software assigned to Device.*

Each operation denotes an algorithm that implements the said operation. For example, to implement the eliminate-function-element operation, the following algorithm is presented.

Algorithm 1: Eliminate-function-element

```
Input: el - an instance of a function element
if el.getLifecycleState() == Dead OR Retired then
    markAsUnresolvable(el)
end
relations = el.getRelations()
for rel IN relations do
    if rel IS Accesses then
        eliminate-meta-class(el)
        CONTINUE
    end
    if rel IS Realizes then
        services = el.getRelatedElementsByRelationType(rel)
        for s IN services do
            if s.getRelatedElementsByRelationType(realizedBy).length = 1 then
                eliminate-service(s)
            else
                CONTINUE
            end
        end
        eliminate-meta-class(el)
        CONTINUE
    end
    if rel IS ComposedOf then
        for c IN el.getRelatedElementsByRelationType(rel) do
            eliminate-function-element(c)
        end
        eliminate-meta-class(el)
        CONTINUE
```

```
      end
    markAsUnresolvable(el)
end
```

First check if the lifecycle state of element *el* is *Gestating* or *Alive* before continuing, otherwise computation must be halted (by calling the markAsUnresolvable function) and human decision required before resuming computation. Afterward, for all the elements' *el* relations, verify the type of relation and heuristic rule (Table 1) that matches the operation's nature, i.e., destructive or refactoring. If no impact whatsoever (NOTHING) then execute the dual co-evolution operation (eliminate-function-element <-> eliminate-meta-class); otherwise if Delete(B) (Table 1), call eliminate-x-element(B) before executing the corresponding co-evolution operation on *el*. If *el* shares other relation types with other elements, computation must be halted (markAsUnresolvable) and human decision required before computation continues.

DEMONSTRATION

Concerning the applicability of the presented co-evolution operations, a migration scenario of the fictitious ArchiSurance case study (Jonkers, Band, & Quartel, 2012) was used, in which a set of operations were executed with respect to specific step-wise meta-model changes. In "Meta-model Evolution Scenario", the changes made to the ArchiSurance meta-model are specified according to precise change requirements. The "Migration scenario" section demonstrates the applicability of the presented co-evolution operations in which a sequence of those were executed regarding the meta-model evolution steps.

Meta-Model Evolution Scenario

The migration scenario depicted in the following section is the outcome of evolving ArchiSurance's meta-model to address the organization's strategic requirements and needs. Figure 3 and Figure 4 illustrate the evolution of the ArchiSurance's meta-model. Figure 3 highlights two elements that will be part of the *TO-BE* architecture: Application Module and Infrastructure Service RelatedClass. The first element is the result of applying a *Rename Active Element* operation to the Application Component element whereas the second results from executing the *Relation to Active Element* operation between the Infrastructure Service and the elements related by the *usedBy* relation.

Figure 4 illustrates four elements that will no longer be part of the *TO-BE* meta-model. Those elements are Business Interaction, Representation, Business Role, and Data Object. These changes are the result of executing four operations: the *Eliminate Passive Structure Element* giving as argument the Representation element, the *Inline Passive Structure Element* with both Business Object and Data Object as arguments, the *Active Element to Relation* passing as argument the Business Role and a heuristic that determines which relation should be considered, and finally the Eliminate Function Element with Business Interaction as argument. After the application of every operation

Each color presented in both Figures relates to the specific lifecycle state of each element. The green color represents the Gestating state, meaning both the Application Module and Infrastructure Service RelatedClass are presented in the meta-model as elements that will become part of ArchiSurance's architecture. The red color represents the Dead lifecycle state of organizational artifacts. In this case,

Figure 3. ArchiSurance meta-model IT-Atlas blueprint (AS-IS)

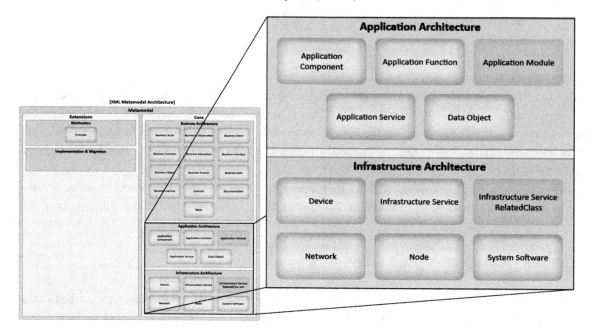

means that the Business Interaction, Business Role, Representation, and Data Object elements will not be part of the future ArchiSurance's architecture.

Migration Scenario

The changes to the ArchiSurance's meta-model triggered the execution of a list of co-evolution operations described in the previous section and presented in Table 3.

The execution of these operations consequently prompted the migration of a number of Passive Structure Elements, Active Elements, Function Elements, Interfaces, Services, and Relations. Table 4 shows the number of transformed elements per meta-types per operation as well as the total number of migrated elements.

Given that meta-model changes commonly occur at secondary stages of EA initiatives, the EA repository often contains tens of thousands of objects, and therefore, the proposed meta-model evolutions imply a significant effort to transform the existing data. ArchiSurance by itself does not provide a complex scenario in terms of number of model elements; however, the point here has to do with the automation and correctness of model transformation, meaning that the same scenario can be applied to more complex EA models with hundreds of elements and relations. If no semantic violation is detected, the automation is complete. Otherwise, human intervention is required to decide between the various possible outcomes, and subsequent execution is automatic. Thus, human intervention is only necessary for decision making and not in actual operation execution. Posterior to the execution of the migration scenario, a total of 12 Passive Structure Elements, 15 Active Elements, 2 Function Elements, 0 Interfaces, 2 Services, and 29 Relations were transformed while maintaining meta-model compliance.

Figure 4. ArchiSurance meta-model IT-Atlas blueprint (Migration Terminus)

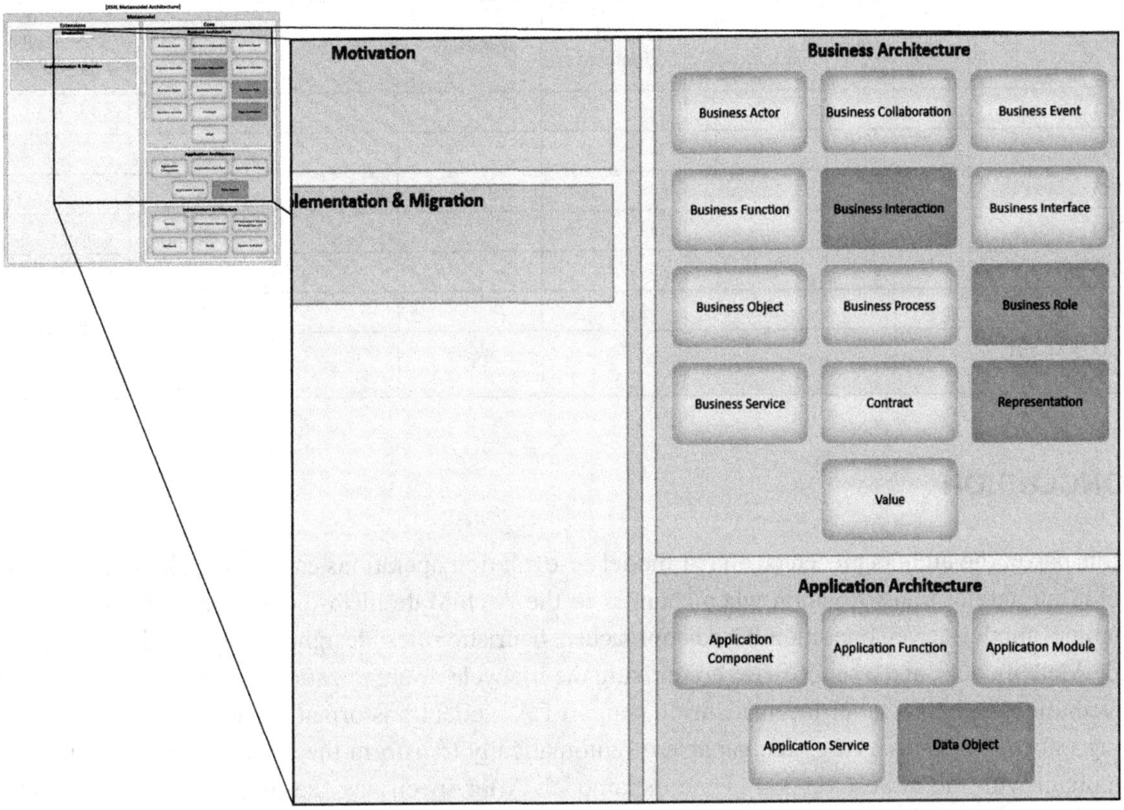

Table 3. ArchiSurance co-evolution operations list

Co-Evolution Operations Applied to the ArchiSurance Case Study
MR1: eliminate-passive-structure-element(Representation)
MR2: rename-active-element(Application Component, Application Module)
MR3: inline-passive-structure-element(Business Object, Data Object, RealizedBy)
MR4: relation-to-active-element(Infrastructure Service, heuristic → ∀ *rel* ∈ Relation : Function Element *uses* Service)
MR5: active-element-to-relation(Business Role, heuristic → ∀ *rel* ∈ Relation : Active Element *assignedTo* Function Element)
MR6: eliminate-function-element(Business Interaction)

FUTURE RESEARCH DIRECTIONS

Future research efforts could encompass an assessment of the remaining ArchiMate relationships (aggregation, flow, specialization) with focus on the completeness of the heuristic rules used in the presented approach. Finally, gathering more data from further applications of the presented EA model co-evolution operations catalog to a wide range of EA initiatives could provide a sounder answer concerning the percentage of representativeness of such operations regarding EA initiatives in general.

Table 4. Number of migrated EA model elements per operation and meta-type

	Passive Structure Element	Active Element	Function Element	Interface	Service	Relation	TOTAL per operation
MR1	7					7	14
MR2		10					10
MR3	5					8	13
MR4					2	2	4
MR5		5				5	10
MR6			2			7	9
TOTAL per meta-type	12	15	2	0	2	29	60

CONCLUSION

In this paper, the authors presented an EA model co-evolution operations catalog (Table 2) to automate ArchiMate model transformation when changes to the ArchiMate meta-model occur. Each operation combines model-driven operation-based approaches, heuristic rules, designed to assure the integrity of ArchiMate models, and a set of states comprising the lifecycle of organizational artifacts. This research contribution enables a set of mechanisms to support EA model transformation, while at the same time being information preserving, i.e., capable of automatically transform the existing models to become compliant with the newest version of the metamodel. After specifying the proposed migration rules, these were implemented in an EA vendor-specific tool to demonstrate its correctness and applicability using the ArchiSurance fictitious organization EA as migration subject.

The systematization of meta-model changes is by itself a relevant contribution since it enables the planning and the definition of common actions by transformation type, that ought to be applied to the EA model data stored in the EA repository. In addition, the automation of co-evolution operations yields practical gains, both in the necessary modeling effort as well as in the avoidance of modeling inconsistencies due to human error.

The authors do not claim however that the presented co-evolution operations cover a wide and known percentage of all possible evolution cases, since no sufficient data has yet been gathered to support such claim. As for the identified limitations, at its current stage: the work of (De Boer et al. 2005) only provides a subset of ArchiMate relationships up to date. Even though the ArchiMate generic meta-model does not express other relationships, the assumption that those relationships ensure completeness of the heuristic rules may be flawed since ArchiMate models use other relationships besides the ones identified in the generic meta-model, hence possibly impacting related elements that are connected by such relationships. Secondly, there is still insufficient data to conclude that the applied changes are representative of most EA initiatives. Hence, the authors cannot at the time of writing give a conclusive answer regarding whether or not the percentage of automated meta-model/model changes is representative of EA initiatives in general.

ACKNOWLEDGMENT

This research was supported by the Link Consulting's project IT-Atlas (n° 11419, under the IAPMEI, 2020 Portuguese PO CI Operational Program).

REFERENCES

Antunes, G., Bakhshandeh, M., Mayer, R., Borbinha, J., & Caetano, A. (2013). Using Ontologies for Enterprise Architecture Analysis. In *2013 17th IEEE International Enterprise Distributed Object Computing Conference Workshops* (pp. 361–368). IEEE. 10.1109/EDOCW.2013.47

Buckl, S., Ernst, A. M., Matthes, F., & Schweda, C. M. (2009). Visual roadmaps for managed enterprise architecture evolution. In *10th ACIS Conference on Software Engineering, Artificial Intelligence, Networking and Parallel/Distributed Computing, SNPD 2009* (pp. 352–357). ACIS. 10.1109/SNPD.2009.99

Buschle, M., Grunow, S., Matthes, F., Ekstedt, M., Hauder, M., & Roth, S. (2012). Automating Enterprise Architecture Documentation using an Enterprise Service Bus. In *Americas Conference on Information Systems (AMCIS 2012)* (pp. 1–14). AMCIS.

Cicchetti, A., Di Ruscio, D., Eramo, R., & Pierantonio, A. (2008a). Automating co-evolution in model-driven engineering. In *Proceedings - 12th IEEE International Enterprise Distributed Object Computing Conference, EDOC 2008* (pp. 222–231). IEEE Computer Society. 10.1109/EDOC.2008.44

Cicchetti, A., Di Ruscio, D., Eramo, R., & Pierantonio, A. (2008b). Meta-model differences for supporting model co-evolution. *Proceedings of the 2nd Workshop on ModelDriven Software Evolution MoDSE'2008.*

De Boer, F. S., Bonsangue, M. M., Groenewegen, L. P. J., Stam, A. W., Stevens, S., & Van Der Torre, L. (2005). Change impact analysis of enterprise architectures. In *Proceedings of the 2005 IEEE International Conference on Information Reuse and Integration, IRI - 2005* (Vol. 2005, pp. 177–181). IEEE. 10.1109/IRI-05.2005.1506470

Florez, H., Sánchez, M., Villalobos, J., & Vega, G. (2012). Coevolution assistance for enterprise architecture models. *Proceedings of the 6th International Workshop on Models and Evolution - ME '12*, 27–32. 10.1145/2523599.2523605

Gruschko, B., Kolovos, D., & Paige, R. (2007). Towards synchronizing models with evolving metamodels. In *Proceedings of the International Workshop on Model-Driven Software Evolution* (p. 3). Academic Press.

Herrmannsdoerfer, M., Benz, S., & Juergens, E. (2009). COPE - automating coupled evolution of metamodels and models. Lecture Notes in Computer Science, 5653, 52–76.

Herrmannsdoerfer, M., Vermolen, S., & Wachsmuth, G. (2011). An extensive catalog of operators for the coupled evolution of metamodels and models. *Software Language Engineering*, 163–182.

Jonkers, H., Band, I., & Quartel, D. (2012). *ArchiSurance Case Study*. The Open Group.

Lankhorst, M., Iacob, M. E., Jonkers, H., Van Der Torre, L., Proper, H. A., & Arbab, F. ... Janssen, W. P. M. (2013). Enterprise architecture at work: Modelling, communication, and analysis (3rd ed.). Springer-Verlag Berlin Heidelberg.

Lankhorst, M. M. (2004). Enterprise architecture modelling - The issue of integration. *Advanced Engineering Informatics*, *18*(4), 205–216. doi:10.1016/j.aei.2005.01.005

Mantz, F., Taentzer, G., Lamo, Y., & Wolter, U. (2015). Co-evolving meta-models and their instance models: A formal approach based on graph transformation. *Science of Computer Programming*, *104*, 2–43. doi:10.1016/j.scico.2015.01.002

Roth, S., & Matthes, F. (2014). Visualizing Differences of Enterprise Architecture Models. *International Workshop on Comparison and Versioning of Software Models (CVSM) at Software Engineering (SE)*.

Sousa, P., Lima, J., Sampaio, A., & Pereira, C. (2009). An approach for creating and managing enterprise blueprints: A case for IT blueprints. *Lecture Notes in Business Information Processing*, *34*, 70–84. doi:10.1007/978-3-642-01915-9_6

The Open Group. (2013). *ArchiMate® 2.1 Specification*. Retrieved from http://pubs.opengroup.org/architecture/archimate2-doc/

Tribolet, J., Sousa, P., & Caetano, A. (2014). The Role of Enterprise Governance and Cartography Enterprise Engineering. *Enterprise Modelling and Information Systems Architectures Journal*, *9*(1), 38–49.

Wachsmuth, G. (2007). Metamodel adaptation and model co-adaptation. In *The European Conference on Object-Oriented Programming* (Vol. *4609*, pp. 600–624). Academic Press.

KEY TERMS AND DEFINITIONS

ArchiMate: A modeling language used in the enterprise architecture domain with a set of default iconography (expressing enterprise entities and relationships) for describing, analyzing, and communicating the stakeholder's concerns regarding enterprise architectures.

Co-Evolution: When two or more entities reciprocally affect each other's evolution. In the present scope, meta-model evolution has repercussions on its conforming models, consequently forcing these to also evolve accordingly.

Enterprise Architecture: A well-defined practice for conducting enterprise analysis, design, planning, and implementation towards a successful development and execution of the enterprise's strategy.

Lifecycle: The set of states in the timeline of an organizational artifact.

Meta-Model: A model that defines the ontology behind a specific domain or system. It provides an explicit description of how a domain-specific model is built.

Model: A representation of a particular domain or system.

Operation: A formalization of a set of steps used to either create, delete, alter, or manipulate model elements.

ENDNOTES

[1]   Eliminate Active Element, Eliminate Function Element, Eliminate Passive Structure Element, Eliminate Service, Eliminate Interface, Flatten Active Element Hierarchy, Flatten Function Element Hierarchy, Flatten Passive Structure Element Hierarchy, Flatten Service Hierarchy, Flatten Interface Hierarchy, Rename Active Element, Rename Function Element, Rename Passive Structure Element, Rename Service, Rename Interface, Split Active Element, Split Function Element, Split Passive Structure Element, Split Service, Split Interface, Eliminate Relation, Move Relation, and Push Relation.

[2]   Merge Active Elements, Merge Function Elements, Merge Passive Structure Elements, Merge Services, Merge Interface, Active Element to Relation, Function Element to Relation, Passive Structure Element to Relation, Service to Relation, Interface to Relation, Relation to Active Element, Relation to Function Element, Relation to Passive Structure Element, Relation to Service, and Relation to Interface.

Chapter 2
Exploring Business Process Agility From the Designer's Perspective:
The Case of CMMN

Ioannis Routis
Harokopio University of Athens, Greece

Mara Nikolaidou
Harokopio University of Athens, Greece

Nancy Alexopoulou
Harokopio University of Athens, Greece

ABSTRACT

Business process agility remains an intriguing issue for business process management (BPM) when it comes to modeling human-centric processes. Several attempts were made from academia to find alternative approaches, with the reputable adaptive case management to be introduced recently as an alternative to BPM methodology and case management modeling and notation (CMMN) standard, as an alternative language of business process management notation (BPMN), targeting the modeling of human-centric processes characterized by agility. This chapter identifies the nature of human-centric processes, as its main objective is to examine whether using CMMN for the design and modeling of such processes could cover their agility requirements.

INTRODUCTION

When considering business processes design, what comes to mind is a predefined set of specific actions that must be accomplished in a predetermined order. Indeed, BPMN had been used seamlessly for the design of action-driven processes. In such processes, a rigid sequence is defined as tasks are being performed according to the order imposed. However, there are processes for which task sequence cannot

DOI: 10.4018/978-1-5225-7271-8.ch002

be prescribed, as which activities are to be performed is strongly based upon human decision influenced by the circumstances as well as unpredicted contingencies. Such processes are characterized by dynamic behavior and intense human involvement and cannot be described by a specific order of actions. (Alexopoulou, et al., 2009) Human-centric processes is an identical example of such processes, making agility a challenging and important factor for them, due to the fact that these processes are not so well defined. Many research attempts refer to this topic, including (Alexopoulou, et al., 2013), where it is indicated that business process design is an equally important phase of the business process lifecycle and that the exploration of agility from the designer's perspective has not been given the attention it deserves.

The objective of this chapter is to explore agility at the designing phase of human-centric processes introducing ACM as a methodology that will ensure agility in human-intensive processes and CMMN as the modeling language that could cover the agility requirements of such a process presented in (Alexopoulou, et al., 2013). For this purpose, a typical human-centric process is used as a case study, the one of Patient Treatment.

This chapter is organized as follows. The background of the notions discussed during this work is presented in the second section. In the third section, a holistic approach towards business process agility is analytically presented. The nature of human-intensive processes is identified in the fourth section. The fifth section presents Adaptive Case Management and its perspective of agility, in comparison to BPM, while the sixth section projects how the CMMN could be used for the agile modeling of human-centric processes. The Future Research Directions and the Conclusion of this chapter are presented in the final two sections, outlining both possible future extensions to the research presented in this work and useful conclusions as far as how the agility of human-centric processes modeled with CMMN could be improved.

BACKGROUND

Business Process Agility

Business process agility (or flexibility) has been a matter of interest for numerous researchers (Milanovic et al., 2011; Van der Aalst et al., 2009; Snowdon et al., 2007; Pesic et al., 2007; Daoudi & Nurcan, 2007; Reijers, 2006; ShuiGuang et al., 2004; Rinderle et al. 2004; Mangan & Sadiq, 2002; Millie & Balasubramanian, 1997). Agility in the context of business processes can be defined as the ability of an organization to effect changes in the process components (activities, roles, resources, information etc.) in a timely manner, usually in response to changes in business environment and stakeholders' needs (Alexopoulou et al., 2008). The intense interest on business process agility stems from the fact that business process automation supported by the utilization of process-aware information systems (Dumas et al., 2005) has increased accuracy and efficiency in process execution on one hand, but it has also rendered business process modification a complex and time-consuming task. This is because well-structured business process models executed by Business Process Management Systems (BPMS) (Dumas et al., 2005) proved to be inflexible to change. Since modern enterprises operate in highly turbulent environments having to cope with a frenetic pace of change (Oosterhout et al., 2006) and continuously sense opportunities for competitive action in their product-market spaces, it is business process agility, which underlies enterprises' success in constantly enhancing and redefining their value creation in highly dynamic environments (Sambamurthy et al., 2003).

In an effort to make business process agility true, researchers propose various methods, techniques or approaches in general, focusing on business process automation. Therefore, although business process design is an equally important phase of the business process lifecycle (Weske, 2007), the exploration of agility in the design phase, associated with the ability of the process designer to easily and effectively describe business process modifications, has not been given adequate attention.

Agile Business Process Modeling

A plethora of business process modeling approaches have been proposed in the literature (Scheer 1999; Muller et al., 2006; Balabko et al., 2004). Most business process modeling approaches are activity-driven (Scheer 1999) and concern well-structured business processes. The reason is that well-structured processes (e.g. manufacturing processes) were the first to be automated as they have well-defined steps. Basically, the objective of activity-driven business process modeling is to identify the activities of a specific functionality context and combine them appropriately in a process graph so that a goal is satisfied. In that sense, the emphasis is laid on how. The activity-driven paradigm is eligible for cases where the actors should be enforced to follow a specific flow of steps.

While activity-driven modeling is characterized by a complete and rigid process logic, in data-driven modeling, process logic is more loosely and partially defined. This is why data-driven modeling is more suitable for cases where the business process graph is extremely complicated and thus cannot be easily depicted. Such complexity may stem, for example, from multiple nested conditions or multiple reverses to the same prior actions causing a chaotic structure. Data-driven approaches (Muller et al., 2006) focus on identifying the data entities managed within a specific functionality context, an i.e. emphasis is given on what, not on the specific process steps followed.

When organizational functionality is modeled, there may be cases that an activity is not initiated due to data modifications or because a sequence in activities has to be followed. Rather it is initiated because something happened that needs to be handled somehow. In such cases, the conditions under which an activity should be initiated can be expressed in a more abstract manner through events. Such conditions may arise from data modifications, human decisions, timing states or anything that could lead to a situation that should be handled, which can even be of an unknown source. Anything that happens signifies an event. An event denotes when (not necessarily in terms of time) an activity should be initiated. Events have been mainly used in ECA model (Dayal et al., 1990). The event-driven paradigm inherently supports the description of processes that are affected by unpredicted contingencies. Since contingencies are unpredicted events, following an event-driven approach would better facilitate the incorporation of the new events in the current model. While not common, there are also role-driven modeling approaches (Balabko et al., 2004). In role-driven approaches, modeling usually focuses on the identification of roles i.e. actor categories, involved in a specific functionality context. In that sense, an emphasis is laid on who. Role-driven approaches focus on specifying interactions between roles. As such, they can be suitable for modeling communication-based processes, e.g. B2B process.

The modifications in business process models can be static or dynamic (Casati et al., 1996). Static changes concern model modifications during the design phase. If there are active instances of the modified model, these instances, depending on the policies and decisions of the company, can be aborted, flushed (i.e. completed following the previous version of the model) or adjusted so that their execution can be continued based on the modified model. The third case corresponds to dynamic modifications. Dynamic modifications include also the case of adjusting a specific instance due to special conditions without altering the respective model (ad hoc changes). Obviously, dynamic changes constitute a greater challenge than static. However, taking into account that organizational functionality is often described through large-scale business processes of high complexity, static changes are not a trivial task and as such, they should be equally emphasized for a spherical approach to business process agility.

Adaptive Case Management

A deeper look in Adaptive Case Management is following, reviewing the basic characteristics for this approach. In order to have a deep understanding of the ACM and its features, it is essential to understand which the characteristics of knowledge work are, how these characteristics are implemented in Case Management, and how are finally translated in Adaptive Case Management features. In addition, the standard for Case Management which was published by Object Management Group (OMG) named as Case Management Modeling and Notation (CMMN) is presented.

Firstly, a case is not a common business process. It requires knowledge work, namely thinking, skills, expertise, and experience as far as the details of the situation are concerned in order to make all the essential process design appropriately. The human resource in those domains is described as knowledge workers, people with high degrees of expertise, education or experience. (Mundbrod, et al., 2012) In knowledge work systems like healthcare, legal and social work, the knowledge workers that are involved in the case process are expected to interfere in multiple contexts and adapt to different roles. That means that they have to interact with each other, to collaborate, with the aim to produce better results in their changing and adaptive activities. To that end, the meaning of collaborative knowledge work, described as a type of knowledge work which is jointly performed by a team of knowledge workers with the aim to fulfil a common organizational goal, (Mundbrod, et al., 2012) leads to a practice used to organize and structure case handling actions in organizations with changing workflows, the Case Management or as it is most commonly known in conference papers and proceedings Adaptive Case Management (ACM).

Case management as a practice is not something new; references to the term "case management" go back to the 1980s or earlier and the Case Management Society of America was founded back in 1990. This type of management refers not only to the coordination of work in one organization that is not routine and unpredictable, and requires human judgment in order to be executed, but it also refers to gathering all of the relevant information in one place, which is called case folder, and acting upon this source of information to fulfill any organizational requests. (Motahari-Nezhad, et al., 2013)

As described above, ACM refers to a practice that when certain requirements are met, optimizes knowledge work in domains such as healthcare, legal and social work. An appropriate definition for an Adaptive Case Management system would be "a system that is able to support decision making and data capture while providing the freedom for knowledge workers to apply their own understanding and subject matter expertise to respond to unique or changing circumstances within the business environment." (Swenson, 2010)

Moreover, the center of attention in Adaptive Case Management is data exchange. Data that represent either the input streams in the Case Management process or the outputs of the Case Management tasks. By capturing data, what is really captured is knowledge about the case that is executed and experience that will be valuable to future similar knowledge work. Valuable data about the case that is executed, are often outside the main case process, usually in inboxes of knowledge workers that are involved, isolated and useless to the case. (Motahari-Nezhad, et al., 2013)

In addition, supporting decision making means that the system except not defining what the "next move" for the case workers should be, it also assists them to choose which one is the best option for the executed case. In some extent, the system leaves its users (knowledge workers) free to prioritize the sequence of their activities in their own way, even to change it on runtime as there is great need to be agile and adaptive in these human-centric environments.

CMMN

In this standard, the key features of Case Management are described vastly with extended and special terminology, as well as the appropriate notation that represents its features graphically. What needs to be taken into account is the fact that in a Case model processes, as are known through BPM are also included. The philosophy through which structured workflow is implemented in agile environments does not change.

Firstly, in this general concept description about Case Management, the Case is described as "a proceeding that involves a set of actions that need to be taken regarding a subject in a particular situation in order to achieve the desired outcome." (OMG, 2014) In the medical treatment case study that is to be examined, the subject is the patient and the desired outcome is represented as the patient's hospitalization and medical treatment.

In addition, according to the CMMN standard the notion of Case Management evolves from the fact that as experience grows in resolving similar Cases over time, a common set of practices and responses can be considered appropriate to manage Cases in a more repeatable manner. Case management seems to have as a fundamental characteristic, the planning at run-time and not in design time phase. During run-time planning, the appropriate Tasks are selected by the Case Manager or the team of Case Workers, the above-mentioned knowledge workers, people with high level of expertise and experience in the undergone situation. (OMG, 2014) According to the standard, the determination of which Tasks are applicable or which Tasks are to be executed next is not predefined and require decisions to be made. However, these decisions may be triggered by some Case Events, which vary from completing certain Tasks to achieving some Case Milestones, under certain circumstances though, some Tasks may be predefined procedural Processes, but the overall Case cannot be considered as a predefined sequence of Tasks. (OMG, 2014)

Moreover, in order to make important decisions about the Case's execution, Case workers need to have access to data about the situation or the subject that the actions to be taken are concerned. This collection of Case data is often described as Case File, within which documents and either structured or unstructured data about the Case are captured for later reference by the Case Workers in order to make decisions. Except for references to data, decision making is enhanced and slightly redirected by Case Management rules, that apply in specific phases of Case's execution and are triggered by Case events. These are rules and data from the knowledge that the Case produces, and that enable case workers to potentially change the planning in run-time. (OMG, 2014)

A HOLISTIC APPROACH TOWARDS BUSINESS PROCESS AGILITY

Business process agility should be analyzed from two separate views: both execution and design. This means that business process agility, as a concept, comprises two equally important constituents: design agility and execution agility. While one may intuitively feel familiar with this conclusion, it is evident, however, in the literature that design agility has not been given the attention it deserves. This stems from the fact that researchers often propose a modeling approach having in mind the execution phase, i.e. they focus on the achievement of flexible process instance adaptations rather than the effort required for the modification of a model at design time (ShuiGuang et al., 2004; Dadam & Reichert, 2009). But how can design agility be interpreted?

As revealed in (Alexopoulou, et al., 2013), the majority of the current research approaches, which restrict agility exploration to a technological framework, business process agility should also be examined beyond the boundaries of IT infrastructure. The technology-neutral dimension in the exploration of business process agility is necessary to unearth requirements that have to do with the process itself, independently of the underlying technology. Therefore, we suggest analyzing design business process agility separately from execution agility.

As indicated in Figure 1, enactment and configuration correspond to the execution view, since the automated execution of business processes entails that these phases are directly related to the IT infrastructure. On the other hand, design and evaluation concern the business process itself and even if they are supported by a software tool, they do not consider the means that will be used for business process execution. As such, they are associated with the design view, which is regarded as technology-neutral.

The requirements for achieving business process agility were confirmed through our study, and are identified as follows:

- **Design View:**
    - The modeling approach should be in harmonization with the nature of the actual business process to be modeled.
- **Execution View:**
    - The business process models executed by the BPM engine should be modular.

Figure 1. Mapping design and execution views to business process lifecycle phases (Alexopoulou, et al., 2013)

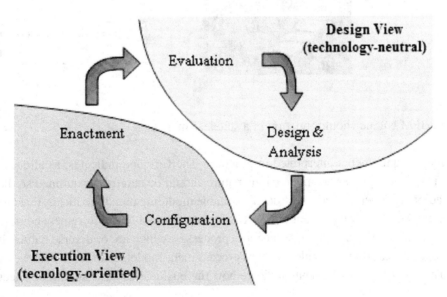

Figure 2. The integrated picture regarding the attainment of business process agility (Alexopoulou, et al., 2013)

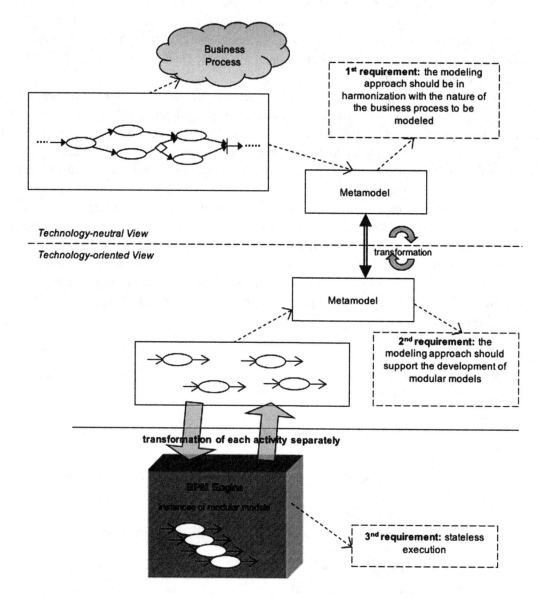

○   The BPM engine should function in a stateless manner.

How are these requirements interpreted in practice? The first one indicates, as already stated, that when a specific business process is modeled, its nature should be carefully examined so that a suitable modeling paradigm is selected. The selection of a suitable modeling paradigm means that an appropriate meta-model is adopted (upper part of Figure 2). Taking into account this requirement combined with the fact that enterprises own usually multiple business processes, which are of diverse nature, it is entailed that an enterprise should adopt multiple business process meta-models in order to achieve business process agility. The other two requirements indicate how the business process should be executed so that agility is ensured. The main point of these two requirements is that the models executed by the BPM engine should be generated based on a meta-model that supports modularity (lower part of Figure 2).

Overall, the identified requirements indicate that in order to attain business process agility, an enterprise should adopt multiple modeling paradigms to facilitate the description of all supported business process types and transform these models into modular executable ones in order to achieve agile execution of business processes, as illustrated in Figure 9.

Business process agility was explored by (Alexopoulou, et al., 2013) through a research project we were engaged in, which aimed at the agile automation of medical business processes. This exploration led us to a number of important conclusions, which are listed in the following:

- Agility implications are different for business process design and execution phases. Design agility should be equally emphasized with execution agility for the attainment of business process agility.
- For design agility to be achieved, it should be ensured that the modeling approach is harmonized with the nature of the actual business process to be modeled.
- For execution agility to be achieved in the business process models executed by the BPM engine should be modular and the BPM engine should function in a stateless manner.
- In practice, design agility is a prerequisite of execution agility.
- Business process agility requires design and execution phases to be more "interwoven" with each other.
- A model can be characterized agile only in relation to a specific business process. As such, when a modeling approach is proposed, the type of business processes it is appropriate for should also be specified.
- An agile enterprise should support multiple business process models ensuring, though, their integration and seamless intercommunication.

HUMAN-INTENSIVE PROCESSES: WHAT IS THEIR NATURE?

Human-intensive processes as are presented in (Barghouti, et al., 1994), they are not as amenable to automation as other software processes. In human-intensive processes, activities do not take place in a strict predetermined order. While there may be cases of activities carried out in a regular fashion, most often, they are performed whenever required, following the human decision, a fact that makes it difficult for most tasks of these processes be automated.

Secondly, since these processes require knowledge work, a significant amount of process-related information is maintained, identified as process knowledge. Keeping this information up to date and providing early notification of updates are important requirements for an effective operational model of these processes. This knowledge should be easily accessible to the involved actors, the humans identified as knowledge workers.

Knowledge Workers

A brief definition of knowledge work was given in the introduction of this chapter. It was described as the combination of thinking, skills, expertise, and experience about a situation in which knowledge workers are involved. This type of work is different from a traditional business process, as while it proceeds, the sequence of actions may change depending on the situation and plan is not predefined but is evolving throughout the case execution. The exact opposite of knowledge work is routine work that can be planned in detail up to certain level. The routine work procedures are similarly executed between each other; thus, these procedures can be easily automated. Something that is inevitable in case of knowledge work. (Swenson, 2010) What, in reality, differentiates knowledge work is highlighted below:

Firstly, as was mentioned above, knowledge work is not repeated in the same way, multiple times in a row. There are always some similarities between knowledge work procedures but the differences are so many and the cost in time of automation so big that it can be considered as a realistic technique in knowledge-intensive environments.

Secondly, knowledge work is quite difficult to be predicted in advance. This unpredictability of knowledge work refers to the fact that it is inevitable for a process designer to know in advance the sequence of specific human acts within the situation. Knowledge work context may differ from case to case and may change before the work is finished. But the fact that makes knowledge work so unpredictable is the following one. What really makes knowledge work unpredictable is the fact that it unfolds during execution. Any step that is taken towards the work's completion creates some knowledge. The next step uses the knowledge created previously and unfolds equally creating greater knowledge and so on. That iterative unfolding nature of knowledge work differentiates it the most from routine work. (Swenson, 2010)

The last characteristic of knowledge work is its flexibility in changing conditions. Unlike strictly defined and rigid business processes that in case of change seem extremely fragile, knowledge work can adapt to changing environments.

Patient Treatment as a Typical Example

A significant and representing example of such a case study is Patient Treatment. Patient Treatment is a challenging issue, since it largely depends on human decision often taken in an ad-hoc manner, a fact that makes it highly dynamic. It fits into the domain of Healthcare, which, as it was mentioned above, is a domain where the work procedure needs human worker involvement as the work that has to be done is highly variable. As far as Healthcare is concerned, it represents the largest business segment in the world. According to Organization for Economic Co-Operation and Development on its annual report in 2009, Healthcare was accounting for around 10% of GDP of the developed world, whereas in the non-developed world is still one of the most critical areas for future growth. (Swenson, 2010)

The field of Patient Treatment Process has to be examined closely in order to familiarize ourselves with the variety of Tasks performed by the end users during Patient Treatment. To begin with, the patient is admitted to a hospital's Medicine Clinic if he/she needs to be hospitalized, a decision that is taken in the Emergency Department. The Emergency Department personnel provide the physicians of the clinic with information regarding the clinical status of the patient, such as medical history and any examinations that have been done or scheduled.

Based on this initial information, the physicians of the Medicine Clinic start the treatment of the patient. They specify a diagnosis for the patient and prescribe the medication accordingly. Such information is registered into the patient's file. During treatment, a clinical examination takes place every morning by the physicians, aiming at monitoring the patient's clinical course. To this end, laboratory and/or imaging examinations may be scheduled. The results, which are also registered into the patient's file, are evaluated by the physicians and if necessary the diagnosis and medication are revised. There may be cases that the physicians will need to consult a specialist in order to conclude about the patient's health problem or about the way the patient should be treated.

The nursing personnel aids in the treatment process through operations regarding, for example, the preparation and administration of the specified medication, blood drawing and measurements of vital signs (e.g. temperature, blood pressure, etc.). Medication administration and measurements are performed at the times specified by the physician. The measured values are written in the patient's chart. Moreover, the nursing personnel keeps notes of anything remarkable regarding the patient, for example, a sign they observed, as well as of any action they performed by their own initiative, for example, any ad hoc medication they may have administered to the patient (e.g. the administration of an analgesic pill in case the patient suffers from a headache).

During treatment, several unexpected situations may arise, which may lead to ad hoc clinical, laboratory or imaging examinations, as well as to reconsideration of the medication administered or even of the diagnosis specified so far. The patient may need to be transferred to the Intensive Care Unit or to undergo an urgent surgery. The need for a patient to remain hospitalized is daily examined after the morning clinical examination based on the data gathered up to that point. If it is decided that the patient does not need further hospitalization, the treatment process ends and the patient is discharged (Alexopoulou, et al., 2009).

As it can be easily identified, users are the highlighted ones, who respectively are responsible for the execution of specific tasks within the Patient Treatment Process. An interaction between users is identified, as well as a fluidness in tasks' sequence of execution, characteristics that create a variable human-based process environment.

Patient Treatment: Users and Tasks

As a better identification of the correspondence between users and tasks needs to be made a classification of tasks per user is presented in Table 1.

As a comment for this first representation (Table 1) of Patient Treatment Case main activity elements (users and tasks), it can be highlighted that the main users such as Physicians and Nursing Personnel have more responsibilities than the secondary users who work in other departments but are ready to get involved in the patient treatment process when needed.

Secondly, another fact that is needed to be mentioned is that although there might be a slight sequence and dependence between some tasks, there are some ad-hoc actions that are conditionally taken or emergency tasks that are not in the process main workflow.

ADAPTIVE CASE MANAGEMENT: AN APPROACH TO ENSURE HUMAN-INTENSIVE PROCESS AGILITY

In order to achieve a better understanding of the key features that comprise ACM, it would have been better if the term "Adaptive Case Management" was analyzed in two parts. The first one would be "Adaptivity" or as it can also be seen in literature "Agility", while the second one would be the above-mentioned term "Case Management" and how it can be adaptive or agile in context. Then, the identification of both terms characteristics would lead to a spherical understanding of Adaptive Case Management's most important elements.

Table 1. A first reading of the Patient Treatment Process case study's main elements

Users	Tasks
Emergency Department Personnel	Provide health status information
Physicians	Start treatment
	Specify diagnosis
	Prescribe medication
	Clinical examination
	Schedule examination
	Evaluate examination results
	Revise diagnosis / medication
	Consult a specialist
Nursing Personnel	Administrate medication
	Blood Drawing
	Vital signs measurements
	Record measurements
ICU Personnel	Urgent surgery

Adaptivity and Agility

Firstly, as it was defined in the introduction, adaptivity refers to the ability to adjust behavior to changes in context. (Sem, et al., 2013) The ability to change, for an organization, is essential when is established in a human-centric business environment. Being adaptive equals to the organization undergoing internal changes, caused by outside conditions that become permanent and make the organization more fitting to those new conditions. (Swenson, 2010) On the other hand, being agile refers to the ability to move quickly from one state to another and without preparation or support. What is needed to be identified is how difficult is it for an organization to achieve agility within its workflow.

Because of the pressing challenges organizations face today, agility has become vastly important to them. Not only for this, but also because agility enables organizations reacting to those challenges positively and covering higher and higher expectations getting a competitive advantage over its rivals. In globalization, where competitors can appear out of nowhere, enterprises are bound to be open to global opportunities. That is what characterizes an agile organization. The ability to sense the opportunity or threat, prioritize the potential responses, and act both efficiently and effectively. (Swenson, 2010)

This how agility is achieved. At first by sensing the threats, namely being aware of its operating environment and the interactions within it, as well as its competitor's capabilities and their ability to respond, on their turn, to changing realities. Secondly, by analyzing the organization's purposes, bringing them to its people's attention, making them aware of the demanding conditions and the corporative strategy that creates responses to these difficulties and setting the goals which are pursued by the organization's staff. Finally, acting efficiently and effectively means that the prioritized actions and the organizational strategy are executed exceptionally well in order to adapt in business needs change. (Swenson, 2010)

Agility in Case Management

Being agile enables corporations that are characterized within their context with knowledge work, to gain a competitive advantage and makes these organizations more efficient. What is more, it enables organizations to adapt their strategy while the business processes are executed. Accordingly, being adaptive or agile reinforces organizations that implement case processes.

In case of Case Management, knowledge workers need to be free to be adaptive. So, they would be able to sense, prioritize and act. Namely, they would be able to understand the circumstances under the case is to be implemented, ensure that case management activities fit with the organizational goals and finally execute these activities so as to have the best possible results.

Comparison to Business Process Management

After defining Adaptive Case Management and its basic characteristics, a comparison between ACM and BPM is needed to be made. With that, we get a view of what really differentiates these two approaches in the level of their scope and their features.

Firstly, Business Process Management is concerned with the lifecycle of the process definition. It differs from Adaptive Case Management in that its focus is the process which is to be executed and it is used as an organizing paradigm. In addition, process models are prepared in advance. On the other hand, ACM differs from Business Process Management in that the case information is the center of attention and the thing around which the other artifacts are organized. (Swenson, 2010)

Adaptive Case Management and Business Process Management aim to achieve different goals by separating the work that has to be done in different ways. (Jalali, et al., 2014) Business Process Management is highlighted as an important area, which aims in supporting operational activities in business processes within the enterprise boundaries so as to achieve business goals, while Adaptive Case Management is described as a paradigm created to support adaptivity of processes in more fluid and changing environments. It is also endorsed that in opposition to BPM systems which handle the business processes as a strict workflow, ACM allows a high level of flexibility in systems since knowledge workers need more freedom in order to complete their work. (Jalali, et al., 2014)

The question that arises from the comparison above, is whether these two approaches can co-exist in a common environment, namely to be used in order to achieve common organizational goals. Keith D. Swenson, in one of his positions he makes a statement in order to argue with that and come to a conclusion. (Swenson, 2012) He says: "Any work support system that depends upon processes that designed with BPM cannot be considered as ACM systems". In order to support this statement, he provides some further explanation about some types of BPM-oriented systems such as Human Process Management (HRM) systems and Production Case Management (PCM) systems, a type of Case Management system used in production-related organizational environments. He highlights the fact that these two types of systems need programming skills to model a workflow in contrary to ACM systems whose activities are designed by case – knowledge workers who are the end-users for these systems (Swenson, 2012).

ACM Tools

Different modeling tools have been developed to support the theory of ACM, in addition to ACM platforms that had been designed, implementing the core philosophy of this approach. The main characteristics that were identified for the majority of these tools are the following: design support, execution support, BPMN integration, CMMN conformance, Agility. For each one of these, we chose an identical tool example, in order to examine their capability of conforming to the characteristics presented above. To measure this, we set a scale of measurement, which consists of three levels of conformance. Each level is represented with a different graphical representation, namely, the lowest level of conformance with ACM characteristics is represented as a white circle, the intermediate level of conformance is represented as a gray circle, while the highest level of conformance is represented with a black circle.

To be more specific, in Table 2, several ACM-empowered platforms and modeling tools are projected. Firstly, Cognoscenti, an experimental system for exploring different approaches to supporting complex, unpredictable work patterns. Cognoscenti is freely available as an open source platform with a basic set of capabilities for tracking documents, notes, goals, and roles which might be used for further exploration into knowledge worker support patterns (Swenson, 2014). Secondly, Casebook was chosen, a Cloud-Based System of Engagement for Case Management. Casebook's main capabilities include case planning, execution, and assistance, measuring and learning, and a community-curated case catalog, alongside with the fact that it enables collaboration among case workers to facilitate case resolution in a social environment (Motahari-Nezhad et al., 2013). Moreover, *Camunda Platform*, an open source platform for workflow and decision automation, mainly designed for BPMN, which also supports the design of CMMN models through a modeling tool named as Camunda Modeler. Additionally, *Visual Paradigm*, a modeling IDE for various standardized methodologies like UML and BPMN, now supporting modeling with CMMN. *Oracle BPM Suite* for ACM was another option.

What can be commented, lies in the fact that the above-mentioned platforms and tools cannot be considered as completely standardized and completely compliant with the theory of Case Management. The main reason behind this assumption lies in the fact that there is no common view for these tools and platforms that these could be based upon, in order to support agile process design and modeling. Thus, what is required is a more standardized concept for ACM and Case Management theory in general. The examined tools and platforms either rely on the design phase of Cases, without promoting agility, or rely on handling Cases from a higher level, which on the one hand promotes agility to the Case Management, but on the other hand, leaves no design options to its users.

Table 2. ACM Characteristics Conformance table

Tools	Main Characteristics				
	Design Support	Execution Support	BPMN Integration	CMMN conformance	Agility
Cognoscenti Collaborative Platform	○	●	○	○	●
Casebook Social Platform	○	●	○	○	●
Camunda Platform & Modeler	●	◐	●	●	○
Visual Paradigm IDE	●	○	◐	●	◐
Oracle BPM Suite	○	●	●	◐	○

USING CMMN FOR THE AGILE MODELING OF HUMAN INTENSIVE PROCESS

The theory of ACM seems to have a continuously growing reputation and competitiveness as far as the business process modeling approaches are concerned, a fact that justifies its growing establishment in research. Thus, it is important for ACM the fact that CMMN has to be widely adopted. What is presented in the following subsections is our experience of using CMMN for the agile modeling of the human-centric process of patient treatment which was presented previously. Firstly, what is projected is how we identify the connection between the CMMN basic elements, represented as a meta-model for CMMN. Secondly, we present the notation of CMMN, focusing upon the elements that will be utilized in the third part of this chapter which is our model for the agile modeling of patient treatment case.

CMMN Basic Elements

In CMMN, ACM data objects and case artifacts are projected as Casefile items, representing a piece of information of any nature, ranging from unstructured to structured, and from simple to complex. (Object Management Group, 2016). On the other hand, tasks are handled as an atomic unit of work and are divided into different task types, namely, human tasks, process tasks or decision tasks. Sentries as a combination of an event and a condition (criterion) are not used as a standalone CMMN element. At first, sentry criteria are used, categorized into two different types, entry and exit criteria of a sentry. Secondly, events are displayed and described into the CMMN standard as anything that can change the case state as far as either the case data or the sequence of case stages, case tasks or case milestones, is concerned, and are divided into two different types, as timer events and user events. Additionally, a milestone represents an achievable target, defined to enable evaluation of the progress of the Case. No work is directly associated with a Milestone, but completion of a set of tasks or the availability of key deliverables typically leads to achieving a Milestone. (Object Management Group, 2016)

Based upon the CMMN standard the authors designed the meta-model, which is projected below, for CMMN from scratch, in order to present the relation between its main elements.

These Case management features represent the main characteristics of a human-centric environment. It includes Cases that need to be analyzed and handled properly, while it also includes, the appropriate Human Tasks that are required for a Case to be completed and are assigned to the involved Roles. Moreover, case data, presented in CMMN standard as Casefile items, are handled as another important factor of the Case Management theory. These represent the case information that is been created and exchanged throughout the Case lifetime, and are being queried from Sentries in order to determine whether the necessary information, for a human task to commence, is available, or a human task has been completed, producing the expected outcome, creating the necessary data or reaching a specific Milestone, based upon specific Criteria. Sentries, alongside with the appropriate criteria, are the connecting point between individual Case plan fragments, which are enabled according to the occurrence of specific events.

Basic Notation

CMMN standard provides a plethora of notation for the Case Management elements in order to cover all the aspects of human-centric modeling elements required to represent a Case model. During our modeling of the Patient Treatment Case which is projected in Figure 4, we utilized some of them, so in

Figure 3. Core CMMN meta-model

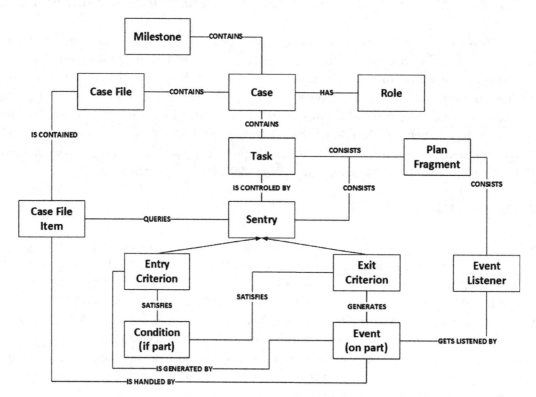

Table 3, we provide a brief description of the elements used in the CMMN model, in order to make it easy for someone to understand the following CMMN model.

Patient Treatment CMMN Model

Having the main CMMN elements presented and described as Case Management entities in the CMMN meta-model presented in Figure 3, it is about time to present our perspective of the agile modeling of the Patient Treatment Case.

To begin with, when a patient arrives at the Emergency Department of a hospital, what initiates the stage is Patient Medical Record casefile item. It provides the stage plan item with all the necessary information for its included tasks. If no hospitalization is being decided for the patient, he is being dismissed, which is a milestone achieved for the Case, and the Case is being terminated automatically. On the other hand, if there is an admission need for the patient, the Patient Medical Record casefile is being updated with the file of the patient's clinical status, while in parallel the physicians of the Medical Clinic are notified that the patient treatment should start.

These two CMMN elements, namely the user event listener and the updated Patient Medical Record casefile are the entry criteria for the next Case stage to commence, the Admission to Medical Clinic stage plan item. This stage includes a mandatory human task of the diagnosis specification of the Clinic's physicians alongside with the discretionary human tasks of Medication Prescription, the scheduling of optional examinations, the consulting of a specialist physician, or even the revision of a previous diag-

Table 3. A list of utilized notation in the CMMN model

Name	Representation	Description
Case Plan Model		Representation of a case to process or resolve. It contains all the case elements that are involved representing the content of the case as well as the way to process and resolve the case.
Case File Item		Any kind of documents that are used in processing a case.
Stage Plan Item		A logical container of tasks to be performed within the course of a case.
Human Task Plan Item		A task that is performed by someone whose job is to process and resolve the case.
Decision Task Plan Item		A task that invokes a decision.
Milestone Plan Item		Represent a specific state within a case.
Timer Event Listener Plan Item		Used to capture the elapse of time that may enable, activate and terminate stages and tasks, or result in the achievement of milestones.
User Event Listener Plan Item		Used to capture user events and may enable, activate and terminate stages and tasks, or result in the achievement of milestones.
Entry Criterion		Represents the condition for a plan item to become available.
Exit Criterion		Represents the condition for a plan item to terminate.

nosis or medication prescription. This stage, when terminated, updates the Patient Medical Record case file with the diagnosis data.

This casefile item initiates the daily Treatment stage, which takes place on a daily basis. For this purpose, a timer event listener is used in order to define this repetition. This stage, the Daily Treatment, includes two separate sub-stages that take place sequentially. At first, the Clinical Examinations human task takes place, which when completed, the Patient Medical Record should be updated with the examinations results. Elsewhere, the nursing personnel execute their tasks accordingly and create a casefile item which includes their daily nursing notes for the patient's health status or any abnormalities in the measurements. These two casefile items, namely the updated with examinations results Patient Medical

Figure 4. CMMN model for patient treatment case

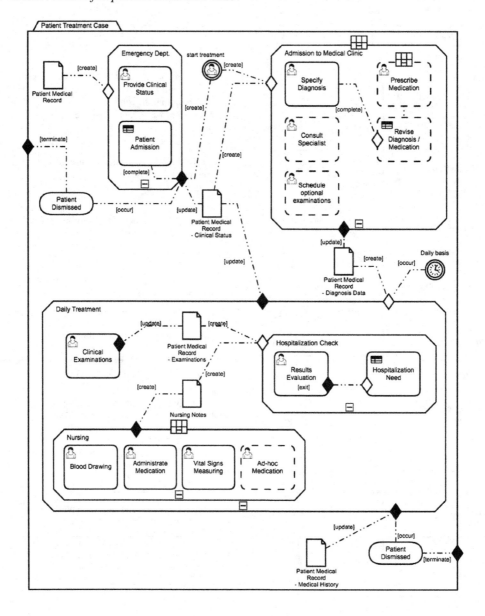

Record and the Nursing Personnel notes, are required for the next substage, the one of Hospitalization Check, to take place. This stage is where the patient's need for hospitalization is being reviewed. According to the decision made on the later, the patient will continue to remain hospitalized or not. In case the patient needs to remain hospitalized, the Patient Medical Record casefile is being updated with the updated patient's clinical status and there is a review in the instructions given to the nursing personnel for the patient's daily treatment. On the other hand, Patient Medical Record casefile is being updated with his/her medical history and any medication that has been prescribed, while the milestone of the patient's dismissal is achieved and the Case is terminated.

Fulfilling Agility Requirements

What can be commented for the modeling approach presented in (Figure 4 is that importance is given to the data flow into the case lifetime. Each casefile item is the initiating and terminating factor for each case stage. So, flow is given to the Case only through the exchange and querying of data. Additionally, events are driving parts of the Case implementation, however, these are in general triggered by the creation of Case data.

1st Requirement: The Modeling Approach Should Be in Harmonization With the Nature of the Business Process to Be Modeled

Patient Treatment Case nature is characterized by the need for continuous data updating and agility as far as the activities defined. Moreover, it requires the capability of its involved actors to take ad-hoc decisions when an emergency arises. On the one hand, the modeling approach presented in Figure 4, implements the notion of Patient Medical Record as a Case Folder element. Casefile items are just parts of this folder containing all the information about patient's health, are updated at every stage of the Case, and are accessible from each case stage separately. This way, data access is given only to the appropriate case actors and data management is easier, while importance is given to the sensitivity of the data queried. On the other hand, the fact that stages are used for the representation of the case individual parts enables the use of less interconnected case plan items. Furthermore, a high level of agility is given to the case, due to the fact that flow is provided only through the use of data querying without a strict sequence of tasks inside of each case stage.

2nd Requirement: The Modeling Approach Should Support the Development of Modular Models

As it was highlighted above, the modeling approach presented in Figure 4, implements the notion of Case stages. This provides the model with the ability to be examined stage-to-stage as an individual part of the Case. Thus, each stage could be examined as an individual sub-model, or an individual module that has its own lifetime and the agility to be executed separately. More specifically, each case stage – module has its entry and exit criteria as sentries, and its own starting or finishing conditions. It has its own requirements to commence and its own results when completed. Additionally, it queries different data and achieves different milestones. As a result, the modeling approach for the human-centric Patient Treatment Case covers the second requirement set in Figure 2 in supporting the development of modular models.

FUTURE RESEARCH DIRECTIONS

As future research, the authors of this chapter primarily aim in identifying the terms according to which CMMN could cover the 3rd requirement set in Figure 2, namely the conditions that could lead human-centric processes and the designed CMMN models in stateless execution. What is required to be examined is how these processes should be executed in specific CMMN compatible tools or platforms. In order to ensure agility, one should examine how the modular nature of agile models presented in Figure 4 could be enhanced.

CONCLUSION

At this chapter, what was intended was the exploration of agility at the designing phase of human-centric processes, through the examination of whether using CMMN for the design and modeling of such processes could cover their agility requirements. The use of the identical human-centric process of Patient Treatment as a case study assisted in reaching the conclusion that on the one hand, CMMN could depict agile models that could be in harmonization with the process nature, while, on the other hand, CMMN supports the development of modular models, as it can be clearly identified in Figure 4, that could lead in executing each module separately in order to ensure agility. What is more, the authors of this chapter attempted to evaluate CMMN as a modeling language based on the agility requirements identified in (Alexopoulou, et al., 2013), reaching the conclusion that CMMN can be used for agile and modular modeling, even if the fact that there is room for improvement. What is required for CMMN is a better engine than the BPM engine, regarding the manner in which it calls each one of the modules designed.

REFERENCES

Alexopoulou, N., Kanellis, P., Nikolaidou, M., & Martakos, D. (2008). A holistic approach for enterprise agility. In *Handbook of research on enterprise systems*. Hershey, PA: IGI Global.

Alexopoulou, N., Nikolaidou, M., Anagnostopoulos, D., & Martakos, D. (2009, September). An event-driven modeling approach for dynamic human-intensive business processes. In *International Conference on Business Process Management* (pp. 393-404). Berlin, Heidelberg: Springer.

Alexopoulou, N., Nikolaidou, M., & Martakos, D. (2013). Exploring the business process agility issue: An experience report. *International Journal of Information System Modeling and Design*, *4*(1), 25–41. doi:10.4018/jismd.2013010102

Balabko, P., Wegmann, A., Ruppen, A., & Clement, N. (2004). *The Value of Roles in Modeling Business Processes*. Paper presented at BPMDS.

Barghouti, N. S., & Rosenblum, D. S. (1994, October). A case study in modeling a human-intensive, corporate software process. In *Software Process, 1994.'Applying the Software Process', Proceedings., Third International Conference on the* (pp. 99-110). IEEE. 10.1109/SPCON.1994.344418

Casati, F., Ceri, S., Pernici, B., & Pozzi, G. (1996). Workflow Evolution. *Proceedings of ER '96*, 438–455.

Dadam, P., & Reichert, M. (2009). The ADEPT project: A decade of research and development for robust and flexible process support. *Computer Science—Research for Development*, *23*(2), 81–97.

Daoudi, F., & Nurcan, S. (2007). A benchmarking framework for methods to design flexible business processes. *Software Process Improvement and Practice*, *12*(1), 51–63. doi:10.1002pip.304

Dayal, U., Hsu, M., & Ladin, R. (1990). Organizing Long-Running Activities with Triggers and Transactions. *Proceedings of ACM International Conference on Management of Data*, 204-214. 10.1145/93597.98730

Dumas, M., Aalst, W., & Hofstede, A. (2005). Process-Aware Information Systems. John Wiley & Sons Inc.

Mangan, P., & Sadiq, S. (2002). *On Building Workflow Models for Flexible Processes. 13th Australasian Database Conference (ADC2002)*, Melbourne, Australia.

Milanovic, M., Gasevic, D., & Rocha, L. (2011). Modeling Flexible Business Processes with Business Rule Patterns. *Distributed Object Computing Conference (EDOC) 15th IEEE International*, 65 – 74. 10.1109/EDOC.2011.25

Millie, M. K., & Balasubramanian, P. R. (1997). Dynamic Workflow Management: A Framework for Modeling Workflows. In *Proceedings of 13th HICSS*. IEEE.

Motahari-Nezhad, H. R., Spence, S., Bartolini, C., Graupner, S., Bess, C., Hickey, M., ... Rahmouni, M. (2013). Casebook: A cloud-based system of engagement for case management. *IEEE Internet Computing*, *17*(5), 30–38.

Motahari-Nezhad, H. R., & Swenson, K. D. (2013). *Adaptive Case Management: Overview and Research Challenges*. Conference on Business Informatics, Vienna, Austria.

Müller, D., Reichert, M., & Herbst, J. (2006, September). Flexibility of data-driven process structures. In *International Conference on Business Process Management* (pp. 181-192). Berlin, Heidelberg: Springer.

Mundbrod, Kolb, & Reichert. (2012). Towards a System Support of Collaborative Knowledge Work. In *Business Process Management Workshops*. Springer-Verlag.

Object Management Group. (2016). *Case Management Model and Notation v1.1*. Object Management Group. Retrieved from http://www.omg.org/spec/CMMN/1.1/CMMN

OMG CMMN & the Object Management Group. (2014). *Object Management Group Web site*. Retrieved from http://www.omg.org/spec/CMMN/1.0/PDF/

Pesic, M., Schonenberg, M. H., Sidorova, N., & van der Aalst, W. M. P. (2007). Constraint-Based Workflow Models: Change Made Easy. In *Proceedings of the OTM Conference on Cooperative Information Systems (CoopIS 2007) (vol. 4803, pp. 77-94)*. Springer-Verlag.

Reijers, H. A. (2006). Workflow flexibility: The forlorn promise. In 15th IEEE International Workshops on Enabling Technologies: Infrastructures for Collaborative Enterprises (WETICE 2006) (pp. 271–272). IEEE Computer Society.

Rinderle, S., Reichert, M., & Dadam, P. (2004). *On Dealing with Structural Conflicts between Process Type and Instance Changes*. BPM. doi:10.1007/978-3-540-25970-1_18

Sambamurthy, V., Bharadwaj, A., & Grover, V. (2003). Shaping Agility through Digital Options: Reconceptualizing the Role of Information Technology in Contemporary Firms. *Management Information Systems Quarterly*, *27*(2), 237–263. doi:10.2307/30036530

Scheer, A. W. (1999). *ARIS-Business Process Modeling* (2nd ed.). Berlin: Springer. doi:10.1007/978-3-642-97998-9

ShuiGuang., D., Zhen, Y., ZhaoHui, W., & LiCan, H. (2004). Enhancement of Workflow Flexibility by Composing Activities at Run-time. *Proceedings of the ACM Symposium on Applied Computing*, 667-673.

Snowdon, R. A., Warboys, B. C., Greenwood, R. M., Holland, C. P., Kawalek, P. J., & Shaw, D. R. (2007). On the architecture and form of flexible process support. *Software Process Improvement and Practice*, *12*(1), 21–34. doi:10.1002pip.307

Swenson, K. D. (2010). *Mastering the Unpredictable: How Adaptive Case Management Will Revolutionize the Way That Knowledge Workers Get Things Done*. Tampa, FL: Meghan-Kiffer Press.

Swenson, K. D. (2014). Demo: Cognoscenti Open Source Software for Experimentation on Adaptive Case Management Approaches. *2014 IEEE 18th International Enterprise Distributed Object Computing Conference Workshops and Demonstrations*, 402-405. 10.1109/EDOCW.2014.67

Swenson, K. D. (2012). Position: BPMN Is Incompatible with ACM. In Business Process Management Workshops. Springer-Verlag.

Van der Aalst, W. M. P., Pesic, M., & Schonenberg, H. (2009). Declarative workflows: Balancing between flexibility and support. *Computer Science— Research for Development*, *23*(2), 99–113.

Van Oosterhout, M., Waarts, E., & van Hillegersberg, J. (2006). Change factors requiring agility and implications for IT. *European Journal of Information Systems*, *15*(2), 132–145. doi:10.1057/palgrave. ejis.3000601

Weske, M. (2007). *Business Process Management: Concepts, Languages, Architectures*. Springer-Verlag.

KEY TERMS AND DEFINITIONS

Action-Driven Processes: Processes designed and implemented having the tasks that should be executed as the center of attention.

Case Management: The organization of activities within the context of a case so as it can be completed.

Dynamic Behavior: The behavior of a process to continuously change according to some conditions.

Human-Centric Processes: Processes designed and implemented, having the human factor as the center of attention.

Modular Models: Models that could be examined in modules, namely, independent parts of the model.

Process Modeling Language: A combination of terms and notation that aim to model a process according to an approach.

Process Nature: The characteristics and key features of the process that could affect the way it is designed and implemented.

Chapter 3
Practical Guidance in Achieving Successful Change Management in Information System Environments

Jeffrey S. Zanzig
Jacksonville State University, USA

Guillermo A. Francia III
Jacksonville State University, USA

Xavier P. Francia
Jacksonville State University, USA

ABSTRACT

Situations such as improvements in business transaction processing and various security issues keep today's information systems in a constant state of change. Serious disruption of company operations can occur when changes are improperly planned and/or carried out. In addition to technological issues, an equally important consideration is in regard to how information system changes will affect organizational personnel. The Institute of Internal Auditors has identified seven steps that can be used to effectively implement change in an information system environment. This along with a discussion of significant issues in managing system patches provides an appropriate background to consider a model for evaluating the maturity of an organization's change management process in an information system environment. The highly respected COBIT guidance from the ISACA is included throughout much of the discussion to provide support for many of the suggested change management practices.

DOI: 10.4018/978-1-5225-7271-8.ch003

INTRODUCTION

In the rapidly changing world of information technology it is imperative that organizations maintain a constant vigilance to ensure that their computer systems stay up-to-date. Some common problems in applying change management to an information system environment are delays in implementing software updates and the errors occurring during the update process. Schmidt and White (2017) point out that it is commonly understood that any significant piece of software has vulnerabilities that will eventually be discovered and require an update to correct them. For the average person, this can be as simple as pressing a button to agree to the update. However, it is common for many companies to make use of a complicated set of interacting software components where changing one thing can affect the system in a variety of unanticipated ways. In such situations, companies lacking sufficient financial resources and/ or expertise may be more likely to postpone system changes.

A recent hacking of the personal data of approximately 143 million persons at Equifax illustrates what can happen when a company uses software that has known security weaknesses that are not addressed in a timely manner. As is true with many Fortune 100 firms, Equifax made use of an open-source software to run parts of its website. One explanation for the security breach suggests that Equifax had a history of outsourcing software development to off-shore locations with no one internally who had any significant experience with software that needed updating (Schmidt and White, 2017). However, software issues can also be attributed situations where incorrect changes are made to address a vulnerability or make an improvement. For example, Goldman Sachs ended up paying a $7 million penalty that resulted from a software configuration error that mistakenly "converted the firm's 'contingent orders' for various options series into live orders and assigned them all a price of $1." The Securities and Exchange Commission (SEC) determined that "Goldman's written policies relating to the implementation of software changes did not require several precautionary steps that, if taken, would likely have prevented the erroneous options incident (SEC, 2015)."

The ISACA is well known for its development of international information system auditing and control standards. One of their most significant contributions is a continuing project known as the Control Objectives for Information and related Technology (COBIT) framework. COBIT 5 "helps enterprises create optimal value from information technology (IT) by maintaining a balance between realizing benefits and optimizing risk levels and resource use." The management process of COBIT 5 contains four domains:

- Align, Plan and Organize (APO)
- Build, Acquire and Implement (BAI)
- Deliver, Service and Support (DSS)
- Monitor, Evaluate and Assess (MEA)

COBIT 5 contains explanations of specific management practices than can be tailored to the development of various objectives that a company may wish to accomplish within each domain. COBIT 5 states that "each enterprise must define its own process set, taking into account its specific situation." In addition, the ISACA provides a process capability model in COBIT 5 that possesses some overlap with the maturity model of COBIT 4.1 (ISACA, 2012a).

The Institute of Internal Auditors (2012) issued an updated Global Technology Audit Guide (GTAG) entitled *Change and Patch Management Controls Critical for Organizational Success*. It contains information to guide internal auditors when working in conjunction with information technology professionals to manage information system changes. The concepts of change and patch management include processes "designed to manage the enhancements, updates, incremental fixes, and patches to production systems."

This chapter is an extended version of a previous article entitled "A Consensus of Thought in Applying Change Management to Information System Environments" (Zanzig, Francia & Francia, 2015). It considers the COBIT and GTAG guidance along with current change and patch management literature for the purpose of providing guidance to address challenges in applying change management to information system environments. This guidance offers valuable insight that can be used to help organizations reach a higher level of process capability over change management. Specific COBIT 5 management practices are provided within the discussion to provide additional support for the suggested change management practices. The remaining sections of this chapter provide: some background on the change management process, a description of the steps of change management, an overview of patch management including a discussion of proposed patching process metrics, measuring maturity of the change management process, and some future research directions and conclusions.

BACKGROUND

Prior to the use of computer technology, the proper processing of information was largely attributable to the employment of honest persons who underwent regular training to maintain a reasonable level of competency. The ability of the human mind to reason and work through problems is beyond measure in its potential value. However, human beings are subject to occasional mistakes and circumstances that may tempt them to manipulate information.

Control procedures can be built into information system technology to catch errors and help in keeping people honest. In addition, technology offers the capability to capture well defined aspects of human processing while allowing for a more consistent application of processing steps. However, the value of consistency over time comes with some potential limitations. One is that time allows for system vulnerabilities to be identified and exploited. A second problem is that an incorrectly defined method of processing can result in processing errors that are repeated on a continuous basis. It is therefore imperative that society have respect for the limitations of technology and continually use human reasoning and evaluation to make changes as the need arises. Any program of change management must maintain a successful balance between the way it affects organizational personnel in addition to certain required elements to ensure that the program functions appropriately.

Human Issues and Change Management

The Association of Change Management Professionals defines change management as "the practice of applying a structured approach to transition an organization from a current state to a future state to achieve expected benefits." Harpham (2018) describes some common reasons that change management efforts fail and suggests potential solutions:

- There is a poor understanding of stakeholders affected by the change. To assess the impact of the project on stakeholders, an organization can begin by constructing a map of important stakeholder groups and asking:
  - What is known about them?

- ○ What interests do the stakeholders have in the project?
- ○ How do stakeholders obtain information?

- Company leaders may inadvertently signal a lack of support for change. Leaders need to keep in mind that employees are watching them in regard to things like whether they attend meetings, personally attempt to undertake the change, and whether they show enthusiasm for getting the change accomplished.

- Keeping quiet about uncertainties can result in stakeholders thinking that they are purposefully being kept out of the loop. Change managers often share "knowns" about a project but may be reluctant to share "unknowns" until they can be worked out. This can result in employees assuming the worst. In order to minimize anxiety, change managers should be upfront about "unknowns" and be open to stakeholder suggestions in dealing with them.

- Employees may not understand the reason for the change. Although the basis for change sponsored by upper management may be readily apparent as a result of long-term planning, it should be recognized that other employees may not have this insight. It is important for management to walk employees through from the beginning so that they understand the how the change will be beneficial.

- Keeping too many business users out of the loop until the change is implemented. A significant representation of system users should be involved from the early stages of design. This provides benefits in terms of correctly identifying the problem and obtaining appropriate thought as to how it can be addressed. Change is unlikely to be successful if employees do not understand what it means for them personally.

- There may not be enough resources allocated to the project to accomplish the change. Companies need to recognize that it is often the case that the same employees cannot be expected to simultaneously keep up with everyday operations and also take on a large-scale change project. Such projects could be facilitated by making use of contractors or consultants to help balance the work load.

Important Elements of Change Management

Too many times significant effort in information system environments is exhausted in regard to unplanned work to put out fires resulting from poor planning. The GTAG (2012) points out that having an effective change management program can result in more time being spent on new projects and achieving business goals. In addition, it points out that internal auditors should evaluate whether important elements of a change management process exist and are understood by organizational personnel:

- Any changes should be categorized and assessed for impact.
- Appropriate testing should be conducted by both business and information technology personnel to ensure that changes are satisfactory before being placed into operation,
- An appropriate level of management should approve all changes.
- An appropriate back-out plan should exist in case a problem occurs after changes are put into operation.
- Changes should be communicated and scheduled with affected parties before they are placed into operation.

- Although emergency changes should be kept to a minimum, procedures should exist to identify, evaluate, and approve such changes. The importance of this GTAG element is also addressed as a management practice in COBIT 5:

BAI 06.02 Manage Emergency Changes

Carefully manage emergency changes to minimize further incidents and make sure the change is controlled and takes place securely. Verify that emergency changes are appropriately assessed and authorized after the change (ISACA, 2012b).

Preventive controls such as the above elements can help to ensure that system changes are appropriately approved and carried out. Detective controls should also be in place to identify problems in case preventive measures fail. Some common detective control metrics to measure a breakdown in the change management process include:

- Number of unauthorized changes that circumvent the change process.
- Number of emergency changes (including patches).
- Percentage of time spent on unplanned work.
- Percentage of projects delivered later than planned. (GTAG, 2012)

THE STEPS OF CHANGE MANAGEMENT

Changes should be anticipated well in advance of problems with a large percentage being performed to address system improvements that make a business more productive. The application of an immature process of change management often results in information system changes being made in a reactive manner to address some unanticipated problem that is in need of a quick fix.

IT assets are easiest to manage and control when there is no pressure to implement or deliver change. In low-performing organizations, patch deployment is often characterized as ad hoc, chaotic, and urgent. High-performing organizations are more likely to treat a new patch as a predictable and planned change subject to the normal change management process (GTAG, 2012).

The Institute of Internal Auditors suggest a series of seven steps, that are described in the following paragraphs, that can be used to standardize a system of change management so the it functions in an efficient manner. Specific management practices from COBIT 5 and other supporting literature are included to more fully describe the steps. In addition, a comprehensive example illustrates how the steps could be used to improve a company's control over verifying invoices for payment.

Step 1: Identifying the Need for the Change

The process of initiating change should not be left exclusively in the hands of upper management since they may not even be aware that there is a problem until the situation has grown to the point of requiring drastic measures. Employees at all levels should not be scared to suggest changes in operations (Pollock,

2016). The significant experience that employees have regarding how the company functions can provide a good source of thought that can be used to achieve more effective and efficient operations. Pierce (2008) suggests that regular meetings with employees should be held so that a better understanding can be achieved regarding how employees use the system along with the difficulties they face that could be solved with innovations. Pierce also notes that dissatisfied system users tend to focus on current system problems while more satisfied persons are more likely to consider long-term innovations. In any case, both types of issues can identify needed change.

In encouraging employees to submit their suggestions, Silverman (2011) makes the point that although financial rewards can provide an incentive for contributions, employees may be even more motivated by simply having an opportunity to have ideas adopted that allow them to perform their work in a more efficient manner. In addition, it should also be considered that more technical persons such as software engineers could be a good source of ideas associated with emerging technologies that employees with less technical skill may not consider (Mathiassen, Ngwenyama, and Aaen, 2005).

The importance of establishing an environment to identify areas where changes could make improvements is addressed in COBIT 5:

APO 04.01 Create an Environment Conducive to Innovation

Create an environment that is conducive to innovation, considering issues such as culture, reward, collaboration, technology forums, and mechanisms to promote and capture employee ideas.

APO 09.01 Identify IT Services

Analyze business requirements and the way in which IT-enabled services and service levels support business processes. Discuss and agree on potential services and service levels with the business, and compare them with the current service portfolio to identify new or changed services or service level options (ISACA, 2012b).

Step 1 Illustration

A company would like to improve its controls over expenditures in that some situations have arisen where the company has been paying for items that were purchased but not received. Although the company requires that purchase orders be identified before accepting any incoming shipments, discrepancies between incoming shipments and related purchase orders are not always forwarded to Accounts Payable where vendor invoices are approved for payment. An employee in Purchasing has suggested that the company implement a system of electronic receiving reports.

Step 2: Preparing for the Change

It is important that a formal structure for submission of change proposals be established so that appropriate components are included such as implementation steps, a plan to test the change, and an approach to roll back the change should problems occur (GTAG, 2012). Employees can submit recommendations for improvements through a change inquiry form. Buckley (2011) points out that the change inquiry should include a description of the type of the change, the likely impact, and a proposed date of implementation. Due to the detailed thought that must go into such a proposal it is important that staff be available to assist employees in the proper submission of a change inquiry.

The necessity of a change manager is an important consideration in this step to evaluate whether the change has adequate potential to be moved forward. In considering the merit of a proposed change COBIT 5 suggests a gap analysis:

APO 02.04 Conduct a Gap Analysis

Identify the gaps between the current and target environments and consider the alignment of assets (the capabilities that support services) with business outcomes to optimize investment in and utilization of the internal and external asset base (ISACA, 2012b).

Internal auditors can help to ensure that any change inquiries appearing to have merit are elevated to a change request and assigned a unique number that will allow them to be tracked throughout the change management process (Buckley, 2011).

Step 2 Illustration

A change inquiry form is submitted for the electronic receiving report suggestion. For each incoming shipment, the report that would collect information regarding: the purchase order number that established the purchase agreement with the vendor, a description of the items, the quantity of the items received, and a comments section. Using purchase order information, item descriptions would automatically populate the receiving report, with the quantities omitted to ensure that receiving personnel actually count the items delivered. The receiving supervisor would then compare the counted quantities to the items on the purchase order and note any discrepancies as a comment on the report. The change proposal suggests that it should be possible to have the change implemented within a three-week period.

After considering the change proposal, the change manager determines that the idea has merit and should elevated to the level of a change request and be assigned a unique tracking number. The implementation of the change would involve the development of an electronic receiving report, linking the report to the purchase order filed with the vendor, and entry of quantities received with the shipment.

Step 3: Developing a Business Justification

In many cases, the business justification for mandatory changes is in regard to some legal or regulatory requirement. In contrast, discretionary changes should provide a benefit in terms of achieving a business objective while considering the impact, cost, and benefits associated with the change (GTAG, 2012). The importance of continually evaluating reporting requirements and developing a business justification for changes is addressed in COBIT 5:

APO 01.01 Define the Organizational Structure

Establish an internal and extended organizational structure that reflects business needs and IT priorities.

BAI 01.02 Initiate a Program

Initiate a program to confirm the expected benefits and obtain authorization to proceed (ISACA, 2012b).

Internal auditors can help to ensure that someone with sufficient authority from the affected area supports the change, and that sufficient information is contained within the change request to make an authorization decision.

Step 3 Illustration

A manager in Accounts Payable believes that the information collected on the electronic receiving report would be of tremendous value in ensuring that any discrepancies between items ordered and received are identified. The current system of handwritten notations in Receiving does not always result in such discrepancies being considered in approving invoices for payment.

Step 4: Authorizing the Change Request

Appropriate personnel should evaluate and authorize change requests before implementation is attempted. This process can be facilitated through the use of a change advisory board (Melancon, 2006). Buckley (2011) indicates that change requests should be categorized and suggests the following:

- **Accepted:** The change request provides a practical business benefit and is worth further consideration with the chance for eventual implementation.
- **Rejected:** The change request should be turned down because it fails to demonstrate a reasonable business benefit.
- **On Hold/Further Work Is Needed:** More information is needed before a decision can be made.

Meyer and Lambert (2007) make the point that change requests should also be prioritized by considering the disruption that could occur if the change is not implemented. In further consideration of this point, Buckley (2011) states that the change can classified by considering how extensively the change affects the overall system:

- **Type A:** The change affects numerous systems and therefore involves a high level of technical complexity.
- **Type B:** The change affects only a single system with a medium level of technical complexity.
- **Type C:** The change affects only a single system with a low level of technical complexity.

Step 4 of the change management process is also addressed as a COBIT 5 management practice:

BAI 06.01 Evaluate, Prioritize and Authorize Change Requests

Evaluate all requests for change to determine their impact on business processes and IT services, and to assess whether change will adversely affect the operational environment and introduce unacceptable risks. Ensure that changes are logged, prioritized, categorized, assessed, authorized, planned and scheduled (ISACA, 2012b).

Internal auditors can assist in this step of the process by making certain that appropriate persons are evaluating change requests and that the roles and responsibilities of the advisory board are properly documented in its charter. Internal auditors can also help to confirm that each change request undergoes a proper process of risk assessment (Buckley, 2011).

Step 4 Illustration

The change advisory board concludes that the change request for the electronic receiving report should be approved for two primary reasons. First, it should not be left to chance that vendor invoices for items received are always correct. Secondly, the approval of invoices for payment should not be left to the possibility that an ad-hoc process of communicating hand-written discrepancies identified in Receiving will make their way into the process of invoice verification.

The change advisory board assigns the change as a "Type B" risk because it primarily affects the area of business expenditures. It is felt that the change warrants a medium level of complexity because the report must tie in with the purchase order filed with the vendor, evidence actual receipt of goods in Receiving, and permit Accounts Payable to perform a more careful evaluation in the approval of invoices for payment.

Step 5: Scheduling, Coordinating, and Implementing the Change

There should be an oversight team over the process of change management that includes a variety of skills including persons from the areas of corporate accounting, information technology, internal audit, and others possessing the necessary skills to be addressed by the particular requirements of the change (Meyer and Lambert, 2007). The oversight team can help to ensure that approved changes are appropriately coordinated and prioritized with other changes that are to be put into operation. COBIT 5 addresses the importance of the oversight team to implement and track changes:

BAI 05.02 Form an Effective Implementation Team

Establish an effective implementation team by assembling appropriate members, creating trust, and establishing common goals and effectiveness measures.

BAI 06.03 Track and Report Change Status

Maintain a tracking and reporting system to document rejected changes, communicate the status of approved and in-process changes, and complete changes (ISACA, 2012b)

Buckley (2011) suggests a number of points that should be addressed before changes are released into operations:

- Testing is complete with results agreeable to authorized parties. COBIT 5 addresses a number of important testing issues:

BAI 03.08 Execute solution testing

Execute testing continually during development, including control testing, in accordance with the defined test plan and development practices in the appropriate environment. Engage business process owners and end users in the test team.

BAI 07.05 Perform Acceptance Tests

Test changes independently in accordance with the defined test plan prior to migration to the live operational environment.

BAI 07.06 Promote to Production and Manage Releases

Promote the accepted solution to the business and operations. Where appropriate, run the solution as a pilot implementation or in parallel with the old solution for a defined period and compare behavior and results. If significant problems occur, revert back to the original environment based on the fallback/ backout plan (ISACA, 2012b).

- An estimate has been made regarding the amount of time that the system will be unavailable during implementation.
- Appropriate communications regarding the planned outage for implementation have been made with those directly impacted by the change.
- Appropriate back-out procedures have been documented.
- System documentation has been updated to reflect changes. COBIT 5 recognizes the importance of system documentation:

BAI 06.04 Close and Document the Changes

Whenever changes are implemented, update accordingly the solution and user documentation and the procedures affected by the change (ISACA, 2012b).

- Operational teams stand ready to provide support for the change.

Internal auditors can help to ensure that the above activities are conducted before changes are released into operations. In addition, auditors can verify that changes are implemented by persons independent of the development team by reviewing the security access profiles of the developers. Independent implementation helps to ensure that unauthorized changes are not put into operations (Buckley, 2011).

Step 5 Illustration

The task of implementing the change is delegated to an oversight team composed of representatives from Purchasing, Receiving, Warehousing, Accounts Payable, Information Technology, and Internal Audit. The team feels that the proposed three-week time frame for implementation is appropriate.

Step 6: Verifying and Reviewing the Implemented Change

An evaluation should be made to determine if the implemented change has been successful and that it appropriately meets its design specifications. COBIT 5 states the importance of providing initial user support and reviewing the implemented change:

BAI 07.07 Provide Early Production Support

Provide early support to the users and IT operations for an agreed-on period of time to deal with issues and help stabilize the new solution.

BAI 07.08 Perform a Post Implementation Review

Conduct a post-implementation review to confirm outcome and results, identify lessons learned, and develop an action plan. Evaluate and check the actual performance and outcomes of the new or changed service against the predicted performance and outcomes (i.e., the service expected by the user or customer) (ISACA, 2012b).

Integration testing should be completed early in the review process to consider whether implemented changes function properly with the various system modules with which the change will need to interact. In contrast, user acceptance testing is performed as part of the final review to help ensure that the agreed-upon requirements have been met (Kaitano, 2007). In reviewing the change management process, it should be determined whether appropriate procedures have been followed. It is also important that information has been gleaned as to what has been learned from the implementation of a particular change that can be carried forward into future change management projects (GTAG, 2012).

Step 6 Illustration

Although test data provided by Purchasing works well in evaluating the functioning of the new electronic receiving report, the Warehousing manager points out that it is possible that items identified on the receiving report may not always make it to the warehouse. He suggests that receiving reports be forwarded to Warehousing along with the incoming goods. This would permit Warehousing to verify the accuracy of the receiving report in connection with what actually makes its way into the warehouse. Management in both Receiving and Warehousing are in agreement that this additional verification of the receiving report could be of value. The issue is corrected by requiring the forwarding of both the goods and the receiving report to Warehousing. It is also agreed that the copy of the receiving report acknowledged by Warehousing will be used in the process of verifying vendor invoices for payment.

Step 7: Backing Out of the Change (If Necessary)

A basic tenet in regard to backing out of unsuccessful changes to software is that programmers should make changes to copies of a program rather than the actual software that is used in operations (Kaitano, 2007). When changes are made directly to operational copies, it is more likely that quick fixes and inappropriate levels of testing will be conducted to minimize the downtime of the system. Serious disruption of company operations can occur if the change later develops issues that could have been detected if more time had been available for implementation and testing. Even if changes are successful and are placed in operation, situations could arise under which the organization would need to return to a prior operating version of the software. An appropriate system of numbering versions of software could be invaluable should such a situation arise.

Step 7 Illustration

The electronic receiving report was implemented by making the changes to a copy of the software to allow return to the original processing in case any significant implementation problems arose. This was unnecessary as the implementation was successful.

PATCH MANAGEMENT PROCESS

The process of patch management is an essential part of overall system management that involves the acquisition, testing, and deployment of system or application updates, known as patches, to lessen perceived system vulnerabilities or improve operational efficiency. The concept of patch management can logically be considered as a smaller scale version of the process of change management which is concerned with major system-wide modification activities (Zanzig, Francia & Francia, 2014).

Scheduling Patch Management

All too often organizations are hesitant to develop an appropriate time table that will enable them to efficiently implement their patching activities. Cavusoglu, Cavusoglu and Zhang (2004) point out that asynchronous patch update is common in practice due to both the managerial costs of patching and concern over the operational risks involved. The unfortunate result is that many systems remain unpatched for months or even years due to a sporadic approach to making needed modifications that provides little, if any, consideration of prioritization and scheduling issues (Shostack, 2003).

A survey conducted by SolarWinds (2012) reveals the following points that could possibly explain the reluctance by some to engage in regular patch management activities:

- An average of 46% of respondents claim that researching, scripting, and testing a patch takes between 3 to 4 hours.
- 40% reported that after vetting the patch, it takes another 2 to 7 days to full deployment.

Even though the above findings indicate a relatively short period of time, it is possible that patches are often delayed because the risk of introducing system vulnerabilities seems high when compared to the benefit of what the patch accomplishes in contrast to a more major system modification. Such an assessment could have far-reaching consequences when ignoring security issues permits outsiders to cause chaos in the functioning of an organization's information system. A data breach report by Verizon (2015) attests to the fact that in 71% of vulnerability attacks, patches to address the vulnerability were available more than a year prior to the incident. It is also interesting that responses to the SolarWinds (2012) survey indicate that over 20% of the experienced security incidents could have been prevented by timely patching.

Okhravi & Nicol (2008) suggest that it is not possible to eliminate all system vulnerabilities regardless of whether systems are changed. On the one hand, familiarity with systems that remain unchanged allows potential perpetrators time to identify and exploit system weaknesses. In contrast, patches and other updates may introduce system vulnerabilities that have not adequately been addressed. However, they also suggest that exploitation of patches will eventually hit zero. This could be due to eventual disinterest in the software as newer versions are released. If this is true, the amount of resources spent to deal with vulnerabilities should be less as software approaches the end of its useful life.

Patch management involves a strategic decision to balance security risks and operational costs. However, there is a lack of quantitative security models to find the optimal equilibrium or managerial implications. Studies have shown that a more quantitative approach to the security attributes that satisfy quality-of-service (QoS) requirements, such as reliability, availability, and performance, is needed (Madan, Goseva-Popstojanova, Vaidyanathan, & Trivedi, 2004).

The question that begs to be asked is "When is the most opportune time to apply an available patch?" This, in essence, is referring to the optimal time of patching or, looking at it in a different perspective, to the time when patching becomes irrelevant. Ultimately, it is a matter of trade-off between security and productivity.

Patch Management Challenges

Although it is imperative that a proper process of patch management be carried it, the process is plagued with so many challenges that, more often than not, put incredible pressure on IT security personnel. In a whitepaper, LanDesk (2014) describes the following three major patch management challenges:

- Patching non-Microsoft products - patching Microsoft products is made easy by the automatic deployment of the Windows Server Update Services. However, an undue reliance on such service opens the gateway to complacency and neglect of other critical non-Microsoft application updates.
- Patching mobile devices and systems - the unpredictable connectivity of mobile users to the enterprise network provides an update challenge to IT administrators. If left unpatched, these system end-points could become the staging point of attack on the enterprise systems.
- Automating patch management processes - patch management is a very process-oriented activity and could become unwieldy when manual techniques are employed to enable patching on mid-to-large IT infrastructures.

Patch Management Maturity

Successful patch management programs can differ in design and implementation because of the varying technology needs across organizations (Chan, 2004). However, there does appear to be a common thread across approaches. Gerace & Cavusoglu (2009) enumerate the following critical elements in patch management that could have a significant effect on its success:

- Senior management support and direction of resources for the patching processes.
- Dedicated resources and clearly defined responsibilities.
- A current hardware and system inventory.
- A record of system and available patch inventories.
- A periodic scanning and monitoring of networks to assess risk levels and patch levels in systems.
- Pre-deployment testing of patches in a controlled environment to determine their overall effects.
- Post-deployment scanning and monitoring to ensure the effective application of patches.

System Users and Patch Management

An important component in the patch management process is ensuring user compliance with update and vulnerability issues regarding patch management. This section discusses approaches that have been used to help ensure that the end user complies with appropriate security and update issues. Higby, Bailey, & Michael (2004) introduce an automated wireless patch management system to update wireless clients with current security patches, antivirus software, and configured firewall settings. This is implemented by refusing user access to the wireless network unless the user has the specified virus protection software, up-to-date virus definitions, and system updates. If a scan identifies that one of these elements is missing, the patch management system provides the user with an available download. Additionally, a Microsoft Radius server is used to authenticate users. Only when authentication and patch updates are applied can the user's device be able to join the network.

Gerace & Mouton (2004) discuss the challenges and successes of implementing an enterprise patch management system, HFNetChkPro 4, in a college campus. HFnetChkPro 4 allows for agentless patch management to update machines on the network without requiring installed programs. It also features a patch scanner to identify which machines do not have a particular patch or update. The patch management tool also features the ability to control reboots of customizable groups of machines. This can allow for updates of broad areas of a system such as for laboratory and classroom computers without the necessity of involving the end user in the implementation of the patch.

Other Methodologies

The patch management process described in the preceding discussion is based on established methodologies such as the Plan-Do-Check-Act (PDCA) model (Deming, Out of the Crisis, 1986), the Plan-Do-Study-Act (PDSA) (Deming, 1993) (Langley, Nolan, & Nolan, 1994), and the Model for Improvement (Langley, et al., 2009). The PDCA model implements a cycle of continuous improvement. The initial step looks into defining the improvement opportunities and the planning for the changes. The second stage executes the changes and the third stage of the cycle checks the changes and the corresponding results. The final stage of the cycle acts on the results before the cycle gets to be repeated. The PDSA model is a modified version of Deming's PDCA cycle. In this modified version, the planning stage is augmented with prediction and associated theory and the "Check" stage is improved with the need to build knowledge by predicting whether the change will yield the anticipated change. In the Model for Improvement, the PDSA model is further refined by supplementing the cycle with the following project information: project goal, metrics of improvement, and the possible changes that can be put into effect.

The previously described patch management process implements the Model for Improvement methodology in a more detailed fashion. For instance, during the planning stage, the patching objectives are defined by first identifying the current vulnerabilities of the system. Also during the preparation for patching, metrics are established and anticipated system changes are documented.

Patching Process Metrics

One of the most quoted phrases in management that is attributed to Peter Drucker is "If you can't measure it, you can't improve it." He is simply stating the fact that there is no way to find out if the actions that you have undertaken are making a difference if there is no basis upon which they can be measured. A good metric should measure the relevant data that satisfies the needs of decision makers and should be quantitatively measurable, accurate, validated on a solid base, inexpensive to execute, able to be verified independently, repeatable, and scalable to a larger scale (Saydjari, 2006). Stoddard (2005) describes how security metrics are organized into three characterizations: organizational, operational, and technical. These categories are not mutually exclusive. Organizational metrics assess the effectiveness of the organization's standards, polices, and procedures used to enhance security. Operational metrics describe how organizational policies and procedures are implemented by technical staff. Finally, the technical set of metrics assesses the adequacy of security imposed on system components. Based on the same delineation by characterization, the authors propose the following set of patching process metrics:

Organizational Metrics

- **Adequacy of Patching Policy:** This metric indicates the thoroughness of the patching policy, if any.
- **Adequacy of Contingency Plans:** A complete success of a patching process must never be assumed. Thus, a contingency plan must be in place before the actual patching process takes place. However, the adequacy of the contingency plan must also be evaluated. If a patch goes bad, a solid contingency plan must be put into action as a defense-in-depth mechanism.
- **Appropriateness of Patching Guidelines:** This metric measures the adequacy of the guidelines to conduct an effective patching process. Do the guidelines provide comprehensive and detailed procedures to carry out the patching process?
- **Adequacy of User Training:** Are the users properly and regularly trained to put into action an effective patching process as needed? An evaluation of the training and all of the materials used in conducting the training sessions must be made for continuous improvement.

Operational Metrics

- **Adequacy of Plans for Patching:** The patching process must be planned way ahead of the actual process due to its widespread operational consequences, intended or unintended. A measure of the adequacy of the plan may provide a tool whether to procced or postpone the patching process.
- **Adequacy of Patching Documentation:** Any process must be fully documented in order to be able to enforce an adequate control. If a patch goes bad during the operational stage, it is possible to undo the patch and prevent it from recurring if proper documentations of past actions are available.
- **Amount of System Downtime:** Another operational metric that must be seriously considered is the amount of operational downtime. Naturally, as in any enterprise, production uptime is prime. However, management must always find a balance between production, efficiency, and security.

Technical Metrics

- **Number of Systems or Applications Requiring a Patch:** This metric indicates the extent and even the urgency of a patch process. The number of systems or applications requiring a patch is divided by the total number of systems or applications to indicate the coverage of the patching process. The metric assumes that a patch is available for a discovered vulnerability. The extent of the patching process may also be considered as an operational metric.
- **Number of Discovered System or Application Vulnerabilities Without a Patch:** This security related metric indicates the extent of the vulnerability that the enterprise is subject to. This metric could be an indicator of the urgency of the patching process as soon as a patch becomes available.
- **Vulnerability Score:** How severe is the discovered vulnerability? Is it severe enough that it will require immediate patching to mitigate its effect? These are the technical questions that must be answered before considering the initiation of the patching process (i.e., if a patch is even available).
- **Adequacy of the Patch:** This metric measures the effectiveness of the patch against the discovered vulnerability. Together with the vulnerability score of the vulnerability, a decision may be made whether to proceed with the patching process. For instance, if the available patch is deemed inadequate and the severity of the vulnerability is not critical, then the patching process may be postponed until such time when an adequate patch is available.

MEASURING MATURITY OF THE CHANGE MANAGEMENT PROCESS

Configuration management is defined in COBIT 5 as "the control of changes to a set of configuration items over a system life cycle." COBIT 5 considers a change management system to be a subset of a configuration management system (ISACA, 2013). The Institute of Internal Auditors appears to agree by stating that change management "does not include the entire systems development lifecycle process, such as application development or configuration management (GTAG, 2012)."

Within the realm of information technology, some persons may consider change management as a major system modification in contrast to patch management which is applied to smaller modifications. However, both concepts are concerned with producing appropriate system modifications with controls in place to ensure that changes are properly evaluated, prioritized, and scheduled. With the continual evolution of both change management theory and technological advancements for patching programs, the process of change management should continually be monitored to ensure that any changes are managed in an effective and efficient manner. COBIT 5 emphasizes the importance of achieving an appropriate level of process maturity:

APO 01.07 Manage Continual Improvement of Processes

Assess plan and execute the continual improvement of processes and their maturity to ensure that they are capable of delivering against enterprise, governance, management and control objectives (ISACA, 2012b).

The Change Management Maturity Model: COBIT 4.1

The Acquire and Implement domain of COBIT 4.1 provides a description of a maturity model as it could be applied specifically for change management:

0 Non-Existent

There is not a defined process of change management and changes can therefore occur with practically no controls. There is no understanding of the value of good change management or the disruption that can occur when effective practices are not present.

1 Initial / Ad Hoc

There is an awareness that changes need to be managed and controlled. However, there is not a consistent approach which results in a high likelihood of unauthorized changes and poor change documentation.

2 Repeatable but Intuitive

An informal but unstructured change management process has been developed with only limited amounts of planning and impact assessment.

3 Defined

The process of change management is defined to include emerging signs of categorization, prioritization, change authorization, release management, emergency procedures, and controls. There are signs of a formal method of analyzing the impact of technology changes on business operations.

4 Managed and Measurable

The process of change management is well developed and consistently followed and monitored. Changes undergo a formal approval process and are the result of good planning and impact assessment. Although effective and efficient, quality is achieved through considerable use of manual procedures and controls.

5 Optimized

There is a regular review of the change management process to keep it up to date with good practices. Sophisticated methods of tracking changes exist to detect unauthorized changes and software. The change management process has also become well integrated with its counterpart in business so that changes to increase business opportunities with information technology are being planned. (IT Governance Institute, 2007)

The Process Capability Model: COBIT 5

COBIT 5 is the most current version of the COBIT guidance. COBIT 5 (2012a) states that "the maturity attributes in COBIT 4.1 and the COBIT 5 process capability attributes are not identical".

Figure 1 provides a description of the COBIT 5 process capability model that replaced the maturity model of COBIT 4.1 (ISACA, 2013). Although it is referring to the more general description of the COBIT 4.1 maturity attributes (i.e., not applied specifically to change management), COBIT 5 does show a comparison table indicating that the attribute levels may have some overlap with COBIT 4.1:

Figure 1. COBIT 5 process capability model

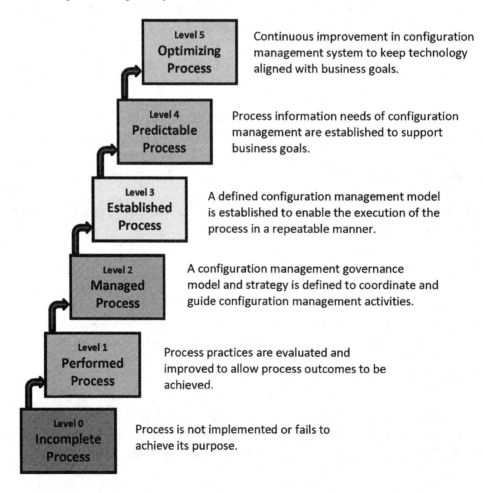

- Level 1 of COBIT 5 is comparable to Levels 1 and 2 of COBIT 4.1.
- Level 2 of COBIT 5 is not comparable to any specific level in COBIT 4.1.
- Levels 0, 3, 4 and 5 of COBIT 5 are comparable to those same levels in COBIT 4.1.

Change Management Maturity Model for Construction Projects

The above discussion of process maturity emphasizes the concept of change management in regard to the realm of information systems as described in COBIT. However, it is likely that many of the factors influencing effective change management are not restricted to information technology. For example, Arowosegbe and Mohamed (2015) developed a change management capability maturity model in regard to the many changes that occur with construction projects. The following maturity levels of their model were identified:

ML 1: Absent or Adhoc

There are no change management processes in place and success is largely dependent on individual effort and experience.

ML 2: Isolated Project

Informal change management processes exist for isolated projects.

ML 3: Multiple Projects

Some groups within the organization have established systematic procedures for managing change.

ML 4: Organization Standard

From the inception of every new project, the organization has a common approach and standards for applying change management.

ML 5: Organizational Competency

All steps of change management are fully integrated with a focus on learning and continuous improvement to avoid repeat failures.

It can be seen that the maturity levels of this model have similarities with those of COBIT 4.1 in that an organization's maturity level is improved as change management practices increasingly become part of normal project management. It is also interesting that the researchers identified the following five Key Capability Areas that they believe largely influence the maturity level of an organization's change management process:

KCA 1: Leadership

Senior management must demonstrate a commitment in being available to the project team and ensure that the team has the necessary skills and training.

KCA 2: Application

Considers the availability of funding to sponsor change management practices along with the scope with which those practices are actually implemented in projects.

KCA 3: Competencies

The organization must demonstrate the ability of organizational personnel to implement change as evidenced by the availability of training programs.

KCA 4: Standardization

Change management processes are fully integrated with project management.

KCA 5: Socialization

Organizational personnel at various levels demonstrate a high level of commitment to achieving successful change implementation.

Similar to the descriptions contained within the COBIT maturity model, the above Knowledge Capability Areas emphasize the importance having a well-defined approach along with management support and acceptance of personnel in regard to both the process of change management and the projects to be implemented.

FUTURE RESEARCH DIRECTIONS

Current and developing trends in change and patch management literature clearly identify the need for a well-defined process for evaluating information system changes that makes use of best practices. Despite significant efforts in defining an approach, there are gaps in current research in regard to the development of formal frameworks and metrics for these processes. It is also apparent that various human and organizational aspects of change and patch management should be linked to an appropriate model of change management maturity. Recognizing these needs, we propose the following research directions:

- Design and develop an awareness training program on change and patch management for both IT practitioners and internal auditors;
- Develop a formal framework for modeling the states of change and patch management processes;
- Develop verification processes for change management;

- Define specific attributes of change and patch management processing associated with the levels of the process capability model of COBIT 5; and
- Strive to find commonality among various maturity models of change management that consider human and organizational elements in addition to technical issues specific to an information system environment.

CONCLUSION

Organizations are continually evolving in their ability to harness technology to enhance information processing in a manner that improves efficiency of operations while maintaining the security of confidential information. In its change and patch management guidance, The Institute of Internal Auditors provides steps in applying change management that can be linked to best practices for information system changes in current literature including the COBIT 5 framework developed by the ISACA. The importance of having an appropriate process of change management is addressed as a management practice in COBIT 5:

APO 02.03 Define the Target IT Capabilities

Define the target business and IT capabilities and required IT services. This should be based on the understanding of the enterprise environment and the requirements; the assessment of the current business process and IT environment and issues; and consideration of reference standards, good practices and validated emerging technologies or innovation proposals (ISACA, 2012b).

A proper approach to change and patch management in the realm of information systems must consider a variety of issues involving technology and its interaction with the organization it serves. It is essential that a formal process exists that considers the importance of the human element from solicitation of ideas to getting appropriate organizational personnel to value and support the benefits of the change. People are unlikely to support even a good change unless they can be convinced that it is being implemented to improve their ability to function productively.

In regard to more technological aspects of the process, it should be considered that change management for information system environments is commonly applied on a smaller scale through patch management. It is essential that an organization be able to consider the maturity of the patching process along with metrics that can be used to evaluate continuous improvement. On a larger scale, an organization should also consider the maturity of its overall change management process. Using comparisons from COBIT 5, some tentative mapping of the attributes of the COBIT 4.1 maturity model as applied to change management can be made to COBIT 5's model for process capability levels. Additional research is needed to study the application of specific change/patch management characteristics to the process capability model. Internal auditors and information technology personnel can work together to help management to achieve significant improvements in their ability to securely process information while achieving a greater focus on improving operations. This can be accomplished by following the practical guidance of a structured approach that incorporates the best practices of change/patch management to an information system environment.

REFERENCES

Arowosegbe, A., & Mohamed, S. (2015). A Systematic Change Management Capability Maturity Assessment Framework for Contracting Organizations. *American Scientific Research Journal for Engineering, Technology, and Sciences, 13*(1), 88–96.

Buckley, S. (2011). IT Change Management. *Internal Auditor*. Retrieved from http://www.theiia.org/intAuditor/itaudit/2011-articles/it-change-management/

Cavusoglu, H., Cavusoglu, H., & Zhang, J. (2004). Economics of Security Patch Management. *Annual Workshop on the Economics of Information Security*. Retrieved November 14, 2012, from http://ns2.honlab.dc.hu/~mfelegyhazi/courses/BMEVIHIAV15/readings/06_Cavasoglu2006security_patch.pdf

Chan, J. (2004). *Essentials of Patch Management Policy and Practice*. Retrieved January 20, 2013, from http://www.patchmanagement.org/pmessentials.asp

Deming, W. E. (1986). *Out of the Crisis*. Cambridge, MA: MIT Press.

Deming, W. E. (1993). *The New Economics*. Cambridge, MA: MIT Press.

Gerace, T., & Cavusoglu, H. (2009). The Critical Elements of Patch Management. *Communications of the ACM, 52*(8), 117–121. doi:10.1145/1536616.1536646

Gerace, T., & Mouton, J. (2004). The Challenges and Successes of Implementing an Enterprise Patch Management Solution. In *Proceedings of the 32nd Annual ACM SIGUCCS Fall Conference* (pp. 30-33). ACM. 10.1145/1027802.1027810

Global Audit Technology Guide (GTAG) 2 Change and Patch Management Controls Critical for Organizational Success. (2012). (2nd ed.). The Institute of Internal Auditors.

Harpham, B. (2018). 8 ways you're failing at change management. *CIO*. Retrieved from http://lib-proxy.jsu.edu/login?url=https://search-proquest-com.lib-proxy.jsu.edu/docview/1983884418?accountid=11662

Higby, C., & Bailey, M. (2004). Wireless Security Patch Management System. In *Proceedings of the 5th Conference on Information Technology Education* (pp. 165-168). ACM.

ISACA. (2012a). *COBIT 5: A Business Framework for the Governance and Management of Enterprise IT*. ISACA.

ISACA. (2012b). *COBIT 5: Enabling Processes*. ISACA.

ISACA. (2013). *Configuration Management Using COBIT 5*. ISACA.

IT Governance Institute. (2007). COBIT 4.1. Author.

Kaitano, F. (2007). Change Control Audits – A Must for Critical System Functionality. *Internal Auditor*. Retrieved from http://www.theiia.org/intAuditor/itaudit/archives/2007/march/change-control-audits-a-must-for-

LanDesk. (2014). Resolving the Top Three Patch Management Challenges. Retrieved from http://info.landesk.com/NA-EN_LANDESKWeb_WhitePapersDynamic.html?wp=resolving-the-top-three-patch-management-challenges-LSI-1192&_ga=1.11167101.898317616.1445994114

Langley, G. J., Moen, R., Nolan, K. M., Nolan, T. W., Norman, C. L., & Provost, L. P. (2009). *The Improvement Guide: A Practical Approach to Enhancing Organizational Performance* (2nd ed.). San Francisco, CA: Jossey-Bass.

Langley, G., Nolan, K. M., & Nolan, T. W. (1994, June). The Foundation of Improvement. *Quality Progress*, 81-86.

Madan, B. B., Goseva-Popstojanova, K., Vaidyanathan, K., & Trivedi, K. S. (2004). A Method for Modeling and Quantifying the Security Attributes of Intrusion Tolerant Systems. *Performance Evaluation*, *56*, 167–186.

Mathiassen, L., Ngwenyama, O., & Aaen, I. (2005, November). Managing Change in Software Process Improvement. *IEEE Software*, 84–91.

Melancon, D. (2006). The Three Cs of IT Change Management. *Internal Auditor*. Retrieved from http://www.theiia.org/intAuditor/itaudit/archives/2006/april/the-three-cs-of-it-change-management/

Meyer, M. J., & Lambert, J. C. (2007, November). Patch Management: No Longer Just an IT Problem. *The CPA Journal*, 68–72.

Okhravi, H., & Nicol, D. M. (2008). Evaulation of Patch Management Strategies. *International Journal of Computational Intelligence: Theory and Practice*, *3*(2), 109–117.

Pierce, R. (2008). Using Customer Input to Drive Change in User Assistance. In *Proceedings of the 26th annual ACM international conference on Design of communication*. ACM. 10.1145/1456536.1456541

Pollock, S. (2016). Change management: It is not a choice. *Talent Management Excellence Essentials*. Retrieved from http://lib-proxy.jsu.edu/login?url=https://search-proquest-com.lib-proxy.jsu.edu/docview/1955087691?accountid=11662

Saydjari, O. S. (2006). Is Risk a Good Security Metric? In *Proceedings of the 2nd ACM Workshop On Quality of Protection (QoP'06)* (pp. 59-60). New York, NY: ACM. 10.1145/1179494.1179508

Schmidt, D., & White, J. (2017). *Why don't big companies keep their computer systems up-to-date. The Conversation, September 26.* Vanderbilt University.

Securities and Exchange Commission (SEC). *SEC Charges Goldman Sachs With Violating Market Access Rule.* Retrieved from http://www.sec.gov/litigation/admin/2015/34-75331.pdf

Shostack, A. (2003). Quantifying Patch Management, Secure. *Business Quarterly*, *3*(2), 1–4.

Silverman, R. E. (2011, Oct. 17). Managing & Careers: For Bright Ideas, Ask the Staff --- Companies, Striving to Cut Costs and Encourage Innovation, Seek Suggestions from Rank and File. *Wall Street Journal*. Retrieved from http://search.proquest.com/docview/898496273?accountid=11662

SolarWinds Press Release. (2012). Results Of Patch Compliance Survey Reveal Increased Need For Automated Patch Management Tools. *Security Dark Reading (Online)*. Retrieved from http://www. darkreading.com/vulnerability-management/167901026/security/news/240007602/results-of-patch-compliance-survey-reveal-increased-need-for-automated-patch-management-tools.html

Stoddard, M. B. (2005). Process Control System Security Metrics–State of Practice. *I3P Institute for Information Infrastructure Protection Research Report*.

Verizon. (2015). *2015 Data Breach Investigations Report*. Retrieved from http://www.verizonenterprise.com/DBIR/2015/

Zanzig, J. S., Francia, G. A. III, & Francia, X. P. (2014). Internal Control Considerations for Information System Changes and Patches. In H. Rahman & R. de Sousa (Eds.), *Information Systems and Technology for Organizational Agility, Intelligence, and Resilience* (pp. 161–179). Hershey, PA: IGI Global; doi:10.4018/978-1-4666-5970-4.ch008

Zanzig, J. S., Francia, G. A. III, & Francia, X. P. (2015). A Consensus of Thought in Applying Change Management to Information System Environments. *International Journal of Information System Modeling and Design*, *6*(4), 24–41. doi:10.4018/IJISMD.2015100102

ADDITIONAL READING

Avila, O., & Garcés, K. (2017). Change management support to preserve Business–Information technology alignment. The Journal of Computer Information Systems, 57(3), 218-228. doi:http://dx.doi.org.lib-proxy.jsu.edu/10.1080/08874417.2016.1184006

Lessa, L., & Saravanan, D. (2014). Change Management as a Critical Sustainability Factor to Prevent Failure of E-government Initiatives. In *Proceedings of the 8th International Conference on Theory and Practice of Electronic Governance (ICEGOV '14)*. (pp. 474-475). ACM, New York, NY, USA. 10.1145/2691195.2691232

Li, F., & Paxson, V. (2017). A Large-Scale Empirical Study of Security Patches. In *Proceedings of the 2017 ACM SIGSAC Conference on Computer and Communications Security (CCS '17)*. (pp. 2201-2215). ACM, New York, NY, USA. 10.1145/3133956.3134072

Litty, L., & Lie, D. (2011). Patch Auditing in Infrastructure as a Service Clouds. In *Proceedings of the 7th ACM SIGPLAN/SIGOPS international conference on Virtual execution environments (VEE '11)*. (pp. 145-156). ACM, New York, NY, USA. 10.1145/1952682.1952702

Kilkelly, E. (2014). Creating leaders for successful change management. Strategic HR Review, 13(3), 127-129. Retrieved from http://lib-proxy.jsu.edu/login?url=https://search-proquest-com.lib-proxy.jsu.edu/docview/1542372976?accountid=11662

Noufou, O., & Ouakouak, M. L. (2018). Impacts of personal trust, communication, and affective commitment on change success. Journal of Organizational Change Management, 31(3), 676-696. doi:http://dx.doi.org.lib-proxy.jsu.edu/10.1108/JOCM-09-2016-0175

Nwokeji, J. C., Clark, T., Barn, B., & Kulkarni, V. (2015). A Conceptual Framework for Enterprise Agility. In *Proceedings of the 30th Annual ACM Symposium on Applied Computing (SAC '15)* (pp. 1242-1244). ACM, New York, NY, USA. 10.1145/2695664.2699495

Nwokeji, J. C., Clark, T., Barn, B., Kulkarni, V., & Anum, S. O. A Data-centric Approach to Change Management. In *Proceedings of the 2015 IEEE 19th International Enterprise Distributed Object Computing Conference (EDOC)*, Adelaide, Australia, 2015, pp. 185-190. 10.1109/EDOC.2015.34

Otsuka, H., & Lutfiyya, H. (2011). Using Strategy Trees in Change Management in Clouds. In Proceedings of the 7th International Conference on Network and Services Management (CNSM '11). International Federation for Information Processing, Laxenburg, Austria, pp. 133-142.

Palumbo, T. (2015). The Importance of Implementing Central Patch Management and Our Experiences Doing So. In *Proceedings of the 2015 ACM Annual Conference on SIGUCCS.*, St. Petersburg, FL. (pp. 105-108). ACM, New York, NY, USA. 10.1145/2815546.2815561

Singleton, T. CISA.C.G.E.I.T., C.P.A. (2014). IS audit basics: The logical reason for consideration of IT. ISACA Journal, 3, 16. Retrieved from http://lib-proxy.jsu.edu/login?url=https://search-proquest-com.lib-proxy.jsu.edu/docview/1536921329?accountid=11662

Thompson, C. F., Anderson, R. I., Au, I., Ratzlaff, C., & Zada, N. (2010). Managing User Experience: Managing Change. In *CHI '10 Extended Abstracts on Human Factors in Computing Systems (CHI EA '10)* (pp. 3143–3146). New York, NY, USA: ACM.

Zelenkov, Y. (2016). Impact of Knowledge Management and Change Management on the Effectiveness of the Firm: Evidence from the Russian Companies. In Proceedings of the 11th International Knowledge Management in Organizations Conference on The Changing Face of Knowledge Management Impacting Society (KMO '16). ACM, New York, NY, USA, Article 51, 7 pages. 10.1145/2925995.2926037

Zhang, F., & Li, Q. (2018). Security Vulnerability and Patch Management in Electric Utilities: A Data-Driven Analysis. In *Proceedings of the First Workshop on Radical and Experiential Security (RESEC '18)* (pp. 65-68). ACM, New York, NY, USA. 10.1145/3203422.3203432

KEY TERMS AND DEFINITIONS

Change Management: The application of a well-defined approach to transition an organization from a current state to a future state so that expected benefits can be accomplished.

Configuration Management: The practice of controlling logical or structural arrangement within an organization to enhance productivity.

Control Procedures: Policies put in place to aid in the mitigation of risks in the accomplishment of organizational objectives.

Detective Controls: Controls put in place to identify errors or irregularities that have occurred.

Internal Audit: An objective approach of assurance and consulting that improves the operations of an organization by further developing its risk management and control processes.

Maturity Model: A technique to measure the ability of an organization to implement continuous improvement processes.

Operational Metrics: The measure of the effectiveness of the implementation of an organization's standards, policies, and procedures.

Organizational Metrics: The measure of the effectiveness of an organization's standards, policies, and procedures in enhancing security.

Patch Management Process: A process that involves the acquisition, testing, and deployment of system or application updates.

Preventive Controls: Controls put in place to lessen the probability that errors or irregularities will occur.

Chapter 4
FME Technique for Reduced Method Rejection

S. B. Goyal
City University, Malaysia

ABSTRACT

In situational method engineering (SME), there are two core intentions that method engineers look for: 1) a set method engineering goal that is the kind of method needed and 2) a method allowing him to satisfy this goal. This chapter can capture method engineering's goal using a generic process model (GPM) that guides the method engineering in the definition of his project method engineering goal and in the selection approach that best allows him to achieve it. The authors wish to move to functional method engineering so as to explore the context of method engineering/situational method engineering more fully based on functional and non-functional method situation. The implications of the approach on CAME tool design are considered and illustrated through a running example.

INTRODUCTION

Method Engineering, ME is the discipline of developing information systems development methods. Initially, it was thought that a universal method (Saeki M. & Wenyin K., 1994) that was capable of addressing the needs of all information system development projects could be defined. However, this view was rejected (Hoef, Rob, Rolf & Vincent 1997), (Karlsson F. & Ågerfalk P J, 2004). Since project needs vary with projects and projects vary in their characteristics, development of methods may require specific adaptations (Anat & Iris, 2011). Therefore, an engineering technique for this is required. The area of Situational Method Engineering, SME was developed to build methods for specific development situations. Situational Method Engineering, SME, assumes the existence of a method base from which method components could be retrieved and assembled to form the desired method (Xavier, Jolita, Anna, Alberto, David, Jesús, Sergi, Marc, Norbert, Alberto, Angelo, 2018).

The assembly process has been illustrated in (Brinkkemper, Saeki & Harmsen 1998) where state chart and object models have been assembled together to form a new method.

DOI: 10.4018/978-1-5225-7271-8.ch004

Ralyte (Ralyté, Rébecca & Rolland, 2003) proposed a two-step goal oriented SME process: first, a method engineering, ME, goal is established, second, assembly based method engineering task is carried out by eliciting ME intentions. Prakash (Prakash, Srivastava, Gupta & Arora, 2007) proposed a three stage SME process: intention matching, architecture matching, and method implementation matching.

The situation of SME can be conceptualized in many ways, as descriptors (Rolland & Prakash, 1996), contingency factors (Slooten & Brinkkemper, 1993; Lemmen & Punter, 1994; Swede & Vliet 1994; Slooten 1995), project factors (Harmsen, Brinkkemper, Han Oei, 1994), situation factors (Harmsen, Lubbers I. & Wijers 1995), context type (Deneckere, Elena & Bruno 2010) and project type (Bucher, Klesse, Kurpjuweit &Winter 2007), (Bucher & Winter 2008). Table I summarizes the proposals made by different authors for the notion of a situation.

In spite of the large number of proposals that exist, there is some dissatisfaction with the notion of situation. Bucher (Bucher, Klesse, Kurpjuweit &Winter, 2007) is concerned about the poor understanding of the notion of a situation. According to (Borner R., 2010), there is need to find a way to reduce the number of possible situations.

The authors first observe that almost all situation characteristics in Table 1 relate to project/method implementational aspects. These do not directly define the characteristics of the needed method but are the factors that influence the successful use of a method. The chapter propose here the introduction of factors that directly affect method selection from a technical viewpoint.

Motivated by information systems that have functional and non-functional aspects, the authors see a situation as having functional and non-functional aspects. The former relates to the tasks that a method must carry out whereas the latter relates to the project/method implementational environment issues that the methods must be sensitive to. A complete resolution to the SME problem shall occur when both functional and non-functional situational aspects are addressed. Consequently, the authors propose the move shown in figure 1.

The figure shows that a method is located in a situation. On the left-hand side, is the current proposal where the situation is non-functional in nature whereas on the right-hand side, the method is situated in its functional and non-functional aspects.

Evidently, the interesting question is the use of functional characteristics in building situated methods. The authors refer to the handling of functional aspects as Functional Method Engineering, FME.

This chapter proposes method as a function to meet the functional characteristics of a situation. From the notion of a function, the authors see that the important factors to be considered are input, output and process. Additionally, the actors who interact with the method and the immediate application environment in which the method component fits are also needed. The chapters treat these as functional situation characteristics. Once method components have been selected by matching functional needs, then these are to be assembled together. We propose a functional assembly process by which appropriate functional components are assembled together to realize the larger method function.

To obtain the notion of 'method as a function', the authors introduce the idea of functional method. The top-level function of a method is decomposed, which yields a nested structure reflecting the functional properties of the desired method. Functional methods and components are available in one part of our two parts of the method repository.

A functional method needs to be implemented. Since, it is a class of methods, it can be implemented in several ways. Every implementation is a definition of internal features and their connection to yield the desired functionality. Method implementations are available in the second part of the repository.

Table 1. Situation Characterization Criteria

Situation Characterization Based on	Example
Situation factors (Harmsen, Lubbers I. & Wijers 1995)	Environment: management commitment, resources; Project Method implementation: Size of project team, capability of project team Projects: Innovation level, Clarity of project goal, complexity of project
Project Characteristics (Harmsen, Lubbers I. & Wijers 1995)	Team size Domain Characteristics etc.
Project Context based on Contingency factors and constraints (Slooten & Hodes 1996)	Contingency Factors: Management Commitment; Importance; Impact; Resistance and conflict; Time pressure; Shortage of human resources; Shortage of means; Formality; Knowledge and experience; skills; Size; Relationships; dependency; Clarity; Stability; Complexity; Level of innovation Values of contingency factors: Low, Normal, High Constraints: Type of information systems, Standards, Technical constraints, external factors etc.
Project Environment (Harmsen 1997)	Existing information infrastructure, the users, the method implementational culture of both the supplier method implementation and the customer method implementation
Project Characterization based on Project or contingency factors (Harmsen 1997)	Examples of project or contingency factors are Application/ domain characteristics, external factors, technical factors, and the available development expertise
Situation Factors (Harmsen 1997)	Environment: management commitment, importance of the information system, impact of the information system, amount of resistance and conflict, scarcity of available resources, stability and formality of the environment, knowledge and experience of the users Project method implementation: skill of the project team, size of the project team, quality of information planning, interfaces with other projects and systems, dependency on other projects and parties Project: clarity and stability of project goal, quality of the specifications, size of the project, complexity of the project, novelty of the project Constraints: (contractual) agreement with the customer, project goal, established standards, technical restrictions Values of individual parameters are Low, medium and High.
Project Characteristics (Karlsson F. & Ågerfalk P J, 2004)	Configuration Packages Configuration Templates
Situation Factors (Bekkers, Brinkkemper & Mahieu 2008)	27 Situation Factors and categorize in five categories Method implementational characteristics Customer characteristics Market characteristics Product characteristics Stakeholder involvement
Vector of Characteristics (Anat & Iris, 2008)	Organisation Project Development team Customer
Context Factor (Borner R., 2010)	service consumer: internal, external, both, budget: restrictive budget, generous funding, SOA concepts: business services, software services, hierarchy of services SOA maturity level: SIMM level 1-3, SIMM level 4-7, Compliance: general laws, industry-specific, regulations, internal policies, IT department: existent, not existent, and Interaction: customer interaction, employee interaction
Context Factor (Borner, Goeken, Kohlborn, & Korthaus, 2011; after Borner R., 2010)	Compliance: general laws, industry-specific, regulations, internal policies IT department: existent, not existent Interaction: customer interaction, employee interaction

Figure 1. Position of our proposal

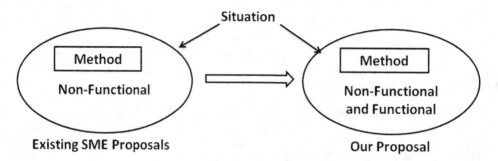

This chapter proposes functional method engineering in two stages, functional matching and implementation matching. Consequently, the chapter has been arranged in two broad parts. In the first, the authors develop the functional method meta-model, the functional situation and the process of functional matching. In the second the authors introduce the notion of method implementation, its matching operations and the process of matching.

The layout of this chapter is as follows. In Functional Situation, the authors use the life cycle developed in (Prakash & Goyal, 2007) to show the place of functional method engineering in this life cycle. In Operations for Functional Method Engineering: First Stage, the authors define our notion of functional method, introduce the functional method meta-model and postulate the attributes of a functional situation. The operations required to perform matching with the functional situation are also considered. In Functional Method Engineering: The First Stage, the first stage of the process of functional method engineering, that which engineers the desired functional method is considered. In Method Implementation, the authors introduce our notion of method implementation and the matching operations. In Functional Method Engineering: The Second Stage, the manner in which the second stage of the functional method engineering process is carried out and considered. Finally, the authors compare our work with related literature.

FUNCTIONAL SITUATION

This chapter relates Functional Method Engineering, FME to the method engineering life cycle proposed in (Prakash & Goyal 2007). In this life cycle, discovery and representation of method intentions is in the requirement's engineering phase, definition of the functional method is in the design phase, and finally development of method implementation is in the construction phase. FME starts with functional method and is therefore located in the Design & Construction Engineering stages of this life cycle (see Figure 2).

This chapter defines a functional method (Prakash & Goyal, 2008) as follows:

Functional Method = {method | method performs Function F}

In other words a functional method represents a set of methods. For example, an attribute can be defined in different ways in different methods. Variations can be to allow single valued attributes, multi-valued attributes & derived attributes. These can be abstracted out into one function, Draw Attribute. Similarly,

Figure 2. The method development life cycle

	Stage & Process	Input	Output
	Requirements Engg./ Intention Matching	Intention of the method To Be obtained from Interviews etc.	Intentionally similar methods to the method To Be
Functional Method Engineering	Design Engg/ Functional Method Matching	Functional Methods of intentionally similar methods	Functionally similar methods
	Construction Engg./ Implementation Matching	Implementations of functionally similar method	Method To-Be

different methods define an ISA hierarchy differently, for example, with strict or loose inheritance. A functional method could then be "draw ISA hierarchy".

A functional method (Prakash & Goyal 2008) is named and the name reflects the function performed by the class of methods abstracted in it. For example, the authors can define a functional method named Create Relationship to abstract out the common functionality of creating relationships in OOSE and ER model. This functional aspect is applicable to agile process of method also (Lidia, Woubshet, Pretti, Jolita, Xavier, Markku, 2017).

Our functional method meta-model is shown in figure 3 in UML notation. This meta-model says that there are three kinds of methods: atomic, complex and abstract. An atomic functional method cannot be broken down into simpler ones. A complex functional method is an aggregate of simpler functional methods and displays a composed-of relationship between the aggregate method and the component methods. An abstract functional method is a generalization/ specialization of another functional method. All functional methods atomic, complex or abstract must be available in the method repository for retrieval and adaptation.

A functional method has five fundamental attributes, as shown in figure 3. These attributes are based in the notion that a method is an abstraction of a function. This suggests three clear attributes, input, output and the concepts used. The authors adopt the first two of these directly. For the concepts used, the authors identify the concepts used in the method to produce the output. In addition to these three attributes, the authors introduce the name of functional method and the environment in which it is defined. Thus authors have the following:

Name of the method reflects the function performed by the method and is unique among all functional method names.

- **Input:** This identifies the input information contents needed for starting off the method.
- **Output:** Is the information produced by the method i.e. resulting from the enactment of the method.
- **Concepts Used:** These are the most important, discriminating notions that go into the function of the method. A used concept refers to the structure, policies and strategies of the process underlying the function represented by the method. For example, a method may use the notion of a transi-

Figure 3. Functional method meta-model for FME

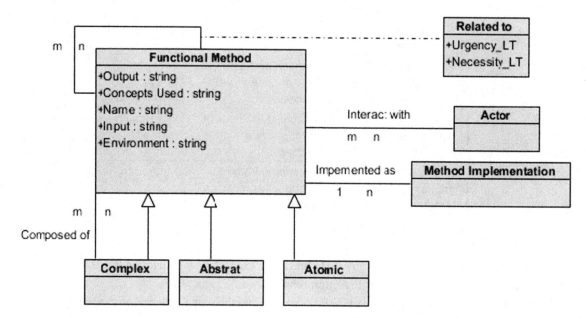

tion diagram model that another functionally similar method may not use. Therefore, the Concepts Used attribute for this method shall have 'state' and 'state transition' as its values.

- **Environment:** is the context of the architecture. It provides the settings or the domain, within which the method has been defined.

These attributes are useful for retrieving functional methods from the repository. Method components retrieved from the repository based on attributes matching are, prima facie, functionally similar to the needed method. Therefore, they are candidates for adaptation when developing the new method.

In figure 3, functional methods enter into a number of relationships, Related to, Interacts with, and Implemented as. This chapter explain each of these below:

Related to: Functional methods are related to one another. This relationship establishes a predecessor and successor relationship between the participating methods. Link Type (LT) is used to elaborate the nature of the relationship between these. It consists of two properties Urgency and Necessity.

Table 2. Types of links

Link Type	Urgency	Necessity	Abbreviation
1	Immediate	Must	IM
2	Immediate	Can	IC
3	Deferred	Must	DM
4	Deferred	Can	DC

Given a pair of related methods, Urgency refers to the time at which a method is to be enacted relative to the enactment of the other. If it is to be enacted immediately after the first, then this attribute takes on the value Immediate. If it can be enacted any time, immediately or at any later moment, after the first, then urgency takes on the value Deferred. Necessity refers to whether or not a method is necessarily to be enacted after the first has been enacted. If it is necessary to enact it, then this attribute takes the value Must otherwise it has the value Can. This gives us four types of inter-relationships between functional methods. These are summarized in Table 2.

Interacts with: Given a method, the question arises as to who can use it. Therefore, it is useful to associate with the functional method its main actors. This chapter defines actors as other functional method, humans, etc. responsible for invoking the services offered, since there can be many actors for a method, and a given actor can work with many functional methods, figure 3, shows that the Interacts with relationship is M:N.

Again, knowledge of actors helps in selecting functional methods for adaptation. If the actors of the method To-Be are the same as those of some methods found in the repository then it reinforces the belief that the latter are candidates for adaptation.

Implemented as: This relationship says that a functional method can be implemented in one or more ways. This is shown by the 1:N relationship between functional method and method implementation in figure 3.

Representing Functional Situation

This chapter can now define a functional situation in terms of the concepts of the meta model. A functional situation is described by

- The five attributes: Name, Input, Output, Concepts used and Environment.
- The three relationships: Related to, Interacts with, and Implemented as.

OPERATIONS FOR FUNCTIONAL METHOD ENGINEERING: FIRST STAGE

In this section, the authors lay the basis for performing the first stage of FME. We first consider the graphical representation of the functional method. Thereafter the authors define operations that can be used in doing FME.

This chapter represent functional method as a labeled rectangle; and the relationship, between functional methods as directed labeled edges between rectangles. These edges are labeled with the values of the link types.

Complex functional methods are built from atomic ones. Figure 4 shows two ways of representing them. The first of these shown in row 6 displays the complex functional method in its full complexity at one level. It is also possible to show a complex functional method as a double rectangle (row 7) which can be expanded to reveal its full details at a lower level (row 8).

Abstract functional methods are shown by the standard ISA link between functional methods. Functional methods that have nothing nested in them are assumed to be atomic.

Now consider figure 5 that shows the functional method named Draw ER schema. This is a complex functional method that represents a method for building ER schema. It consists of two simpler functional methods, Draw Entity and Draw Relationship respectively. The link types between these show that Draw Relationship can be enacted any time after (urgency= D) Draw Entity has been done, and that it may optionally be performed (Necessity=C). Since it is possible to Draw Entity or Draw Relationship in any order, two labeled "is related to" edges are defined in figure 5.

Both these edges have the same link types, namely, DC. The attributes of Draw ER Schema are as follows:

Figure 4. Notations for functional method

Graphical Notation	Meaning	Significance
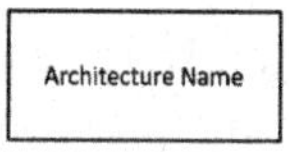 Architecture Name	Labeled Rectangle	Functional Method
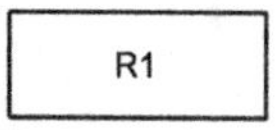 R1	R1 is functional method	Atomic functional method
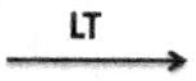 LT →	Labeled Edge: LT is a link type	Link Type (Refer Table 3)
/ \	Without labeled edge used for abstract method type	Edge for abstract type
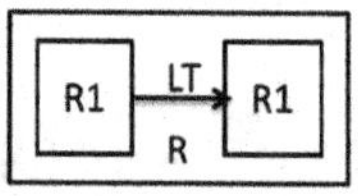 R1 —LT→ R1 / R	R is complex functional method and contain another R1 & R2 two atomic functional method	**Complex Functional Method:** a) Regular
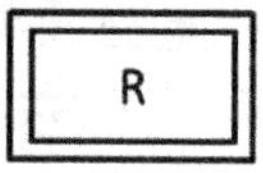 R	R can be collapsed its complex functional method is shown at a lower level.	**Complex Functional Method:** b) Collapsed
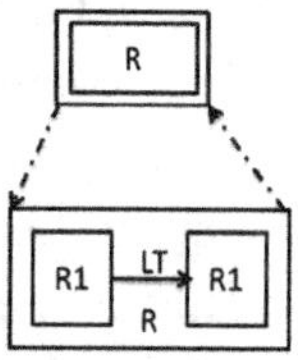 R / R1 —LT→ R1 / R	The expanded functional method corresponding to R is displayed.	**Complex Functional Method:** c) Expandable
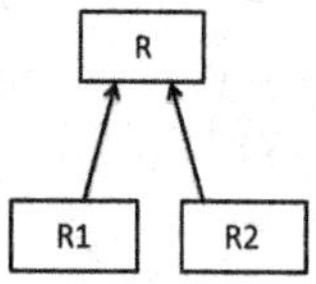 R / R1 R2	R is a generalization of R1 and R2	Abstract Functional Method

- Name: Draw ER Schema
- Environment: Information Systems, Database Systems
- Input: Application concepts
- Output: Conceptual schema
- Concepts used: Attributes, Entities and Relationships
- Related to: NIL
- Implemented as: Submethod
- Interacts with: Application Engineer
- Method type: Complex

The functional situation of Draw ER schema is identified by the foregoing.

The input to the method is the set of application concepts, (employee, department, the employs relationship etc.) that are to be represented in ER form. The output of the method is the conceptual schema in ER form. The concepts used in the method are those of attribute, entity and relationship respectively. The method is stand-alone and is not related to any other one. The actor who uses the method is the application engineer. Finally, the method, since it is complex, is not implemented but has sub-methods. This is represented by "Submethod".

Now, it is possible to consider Draw Entity. Figure 5 shows that it consists of Draw Attribute and Draw Key, which in turn are atomic. There is a relationship between the components of Draw Entity. This relationship has Urgency=D and Necessity=C as before.

The attributes of Draw Entity are as follows:

- Name: Draw Entity
- Environment: ER diagram
- Input: Entities
- Output: Keys, Attributes, Entities
- Concepts used: Attribute, Key
- Related to: NIL
- Implemented as: Submethod
- Interacts with: Application Engineer
- Method type: Complex

As before, the foregoing nine attributes identify the functional situation of Draw Entity. Similar diagrams can be drawn and attributes specified for the other components of Draw ER Schema.

Figure 5. Functional method of draw ER schema

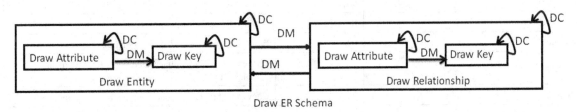

From the attributes of Draw ER Schema and Draw Entity respectively, the authors see that the first eight attributes provide to us information that defines the functional situations in which these methods are useful. In other words, these shall match the functional situation that has the attribute values of these. There is a special attribute called method type which is specific to describing the functional method and has no role to play in defining the situation. This attribute only provides information about the structure of the methods itself. It is used in the functional assembly process described later.

Functional Method Matching Operations

All functional methods are stored in the method repository. The new desired method is built by matching the functional needs of retrieved method components with the functional attributes of the candidate method, and adapting components that are needed and discarding the useless ones. The proposed matching operations are shown in Table 3.

In Table 3, R1, R2, refer to rectangles, and LT, LT1, LT2 to link types. Whereas most of the operations are self-explanatory, perhaps, Nest, Un-nest, Sequence and Eliminate need some explanation. For Nest, the assumption is that R2 is a functional method that is (a) not nested in the nested structure of R1 and (b) is at the same nesting level as R1. For Un-nest, R2 must be at the next lower level of nesting in R1. After the operation is executed, it is available at the same level of nesting as R1.

The sequence operation can be applied to form a sequence of methods with each pair in the sequence having its own link type. It is assumed that the methods participating in a sequence are all at the same level of nesting. After the operation is executed, the sequence remains at the same level of nesting as the methods comprising it. The Eliminate operation is the inverse of sequence. The edge in the sequence is eliminated and the participating methods are separated out and remain at the same nesting level as

Table 3. The functional method matching operations

Operation	Arguments	Description
Rename	R1, Y	Rename R1 and the new name is Y
Create	R1	Creates a new R1 at the outermost level of nesting
Delete	R1	Delete R1, all its internal components and all links into/out of it
Nest	R2, R1	Produce R1 having R2 nested in it.
Un-nest	R2, R1	Make R2 at the same nesting level as R1. Removes all links in R1 coming out of or going into R2
Change	LT1, LT2	Change the link type from LT1 to LT2
Sequence	R1, R2, LT	Produce a sequence of R1 followed by R2 with LT type link.
Eliminate	R1, R2, LT	The sequence is deleted. R1 and R2 are separated
Generalize	R1, R2	Produce R1 generalization of R2
Specialize	R1, R2	Produce R1 specialization of R2
Expand	R1	Expand R1 & show its internal structure
ColReg	R1	Convert and replace collapsed complex R1 with regular complex R1
RegCol	R1	Convert and replace regular complex R1 to collapsed R1

they were in the sequence. The generalize/specialize operations build the ISA hierarchies of methods. Finally, the Expand operation shows the internal structure of a given method. ColReg (i.e. Collapsed to Regular) is use to convert and replace collapsed complex functional method with regular complex functional method. RegCol (i.e. Regular to Collapsed) is the inverse operation of ColReg. The use of these operations is considered in the next section.

FUNCTIONAL METHOD ENGINEERING: THE FIRST STAGE

As already discussed, FME starts with functional method matching (Figure 2). It aims to match the method stored in the method repository with the functional situation. To-Be. The core matching process is described in this section.

This chapter illustrates FME with the same problem as that of Brinkkemper (Brinkkemper, Saeki & Harmsen 1998), namely building an Objectchart from Object Model and Harel's Statechart.

Consider Figure 6 that shows the functional method named Draw an Object Model. This is a complex functional method and consists of three functional methods, Identify Class, Identify Object and Identify Association respectively. The link types between Identify Cass and Identify Object is DM. The link type between these shows that Identify Object must be enacted any time after (Urgency=D) Identify Class has been done, and that it must be performed (Necessity=M). Similarly, the link type between Identify Class and Identify Association is DM. Since it is possible to Identify Association and Identify Class in any order, we define the link type DC between Identify Association and Identify Class. The rest of the link types of Figure 6 can be similarly obtained.

The values of the attributes and relationships of Draw an Object Model are as follows:

- Name: Draw an Object Model
- Environment: Information Systems, Software development
- Input: Application concepts
- Output: Classes, Objects, Associations
- Concepts used: Attributes, Service
- Related to: NIL
- Implemented as: Submethod
- Interacts with: Application Engineer/ method engineer
- Method type: Complex

Figure 6. Functional method to draw an object model

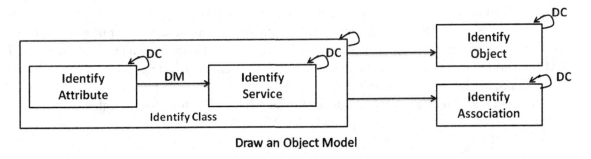

Draw an Object Model

The input of the method is the set of application concepts that are to be represented in the Object Model diagram. The output of the method are the Classes, Objects and Associations in Object Model. The concepts used in the method are those of Attribute and Service respectively. The method is stand alone and is not related to any other one. The method is used for interaction by the application engineer or the method engineer. Finally, the method has sub-methods as represented by the "implemented as" having value "Submethod".

Now, it is possible to consider Identify Class. Figure 6 shows that it is complex and consists of Identify Attribute and Identify Service, which in turn are atomic. The attributes of Identify Class are as follows:

- Name: Identify Class
- Environment: Object Model
- Input: Class
- Output: Class, Attribute, Service
- Concepts used: Attributes, Service
- Related to: NIL
- Implemented as: Submethod
- Interacts with: Application Engineer/ method engineer
- Method type: Complex

Similar diagrams can be drawn and attributes specified for the other components of Draw an Object Model.

Let us now draw Harel's Statechart (see Figure 7). Harel's Statechart is used to understand the behavior of the objects in a system. It specifies how objects react to events or operations. The reaction can be to perform a transition between states and possibly to execute some actions. It defines the run-time behavior of instances of a class.

Figure 7 shows a complex functional method Draw Statechart Schema. It consists of four methods, Identify State, Identify State Change, Identify Triggers and Cluster States. The link type between Identify State and Identify State Change is DM. The link type between these shows that Identify State Change must be enacted any time after (Urgency=D) Identify State has been done and that it must be performed (Necessity=M). Since, it is possible to Identify State and Identify State Change. Link type between Identify State Change and Identify State is DC. Identify State Change is connected to Identify Triggers with link type DM.

Identify Triggers is a complex functional method. It consists of four functional methods, Specify Transaction, Generate Event, Evaluate Firing Conditions and Expand Transaction. Link types between Specify Transaction and Generate Event, and Specify Transaction and Evaluate Firing Conditions are DM and DM respectively. Since it is possible to Specify Transaction and Evaluate Firing Conditions in any order, the authors define the link type DC between Evaluate Firing Conditions and Specify Transaction. The authors must Develop Transaction after Generate Event and Evaluate Firing Conditions. Hence, Generate Event to Develop Transaction and Evaluate Firing Conditions to Develop Transaction are DM and DM respectively. Finally, the link type is DC between Identify Triggers and Cluster States. These Cluster States have a self-loop with link type DC.

The values of the attributes and relationships of Draw Statechart Schema are as follows:

Figure 7. Functional method to draw statechart schema

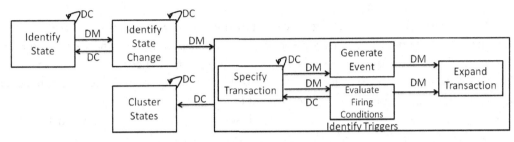

Draw Statechart Schema

- Name: Draw Statechart Schema
- Environment: Information Systems, Software development
- Input: list of events
- Output: States & Transition Diagram
- Concepts used: Event, Firing Condition
- Related to: NIL
- Implemented as: Submethod
- Interacts with: Application Engineer/ method engineer
- Method type: Complex

Diagrams can be drawn, and attributes specified for the other components of Draw Statechart Schema.

Let us now illustrate the first stage of the FME process: to Draw an Objectchart Schema. The method engineer starts the FME process by creating a new method using the operation Create(Draw an Objectchart Schema). At this moment, the diagram consists of a rectangle with no other details available. The name of the created process is entered in the rectangle. The values of the attributes and relationships are as follows:

- Name: Draw an Objectchart Schema
- Environment: Information Systems, Software development
- Input: Application Concepts, List of events
- Output: Class, Object, Associations
- Concepts used: Object Model, Statechart
- Related to: NIL
- Implemented as: Submethod
- Interacts with: Application Engineer/ method engineer
- Method type: Complex

The method engineer searches the repository to retrieve Draw Object Model as shown in figure 6 and Draw Statechart Schema as shown in figure 7. The searching and retrieving is done using the functional situation and is discussed in the next section. The method engineer decides to reuse these two methods to build the new one. Each architectural component of these is checked for suitability by following the matching process described below.

Functional Method Matching

The method engineer applies the matching process shown in figure 8 and uses the operations of Table 3. For each method component thus obtained, the method engineer applies his knowledge and judgment to see if it meets the desired functional situation. If it does, then nested components are examined for their relevance to the method To-Be. This is done recursively till all components have been matched and examined. The next method component is then picked up.

Applying this process to Figure 6, the authors must start with Identify Class and we apply Un-nest(Identify Class, Draw an Object Model).

The authors look inside Identify Class and find two functional methods Identify Attribute and Identify Service. The method engineer feels that Identify Class is not useful but Identify Attribute and Identify Service are useful. The following sequence of matching operations is applied.

- Un-nest(Identify Attribute, Identify Class)
- Un-nest(Identify Service, Identify Class)
- and the results are shown in figure 9.

Figure 8. Functional method matching process

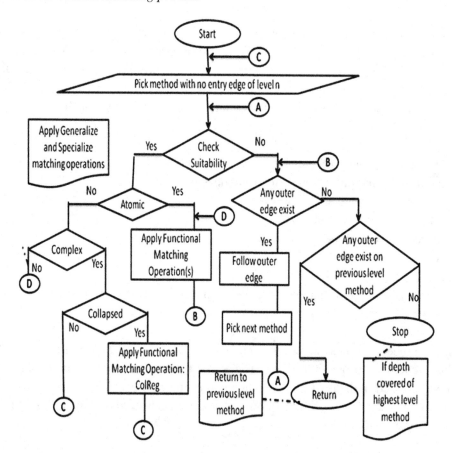

Figure 9. Partial functional method 1

Identify Attribute		Identify Service

Draw an Objectchart Schema

Now, other methods i.e. Identify Object and Identify Association are found to be irrelevant to building the desired method.

The method engineer now processes Draw a Statechart Schema shown in figure 7. The method engineer applies the following matching operation one by one:

- Un-nest(Identify State, Draw Statechart Schema),
- Un-nest(Identify State Change, Draw Statechart Schema),
- Un-nest(Identify Triggers, Draw Statechart Schema),
- Un-nest(Cluster States, Draw Statechart Schema),

The result is shown in figure 10.

Links between architectural components are set up as follows:

- Sequence (Identify State, Identify Attribute, IM)
- Sequence (Identify Attribute, Identify State, DC)
- Sequence (Identify State, Identify State Change, DM)
- Sequence (Identify State Change, Identify State, DC)

At this moment, the new method is as shown in figure 11.

The method engineer now creates self loops to allow iteration. The result is shown in figure 12.

Figure 10. Partial functional method 2

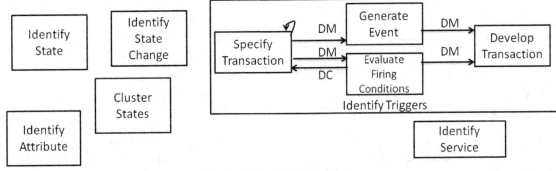

Draw an Objectchart Schema

Figure 11. Partial functional method 3

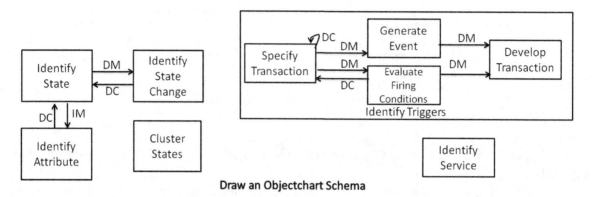

Draw an Objectchart Schema

- Sequence (Identify State, Identify State, DC)
- Sequence (Identify Attribute, Identify Attribute, DC)
- Sequence (Identify State Change, Identify State Change, DC)

To identify triggers the method engineer must use the Identify Service after the Generate Event. This is achieved as follows:

Eliminate(Generate Event, Develop Transaction, DM)
Sequence(Generate Event, Identify Service, DM)
Sequence(Identify Service, Develop Transaction, DM)
Sequence(Identify State Change, Identify Triggers, DM)

The result is shown in figure 13.

To complete the integration of Object Model and Statechart additional method and links as follows are defined

Sequence(Identify Triggers, Cluster States, DM)

Figure 12. Partial functional method 4

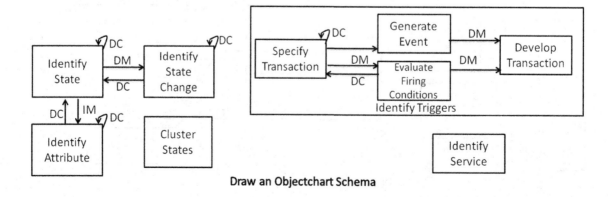

Draw an Objectchart Schema

Figure 13. Partial functional method 5

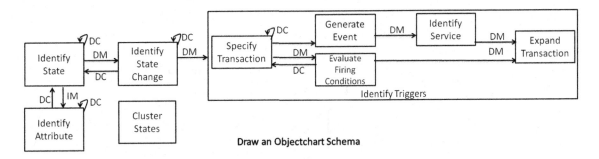

Create(Annotate State)

Sequence(Identify Triggers, Annotate State, DM)

Create(Define Firing Post Cond^n Spec)

Sequence(Identify Triggers, Define Firing Post Cond^n Spec, DM)

Sequence(Define Firing Post Cond^n Spec, Define Firing Post Cond^n Spec, DC)

In Figure 14, the shaded methods show the new functional method that this chapter need to introduce to achieve the objective of Objectchart.

The Method Base and Retrieval

In the previous section, the authors have assumed that a functional method can be retrieved. The authors now consider the retrieval technique and the method base.

The meta-model (Figure 3) suggests a two part method base, see figure 15. One part, called the Functional Method Base, FMB, contains the functional methods available for reuse as well as their properties. The other part, the Method Implementation Base, MIB (explained in Method Implementation section)

Figure 14. The desired method: draw an objectchart schema

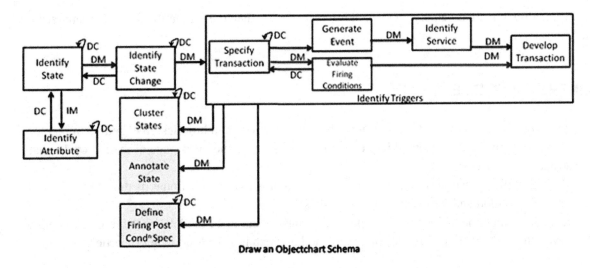

Figure 15. Outline of CAME tool: GEM

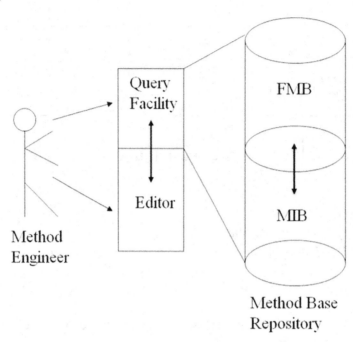

contains available implementations of a functional method and their properties. The 1: N relationship between functional method and method implementation (Figure 3) is captured in the method base by appropriately linking the two parts together. This is shown by the arrow from FMB to MIB in figure 15. Thus it is possible to access in the MIB all the implementations associated with a given functional method in FMB.

Functional methods can be retrieved on the following criteria:

1.   By method name, or
2.   By method attributes & relationships, input, concepts used etc using AND/OR connectives.

If functional methods satisfying the condition are found, then these functional methods are retrieved and presented.

METHOD IMPLEMENTATION

Having explained our notion of functional method, this chapter shall now describe method implementation. As shown in figure 2, method implementation is useful in the third stage of the life cycle, that is, construction engineering.

Method implementation (Figure 3) is a way of realizing a given functional method. It considers the features of a method and the ordering between these.

A method implementation can be expressed in any of the meta models available in the literature. However, the authors are looking for that meta model which has the following properties:

- It integrates the product and process aspects of methods.
- It provides facilities for ordering of method features.
- It is capable of handling the link types between methods.

The first property eliminates the class of product meta models and process meta models respectively, leaving us with the contextual (Rolland & Prakash 1994; Grosz, Rolland, Schwer, Souveyet, Plihon, Si-Said Achour & Griaho 1997) decisional (Prakash N. 1994; Prakash 1996; Prakash 1997), and generic models (Prakash 2006) respectively. The second eliminates the contextual model. The decisional meta model gets eliminated by the third property: its link types are merely instances of the generic link types available in the generic model. Thus, the authors are left with the generic model as a means for representing method implementation.

Generic Method Model

The generic method model (Prakash 2006) builds a dependency graph. Nodes of this graph are method blocks. Reference to figure 16 shows that there are three kinds of method blocks:

1. Atomic method block. Method primitives are the simplest kind of method blocks. A method primitive has two parts, an argument part and an action part. The action part acts upon the argument part to produce the product. These two parts correspond to product and process primitives respectively of figure 16. The product primitive is found in the product model. Process primitives correspond to the operations allowed. This gives to us the basic notion of an activity or task of a method.
2. Complex method blocks are built out of simpler ones following the composition principle.
3. Abstract method blocks establish a generalization/specialization relationship between method blocks.

Figure 16 shows that there is a 'Depends on' relationship between method blocks. A Method Block, MB1, that is dependent upon another, MB2, can only be enacted after MB2 has been enacted.

The generic model associates two main properties with a dependency, namely, urgency and necessity. Urgency refers to the time at which the dependent method block, MB_2, is to be enacted. If MB_2 is to be enacted immediately after MB_1 is enacted then this attribute takes on the value Immediate. If MB_2 can be enacted any time, immediately or at any later moment, after MB_1 has been enacted, then urgency takes on the value Deferred. Necessity refers to whether or not the dependent method block MB_2 is necessarily to be enacted after MB_1 has been enacted. If it is necessary to enact MB_2, then this attribute takes the value Must otherwise it has the value Can. Combining these two properties together, authors get the four possibilities as shown in figure 2.

In this way, there is uniformity between the representation of dependencies at the functional and the implementation levels.

Given a set of method blocks and dependencies between them, the entire method can be represented as a dependency graph. For example, consider the dependency graph of Fig. 17. The IC dependencies are shown. Assume that the rest are IM dependencies.

The graph shows that method blocks O_{10}, O_{11}, and O_2 are to be enacted in parallel after O_9 has been enacted. Similarly, once O_6 is enacted. O7 and O_8 are enacted in parallel, whereas a choice between enactment of O_{13} and O_{14} is to be made.

Figure 16. The generic method model

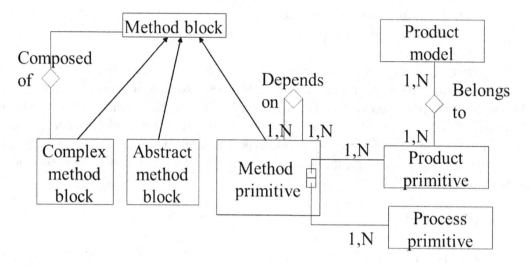

Figure 17. A dependency graph with its properties

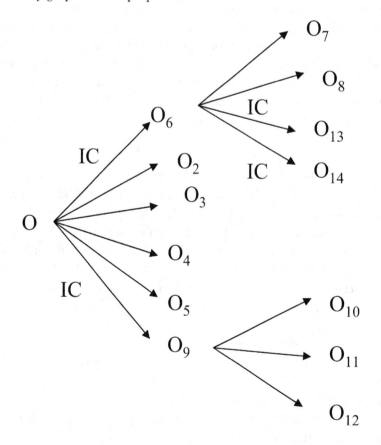

Representing Method Implementation Using Dependency Graph

In this section, authors lay the basis for performing the second stage of FME. The authors first consider the graphical representation of method implementation. Thereafter, this chapter define operations on method implementation that can be used in doing FME.

The authors represent a node of a method implementation as a circle with label <A,B> where A represents an 'argument' (for example 'Attribute') and B represents an 'action' (for example 'Identify'). Relationships between nodes are edges. These edges are labeled with the values of the link types.

Nodes corresponding to complex implementations have their own sub-method implementations. Such a node can be expanded to reveal its full details at a lower level.

Now, consider the two variant method implementations of Draw Attribute, one that does not allow derived attributes and the other, that does. The abstractions of these yields the functional method, Draw Attribute.

Draw Attribute = {M1, M2}

where

M_1 contains both Single-valued/ Multi-valued attributes.

M_2 contains derived attributes in addition to single and multi-valued ones.

It is to be noted that M_1 and M_2 respectively do not represent classes of methods but ways in which Draw Attribute can be implemented. Consequently, they are not functional methods but two different implementations of the functional method Draw Attribute.

This chapter show the implementation for Draw attribute corresponding to M_1 and M_2 in figure 18 and figure 19 respectively. In figure 18, the method starts off by identifying the attribute of interest. This is captured by the node <Attribute, Identify>. It is now possible to determine whether the attribute is atomic or composite. This is captured by the node <nature, Determine>. The nature of the edge connecting this with <Attribute, Identify> is IM as shown. After <nature, Determine> method engineers have two options, if we find that nature of attribute is complex then again we can move to <Attribute, Identify> with the link DC otherwise, method engineer find the valuation of the attribute that is single or multi-valued attribute. This is captured by the node <valuation, Define> as shown in the figure.

Method implementation of the second variant is as in figure 19. Definition of derived attributes is captured by the node <Virtualisation, Find>. The link type is DM between <nature, Determine> and <Virtaulisation, Find>.

As shown in the figure 15, it is possible to navigate from FMB part to the MIB and vice versa by the link connecting functional methods stored in the former to the method implementation stored in the latter. Thus, in our example, it is possible to navigate to the two method implementations of figure 18 and figure 19 respectively from Draw Attribute.

It can be seen that method implementations show the 'hows' for realizing a method. They help in defining

Figure 18. Method implementation for M_1.

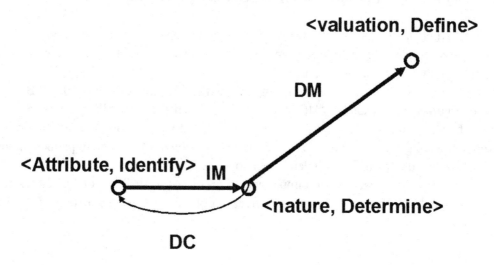

Figure 19. Method implementation for M_2.

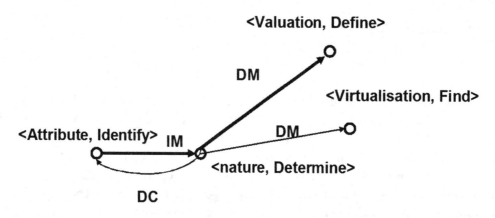

1. The capabilities provided by a method,
2. The interconnections between these capabilities, and
3. The constraints that are applicable.

Variations in these three result in the same functional method getting implemented differently.

Method Implementation Matching Operations

All method implementations are stored in the MIB of the method repository. The new desired method implementation corresponding is built by matching the retrieved method implementation with the desired one.

The proposed matching operations are shown in Table 4. Here N1, N2, N3 refer to nodes and LT, LT1 LT2 to link types. Whereas most of the operations are self-explanatory, perhaps, Sequence, Eliminate and Expand need some explanation.

Table 4. The implementation matching operation

Operation	Arguments	Description
Rename	N1, N2	Rename R1 and the new name is N2
Create	N1	It creates an initial node N1 without any link type.
Delete	N1	Delete N1, links into/out of it
Change	N1,N2, LT1, LT2	Change the link type LT1 to LT2 from N1 to N2
Sequence	N1, N2, LT	Produce a sequence of N1 followed by N2 with LT type link.
Eliminate	N1, N2, LT	The sequence is deleted. N1 and N2 are separated.
Generalize	N1, N2	Produce N1 generalization of N2
Specialize	N1, N2	Produce N1 specialization of N2
Expand	N1	Expand N1 & show all details
InsDetCol	N1	Insert details of complex node.
HideCol	N1	Hide all sub-nodes of N1.

The sequence operation can be applied to form a sequence of two nodes with each pair in the sequence having its own link type. The Eliminate operation is the inverse of sequence. The edge in the sequence is eliminated and the participating nodes are separated out as they were in the sequence. The Expand operation reveals the inner structure of a complex node. Similarly, InsDetCol and HideCol insert and hide details of complex nodes.

Suppose that the method engineer has the method implementation of Figure 18 and wants to create the one of Figure 19. The sequence of operations to yield Figure 19 is as follows:

Create(<Virtualisation, Find>)

Sequence(<nature, Determine>, <Virtualisation, Find>, DM).

FUNCTIONAL METHOD ENGINEERING: THE SECOND STAGE

This chapter illustrate method implementation adaptation by taking the sub-method "Identify Object" of Object Model. Assume that, the method engineer wants to retrieve the method implementation of "Identify Object". Upon entering the name, different method implementations are listed. Let one be selected & let the result be as shown in Fig. 20. The category of object is captured using the node <Category, Detect>. In this context of the Object Model, the category of object includes a person, place, thing, or event. After category detection, the authors must find the type of object that is, tangible or intangible, using the node <Type, Detect>. The nature of the edge connecting from <Category, Detect> is DM as shown. Attributes are captured using the node <Attribute-data, Find> with the link type DM from <Type, Detect>. It is possible that the authors can find more than one attribute. This is captured using a self loop on <Attribute-data, Find> with link type DC. After the identification of attribute values method engineer must identify the behavior of objects using the node <Behavior, Identify> with link type DM from on <Attribute-data, Find>. It is again possible that method engineer can find more than one behavior of an object. This is captured using a self loop on <Behavior, Identify> with link type DC.

Method implementation for Identify Object is shown in figure 21. This method implementation is the same as that in figure 20 except for the introduction of the notion of a state. This is captured by the node <State, Find>. As shown link type is DM between <Attribute-data, Find> and <State, Find>.

COMPARISON AND DISCUSSION

This chapter compare the existing SME with proposed FME and consider the efficacy of our proposals. We show that the notion of the following:

- Method as a Service & Method as a Function
- Situation & Functional Situation
- Situational Method Engineering & Functional Method Engineering
- Comparison of Operators

Method as a Service and Method as a Function

In (Iacovelli, Carine & Rolland, 2008) a proposal has been made to view methods as services. A Method Oriented Architecture, MOA on the lines of Service Oriented Architecture, SOA has been proposed. This notion has been approached from the view point of method components (Deneckere R., Elena K. & Bruno C. (2010), (Iacovelli, Carine & Rolland, 2008) and was argued that there is insufficient support in method engineering for the definition and use of components. The move to 'method as a service' is

Figure 20. Method implementation for identify object

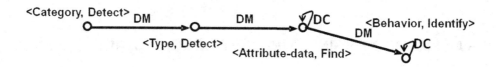

Figure 21. To-be method implementation for identify object

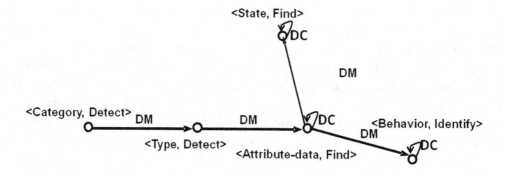

justified because of the ability to handle services in MOA. Though a method descriptor is needed as part of MOA, this work does not consider the impact of method as a service on the notion of situation and situational method engineering.

Situation and Functional Situation

This chapter has showed in Table 1 that a situation is the combination of circumstances at a given moment in a given organization. The **situation** of SME can be conceptualized in many ways, as descriptors, contingency factors, project factors, situation factors, context type and project type etc. As such, a situation does not directly define the characteristics of the *needed method*, but are the factors that influence the *successful use of a method*.

Our proposal for a functional situation considers the factor that affects method selection from a technical viewpoint. The authors have defined a functional situation in terms of the concepts of our meta-model shown in figure 2. It is described by a) the five attributes: Name, Input, Output, Concepts used and Environment, and b) The three relationships: Related to, Interacts with, and Implemented as.

Situational Method Engineering and Functional Method Engineering

Let us now consider the manner in which our proposals compare with those of SME. The basic difference starts from the notion of the situation itself of Functional Method. This has an impact on the way method components are selected and put together. A summary of the differences and similarities are contained in Table 5.

It can be seen from the table that there are substantial differences between FME and SME both from the point of view of CAME support and from the perspective of method knowledge.

By considering method selection and adaptation as a two part activity the authors propose a high level and low level selection and adaptation mechanism. The former provides some assurance that the method engineering task is progressing purposefully before detailed work is done. Thus, the chance of method rejection at a later stage is likely to be reduced.

Comparison of Operators

This chapter can also compare and contrast our operators with other proposals made in the literature. *In Ralyte* (Ralyté, Rolland, & Deneckere, 2004) *four classes of operators have been defined for Method Engineering*. These operators allow engineering Element, Compound, Property and Model Element which are defined in their meta-model. The operators allow name changes, changes in elements and properties and structural changes through changes in model elements.

In our functional view, the authors need all the operators of Ralyte (Ralyté, Rolland, & Deneckere 2004), Xavier (Xavier, Jolita, Anna, Alberto, David, Jesús, Sergi, Marc, Norbert, Alberto, Angelo, 2018). defined on Element. It is possible to change

- The name of the function,
- Add/delete new functions, and
- Change the nature of a function, for example, an atomic function in one method can be treated as a complex one in another method and vice-versa. For this, we need the nest and un-nest operations.

Table 5. Comparison of FME and SME

Criterion	Functional Method Engineering (FME)	Situational Method Engineering (SME)
Method Knowledge	Functional Components: showing externally visible functionality; Implementation components: showing method features	Chunks, fragments, patterns, method blocks, components
Method Base	Two levels: Functional Method and Method Implementation, related by is implemented as	One level that contains method components
Selection strategies	Progressive: 1. Functional Implementation selection 2. Method Implementation selection from short-list of selected functional methods	One shot selection: from universe of method knowledge
Construction Process	Assembly	Assembly
Basis of retrieval/ selection	Name, Input, Output, Concepts used, Environment, Related to; Interacts with, Implemented as, Method type	Non-functional aspects like Contingency factor, project factors, Situation factors, project type, context type

These correspond to the split/merge operation of Ralyte. We also need operators to generalize and specialize and expand functional methods.

Ralyte (Ralyté, Rolland, & Deneckere 2004) allows new properties to be defined and existing ones modified. Our meta-model of Fig. 3 provides the set of concepts as fixed. Thus, we do not see the introduction of other attributes or the dropping of existing ones. Similarly, the relationships in which functional method participates are defined in the meta-model and are given. New relationships cannot be added or existing ones dropped.

Finally, Ralyte (Ralyté, Rolland, & Deneckere 2004) allows 8 operations as shown in Table 6 on Model Element, six of which really cause a structural change. These six operators deal with connections between elements. Notice that in our case, there is only one type of connection between functional methods, a dependency. There are only two cases with a dependency, either it exists or it does not. To handle this, we introduce the sequence operator and its inverse, Eliminate. We do not need operators for 'connection via generalization' etc. found in Ralyte.

Our dependencies can be of different types and we need operations for changing the types of dependencies. This is achieved by the operator, Change.

The total number of operators in our case is 15 whereas that in Ralyte (Ralyté, Rolland, & Deneckere 2004) are 23. This is partly because of the central notion of a method as a function and partly because of the notion of dependency as the only connector.

Table 6 shows that the number of operators in our case is much lower than the number of Ralyte (Ralyté, Rolland, & Deneckere 2004). This is partly because of the central notion of a method as a function and partly because of the notion of dependency as the only connector.

Table 6. Comparison of Operators

Generic ME Operators (Ralyté, Rolland, & Deneckere 2004)	FME Operators from Table 3 and Table 4
Element	
Rename	Rename
Add	Create
Remove	Delete
Merge	Nest
Split	Un-nest
Replace	-
Generalize	Generalize
Specialize	Specialize
Compound	-
Property	-
Model Element	-
-	Sequence
-	Change
-	Eliminate
-	Expand
-	ColReg/ InsDetCol
-	RegCol/ HideCol

CONCLUSION

This chapter proposes that method engineering should consider the functional requirements of methods, perhaps, in addition to project/ organizational requirements. Based on our notion of functional situation, the authors have defined a two stage approach to method engineering. In the first stage the broad functional features of methods stored in a repository are matched with the functional requirements. Thus, a first-cut method is engineered. Thereafter, it is required to define the method features and their interconnections to meet the defined functionality. This is done in the second stage. The forgoing has been implemented in a CAME tool.

Thus, the authors propose a functional method engineering approach supported by our tool called GEM.

The major benefit that method engineer see from our approach is that there is assurance that progress is being made in reaching the required method. As mentioned above, this is achieved in the first stage through the selection of functionally similar methods. The chance of rejection of functionally similar methods is reduced in the second stage.

FUTURE WORK

In this chapter, authors have proposed a life cycle for the task of method engineering and have concentrated on elaborating the design and construction phases of this life cycle. The output of the design phase is the architecture of a method. The meaning of method architecture and its representation was developed by analogy with the notion of architecture found in computer technology. Similarly, the notion of method organization was developed for the construction phase of the life cycle. Future work is centered on an elaboration of the method requirements engineering phase. As mentioned, in our view, this phase is intentional in nature. These intentions are to be elicited by the method engineer from organizational stakeholders, an intentional model is to be built and subsequently intention level matching should be performed between the legacy methods and the method To-Be.

This chapter proposes the following investigations for the future:

1. Method Intention refers to the goal that the method fulfills. These intentions are to be elicited by the method engineer from organizational stakeholders. An intentional meta-model is to be built and subsequently intention level matching should be performed between the legacy methods and the method To-Be.
2. The link between the intentional and architecture levels needs to be defined. Thus, entire life cycle of Table 2 shall be covered.
3. Future work is centered on an elaboration of the method requirements engineering phase. As mentioned, in our view, this phase is intentional in nature.

REFERENCES

Anat, A., & Iris, R. B. (2008). A Domain Engineering Approach for Situational Method Engineering. *ER 2008,* 455-468.

Anat, A., & Iris, R. B. (2011). Semi-Automatic Composition of Situational Methods. *Journal of Database Management, 22*(4), 1–29. doi:10.4018/jdm.2011100101

Aydin, M. N. (2007). Examining Key Notions for Method Adaptation. *Situational Method Engineering, 2007,* 49–63.

Bekkers, W., van de Weerd, I., Brinkkemper, S., & Mahieu, A. (2008). The Influence of Situational Factors in Software Product Management: An Empirical Study. *Proceedings of the 21st International Workshop on Product Management,* 41-48. 10.1109/IWSPM.2008.8

Börner, R. (2010). Applying Situational Method Engineering to the Development of Service Identification Methods. *16th Americas Conference on Information Systems,* 1-10.

Borner, R., Goeken, M., Kohlborn, T., & Korthaus, A. (2011). Context Factors for Situational Service Identification Methods; ICIW 2011, *The Sixth International Conference on Internet and Web Applications and Services,* 35-42

Brinkkemper, S., Saeki, M., & Harmsen, F. (1998). Assembly Techniques for Method Engineering. *CAiSE 1998,* 381-400.

Bucher, T., Klesse, M., Kurpjuweit, S., & Winter, R. (2007). Situational Method Engineering– On the Differentiation of "Context" and "Project Type". *Situational Method Engineering, 2007,* 33–48.

Bucher, T., & Winter, R. (2008). Dissemination and Importance of the "Method" Artifact in the Context of Design Research for Information Systems. *Third International Conference on Design Science Research in Information Systems and Technology (DESRIST 2008),* 39-59.

Deneckere, R., Adrian, I., Elena, K., & Carine, S. (2009). From Method Fragments to Method Services. *CoRR abs/0911.0428,* 80-96.

Deneckere, R., Elena, K., & Bruno, C. (2010). Contextualization of Method Components. *RCIS, 10,* 235–246.

Goyal, S. B. (2012). *From Situational to Functional Method Engineering* (PhD Thesis). Banasthali University, Rajastahn, India.

Goyal, S. B., & Prakash, N. (2008). *From Situational to Functional Method Engineering.* Retrieved on March 17, 2012, from sites.upc.edu/~www-pi/ER2008/PhD/papers /ShyamGoyal.pdf

Goyal, S. B., & Prakash, N. (2013). Functional Method Engineering. *IGI-IJISMD, 4*(1), 79-103.

Grosz, G., Rolland, C., Schwer, S., Souveyet, C., Plihon, V., Si-Said, S., ... Griaho, C. (1997). Modelling and Engineering the Requirements Engineering Process: An Overview of the NATURE Approach. *Requir. Eng., 2*(3), 115–131.

Harmsen, A. F. (1997). *Situational Method Engineering,* Retrieved March, 17, 2012, http://eprints.eemcs. utwente.nl/17266/01/af_harmsen%5B1%5D.pdf

Harmsen, F., Brinkkemper, S., & Han Oei, J. L. (1994). Situational method engineering for informational system project approaches. *Methods and Associated Tools for the Information Systems Life Cycle. CRIS, 94,* 169–194.

Harmsen, F., Lubbers, I., & Wijers, G. (1995). Success-driven Selection of Fragments for Situational Methods: The S3 model. *Second International Workshop on Requirements Engineering: Foundations of Software Quality (REFSQ'95),* 104-115.

Hoef, R., Rob, L. W., Rolf, E., & Vincent, T. (1997). An Environment for Object-oriented Real-time Systems Design. *SEE, 1997,* 23–33.

Iacovelli, A., Carine, S., & Rolland, C. (2008). Method as a Service (MaaS). *RCIS, 2008,* 371–380.

Karlsson, F., & Ågerfalk, P. J. (2004). Method configuration: Adapting to situational characteristics while creating reusable assets. *Information and Software Technology, 46*(9), 619–633. doi:10.1016/j. infsof.2003.12.004

Lemmen, K., & Punter, T. (1994). The Approach Model (2): Methodology Engineering with the MADIS framework. Informatie, 36(6), 368-374.

López, L., Behutiye, W., Karhapää, P., Ralyté, J., Franch, X., & Oivo, M. (2017). Agile Quality Requirements Management Best Practices Portfolio: A Situational Method Engineering Approach. *PROFES, 2017,* 548–555.

Prakash, N. (1994). A process view of methodologies. *CAiSE, 94*, 339–352.

Prakash N. (1996). Domain Based Abstraction for Method Modelling, Ingénierie Des Systèmes d'Information. *AFCET/HERMES, 4*(6), 745-767.

Prakash, N. (1997). Towards a formal definition of a method. *Requirements Engineering Journal, 2*(1), 23–50. doi:10.1007/BF02802896

Prakash, N. (2006). On generic method models. *Requir. Engg., 11*(4), 221–237.

Prakash, N., & Bhatia, M. P. S. (2003). Developing Application-Centric Methods. *CAiSE Short Paper Proceedings*, 225-228.

Prakash, N., & Goyal, S. B. (2007). Towards a Life Cycle for Method Engineering, *Eleventh International Workshop on Exploring Modeling Methods in Systems Analysis and Design (EMMSAD'07)*, 27-36.

Prakash, N., & Goyal, S. B. (2008). Method Architecture for situational method engineering. *RCIS, 2008*, 325–336.

Prakash, N., Srivastava, M., Gupta, C., & Arora, V. (2007). An Intention Driven Method Engineering Approach. *RCIS, 2007*, 281–288.

Ralyté, J., Deneckere, R., & Rolland, C. (2003). Towards a Generic Model for Situational Method Engineering. *CAiSE, 2003*, 95–110.

Ralyté, J., Rolland, C., & Deneckere, R. (2004). Towards a Meta-tool for Change-Centric Method Engineering: A Typology of Generic Operators. *CAiSE, 2004*, 202–218.

Rolland, C., & Prakash, N. (1994). Guiding the Requirements Engineering Process. *APSEC*, 82-91.

Rolland, C., & Prakash, N. (1996). A proposal for context-specific method engineering. *Proceedings of the IFIP TC8, WG8.1/8.2 Working Conference on Method Engineering*, 191-208.

Saeki, M., & Wenyin, K. (1994). Specifying Software Specification & Design Methods. *CAiSE, 1994*, 353–366.

Slooten, K., & Brinkkemper, S. (1993). A Method Engineering Approach to Information Systems Development. Information System Development Process, 30, 167-186.

Slooten, V. (1995). *Situated Methods for Systems Development* (Dissertation). University of Twente.

Slooten, V., & Hodes, B. 1996). Characterizing IS Development Projects. *Proceedings of the IFIP TC8, WG8.1/8.2 Working Conference on Method Engineering*, 29-44.

Swede, V., & Vliet, H. (1994). Consistent Development: Results of a First Empirical Study on the Relation Between Project Scenario and Success. *CAiSE, 1994*, 80–93.

Xavier, F., Jolita, R., Anna, P., Alberto, A., David, A., Jesús, G., … Alberto Siena, A. S. (2018). A Situational Approach for the Definition and Tailoring of a Data-Driven Software Evolution Method. *CAiSE 2018*, 603-618.

Section 2
Social Media in Organizational Transformation

Social media are changing the way we communicate, shop, entertain, work, and consequently, the way we live. This section looks to the effect of social media in organizations and how social media may be used and integrated in the organizations' business processes. The first chapter points out advantages of adoption of social media by organizations and provides a view of a new context of labor faced within digital transformation of organizations. The second chapter ponders about the participation in online social networks and about the technologies that support and promote these as a fundamental role in organizations.

Chapter 5
Enterprise 4.0:
The Next Evolution of Business?

Maria João Ferreira
Universidade Portucalense, Portugal & Universidade do Minho – Azurém, Portugal

Fernando Moreira
Universidade Portucalense, Portugal

Isabel Seruca
Universidade Portucalense, Portugal & Universidade do Minho – Azurém, Portugal

ABSTRACT

Enterprise 4.0 is already referred to as the next stage of the evolution of global business and the global economy. This wave is achieved by technology enablers often referred as digital transformation (DT). Social media represent a subset of these technologies which contribute to organizational transformation. However, the adoption of social media does not imply such a transformation; changes in the organization's culture and behavior are also needed. While the technology enablers allow the production, sharing, and management of information and knowledge within the organization they also require the updating of the supporting information systems (IS). Thus, using technologies in organizations requires an exercise in understanding how to demonstrate their usefulness in relation to the creation, access, and sharing of contents and IS improvements in a safe way. To this end, this chapter envisages a new context of labor faced within DT of organizations, largely boosted by the organizational adoption of social media, and which the authors propose to be implemented through the m_CSDIT framework.

DOI: 10.4018/978-1-5225-7271-8.ch005

INTRODUCTION

Enterprise 4.0 is the next stage of the evolution of global business and the global economy. This parallels Industry 4.0 that relates to factory automation but goes beyond the factory concept into all aspects of the global economy.

This wave of digital transformed enterprises is achieved by technology enablers often referred as digital transformation (DT) enablers which include (1) cloud, (2) mobile, (3) social, and (4) big data – analytics (Uhl and Gollenia, 2016; IDC, 2018). Innovation accelerators like IoT, Robotics, Artificial Intelligence, Augmented and Virtual Reality, Cognitive Systems and Next Generation Security are often also playing part of this process of digital transformation Kane (2017).

It is, therefore, widely acknowledged that organizations have suffered a large transformation at the social, economic and technological levels, where the traditional barriers of transferring information and knowledge have been progressively eliminated. This evolution allowed the elimination of silos, the breaking down of hierarchies, the connection of internal and external stakeholders and the empowering of employees (Berkman, 2014). According to Bear (2015), Social Business has contributed to this end, and has proved its value across nearly every business function, from marketing and commerce, to product development and human resources, to internal collaboration and intelligence.

Social Business (Yunus, 2007; Bear, 2015) can be defined as the ability of an organization to share information, produce knowledge collaboratively, manage knowledge, eliminate communication and sharing barriers, accelerate business processes, approaching the business partners, namely suppliers and customers, and create innovative products, services and business models. It is thus essential that such products, services and models are created and properly documented, managed and shared.

Information systems and technologies (IST) are the essence of up-to date organizations, and changes in this field are occurring at an uncontrollable pace, interrupting traditional business models and forcing organizations to implement new models of business. These changes need to be accompanied by new modeling methods that, for instance, drive the evolutionary changes of requirements, as argued by Gustas and Gustiene (2012). A change of paradigm in what comes to the use of IST in the day-to-day life of every citizen, by itself, does not sustain such a transformation; it is also necessary a change of culture and behavior. On the one hand, the use of IST in an appropriate and integrated way with the organization's processes will depend on an individual and collective effort, which may be called "collective leadership" (Paunova, 2015). On the other hand, the younger generation, accustomed to sharing, often through mobile devices, personal information on Facebook, Twitter, among others, enters the job market looking for similar tools. These new "social tools" allow the production, sharing and management of information and knowledge within the organization between peers and other stakeholders, allowing the barriers elimination of the communication and sharing.

Therefore, we may infer that Social Business is much more than just collaboration and sharing, since the IST that are currently available allow the organizations' processes to be more dynamic, more "social".

Following these developments, and according to the European Commission report "*A Roadmap for Advanced Cloud Technologies H2020 under*", the environment of IST (market research, industry, education, training, etc.) is undergoing constant changes. These changes originate, typically from the conflict between the technical restrictions and the "new" needs experienced by users. Thus, it is necessary to identify the major changes that can be expected in the next years and can, or will, affect the environment of IST. It is expected, for example, storage for all and the internet of and for things (World Economic Forum, 2015).

The growth of social media is already happening at a tremendous rhythm (Schultz, et al., 2015). The arrival and development of mobile internet applications has set to double the intensity of social media use (Gulbahar and Yildirim, 2015).

The arrival of mobile internet has fully democratized the World Wide Web. Yesterday's non-internet users now only need a smartphone and a location with free *wifi* access to go online. In the past, it was needed a workplace, a computer and an internet subscription, which was too expensive for many people. This barrier has now, however, disappeared. As discussed in Van Belleghem (2012), the situation in the United States proves this beyond doubt. The highest smartphone penetration levels are to be found in the poorer Hispanic and Asiatic sections of the community. In 2011, the research company Nielsen found that in the traditionally more affluent white community only 27% had a smartphone. These figures are the reverse of what would be rationally expected, and they mean that all target groups in all social classes will soon be approachable on a large scale via social media.

The combination of internal and external conversations is well suited to take advantage of the changes ushered by mobile internet. If the company staff makes great use of online media, they will be ready and waiting to pick up customer feedback, so that they can avoid or solve possible problems and fully take advantage of conversation potential. If the company's culture and service are good, this will result in positive conversations. Consumers who are looking for online information while they are out shopping will find these conversations in their search results and will be influenced by them. The fact that the internet has been democratized means that organizations have no other option: they must integrate the use of social media into their activities, if they wish to survive. Social media therefore connects the organization, its staff and its customers to each other.

The impact of these developments on the demand has been immense. In the United States, 27% of smartphone users use their phone while they are out of shopping, to find out more about the products they are thinking of buying. They also compare prices and look for promotion offers in other stores. From now on, it is clear that people always have the internet with them, wherever they go and whatever they do. This means they have instant access to all the information in the world. The impact for, namely, the retail industry is, therefore, phenomenal.

Taking advantage of these technologies for organizations within the context of Social Business, in particular nomadic workers, requires a comprehension exercise in how to demonstrate usefulness with regard to the creation, sharing and documentation of information and knowledge in and out of an organization, the organization improving (business processes) and, the education and training of organizational workers and ad-hoc discussion, in a safe way. In this paper, we further develop the m_CSDIT approach early described in Ferreira, et al. (2014; 2015). The Case Study approach (Yin, 2009) will be used as the research method.

We argue that Social Business, supported by different ISTs including mobile devices that comply with the m_CSDIT approach will contribute in a particular way for the organizational well-being (Di Stefano, 2017) raising indicators of the collective intelligence (Barlow & Dennis, 2016) and agility (Lowry& Wilson, 2016) dimensions.

The intelligence dimension, on its different indicators is achieved through "collective leadership", since it is more efficient than hierarchic management, for certain types of tasks, allowing the internal relations of cooperation to increase and improving the flow of knowledge. Broad participation is usually more effective and leads to more information that can be processed and used in decision-making.

The agility dimension is achieved, through collaborative work, supported mainly by nomadic workers, allowing a systemic perception, especially taking advantage of the interconnections between the organization's capabilities and market opportunities.

As a result, this paper will provide a comprehensive view of a new context of labour faced within Digital Transformation of organizations, which we term Enterprise 4.0, largely boosted by the organizational adoption of social media, and which we propose to be implemented through the m_CSDIT framework.

THE DT ENABLER: SOCIAL BUSINESS

The Social Business Concept

The concept of social business was firstly associated with Yunus´ work (Yunus, 2007). According to Yunus, the concept involved both economic and social perspectives: social business is supposed to solve a social problem and to achieve financial sustainability rather than to generate profits.

A new perspective was introduced by Kim (2012) in a blog post where the concept was applied to evolutionary marketing and technology strategies. Social Business, also called Social Enterprise and Enterprise 2.0 (Berkman, 2014; McAfee, 2006; McAfee, 2009) and more recently Enterprise 4.0 (Valentin, 2017), is a recent but popular trend that is revolutionizing organizational work and generating value for all of its elements, i.e. employees, customers, partners and suppliers. It means that all departments in an organization integrate their social capabilities into traditional business processes (Dorn et al., 2007) to change the way of working in order to create value. A Social Business organization uses social software technology to communicate with its rich ecosystem of customers, business partners and employees (Tajvidi & Karami, 2017). More than just a technological concept to Wood & Khan, G. F (2016) social business is also a *"business culture of collaborative innovation and engagement at all levels of business functions"*.

A Business is created and managed by people. The individual or group who is taking decisions will determine either the success or failure of an organization, i.e. if it will survive or will eventually die in market (Hiriyappa, 2008). In order to achieve that success long term goals are needed to be set, i.e. profitability, productivity, competitive position, employee's development, employee relationships, public responsibility, and technological leadership (Hiriyappa, 2008) that are converted into internal efforts and organizational transformations. However, those organizations often fail due to internal (Kotter, 1995) and external forces (Zakić et al., 2008).

An organization in the 21st century, known as Enterprise 4.0 (Valentin, 2017), to achieve success, must be a connected entity that supports internal and external networks of people and knowledge in order to obtain competitive advantage and to face the constant and mutable external environmental forces. The potential of social business allows this challenge. Hagel et al. (2010) claim that *"each of us, individually and together, are now, for the first time in history, in a position to collaborate in a complete reimagination of our biggest private and public-sector institutions that will eventually remake society as a whole"*. Following this imperative, organizations must be open to be supported by social business, which constitutes a shift in how people work, moving from hierarchies to networks. Nowadays, complex work is the most valuable, as well as the type of work that cannot be automated or outsourced. It is work that requires creativity and passion. Doing complex work in networks means that information, knowledge and power no longer flow up and down. They flow in all directions. Brown (2012) claims that to understand complex systems it is necessary to submerge in them. This requires social learning (Romero-Mujalli, 2017). Complex work is not linear. Social business is giving up centralized control and harnessing the power of networks.

Organizations must be able to share knowledge quicker than before. This requires a shift towards something like a starfish framework that not only allows for independent action but also distributes knowledge through all parts. Social learning is about how organizational knowledge gets distributed.

Undertaking social business is not the same of an organization that just uses a Facebook page or/and a Twitter account. Social business means that all departments of an organization, from human resources to marketing, to product development, to customer service, to sales, use social media in the same way they use any other tool and channel to do their job. It is an organization that uses social networking tools often to communicate inside and outside the organization. It is a strategic approach to shaping a business culture, highly dependent upon executive leadership and corporate strategy, including business process design, risk management, leadership development, financial controls and use of business analytics. According to Abbott (2015), for organizations, the use of mobile devices conjugated with social business allow the following benefits: market and sales are more effective; teamwork and collaboration are empowered; crowd-sourcing is facilitated, ideas and creativity are more easily spread; trends can be sooner spotted; meaningful interactions may be elevated, loyalty and trust can be enforced; performance can be optimized; stronger teams may be built and maintained; personalize motivation, and best of all … organizations can grow better, faster, bigger, stronger, happier – for less time, hassles and costs.

Integrating Social Business Into an Organization

Besides the well-known potential for organizations in the use of social media, most organizations show a paradoxical behavior in the way they perform business and in the way they manage their institutional social media. This paradoxical behavior results most often in the underuse of conversation potential. These issues are discussed in Van Belleghem (2012).

Perhaps the two last issues in the list provided constitute the biggest paradoxes of all the mentioned issues. Organizations keep referring that satisfied customers and satisfied staff are important, but very often their actions do little or nothing to reflect these words. These are the fundamental causes of unused conversation potential. This problem is exemplified in a further section with the discussion of real cases study.

The future of organizational work is social, collaborative and mobile (Streitz, 2003). The introduction of social business into an organization requires important changes in the way its collaborators work in all the organization structure (Cortada et al., 2012). According to Cortada et al. (2012), in order to integrate social business in the core of an organization three key issues must be addressed:

1. Organizations need to consider how to incorporate social metrics in themselves and in their processes;
2. Organizations need to understand and manage the risks associated with the integration of social business; and
3. Organizations need to manage change, which is a fundamental requirement to undertake with success social business practices.

Moreover, in SideraWorks (2013) seven dimensions are proposed that must be questioned and defined: (1) vision and goals; (2) cultural readiness; (3) organizational structure; (4) social strategy; (5) communication; (6) social technologies; and (7) training and education.

In this context, the two last dimensions (social technologies and training and education) should allow knowledge to flow in the organization. The primary function of social technologies and training and educating professionals in the networked organization is to connect and communicate based on three core processes:

1. Facilitating collaborative work and learning amongst workers, especially as peers;
2. Sensing patterns and helping to develop emergent work and learning practices; and
3. Working with management to fund and develop appropriate tools and processes for workers.

According to Zhao & Kemp (2012) employees tend to use blogs, wikis and social bookmarks to search and retrieve information about the organization, to connect with coworkers or to build relationships. Another survey, according to these authors, shows that the main goal of using social media tools, such as Facebook in the workplace is to maintain and develop connections with friends not work-related. The adoption of such tools in the workplace has therefore raised several issues and challenges for organizations. One of the most important issues is the virtual disappearance for employees of boundaries between the personal and professional life, as well as personal and professional connections.

Social Business Contributes for a More Competitive Organization

In a few short years, social technologies have given social interactions the speed and scale of the Internet. Whether discussing consumer products or organizing political movements, people around the world constantly use social media tools to seek and share information. And, in this context, business is changing their behavior and social media becomes an important business tool (Tajudeen, 2018).

The value of organizations that use social media tools is determined by how they are harnessed to create value for the organization (Majchrzack et al., 2009). Martin & van Bavel, presents a set of a number of potential benefits, i.e., tangible and intangible gains, when the organizations use social media tools, which they classified in terms of a) employ uses of the technologies, b) customer engagement activities, and c) external partner activities (Martin & van Bavel, 2013).

Those potential benefits are quantified in some studies, namely McKinsey & Company (2016, 2017), and Gaál et al. (2015). McKinsey & Company (2016) study emphasizes that the beneficial features of the social tools, point out by the organizations, are real-time interactions, the ability to collaborate with specific groups, and cross-platform availability (see Figure 1).

The study driven by McKinsey & Company (2017) indicates the increasing relevance of social tools also appears at the organizational process level. The use of social tools remains most common in externally facing processes namely PR, recruiting and hiring, and customer relationship management. But processes like procurement, supply-chain management, and after-sales services have been gaining importance (see Figure 2).

These studies show the importance of social business to organizations, not only inside the organization itself, but also in its relations with the outside, i.e., with the organizational ecosystem.

Figure 1. Beneficial features of social tools [From: McKinsey & Company (2016)]

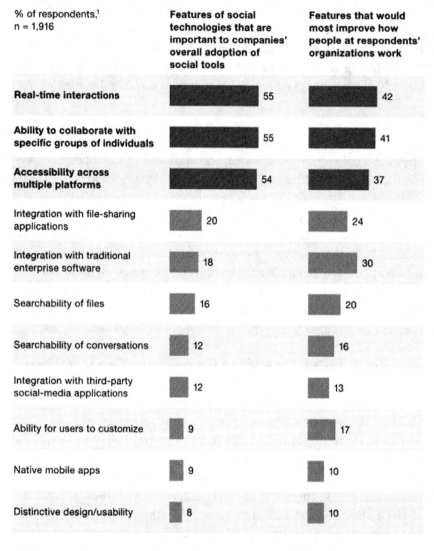

The Contribution of Social Business to the Organizational Well-Being

As referred in previously social business is the creation of an organization that is using social technology to benefit its entire ecosystem by embedding several aspects including collaboration. In this way the core of social business and the activities that it supports will have an impact in the organization through six dimensions (SideraWorks, 2013): adaptability, empowerment, agility, connection, openness and collective intelligence (Malone, et al., 2009). We highlight two of these – the agility and collective intelligence dimensions.

Figure 2. media tools in organizational processes - Comparative analysis [From: McKinsey & Company (2017)

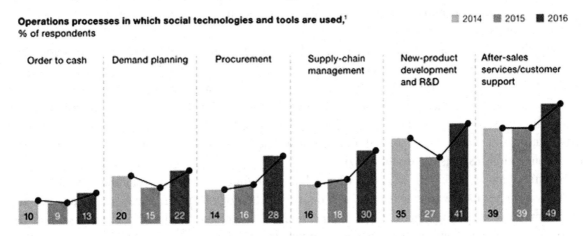

Organizational agility is defined, in the Business dictionary, as the capability of an organization to rapidly change or adapt in response to changes in the market. A high degree of organizational agility can help an organization to react successfully to the emergence of new competitors, the development of new industry-changing technologies or sudden shifts in overall market conditions.

Organizational agility helps balancing speed of response, communication and information sharing with thoughtful coordination and long-term scalability. In this context, according to Charbonnier-Voirin (2011), organizational agility is the organization capacity to incorporate new elements such as innovations or improvements in order to enhance its performance.

Levy (1999) argues that collective intelligence is the *"capacity of human communities to co-operate intellectually in creation innovation and invention"*. Levy also adds that collective intelligence is a *"fully distributed intelligence that is continuously enhanced and synergized in real time"* which results in effective mobilization of skills with social business. And in this context, collective intelligence leverages the capacity to listen and use established information as well as new sources of information. Evaluating and analyzing data is not just to track activity, but to actively support business decisions in order to improve products, services, and processes of an organization (SideraWorks, 2013).

Organizational well-being is the process of creating well-being across an organization (Dodge et al. 2012). Therefore if agility and collective intelligence are incremented in an organization, well-being will also be incremented.

The Support of Social Media Tools in Social Business Context

Organizations worldwide are adopting social media (Kaplan & Haenlein, 2010) tools in many critical applications to create, share and documenting. Some industry executives from advertising and marketing consider their use crucial. Despite its growing ubiquity, social media tools are still not well understood from a strategic business perspective, and also regarding its use in education and training in the workplace (Barczyk & Duncan, 2012).

Studies on the organizational impacts of the use of social media tools to date have been mentioned only speculatively (Vannoy & Palvia 2010). According to (Boyd 2008) a possible explanation for this is the growing use of social media tools outside the organization or explicitly social contexts, which are used mostly by youth and students.

According to Jarrahi & Sawyer (2013) the increase in the number and variety of information and communication technologies in the workplace, as well as the practices of knowledge sharing which are becoming increasingly digital allow traditional organizations to benefit from the wide variety of social technologies. The social media tools constitute the subset of social technologies that have allowed new possibilities for sharing organizational knowledge. The use of social media tools offer opportunities for collaboration and social exchange, and are well positioned to increase and prolong the interpersonal social connections (Skeels & Grudin 2009).

Jarrahi & Sawyer (2013) mention that what is known so far on the use of social media tools at work is based on studies focused on the use of a social media technology by itself. These studies provide useful information about some organizational implications of its use, but do not consider how technologies can be used together. However, it is easy to acknowledge that the vast majority of organizations have employees interacting with several technologies.

For a successful organization to have social business, social media must be understood as a means, not an end. Social media is the ideal partner for such an organization. The advantages are obvious: speed, a wide potential reach, a human method of communicating, no hierarchy, full transparency, creation of communities, etc. It is the only channel where feedback from the outside world is transparent and direct. Social media force organizations to be more honest, quicker and clearer in their communication. This trend has allowed organizations to develop in the direction of genuine customer-orientation.

Despite these advantages, the checklist mentality which some organizations use when dealing with social media is not the right way to maximize the company conversation potential. Regarding Facebook pages and Twitter accounts as some kind of magic trick is not the good way of achieving success and will only lead to disappointment. The reality is that, with a few exceptions, any company is likely to have a million fans on the first day. For the vast majority of organizations, it takes time and effort to build up a community of fans and followers. Besides, wide reach on social media is only one of the important criteria. Building up a strong relationship with the customer is just as important. The role of company employees in helping to make the company's culture tangible is another relevant issue to consider. Social media are then the ideal way to spread the company's culture and stories on a wide scale.

Social media tools refer to social networks (Facebook, Google+, LinkedIn, Twitter), in addition to sharing videos platforms (YouTube), blogging platforms, platforms of communication (Skype, etc.) and visual media (Instagram, Pinterest, Tumbir and Snapchat) (Drell and Davis 2014).

Social media tools provide their users a profile, a list of friends, a chat room and the ability to send public or private messages, create events, comment, get feedback, etc. From a general perspective we can say that they have in common the ease of use, and free use, for good or for evil, representing the day-to-day lives of young people, mostly.

THE USE OF CONVERSATION POTENTIAL

Social media can enable and significantly increase the collaboration and learning from customers in various ways, for instance by novel social ways of providing and receiving feedback of a brand, an organization's products or services and practices. Today's consumers want an organization that is open and receptive to their opinions, an organization that puts the customer first, in a central position.

Thanks to social media, organizations can get their information out to the public faster than ever. However, social media can spread bad information about a business just as fast as it can spread good information, due to its powerful amplifying effect. Social media builds brand awareness in ways that no other form of media can and reaches customers who would be otherwise unreachable. The conversation potential and the reach provided by the use of social media can lay the foundations for an organization's future growth or damage of reputation or brand image.

Designing a social strategy for the organization and learning from the interaction with customers so as to re-design strategy or improve organization procedures and practices should allow the right balance for an organization to ensure success in engaging with social media. The two case studies provided in this section describe real stories of how organizations can use the conversation potential enabled by social media and the consequent impact on the businesses' brand image in both cases.

The 'KLM' Case

This case describes a complete change in how KLM (Haar, 2015; Koetsier, 2015; Mcculloch, 2015) found novel ways to leverage social interactions with customers and improve business processes.

Background

KLM Royal Dutch Airlines has operated, for more than 90 years, flights throughout the world. With more than 32,000 employees serving more than 133 international destinations, KLM is one of the largest international airline companies. Moreover, KLM is dedicated to providing more than a reliable and cost efficient mean of transportation. The company has also taken the initiative for Corporate Social Responsibility involving customers, employees and society.

Since 2009, KLM had only just started exploring this new world with a Facebook page, a Twitter account and, like most companies taking their first steps in social media. At that time, KLM started its contribution to social platforms by posting some pictures of planes and launching a campaign Indeed, the airline company found novel ways to leverage social interactions and improve business processes.

Problem

Few people had ever heard of the so called "Eyjafjallajökull" volcano until 14 April 2010. That was the day this Icelandic volcano erupted, causing most airline traffic to grind to a halt and creating a huge ash cloud above Europe, making plane travel impossible for about five days.

Around 10 million travelers were affected, forcing KLM to seek new ways of communicating with its passengers, and at that moment the company was starting using social media tools. KLM has become a leader in using social media progressively. Ironically, the genesis of its work was more happenstance than a grandiose plan, as already referred. This phenomenon overwhelmed KLM's phone lines, email, and ticket counters. At the time, the company was using social media on a small scale, dabbling with Twitter and Facebook. Willing to get in touch with the airline, thousands of customers were desperately waiting for a response. Within an hour, KLM had created a social media room where company volunteers (about 100 employees used social media) took turns answering questions. Some would arrive at

4am wearing their business suits, so that they could do their shift and head straight through to an 8am meeting. Managers became service agents and some of them experienced direct customer contact for the very first time.

Solution

Because KLM customers used Facebook and Twitter to keep their friends and family updated on their lives, KLM had to be there as well. Hence, the KLM social customer service was born. This service has 150 people dedicated to serving clients via social. And each of them represents almost $170,000 in annual revenue.

Recognizing the potential power of social media, KLM committed to the new communication channel and expanded its efforts. Currently, the airline handles about 75,000 queries a week, 24/7, across a variety of social platforms including Facebook, Twitter, and LinkedIn. The company communicates in 14 languages and recently began tinkering with country-specific social tools, like Sina Weibo, Tencent Weibo, WeChat, and Renren in China and VKontakte in Russia. No automated answers, but a personal reply from one of the KLM service agents. The KLM social media policy is based on the one-stop-shop principle. If someone approaches the company on Twitter, they give them a tailored reply, not just a link to other channels.

KLM answers more questions than any other company on Facebook. There is no other brand that has higher social care demand on Facebook than KLM. Based on the analysis of their Socially Devoted Q4 data, KLM receives 40% of all queries addressed to Dutch companies, and nearly 30% of all queries in the airlines industry globally.

However, it was necessary to 'put the pieces together' in order to use social media to help customers book flights and to address the payment phase of the process. The problem arose as the airline could not easily and safely transmit credit card details through social platforms. Acknowledging the fledgling nature of these tools, the company searched for a payment solution to fix the problem, but could not find one. Thus, the airline had to work with one of its payment service providers and build the platform itself.

The KLM booking system, which costed €3,500 to develop, allowed its social media representatives to offer a quick payment link and stay with the customer from booking to ticket issue. The social media booking application is generating more than €100,000 each business day and the number has been rising every week. In 2014, the system contributed €25 million to the company's year-end revenue.

Customers will get desired flight details, timing, and information on pricing, and, if the transaction proceeds, there is a direct link to a payment page. As soon as the customer credit card is processed, KLM agents are notified and inform the customer that his ticket is booked.

KLM has also put satisfaction measurements in place for its social contact center. The agent enters the measurements at the start and end of each contact center conversation, so as to monitor how customer sentiment changed during the interaction.

The data collected by KLM feeds into its social CRM efforts via Salesforce, where it ties Twitter handles or other social media data to customer records. Customer service agents can see the contextualized data in real time, and air crews can see these in mid-flight. All these data is increasingly being used by KLM's marketing in order to personalize communications and offers.

The 'Become the Doritos Guru' Case

This case describes a complete change in how the Canadian based chips brand Doritos (StuzoGroup, 2013) got through to its teen audience, and the success the organization had with a totally re-imagined, user-generated campaign based on the use of social media. The campaign was based on the proposition: "name the new Doritos flavor, create a 30-second commercial for it and in return we will pay the winner, who will be declared "The Doritos Guru", $25,000 cash and 1% of the flavor's Canadian net sales, forever". Although the effort was centered on the mystery flavor, the impact lifted overall Doritos sales. The case also showed excellent results for brand health and engagement through the use of social media.

Background

In early 2009 Doritos released a new chip flavor and wanted to use this as an opportunity to drive brand awareness and engagement through an innovative promotion that leveraged social media. Working with multiple partners, Doritos decided to pursue a cross-platform promotion focused on a viral video.

The campaign, called "Become the Doritos Guru", was a video upload contest wherein users were tasked to create a catchy TV spot and name for the new chip flavor. Doritos was prepared to offer a prize of $25,000 and 1% of future consumer sales to the winning commercial and name for the new flavor. At the outset of the campaign, Doritos identified the ideal business outcomes for the promotion:

- Reach consumers across multiple social channels to create high brand awareness and engagement;
- Launch brand presence on Facebook and build out a Facebook fan base and Social CRM;
- Drive sales of the brand and the new flavor.

The Solution

The social promotion experts at Stuzo Group (StuzoGroup, 2013) conceived and developed the interactive components of the program. A first of its kind, the Stuzo Group proposed a solution which would launch an interconnected promotion on Facebook, YouTube, and a standalone website using Facebook Connect.

Consumers were able to engage with the promotion in the environment of their choice. Facebook and the Doritos Guru microsite served as the interfaces for video uploads and related promotion interactions, while a branded YouTube Channel was used to host the videos and provide additional exposure. Data such as number of votes, comments, and video views was transferred seamlessly between the three sites. The platform's administrative controls allowed Doritos to screen and approve video submissions before publishing them simultaneously to all three channels. Using the many tactical component features of the platform, users could vote, comment and share submissions, greatly encouraging viral spread. The winning video was based on votes from other users, showing the power of social media.

Campaign Results

This innovative promotion crushed all expectations set by Doritos and its agency partners. The campaign' participants took the opportunity to name the new flavor and to momentarily embody the Doritos brand. Furthermore, massive consumer engagement was achieved. Viewers came out in full force to express their opinions driving an enormous amount of traffic to all three channels. Overall, 75,000 people participated. 4,000 clever and well-produced ads were submitted, 570% more than the original goal. The Doritos YouTube channel became the #1 Subscribed Channel with 2.1 million video views. Viewers spent an average of 6 minutes on the sites, 2 minutes over the original goal. Viewer participation was exceptional with 560,000 votes and 188,000 comments. In one week after its official launch, Doritos' Facebook page gained 31,000 fans. Throughout the campaign, over 900,000 consumers visited the page. As a result of the integrated marketing program, Doritos sales increased dramatically in just two months. In particular, Doritos sales including the new flavor increased by an unprecedented 23% during the campaign period.

ENTERPRISE 4.0: THE DIGITAL TRANSFORMED ENTERPRISE

Digital transformation in organizations is already a reality that needs to be implemented and even, in some cases improved, as already discussed. Acknowledging this context, the m_CSDIT framework was formerly proposed in Ferreira et al. (2014a, 2015) at that stage, the framework was used to introduce and/or systematize social business in organizations. We now propose an extension of the framework to accommodate digital transformation leading to the Enterprise 4.0.

The following subsections present the updated approach, renamed as mobile Create, Share, Document, Improve and Training (m_CSDIT) and the rationale for its use, under a context of organizational DT.

Mobile_Create, Share, Document, Improve, and Training: m_CSDIT

The relevance of conducting Digital Transformation supported by the four technology enablers - Big Data and associated analytics, Cloud Computing, Mobile Connectivity, and Social tools is widely acknowledged and recognized by the scientific community and organizations, as discussed throughout the previous sections. However, there is a lack of approaches that allow the systematization and that guide its implementation within an organization, while improving IS and organizational processes.

To address this end, we propose the m_CSDIT approach as a three-layer framework targeting the following issues:

1. Creation, sharing documentation of information and knowledge in and out of an organization, and improvement of organizational processes based on information and knowledge;
2. Training of organizational workers – driven by the ToOW model Ferreira et al. (2017);
3. Promotion of ad-hoc discussion.

As shown in Figure 3, a context for an Enterprise 4.0 implementation can be settled through the use of the four pillars of digital transformation, so as to achieve the well-being of the organization considering the agility and collective intelligence dimensions. Thus, emphasis is given in the production of value for the organizational ecosystem.

Creating value often occurs in different social contexts. This approach includes individual and organizational contextual factors. It identifies the crucial role that an organization plays in promoting a culture of lifelong learning, collaboration and innovation, in order to achieve the organization's strategic objectives. The model identifies and presents the relationships and interactions namely between employees, technology and tools, the business strategy and business processes.

Figure 3. The m_CSDIT approach

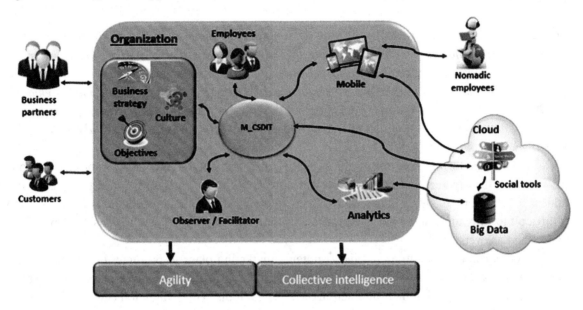

The approach highlights the collaboration issue and its relation with the accomplishment of the organizational goals. The employees are at the centre of the collaboration and are mostly members of social networks. Figure 1 illustrates the nature of the proposed collaboration in the workplace, where mobile devices are used, IS and underlying processes are largely organized and conducted by the organization, and which is based on the social context.

The approach may be briefly described as the collaboration in the workplace based on the four pillars of digital transformation. This means that the organization learns through the participation and involvement of its stakeholders, namely employees, through a network, connecting, interacting and collaborating to obtain or share information and / or knowledge, in order to improve its organizational processes/IS. We propose that the collaboration in the workplace is achieved through the integration of suitable social media tools to the needs of organizational development and learning. To that end, we suggest a mixed form of peer tutoring with an instructor who acts as observer / facilitator. To achieve the potential benefits of collaboration, we recommend that the organization supports rather than restricts the adequate use of tools in the workplace. Thus, organizations have to define the best long-term strategies and implement action plans to take advantage of collaboration based on the DT pillars.

m_CSDIT 1st Layer: Monitoring the Use of Social Media

The effective and full use of social media by organizations, as advocated by the first layer of the m_CSDIT approach, require that these organizations are able to monitor and analyze the high volumes of heterogeneous data that are produced by the use of social media, so as to obtain relevant information and valuable insights for decision making and for conducting their business. This task should be accomplished through the use of social media monitoring tools.

Social Media Monitoring Tools

Janssen (2014) defined social media monitoring as "*a process of using social media channels to track, gather and mine the information and data of certain individuals or groups, usually companies or organizations, to assess their reputation and discern how they are perceived online*". He also adds that "*Social media monitoring is also known as social media listening and social media measurement*". Rouse (2013) puts forward the following definition of the concept: "*Social media listening, also known as social media monitoring, is the process of identifying and assessing what is being said about a company, individual, product or brand*".

Social media monitoring tools are useful in the discovery of what is happening in online environments, in which the organization operates. Furthermore, these tools can also be used to measure the usefulness of the efforts made on interaction with customers and potential customers. Indeed, it can be quite difficult to fully understand the effectiveness of these efforts, only by analyzing subscriptions of customers and answers.

Today's organizations tend to use modern strategic marketing plans to promote their products and services by using social media tools. Hence, organizations can measure customer responses or potential customers' attraction regarding their interactions with social tools. This evaluation can only be carried out efficiently, if it is performed through the use of monitoring tools of the target social media. The results obtained can be used in defining new marketing strategies, address issues and problems identified by customers, etc.

Thus, by using social media monitoring tools, organizations can make better informed decisions about where improvements can be made, spot opportunities and strengthen any weaknesses that they may have in their social media output.

There are a large number of social media monitoring tools. Hence, depending on the goal to be achieved, the right tool may be a series of free Google Alerts or an expensive software suite, including ad hoc analysis and full integration with legacy customer relationship management applications. These tools transfer the desired words and phrases from unstructured to structured database data, for analysis with traditional data mining techniques.

In the private and/or public sector, social media monitoring tools can mine text for specific keywords on social networking websites, blogs, discussion forums and other social media. For example, in the private sector, these tools are useful as companies aim to hear and analyze the complaints about their own products or services, or those of competitors, to help to attract customers; in the public sector, "observing" online conversations may be a way of collecting opinions from people who may not want to fill in a formal survey form.

Classification and Adoption of Social Media Monitoring Tools

Due to the diversity of social media monitoring tools available and wide range of features offered, we envisaged a framework to classify and guide the process of adoption of such a tool (or set of tools) by an organization. The framework called FCASM²T (Framework for classification and adoption of social media monitoring tools) is described in (Moreira et al., 2015) and is composed of five phases as illustrated in Figure 4: (1) Tools and functionalities/features; (2) Profile calculation; (3) Ordering of the index; (4) Definition of ranges of adoption and (5) Suggestion for adoption.

Figure 4. The FCASM²T framework

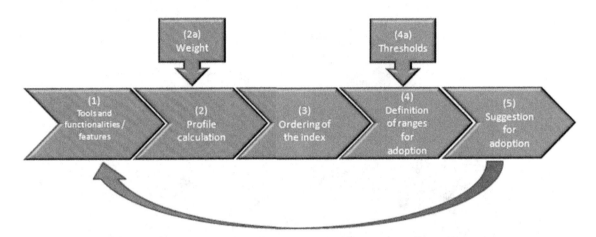

In the first stage (1) tools are collected from the repository of available tools, and their functionalities and features are identified. After building the matrix (tools – functionalities/features), in step (2), weights (2a) are assigned to each of the functionalities, according to the degree of importance that the feature is perceived to have. Subsequently, the profile of each tool is calculated. In step (3) the ordering of the sorting index is performed. This ordering is made based on the profiles calculated for each tool in step (2). In step (4) thresholds are set (4a) so that intervals of choice may be defined. By using step (5) and based on the defined thresholds, it is possible to have as an outcome the suggested tool or tools most suitable for an adoption. At this stage, the following three types of adoption are allowed: (i) full adoption; (ii) conditional adoption, and (iii) should not to be adopted.

The process is iterative, as new tools and functionalities may be considered, and need to be evaluated in the process.

m_CSDIT 2nd Layer: The Training of Organizational Workers (ToOW) Model

The ToOW, originally named EToW (Ferreira et al., 2014b), addresses the 2nd layer of the framework, and is presented in Figure 5 as a cyclic sequence of stages, aiming to use the four pillars of DT in the definition of training strategies for the organizational workers, aligned with the organizational strategy.

As depicted in Figure 5, the ToOW model is designed to train organizational workers supported by social media tools (3) (see section 3). The training strategies of the organization (2) are aligned with the organizational strategy (1) and analytical tools are used to evaluate the employees training, on the basis of their performance, according to the defined organizational strategy (4).

In order to enable a more flexible training scheme, the model also considers training actions proposed by employees; however, training attendance will always be compulsory according to the defined training strategies (2). The definition / adjustment of the training strategies (2) should be made in a periodical basis, so as to pace with the evolution / needs of the organization.

Regarding the use of social media tools, the model considers a complete set of tools to be used within the training activities, which can be used inside and outside the organization, that is, in different learning contexts. The model is designed in such a way as to enable training in the classroom, at distance or in

Figure 5. The ToOW model

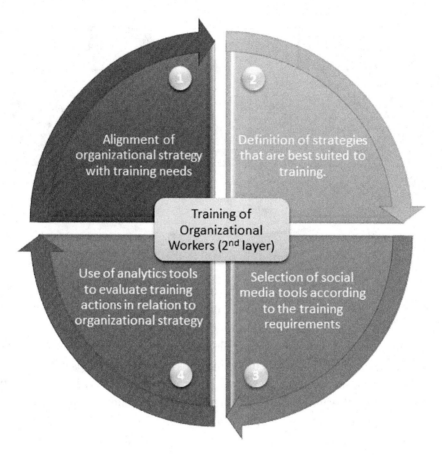

workplace context, in a formal or informal way. In the case of informal training there will always be, as shown in Figure 1, an Observer / Facilitator, who will have a role of moderator on the ongoing training.

As cloud is one of the pillars of DT and social is one of the others, the use of social media tools located in the cloud, will allow to consider the ToOW approach as collaborative learning, as it enables internal training (Figure 3 – Employees) as well as external training (Figure 3 – Nomadic employees), enabling the interaction and collaboration among the participants and, thus, the sharing of information and/or knowledge.

All the training sessions carried out have to be evaluated so that it can be understood if the investment made in training employees meet the needs of the organization and the impact it may have on organizational processes' improvement. Hence, analytics tools – one of the pillars of DT – will be used to monitor and compare training results with the defined metrics goals to improve organizational processes.

The absence of a training culture embedded in the organization's ecosystem may lead to the failure of training strategies set for the employees and for the organization in general. In order to avoid this failure scenario, the model hereby proposed aims to promote the development of a culture of lifelong training, adding value to organizational development and being central to achieve the objectives defined in the alignment of the organizational strategy with the organization training needs.

A Scenario for the Model Usage

In this section, we outline an application scenario for a training plan that uses the ToOW model proposed in this paper. The scenario targets a real estate agency which seeks to be more agile in its interactions with customers and sellers, in order to better promote its properties, while enhancing its selling staff training procedures and staff performance assessment system (Stage 1, Figure 5).

The corporate website is the main institutional platform of communication of the agency with its customers, by advertising the properties offered and providing further sellers contact information; it is also from the website that it is possible to access social media platforms, newsletters and blogs. For internal communication and training purposes, the agency sets up an intranet based on cloud computing technology (e.g. DropBox; Google Drive) for training of its selling staff (Stage 2, Figure 5). In the intranet, there is a folder for each property with the property full description and promotion images, and a video for guiding the seller with the highlights that should be focused on the property visits' with the potential customers. Virtual reality and/or augmented reality applications may also be considered for that purpose. The entire promotion plan for the property (advertisement in the corporate newsletter, web site promotion, social media campaigns, special events, etc.) is also available so that the seller is aware of the agency sales and marketing strategy regarding that property; hence, the seller can record what was the trigger of contact of a customer with the agency regarding a given property. This folder is shared by all the sellers in charge of the property's promotion. After each property visit or customer interaction, the seller uses his/her mobile device to fill a spreadsheet record with the main features of the visit/interaction and results achieved, which may also involve updating the property status. After each visit, the customer is invited to fill an online questionnaire so as to assess his/her satisfaction on the service level provided by the seller and agency. The results of all the questionnaires filled regarding a property are saved into a spreadsheet available in the property folder.

There is also an institutional blog for the real estate agency (accessed from the corporate website) where customers may establish a chat conversation with the sellers and post comments and questions about the property as a result of the contacts or visit they did or even discuss further meetings (Stage 3, Figure 5).

As the history of all the interactions and engagements of the seller with customers about a property is stored, loading a data warehouse of sellers-customers interactions, analytic tools may easily be used to monitor the KPI's set by the real estate agency regarding the performance of the seller (Stage 4, Figure 5). Hence, KPI's like the number of property visits promoted, the visits conversion rate, sales growth, blog engagement, top sellers in sales revenue, website traffic lead ratio, newsletter signup conversion rate, customer satisfaction, customer retention may be measured and contribute to the seller's assessment. Depending on the organizational strategy, some of the KPI's related with the sellers performance may be shared among the sellers team, so as to improve the collective intelligence, generate useful sales and marketing insights and stimulate organizational goals achievement. If the assessment results of sellers are not satisfactory, the reasons may be analysed and the alignment of organizational strategy with the training needs may be resettled, generating a new cycle of application of the ToOW model.

CONCLUSION AND FURTHER WORK

This paper aimed to give an overview of the state-of-the art of the issues underlying the undertaking by organizations of social business supported by social media tools. Then it described our extended m_CS-DIT approach, consisting in a three-layer framework that covers the systematization of (1) the creation, sharing and documentation of information and knowledge in and out of an organization and improvement of organizational processes based on information and knowledge, (2) training of organizational workers and (3) promotion of ad-hoc discussion.

The main difference between a traditional organization with and without social business is the involvement of the customers, business partners and employees in the life of an organization. Both visions present benefits and drawbacks. In particular, it is envisaged that the m_CSDIT approach will allow the implementation of social business in an organization. The approach is focused on the production of value for the customer, reducing whatever does not add value from his point of view as well as to the organization itself. Therefore, the involvement of the organization ecosystem is of paramount importance to achieve this goal. On the contrary, traditional approaches allow the conduction of business within an organization in a closed way.

Despite the successes and progress made to date, many important topics remain open for investigation with respect to providing appropriate approaches to undertake social business in organizations supported by the use of social media tools.

Many of the results achieved so far in social business supported by social media tools have come from joint work between researchers and organizations. Awareness, education and systematization remain three of the biggest issues to develop for those working in social business.

Researchers need to have practical experience as well as a sound theoretical foundation. Practitioners need to be equipped with a variety of approaches to use where appropriate depending on what is best suited to a given situation. Customers need to understand the importance of the process, believe in it, and support the efforts involved in doing it right. That was the context for the proposal of the m_CSDIT approach.

We envisage that the m_CSDIT approach will allow the implementation of a new context of labour, which we term Enterprise 4.0, largely boosted by the organizational adoption of social media, offering a new context to the traditional way of doing business - the context of DT. The approach promotes the organizational well-being considering the agility and collective intelligence dimensions.

Even though we have progressed in the conceptualization of the m_CSDIT approach, the framework needs to accomplish a greater degree of formalization, as well as validated and implemented in an organizational context.

REFERENCES

Abbott, S. (2015). *The Co+Factor - The Exclusively-For-Everyone, Not-To-Be-Kept-Secret Ingredient/ Benefit For Helping You and Your Organization Create, Engage and Prosper.* Retrieved April 2, 2018, from http://bemobileworksocial.com/wp-content/uploads/2015/02/The-Co-Factor-E-Book.pdf

Barczyk, C. C., & Duncan, D. G. (2012). Social Networking Media: An Approach for the Teaching of International Business. *Journal of Teaching in International Business, 23*(2), 98–122. doi:10.1080/08 975930.2012.718703

Barlow, J. B., & Dennis, A. R. (2016). Not As Smart As We Think: A Study of Collective Intelligence in Virtual Groups. *Journal of Management Information Systems, 33*(3), 684–712. doi:10.1080/074212 22.2016.1243944

Bear, M. (2015). Survival of the fittest: Using social media to thrive in the 21st century. *Journal Of Brand Strategy, 4*(2), 106–113.

Berkman, R. (2014). The social enterprise: where does the information professional fit? *Online Searcher*, (6), 45-48.

Boyd, D. (2008). *Taken out of context: American teen sociality in networked publics.* Berkeley, CA: School of Information, University of California-Berkeley.

Boyd, D. M., & Ellison, N. B. (2008). Social network sites: Definition, history, and scholarship. *Journal of Computer-Mediated Communication, 13*(1), 210–230. doi:10.1111/j.1083-6101.2007.00393.x

Brown, J. S. (2012). *Learning in and for the 21st Century.* National Institute of Education.

Charbonnier-Voirin, A. (2011). The development and partial testing of the psychometric properties of a measurement scale of organizational agility. *M@n@gement, 14*(2), 119-156.

Cortada, J. (2012). *The Business of Social Business: What works and how its done.* IBM Institute for Business Value. Retrieved January 28, 2018, from http://www.ibm.com/midmarket/common/att/pdf/ IBV_2012_The_business_of_social_business.pdf

Di Stefano, G., Piacentino, B., & Ruvolo, G. (2017). Mentalizing in Organizations: A Psychodynamic Model for an Understanding of Well-Being and Suffering in the Work Contexts. *World Futures, 73*(4-5), 216–223. doi:10.1080/02604027.2017.1333851

Dodge, R., Daly, A., Huyton, J., & Sanders, L. (2012). The challenge of defining wellbeing. *International Journal of Wellbeing, 2*(3), 222–235. doi:10.5502/ijw.v2i3.4

Dorn, J., Grün, C., Werthner, H., & Zapletal, M. (2007). A Survey of B2B Methodologies and Technologies: From Business Models towards Deployment Artifacts. *Proceedings of 40th Hawaii International Conference on Systems Science.*

Drell, L., & Davis, J. (2014). Getting started with social media success metrics. *Marketing Research, 26*(5), 22–27.

Ferreira, M.J., Moreira, F. & Seruca, I. (2014a). A traditional organization towards a new dimension of labour – social business. In *Information systems and Technology for Organizational Agility, Intelligence, and Resilience* (pp. 180-204). Hershey, PA: Information Science Reference (IGI). doi:10.4018/978-1-4666-5970-4.ch009

Ferreira, M. J., Moreira, F., & Seruca, I. (2014b). Social business – a new dimension for education and training in organizations: The ETOW model. *Proceedings Of 16th International Conference on Enterprise Information Systems (ICEIS)*, 420-427.

Ferreira, M. J., Moreira, F., & Seruca, I. (2015). Social Business: A Way to Promote Organizational Transformation. *International Journal of Information System Modeling and Design, 6*(4), 57-81. Doi:10.4018/IJISMD.2015100104

Ferreira, M. J., Moreira, F., & Seruca, I. (2017). Organizational training within digital transformation: The ToOW model. *19th International Conference on Enterprise Information Systems (ICEIS)*.

Gaál, Z., Szabó, L., & Obermayer-Kovács, N. (2015). The Power of Social Media in Fostering Knowledge Sharing. *Proceedings of the European Conference on Intellectual Capital*, 114-121.

Gulbahar, M. O., & Yildirim, F. (2015). Marketing Efforts Related to Social Media Channels and Mobile Application Usage in Tourism: Case Study in Istanbul. *Procedia - Social and Behavioral Sciences, 195*, 453-462. doi:10.1016/j.sbspro.2015.06.489

Gustas, R., & Gustiene, P. (2012). A Graphical Method for Conceptual Modelling of Business and Software Scenarios. *Proceedings of 11th International Conference on Intelligent Software Methodologies, Tools and Techniques*, 238-253.

Haar, G. (2015). *What Has KLM Learned From 5 Years of Social Media Service?* Retrieved February 03, 2018, from https://blog.klm.com/what-has-klm-learned-from-5-years-of-social-media-service/

Hagel, J., Brown, J. S., & Davison, L. (2010). *The Power of Pull: How Small Moves, Smartly Made, Can Set Big Things in Motion*. New York: Basic Books.

Hiriyappa, B. (2008). *Strategic Management for Chartered Accountants*. New Age International Pvt Ltd Publishers.

IDC. (2018). *Digital Transformation*. Retrieved march 03, 2018, from https://www.idc.com/promo/thirdplatform/fourpillars

Janssen, C. (2014). *Social Media Monitoring*. Retrieved February 03, 2018, from http://www.techopedia.com/definition/29592/social-media-monitoring

Jarrahi, M. H., & Sawyer, S. (2013). Social Technologies, Informal Knowledge Practices, and the Enterprise. *Journal of Organizational Computing and Electronic Commerce, 23*(1-2), 110–137. doi:10.1080/10919392.2013.748613

Kane, G. C. (2017). The evolutionary implications of social media for organizational knowledge management. *Information and Organization*, 2737–2746. doi:10.1016/j.infoandorg.2017.01.001

Kaplan, A. M., & Haenlein, M. (2010). Users of the world, unite! The challenges and opportunities of social media. *Business Horizons*, *53*(1), 59–68. doi:10.1016/j.bushor.2009.09.003

Kim, P. (2012). *The definition of social business.* Retrieved February 05, 2018, from http://dachisgroup.com/2012/06/the-definition-of-social-business/

Koetsier, J. (2015). *KLM's 150 social media customer service agents generate $25M in annual revenue.* Retrieved November 05, 2015, from http://venturebeat.com/2015/05/21/klms-150-social-media-customer-service-agents-generate-25m-in-annual-revenue/

Kotter, J. P. (1995). Leading Change: Why Transformation Efforts Fail. *Harvard Business Review On Point*, 60-67.

Levy, P. (1999). *Collective Intelligence: Mankind's Emerging World in Cyberspace.* Perseus Books.

Lowry, P. B., & Wilson, D. (2016). Creating agile organizations through IT: The influence of internal IT service perceptions on IT service quality and IT agility. *The Journal of Strategic Information Systems*, 25211–25226. doi:10.1016/j.jsis.2016.05.002

Majchrzack, A., Cherbakov, L., & Ives, B. (2009). Harnessing the Power of the Crowds with Corporate Social Networking "How IBM does it". *MIS Quarterly Executive*, *8*(2), 103–198.

Malone, T. W., Laubacher, R., & Dellarocas, C. N. (2009). *Harnessing Crowds: Mapping the Genome of Collective Intelligence.* MIT Sloan Research Paper No. 4732-09. Retrieved February 05, 2018, from http://ssrn.com/abstract=1381502

Martin, A., & van Bavel, R. (2013). *Assessing the Benefits of Social Networks for Organizations.* Retrieved November 06, 2015, from http://ftp.jrc.es/EURdoc/JRC78641.pdf

McAfee, A. (2006). Enterprise 2.0: The Dawn of Emergent Collaboration'. *MIT Sloan Management Review*, *47*(3), 21–28.

McAfee, A. (2009). *Enterprise 2.0: New Collaborative Tools for Your Organization's Toughest Challenges.* Harvard Business Review Press.

Mcculloch, A. (2015). *KLM: Putting Social Customer Care First.* Retrieved November 08, 2015, from http://www.socialbakers.com/blog/2374-klm-putting-social-customer-care-first

McKinsey & Company. (2015). *Transforming the business through social tools.* Retrieved February 05, 2018, from http://www.mckinsey.com/insights/high_tech_telecoms_internet/transforming_the_business_through_social_tools

McKinsey & Company. (2016). *How social tools can reshape the organization.* Retrieved from April 05, 2017 from https://www.mckinsey.com/business-functions/digital-mckinsey/our-insights/how-social-tools-can-reshape-the-organization

McKinsey & Company. (2017). *Advanced social technologies and the future of collaboration.* Retrieved April 05, 2017, from https://www.mckinsey.com/business-functions/digital-mckinsey/our-insights/advanced-social-technologies-and-the-future-of-collaboration

Moreira, F., Seruca, I., & Ferreira, M. J. (2015). Towards a Framework for Classification and Adoption of Social Media Monitoring Tools. *Proceedings Of 2nd European Conference Social Media (ECSM 2015).*

Paunova, M. (2015). The emergence of individual and collective leadership in task groups: A matter of achievement and ascription. *The Leadership Quarterly, 26*(6), 935–957. doi:10.1016/j.leaqua.2015.10.002

Romero-Mujalli, D., Cappelletto, J., Herrera, E., & Tárano, Z. (2017). The effect of social learning in a small population facing environmental change: An agent-based simulation. *Journal of Ethology, 35*(1), 61–73. doi:10.100710164-016-0490-8

Rouse, M. (2013). *Social media listening.* Retrieved February 05, 2018, from http://searchcrm.techtarget.com/definition/Social-media-monitoring

Schultz, M. D., Koehler, J. W., Philippe, T. W., & Coronel, R. S. (2015). Managing the Effects of Social Media in Organizations. *SAM Advanced Management Journal, 80*(2), 42-47.

Sideraworks. (2013). *What Is Social Business?* Retrieved November 11, 2015, from http://www.sidera-works.com/wp-content/uploads/2012/03/WhatIsSocialBusiness_SideraWorks.pdf

Skeels, M. M., & Grudin, J. (2009). When social networks cross boundaries: A case study of workplace use of Facebook and LinkedIn. In GROUP'09. Sanibel Island, FL: ACM. doi:10.1145/1531674.1531689

Streitz, N., Prante, T., Röcker, C., Alphen, D. V., Magerkurth, C., Stenzel, R., & Plewe, D. A. (2003). Ambient Displays and Mobile Devices for the Creation of Social Architectural Spaces. *The Kluwer International series on Computer Supported Cooperative Work, 2*, 387-409.

StuzoGroup. (2013). *Doritos-Become The Doritos Guru.* Retrieved November 08, 2015, from http://www.stuzo.com/case-studies/Stuzo_CaseStudy_Doritos_BecometheDoritosGuru.pdf

Tajudeen, F. P., Jaafar, N. I., & Ainin, S. (2018). Understanding the impact of social media usage among organizations. *Information & Management, 55308–55321. doi:10.1016/j.im.2017.08.004

Tajvidi, R., & Karami, A. (2017). Full length article: The effect of social media on firm performance. *Computers in Human Behavior.* doi:10.1016/j.chb.2017.09.026

Uhl, A., & Gollenia, L. (2016). *Digital Enterprise Transformation: A Business-Driven Approach to Leveraging Innovative IT.* Routledge Taylor & Francis Group.

Valentin, B. A. (2017). Methods of Assessment and Training of a Company Towards the Enterprise 4.0. *Annals of DAAAM & Proceedings, 28*, 1065-1073. doi:10.2507/28th.daaam.proceedings.148

Van Belleghem, S. (2012). *The Conversation Company, Boost your Business Through Culture. People & Social Media.* London, UK: Kogan Page.

Vannoy, S. A., & Palvia, P. (2010). The Social Influence Model of Technology Adoption. *Communications of the ACM, 53*(8), 149–153. doi:10.1145/1743546.1743585

Wood, J., & Khan, G. F. (2016). Social business adoption: An empirical analysis. *Business Information Review, 33*(1), 28–39. doi:10.1177/0266382116631851

World Economic Forum. (2015). Deep Shift - Technology Tipping Points and Societal Impact. *Global Agenda Council on the Future of Software & Society.* Retrieved November 13, 2015, from http://www3. weforum.org/docs/WEF_GAC15_Technological_Tipping_Points_report_2015.pdf

Yin, R. (2009). *Case Study Research: Design and Methods.* London, UK: SAGE Publication, Inc.

Yunus, M. (2007). *Creating a World Without Poverty: Social Business and the Future of Capitalism.* New York: PublicAffairs.

Zakić, N., Jovanović, A., & Stamatović, M. (2008). External and Internal Factors Affecting the Product and Business Process Innovation. *Facta Universitatis Series: Economics and Organization, 5*(1), 17–29.

Zhao, F., & Kemp, L. (2012). Integrating Web 2.0-based informal learning with workplace training. *Educational Media International, 49*(3), 231–245. doi:10.1080/09523987.2012.738015

Chapter 6
Supporting Participation in Online Social Networks

Agostino Poggi
University of Parma, Italy

Paolo Fornacciari
University of Parma, Italy

Gianfranco Lombardo
University of Parma, Italy

Monica Mordonini
University of Parma, Italy

Michele Tomaiuolo
University of Parma, Italy

ABSTRACT

Social networking systems can be considered one of the most important social phenomena because they succeeded in involving billions of people all around the world and in attracting users from several social groups, regardless of age, gender, education, or nationality. Social networking systems blur the distinction between the private and working spheres, and users are known to use such systems both at home and at the work place both professionally and with recreational goals. Social networking systems can be equally used to organize a work meeting, a dinner with the colleagues, or a birthday party with friends. In the vast majority of cases, social networking platforms are still used without corporate blessing. However, several traditional information systems, such as CRMs and ERPs, have also been modified in order to include social aspects. This chapter discusses the participation in online social networking activities and, in particular, the technologies that support and promote the participation in online social network.

DOI: 10.4018/978-1-5225-7271-8.ch006

INTRODUCTION

Social networking systems represent one of the most important social phenomena involving billions of people all around the world, attracting users from several social groups, regardless of age, gender, education, or nationality. In fact, some social networking systems are become the largest information systems accessible to the general public and, because of their neutrality regarding the public-private and the work-home axes, they often assume the role of feral systems.

Social networking systems blur the distinction between the private and working spheres, and users are known to use such systems both at home and on the work place both professionally and with recreational goals. Social networking systems can be equally used to organize a work meeting, a dinner with the colleagues or a birthday party with friends. For example, the chat systems that are embedded in social networking platforms are often the most practical way to contact a colleague to ask an urgent question, especially in technologically oriented companies.

Moreover, several traditional information systems have been modified in order to include social aspects and several organizations: (*i*) allow external social networking platforms to be used (e.g., Facebook was available for Microsoft and Apple employees before the general public launch), (*ii*) have created an internal social networking platform (DiMicco & Millen, 2007), or (*iii*) allow other social platforms for specific purposes (Millen et al., 2006). However, in the vast majority of cases, social networking platforms are used without corporate blessing, maintaining their status as feral systems.

According to DiMicco (2008), most users that use social networking platforms for work purposes are mostly interested in accumulating social capital, either for career advancement or to gather support for their own projects inside the company. Given the close relation between professional usage of social media and social capital.

This chapter has the goal of discussing about the participation in online social network, about the technologies that support and promote their use by individual and organization. The next section introduces online social networks; the third section discussed about the participation in this kind of networks; the fourth section introduces the technologies the support the activities in online social network; the fifth section discusses about the use of online social network and related social media in firms and organizations; and, finally, the last section concludes the summarizing its main contributions and presenting the directions for future work.

BACKGROUND

The result of the interactions among the users in a social networking system is an online social network, i.e., a special case of the more general concept of social network. A social network is defined as a set or sets of actors and the relations defined on them (Wasserman & Faust, 1994). Social networks are typically studied using social network analysis, a discipline that focuses on the structural and topological features of the network. More recently, additional dimensions have been added to the traditional social network analytic approach (Monge and Contractor 2003; Borgatti and Foster 2003; Parkhe et al. 2006; Hoang and Antoncic 2003).

The study of structure of Online Social Networks, expressed as patterns of links among nodes, can exploit models and ideas from classical sociology and anthropology, with particular attention to contextual and relational approaches. In fact, all the results obtained in decades of studies of human networks are also at the basis of the analysis of online social networks. However, these results cannot be simply applied to the different context of online relations. Instead they have to be evaluated and adapted to the new networks, which may have significantly different structure and dynamics.

Moreover, online social networking platforms may greatly vary both technically and in their aims. They may be used by people for organizing quite diverse activities, in different types of virtual communities. In particular, virtual organizations, virtual teams, and online networks of practice are the most discussed. Although there are several differences that clearly set the concepts apart, the *trait d'union* of these virtual communities are: i) the lack of central authority, ii) their temporary and impromptu nature, and iii) the importance of reputation and trust as opposed to bureaucracy and law.

Virtual Organization

According to the definition given by Mowshowitz (1994), a virtual organization is "a temporary network of autonomous organizations that cooperate based on complementary competencies and connect their information systems to those of their partners via networks aiming at developing, making, and distributing products in cooperation." The term was then popularized by the Grid Computing community, referring to Virtual Organizations as "*flexible, secure, coordinated resource sharing among dynamic collections of individuals, institutions, and resources*" (Foster et al., 2001). The premise of Virtual Organizations is the technical availability of tools for effective collaboration among people located in different places, but their definition also emphasizes the possibility to share a large number of resources, including documents, data, knowledge and tools among interested people. Their importance is sustained by continuing trends in production and social forms, including the growing number of knowledge workers, the emergence of integrated industrial district and other aspects developing at an international level, like dynamic supply chains, just-in-time production, sub-contracting, delocalization, externalization, global logistics and mass migrations which collectively are usually named "*globalization*".

Virtual Team

A virtual team is usually defined as a group of geographically, organizationally and/or time dispersed members connected by information and telecommunication technologies (e.g., email, video and voice conferencing services) that work together asynchronously or across organizational levels (Powell et al., 2004; Lipnack & Stamps, 2008; Ale Ebrahim et. al. (2009). Virtual teams can represent organizational structures within the context of some virtual organization, but they can also come into existence in other situations, where independent people collaborate on a project (e.g., an open source project); in these cases, they do not have hierarchy or any other common structure because member may be from different organizations.

Due to the streamlined development of information technologies, today many companies prefer to take advantage of virtual teams for the development of the work of a relevant part of their projects and more and more people work in virtual teams for at least part of the time. In fact, virtual teams allow companies to procure the best competences necessary for their projects without geographical restrictions and usually well-managed virtual teams are more productive than co-located teams (Vlaar et al., 2008). However, the success of the work of virtual team requires new skills, new ways of working and the presence of effective leaders.

Online Network of Practice

An online network of practice represents an informal and emergent virtual community that is represented by individuals connected through social relationships and that supports the exchange of information between its members in order to perform their work and sharing knowledge with each other (Brown & Duguid, 2017). The term practice represents the glue that connects individuals in the network. Usually the glue is the type of work (e.g., journalist, software developer, teacher), but often is the sharing of similar interests (e.g., common hobbies, discussing sports and/or politics). In an online network of practice, individuals may never get to know one another or meet face-to-face. Moreover, their interactions are generally coordinate through means such as blogs, microblogs, mailing lists and bulletin boards (Teigland, (2004).

Networks of practice differ from networks in several significant ways. In fact, individuals not only for their own needs, but to serve the needs of others. One of the most interesting distinctions is that in a network of practice, there is an intentional commitment to advance the field of practice, and to share those discoveries with a wider audience; in fact, its members make their resources and knowledge available to anyone, especially those doing related work (Wheatley & Frieze, 2006).

PARTICIPATION IN ONLINE SOCIAL NETWORKS

In order to understand the reasons that motivate the users in engaging in online social activities in general, and, more specifically, in sharing their valued knowledge in online communities, it is necessary to analyze the nature and the structure of their relationships in the context of a specific community, and to evaluate the possible implications for the involved users.

Social Capital

In particular, an important theoretical foundation for the analysis of participation in social networks is constituted by social capital (Maskell, 2000; Lin, 2017). Social capital represents a person's benefit due to his relations with other persons, including family, colleagues, friends and generic contacts. The concept originated in studies about communities, to underline the importance of collective actions and the associated enduring relations of trust and cooperation, for the functioning of neighborhoods in large cities (Jacobs, 1961).

Erickson (2000) argues that network variety as much as the people that someone knows, is a form of social capital valuable to both employers and employees in the hiring process. In fact, network variety is social "capital" in the same sense that education and work experience are human "capital" because all these forms of capital yield returns in the form of greater employee productivity.

Social capital has been studied as a factor providing additional opportunities to some players in a competitive scenario, and, from this point of view, it has been studied in the context of firms (Backer, 1990), nations (Fukuyama, 1995) and geographic regions (Putnam, 1995). In this sense, social capital is defined as a third kind of capital that is brought in the competitive arena, along with financial capital, which includes machinery and raw materials, and human capital, which includes knowledge and skills. Moreover, the role of social capital in the development of human capital has been studied by Loury and Coleman (Loury, 1987; Coleman, 1988).

Social capital is typically studied: (*i*) by drawing a graph of connected people and their own resources, creating a connection between each player's resources and those of his closest contacts; or (*ii*) by analyzing social structures in their own right, and supposing that the network structure alone can be used to estimate some player's competitive advantage, at the social stance.

The size of the ego-centered social network is an important factor to estimate the social capital of one individual; however, the size alone does not provide enough information. According to Burt (1992) social capital is related with the number of non-redundant contacts and not directly with the simple number of contacts. In fact, although information spreads rapidly among homogeneous, richly interconnected groups, Granovetter (1973) argues that new ideas and opportunities are introduced in the groups by contacts with people from outside the group. In order to explain this phenomenon, Granovetter distinguished among three types of ties: (*i*) strong ties, (*ii*) weak ties, and (*iii*) absent ties.

A quantitative distinction between strong and weak ties has been subject of debate, but intuitively weak ties are simple acquaintances, while strong ties are reserved for close friends and family. The "*absent ties*" indicate missing relations in the network. Burt capitalizes on Granovetter's insight, and emphasizes the importance of absent ties, that create the "*structural holes*" in the network texture. According to Burt, structural holes allow the individuals that create a weak link among two otherwise separated communities to greatly increase their social capital.

Nahapiet & Goshal (1998) discuss the role of social capital in building intellectual capital inside organizations. The authors distinguish the structural, relational, and cognitive aspects of social networks. The structural properties describe the patterns of connection among actors and regard the social system as a whole. The relational properties describe the type of ties people have developed during their interactions, including relationships like friendship, trust, and respect. The cognitive properties refer to basic knowledge, representations, languages and other systems of meaning, shared among actors. Moreover, they focus on the development of intellectual capital, which is essentially an aspect of human capital, but may also be owned by a social collectivity. In fact, they classify knowledge as (*i*) either implicit or explicit, and (*ii*) either individual or social. In the case of social knowledge, they argue that social capital facilitates the creation of intellectual capital primarily by creating conditions for exchange and combination of knowledge.

Evolution of Network Connections

Monge and Contractor (2003) proposed a multi-theoretical and multilevel model for analyzing the evolution of network connections in online social networks. Their analysis considers the following theories: self-interest, mutual interest and collective action, homophily and proximity, exchange and dependency, co-evolution, contagion, balance and transitivity, and cognition.

According to the theories of self-interest, people create ties with other people and participate in team activities in order to maximize the satisfaction of their own goals. The most known theories of self-interest are based on the notion of social capital (Burt, 1992). Another foundation of these theories lies on transaction cost economics (Williamson, 1991).

The mutual interest and collective action theories study the coordinated action of individuals in a team. They explain collective actions as a mean for reaching outcomes which would be unattainable by individual action (Fulk et al., 2004). Thus, individuals collaborate in a community because they share mutual interests.

The principle at the basis of homophily and proximity theories is that connections are mostly structured according to similarity (McPherson et al., 2001). Moreover, connections between dissimilar individuals break at a higher rate.

Another founding motivation for the emergence of groups can be the exchange and dependency theories (Cook, 1982). These theories explain the creation of communities by analyzing the network structure together with the distribution and flow of resources in the network. Example of exchange networks vary from data analysts to bands of musicians.

The underlying principle of co-evolution theories is that evolution based on environmental selection can be applied to whole organizations, and not only to individuals. Thus, they study how organizations compete and cooperate to access limited resources, and how communities of individuals create ties both internally and towards other communities (Campbell, 1985; Baum, 1999).

For explaining the spread of innovations, contagion theories study how people are brought in contact trough the social structure (Burt, 1987). Social contagion is described as a sort of interpersonal synapse through which ideas are spread. Conversely, some sort of social inoculations may prevent ideas from spreading to parts of the network.

Since macroscopic patterns originate from local structures of social networks, balance and transitivity theories cope with the study of the distribution of triads in digraphs and socio-matrixes (Holland & Leinhardt, 1975). In particular, the first applications of these studies identified the most typical distributions of triads configurations in real social networks and from such distributions showed that individuals' choices have a consistent tendency to be transitive.

Finally, cognitive theories explore the role that meaning, knowledge, and perceptions play in the development of teams and the impact of increasing specialization over collaboration. In this sense, the decision to form a collective depends on what possible members know (Hollingshead et al. 2002). These studies are grounded on the concept of transactive memory.

Social Capital and Knowledge Contribution

Chow & Chan (2008) present a study that was one of the first to provide empirical evidence about the influence of a social network, social trust, and shared goals on employees' intention to share knowledge. This study offers insights to practitioners on the value of social capital and reasons why people are or are not willing to engage in knowledge sharing within an organization. Moreover, it found that social network and shared goals directly influenced the attitude and subjective norm about knowledge sharing and indirectly influenced the intention to share knowledge. Finally, this study argues that social trust does not play a direct role in sharing knowledge and that organizational members do not differentiate between tacit and explicit knowledge when they share it.

Wasko & Faraj (2005) present a study that tries to better understand knowledge flows by examining why people voluntarily contribute knowledge and help others through electronic networks. This study starts from the theoretical model proposed by Nahapiet and Ghoshal (1998) and reports on the activities of an online network supporting a professional legal association. Using archival, network, survey, and content analysis data, it empirically tests a model of knowledge contribution. One of the result is that people usually contribute their knowledge when they perceive that it enhances their professional reputations, when they have the experience to share, and when they are structurally embedded in the network. Surprisingly, contributions occur without regard to expectations of reciprocity from others. Moreover, this study attempts to address the question of why people nevertheless contribute knowledge to others in online networks of practice. The study takes the following features into account, as possible enablers of participation: individual motivations, relational capital, cognitive capital and structural capital.

One key aspect of social contribution is given by individual motivations. In fact, an individual's expectation that some new value will be created, as result of his participation in the network. The individual should expect to receive some benefits from his contribution, even in the absence of direct acquaintance with other members of the community and without mechanisms enforcing or encouraging reciprocity. Increasing the reputation is one of the most important forms of return of investment, especially if the online reputation is believed to have a positive impact on the professional reputation.

Another enabling factor for contributions to an online community is represented by the personal relationships among individuals, as members of that community. Relational capital is directly related to the level of an individual's identification with the community, trust with other members, perception of obligation to participate and reciprocate, acceptance of common norms. In particular, commitment can be associated with a community, apart from individuals.

Any meaningful interaction between two members of a community requires some basic shared understanding. All those common semantic resources, including languages, interpretations, narratives, contexts and norms, are usually described as cognitive capital. In fact, an individual can participate in community activities only if he possesses the required knowledge and, more in general, the required cognitive capital.

Communities characterized by dense internal connections are dialectically correlated with collective actions (Structural capital). In fact, individuals who are strongly embedded in a social network, have many direct ties with other members and a habit of cooperation. On the other hand, an individual's position in the network influences his willingness to contribute, thus increasing both the number and quality of interactions.

Those factors have different weight in different social contexts. In the case study analyzed by Wasko & Faraj (2005), reputation plays a crucial role, since it also affects professional reputation. Other factors, though, also have significant correlation with the number and usefulness of contributions in the online community. The final results compare both the level and helpfulness of contributions against the following factors: (*i*) reputation, (*ii*) willingness to help, (*iii*) centrality in the network structure, (*iv*) self-rated expertise, (*v*) tenure in field, (*vi*) commitment, (*vii*) reciprocity.

With regard to individual motivations, results for the case at hand show a stronger influence of reputation over intrinsic motivations, like willingness to help. Social capital, assessed by determining each individual's degree of centrality to the network, is confirmed to play the most significant role in knowledge exchange. Also cognitive capital, assessed by self-rated expertise and tenure in the field, shows a strong influence over participation, but this is mostly limited to the individual's experience in the field, while self-rated expertise is not quite significant. Finally, in the analyzed network of practice, relational capital, assessed by commitment and reciprocity, is not strongly correlated with knowledge contribution, suggesting that these kinds of ties are more difficult to develop in an online network.

TECHNOLOGIES FOR SOCIAL ONLINE SOCIAL NETWORKS

One of the goals motivating the participation in online communities is the benefit of team work over solo work. Various studies (Van de Ven et al., 1976; Malone & Crowstone, 1994) describe the advantages and costs of coordinating team activities. In fact, while an increase in coordination can lead to greater effectiveness, typically it also produces a faster growth of coordination costs. As a consequence, a lot of effort is being devoted in creating tools and technologies that make group work more effective by containing the costs of their coordination (Bergenti et al. 2011; Franchi & Poggi, 2011; Franchi et al., 2016a). Virtual Teams assembly is another problem that online social platforms can help to solve. In fact, the success of a team depends largely on its assembly process, for identifying the best possible members.

Social collaboration platforms should also help to model and manage multidimensional networks. In fact, apart from direct relationships among people, such platforms should also include other resources. For example, in the area of academic research, a network model could include both people and the events they attend (Wasserman & Faust, 1994), thus creating a bimodal network. Su and Contractor (2011) propose a more complex multi-dimensional network model, including people, documents, data sets, tools, keywords/concepts, etc.

Additionally, in some online communities, participation may also strongly depend on adopted mechanisms and policies for preserving privacy, including confidentiality of messages and identity (Mordonini el al., 2017). For personal identity privacy, stable pseudonyms could be assigned at registration (Andrews, 2002). Moreover, in online communities and Virtual Teams, acquaintance may happen online, without previous connection in real life. In those cases, a member's reputation is directly related to his pseudonym, and ratability of his online activities may be more important than his real world identity for creating trust. Complete anonymity may also have a value in some activities of Virtual Teams, apart from encouraging participation in general. For example, an anonymous brainstorm activity may help opening a conversation about trust and ground rules for online meetings (Young, 2009).

For reaching wider and more effective adoption in open and dynamic online communities, including virtual organizations, virtual teams and online networks of practice, we argue that social networking platforms should embrace an open approach (Franchi et al. 2013). In fact, many isolated sites could not satisfy the need for an inter-organizational collaborative environment. On the other hand, organizations are not keen to rely on a single centralized site, which may pose risks to privacy and may control published data. Moreover, openness is important for participation, too. In fact, a closed environment can hardly reach the minimal dimension and variety required for activating the typical dynamics at the basis of the different theories taken into consideration by the multi-theoretical and multilevel model (Su & Contractor, 2011), for explaining participation in online social networks.

Requirements

In online social networks there are at least three distinct functional elements: (*i*) profile management, (*ii*) social graph management and (*iii*) content production and discussion. In fact, by definition, a social network cannot lack social graph management and self-presentation, no matter how minimal. On the other hand, virtually no modern online social network lacks the content generation features. According to these three main functional areas, it is also possible to draw a classification of the online social networks in three main categories: (*i*) systems where the profile and social graph management is prevalent; (*ii*) systems where the content has a prominent role with respect to social networking activities and there are frequent interactions with people not closely related; and (*iii*) systems where the two aspects have roughly the same importance.

The archetypal examples of the first category of systems are business-related and professional online social networks, like Linkedin. People pay a great deal of attention in creating their profile. In this type of systems there are usually various relationships among users, representing the variety of relationships that members may have in real life. Most users do not visit the site daily and do not add content to the system often (Skeels & Grudin, 2008).

The second type include blogging, micro-blogging and media sharing web sites, like Twitter. The "follow" relationships, which are typical for a system of this kind, are usually not symmetric. The focus is in information transmission; often the system does not support a proper profile and sometimes even the contacts may be hidden. Often weak semantic techniques such as Twitter hash-tags are used, in order to read content by subject instead than by author. Through collaborative tagging, the actors of the system may develop a sort of emergent semantics (Mika, 2007), possibly in the form of so-called "folksonomies". Considering that tags usage is a heavy tailed power-law like distribution, i.e., most people actually uses very few tags, collaborative tagging usually produce a good classification of data (Halpin et al., 2007).

The third category includes the personal online social networks, like Facebook. In this type of systems, users have a profile, partly public and partly confidential. Frequently, there is only one kind of relation, "friendship", which is symmetric and requires approval by both users. These sites have extremely frequent updates: a noticeable percentage of users perform activities on the system at least on a daily basis.

Interoperability

Among the open protocols and data formats for conveying profiles and contacts, Portable Contacts (http://portablecontacts.net/) shows some benefits, especially from the point of view of interoperability. In fact, it is quite simple and well supported by existing large social networks and mail systems, to manage lists of "friends" and address books, respectively. It also allows to associate tags and relationship types with each user, thus paving the way for semantically annotated social networks. In order to let users to express their profile, Friend of a Friend (FOAF) is another sensible choice (Brickley & Miller, 2005). In fact, it provides a descriptive vocabulary that allows the definition of profiles that can be searched and filtered through semantic engines.

Content publication and distribution is another important requirement of online social networks. Atom and RSS emerged as two similar technologies, intended to help readers to receive automatic updates of their favorite websites, and possibly from online acquaintances. RSS and Atom protocols use a pull strategy, i.e., the observer periodically checks the observed resource for updates.

As an alternative, online social networks could adopt a push strategy, i.e., the update is automatically announced to the subscribers. The OStatus protocol (http://status.org/) is a minimal HTTP-based specification for realizing a publish-subscribe mechanism designed around a huh that allows an efficient notification of news to the subscribers.

An on-going and well-supported effort to standardize typical users' activities in social networks is Activity Streams (http://activitystrea.ms/). It is an open format specification for the syndication of activities taken in social web applications and services. The activities of a user are represented as a flow and followers can get it through a subscription.

Finally, OpenSocial (http://opensocial.org/) is a set of common APIs, defined in the form of RESTful Web services, that allow developers to access core functions and information at social networks: (*i*) information about a user's profile, (*ii*) information about the social graph connecting users, and (*iii*) activities occurring in the network, including status updates, publishing of new content and media, commenting and tagging. Moreover, OpenSocial also allows the development of social applications by composing gadgets for collecting and organizing data from different services in a single user interface.

For verifying authorization across different applications, OAuth is often used. An OAuth security token can be used to grant access to a specific site (e.g., a video editing site) for specific resources (e.g., just videos from a specific album) and for a defined duration (e.g., the next 2 hours). This approach allows different social-aware systems to cooperate, and to reduce the necessity for users to maintain and use too many different passwords (Tomaiuolo, 2013; Franchi et al., 2015).

ORGANIZATIONS AND ONLINE SOCIAL NETWORKS

The initial adoption of online collaboration tools and social networking platforms in the work environment has occurred largely on an individual basis. Faced with an increasingly decentralized, expanded and interconnected environment, workers and members of organizations began adopting social networking platforms as better tools for connecting and collaborating with colleagues and partners (Einwiller & Steilen, 2015; Ellison et al., 2015). Thus, social media made their first appearance in firms and organizations mostly without indications from the management and without integration with internal information systems. In this sense, they took the form of feral systems. In fact, (*i*) they were not "part of the corporation's accepted information technology infrastructure", and (*ii*) they were "designed to augment" that infrastructure, along with the definition of Feral Information Systems provided by Houghton & Kerr (2006).

Challenges

In a study published by AT&T (2008), ten main challenges are listed for the adoption of social media by businesses. In fact, these challenges can be grouped in three main areas: (*i*) organizational costs, (*ii*) risks of capital loss, and (*iii*) technical challenges.

About organizational costs, the first issue is that social networking have indirect benefits, which often are not fully appreciated. It is probably the main area of resistance, due to the perceived costs of networking time, not seen as cost efficient activity, and the necessity to allow employees to manage their working time with more freedom. However, traditional ROI methods make it difficult to incorporate all the benefits of social media, both direct and indirect. Thus new performance indicators will be needed. Another issue is the definition of an effective plan to reach the critical mass for the social network to be functional. In fact, common figures of users creating content and collaborating through social media are pretty low, typically from 1% to 20%. Resistance to adoption can come from both regular employee and cadres, possibly including managers and executives. Such a plan would also face the problem of timeliness. In fact, developments in the Web 2.0 environment occur very fast: successful applications may reach millions of users in a couple of years, sometimes creating a new market.

Other challenges are related to the risk of loss of capital, faced by organizations in the adoption of social media. The capital at risk can include intellectual property, as well as human and social capital. In fact, organization members may easily and inadvertently leak sensible and protected content on social media, and such content may face rapid diffusion by "word of mouth" mechanisms. An even greater risk, however, may come from the increased mobility of organization members and employees. This risk is increased by the exposure of members' profiles to the outside world, including other organizations and competitors.

Finally, the adoption of online social networks implies technical costs for creating and maintaining a more complex and open infrastructure. Some important challenges regard security, which is harder to enforce as intranets need to open to the external world, for enabling social collaboration. The risks include the malicious behavior of users, as well as the proliferation of viruses and malware. Also on the technical front, social media applications require increased levels of bandwidth, storage and computational capacity, to support interactions through videos and other form of rich content. Moreover, the increased and differentiated use of social media will pose challenges for the interoperability of different applications, especially with regard to security and authentication schemes.

While the study of AT&T is formulated in reference to the business context, it is interesting to notice that similar considerations are also referred to government agencies and other types of organizations. For example, Bev et al. (2008) describe the case of government agencies. Among other issues, the study underlines the problems of (*i*) employees wasting time on social networks, (*ii*) risk of malware and spyware coming from high traffic sites, and (*iii*) bandwidth requirements. About the first issue, that we described as one aspect of the organizational costs, the authors of the document argue that the problem is not specific to Web 2.0 technologies. In fact, a similar argument was used with respect to mobile phones, emails, etc. For this reason, it is better treated as a management problem instead of a technology problem. About security, efforts should be dedicated to at least mitigate the risks, if they cannot be canceled. Finally, with regard to bandwidth and other technological issues, enough resources should be deployed, to allow at least some selected employees to use rich-content media to communicate with the public, in the most effective way.

Augmenting Information Systems

Although often social networking technologies are not condoned as part of the official information system, yet people use them routinely, at least on an individual basis. In fact, many work activities, in many different sectors, benefit from social media. The use of social media can help workers in their activities (Isari et al., 2011). Social media are a suitable means for coordination among people. Usually it happens across firm boundaries, but they can help in the coordination of activities within a same firm with a big help when employees work in different sites. In this last case, they can provide a complete environment to enable employees to self-organize online, report their status, and stay aware of the status of the other employees of course, considering all the information necessary for coordinating or helping their work. Moreover, the access to social media and, in particular, to community discussing about the technologies and the business of the company can help in the distribution of knowledge within the company and minimizing misunderstandings between colleagues who do not meet face-to-face frequently. Of course, the use of corporate microblogs, either feral or officially supported, can help in the previous cited tasks, but also it allows employees to spread knowledge, ideas, and suggestions about the ways of improving their work.

It is quite easy to find many concrete cases of use of social media for work activities, adopted at first on an individual basis. Just as examples, we will briefly cite the two quite different cases of (*i*) journalism, and (*ii*) software development.

In the field of journalism, social media have already acquired an important role, especially for reporting on breaking news. In those cases, when journalists lack direct sources, social media can guarantee an alternative flow of information, produced by eyewitnesses and other non-professional reporters, who happen to be on the scene at the right moment. However, this new flow of information poses new challenges, as professionals have to discern interesting and trustworthy sources and pieces of content in a magma of information overflow. Professional journalists, in particular, should be wary of rumors and misinformation which are easy to spread on social networks. They should avoid to augment their epidemic potential, to provide credible reports to the public and protect their own professional reputation. For this reason, some research works are targeting specifically the problem of filtering and assessing the veracity of sources found through social networks (Diakopoulos et al., 2012).

Another, very different, example is software development, where Virtual Teams are quite a common practice. In fact, individual developers increasingly use social networks to self-organize both with colleagues in the same organization, and across organizational boundaries. Also, some large communities have emerged as a grassroots process, empowered by new social media and motivated by common interests and emerging attractive targets. In particular, Begel (2010) apply a specific model of teaming to the process of software development. The teaming problems are central in the process, and thus it is highly dependent on developers' abilities to connect and relate with colleagues with similar interests and sufficient skills. The role of social media can then be analyzed in the various aspects of teaming: (*i*) forming, i.e., to select and organize developers into a team; (*ii*) storming, i.e., to reach consensus about the team's goals; (*iii*) norming, i.e., to define guidelines and development methodologies; (*iv*) performing, i.e., to actually develop the new product, through coordinated activities; (*v*) adjourning, i.e., to evaluate accomplishments and failures and improve the team's functioning.

More in general, social media are appreciated by individuals and organizations as they improve collective thinking a thus foster innovation. In fact, creativity and innovation have long been the subjects of organizational studies and social network analysis. Though not all creative ideas lead to innovation, yet it is from creativity that innovation may arise, if followed by successful implementation. Fedorowicz et al. (2008) note that creative ideas rarely come from individuals. More often, they come from teams and groups. Today, this frequently happens in Virtual Teams, through social media and e-Collaboration. Studies focus on various important aspects, such as: (*i*) the impact collaborative tools; (*ii*) the impact of e-Collaboration processes; and (*iii*) the design requirements for tools supporting creativity and innovation. Dwyer (2011) argues that, apart from the number of collaborators, it is also important to measure the quality of collaboration. In fact, various collaborator segments can be identified, with significant differences in the value of contributed ideas and the timing of participation. Thus, new metrics should be used, taking those differences into account and being based on information content. Hayne & Smith (2005) note that groupware performance depends on the fit between the structure and task of the group. However, they argue that an important role may also be played by the cognitive structure, which also maps to the group structure. In fact, collaborative tasks may push human cognitive capabilities to their limits, in terms of perception, attention and memory. Thus, the authors argue for the integration of different areas of study, such as: psychology, especially with regard to abilities and limitations; theories of social interactions, with regard to group communication and motivation; studies of groupware structures and human interactions mediated by artifacts.

To leverage the advantages of social networking, organizations and firms should support their transition from the individual adoption as feral systems to the formal incorporation into existing information systems. To achieve this goal, knowledge management professionals should act as social networking architects, in conjunction with other managers and IT professionals. In fact, social network analysis can highlight the patterns of connection among individuals and the main knowledge flows in a whole organization. Thus, it can be used by managers as a basis for reshaping the organization and advancing towards the business goals. Anklam (2004) describes three main types of intervention, to conduct after a social network analysis: (*i*) structural/organizational, i.e. change the organigrams to improve the knowledge transfer; (*ii*) knowledge-network development, i.e. overcome resistance to action on the basis of evidence, instead of intuition; (*iii*) individual/leadership, i.e. resolve problems with the particular role of individuals, for example acting as factual gatekeepers and resulting in a knowledge bottleneck. More in general, social network analysis can be useful to cope with common business problems, including: launching distributed teams, retention of people with vital knowledge for the organization, improve access to knowledge and increase innovation.

Along the same lines, Roy (2012) discusses the profile of leaders in Virtual Teams. In fact, apart from usual technical and leadership capacities, to work effectively in a virtual environment, they also need abilities to build relationships among participants and to defuse frustrations. In fact, on the one hand, they need particular communication skills, as well as good knowledge for operating video conferencing software and other CSCW tools. On the other hand, they must be able to establish trust, embrace diversity, motivating team members and fostering the team spirit.

Adaptation

The trend toward introducing social media systems in the work environment has seen a massive increase in importance in recent years. At their first appearance, without indications from the management and without integration with internal information systems, social media took the form of feral systems. However, organizations and firms are finally becoming to accept this situation as a matter of fact, trying to gain benefits from the same features that drove the introduction of social platforms in the first place. Thus, information systems are moving from the communication level, to the coordination and collaboration levels, increasingly acknowledging and leveraging the various dimensions of social relations among people, both internally and across organization boundaries.

A first strategy, that some organizations and brands are adopting, is to use social media for improving their Customer Relationship Management (CRM). In fact, social media can be a means for firms and organizations to listen to customers and to cope with the difficulties in collecting data through interviews (Murphy et al., 2011). Social media allow the use of online sources of information, sometimes for free. So firms and organizations are moving to reduce costs and time needed by traditional survey researches. Moreover, in the last years several social media monitoring tools and platforms have been developed to listen to the social media users, analyze and measure their content in relation to a brand or enterprise business and so it is reducing the time necessary for extracting the useful information through the huge data provided by social media (Stavrakantonakis et al., 2012). However, this quite popular trend towards so-called "*Social CRM*" has not always been satisfactory. A study by IBM (2011) shows that there's a quite large gap between the expectations of brand managers and social media users. In fact, only the 23% of users are keen to engage with brands on social media, and only 5% of users declare active participation. The majority, instead, limit their communications and shares with parents and relatives. Among the potentially interested people, many expect tangible benefits, including discounts, services, additional information and reviews about products. The study is in accordance with the difficulties that brands face to engage with users and to launch viral campaigns. Nevertheless, businesses continue to be greatly interested in using social media for rapid distribution of offers and content, reaching new people trough trusted introducers, but also for improving customer care and research.

A second type of effort is directed to augment internal tools, in particular Knowledge Management (KM) systems, with explicit and rich data about relationships among involved people. The long term goal of KM, in fact, is to let insights and experiences existing in implicit way into an organization emerge and become easily accessible for wider internal adoption. Such knowledge can be either possessed by individuals or embedded into common practices. To provide effective access to valuable internal knowledge and expertise, it is essential to recognize and value the particular knowledge possessed by different persons, and then to have means to contact the relevant persons in a timely manner, thus making information-seeking an easier and more successful experience. In many regards, such a scenario can be fully developed only on the basis of the evolution of existing ICT tools and the creation of new ones, by making some typical features of social networking applications available in tools for daily activities.

This trend regards existing Information Systems and also, for some aspects, platforms for Enterprise Resource Planning (ERP). In fact, some aspects of traditional ERP systems are integrating features of social networking platforms, fostering collaboration among people on the basis of direct interpersonal links and simple knowledge sharing tools. The centralized and inward approach of early systems is being challenged also in the core area of production management software. The drift towards network of integrated enterprises is testified by an increasingly dynamic production environment, arranged in the form of complex Virtual Organizations and Virtual Enterprises. In this context, the tasks of supply chain management, project and activity management, data services and access control management require the participation of actors of different organizations and possibly different places and cultures.

Finally, a third type of effort is directed to offer a large-scale knowledge sharing inside an organization through an enterprise social network (Ellison, 2015). This kind of site includes the fundamental features of online social network, but is implemented within an organization and have the ability to restrict membership or interaction to members of a specific enterprise.

FUTURE RESEARCH DIRECTIONS

The importance of online social network and the importance of the data that can be extracted from them determined a strong need of research on new techniques and models for their analysis. Our idea is agent-based techniques can easily deal with the modelling and the analysis of online social networks that represent a massive number of individuals and organizations with different behaviors and behaviors changing over time. In fact, agents are suitable to model and simulate both the low level and complex interactions among the parties. Moreover, agent-based applications can be easily executed in a distributed computing environment that can scale with the size of the online social network. We are working for some year on the use of agents for modelling and analyzing online social networks (Bergenti et al, 2013). In particular, we developed a software framework, that will be the basis for an easy and fast development of distributed applications working on online software networks (Bergenti et al., 2014), and started a first experimentation oriented to the analysis on their data (Fornacciari et al., 2017). Of course, we still working on it with the goal of providing interesting results by extending the experimentation to the modelling of online social network and involving in the experimentation two of the most known and used online social network (i.e., Facebook and Twitter).

CONCLUSION

This chapter discussed about social networking systems and how they assumed a fundamental role in both the private and working spheres. In fact, individuals use them both at home and on the work place both professionally and with recreational goals. Moreover, the chapter discussed about the importance of social capital in online social networks and showed how it or at least the idea of being able to accumulate it, either directly or indirectly, is an important factor in the participation in online social networking activities. Finally, the chapter discussed how social elements have been introduced into more traditional business systems.

The most known and used social networking platforms utilize a traditional client-server architecture. This means that all the information is stored and administered on central servers. Although this approach supports highly mobile user access since users can log-in from any web browser, it also presents many drawbacks, e.g., lack of privacy, lack of anonymity, risks of censorship and operating costs. The integration between peer-to-peer technologies and multi-agent systems may be used for developing social networks that do not present the previous drawbacks Moreover, the use of m multi-agent systems is the right solution to offer strong coordination techniques to the users of social networks and provide them more sophisticated and usable services. In the last years, we worked to study and to develop prototypes to support an evolution in this new direction, we achieved some interesting results (Franchi et al., 2016b; Bergenti, et al., 2018), but we are still working to improve such first results and to experiment some new prototypes in a real setting.

REFERENCES

Ale Ebrahim, N., Ahmed, S., & Taha, Z. (2009). Virtual R&D teams in small and medium enterprises: A literature review. *Scientific Research and Essays*, *4*(13), 1575–1590.

Anklam, P. (2004, May). KM and the Social Network. *Knowledge Management Magazine*, 24-28.

AT&T. (2008). *The Business Impacts of Social Networking*. Retrieved 2012-10-20 from http://www.business.att.com/content/whitepaper/WP-soc_17172_v3_11-10-08.pdf

Baker, W. E. (1990). Market networks and corporate behavior. *American Journal of Sociology*, *96*(3), 589–625. doi:10.1086/229573

Baum, J. A. (1999). Whole-part coevolutionary competition in organizations. *Variations in organization science*, 113-135.

Begel, A., DeLine, R., & Zimmermann, T. (2010). Social media for software engineering. In *Proceedings of the FSE/SDP workshop on Future of software engineering research* (pp. 33-38). ACM. 10.1145/1882362.1882370

Bergenti, F., Franchi, E., & Poggi, A. (2011). *Agent-based social networks for enterprise collaboration. In 20th IEEE International Workshops on Enabling Technologies: Infrastructure for Collaborative Enterprises* (pp. 25–28). IEEE.

Bergenti, F., Franchi, E., & Poggi, A. (2013). Agent-based interpretations of classic network models. *Computational & Mathematical Organization Theory, 19*(2), 105–127. doi:10.100710588-012-9150-x

Bergenti, F., Poggi, A., & Tomaiuolo, M. (2014). An actor based software framework for scalable applications. In *International Conference on Internet and Distributed Computing Systems* (pp. 26-35). Springer. 10.1007/978-3-319-11692-1_3

Bergenti, F., Poggi, A., & Tomaiuolo, M. (2018). Agent-Based Social Networks. In Encyclopedia of Information Science and Technology, Fourth Edition (pp. 6950-6960). IGI Global. doi:10.4018/978-1-5225-2255-3.ch602

Bev, G., Campbell, S., Levy, J., & Bounds, J. (2008). *Social media and the federal government: Perceived and real barriers and potential solutions*. Federal Web Managers Council.

Borgatti, S. P., & Foster, P. C. (2003). The network paradigm in organizational research: A review and typology. *Journal of Management, 29*(6), 991–1013. doi:10.1016/S0149-2063(03)00087-4

Burt, R. S. (1987). Social Contagion and Innovation: Cohesion versus Structural Equivalence. *American Journal of Sociology, 92*(6), 1287–1335. doi:10.1086/228667

Burt, R. S. (1995). *Structural holes: The social structure of competition*. Harvard University Press.

Campbell, J. H. (1985). An organizational interpretation of evolution. *Evolution at a crossroads*, 133.

Chow, W. S., & Chan, L. S. (2008). Social network, social trust and shared goals in organizational knowledge sharing. *Information & Management, 45*(7), 458–465. doi:10.1016/j.im.2008.06.007

Coleman, J. S. (1988). Social capital in the creation of human capital. *American Journal of Sociology, 94*, 95–120. doi:10.1086/228943

Cook, K. (1982). Network Structures from an Exchange Perspective. In *Social Structure and Network Analysis*. Sage Publications.

Diakopoulos, N., De Choudhury, M., & Naaman, M. (2012, May). Finding and assessing social media information sources in the context of journalism. In *Proceedings of the 2012 ACM annual conference on Human Factors in Computing Systems* (pp. 2451-2460). ACM. 10.1145/2207676.2208409

DiMicco, J. (2007). Identity management: multiple presentations of self in facebook. *6th International Conference on Supporting Group Work (GROUP'07)*, 1–4. 10.1145/1316624.1316682

DiMicco, J., Millen, D., & Geyer, W. (2008). Motivations for social networking at work. *Conference on Computer Supported Cooperative Work*, 711–720.

Dwyer, P. (2011). Measuring Collective Cognition in Online Collaboration Venues. *International Journal of e-Collaboration, 7*(1), 47–61. doi:10.4018/jec.2011010104

Ellison, N. B., Gibbs, J. L., & Weber, M. S. (2015). The use of enterprise social network sites for knowledge sharing in distributed organizations: The role of organizational affordances. *The American Behavioral Scientist, 59*(1), 103–123. doi:10.1177/0002764214540510

Erickson, B. H. (2017). Good networks and good jobs: The value of social capital to employers and employees. In *Social capital* (pp. 127–158). Routledge.

Fedorowicz, J., Laso-Ballesteros, I., & Padilla-Meléndez, A. (2008). Creativity, Innovation, and E-Collaboration. *International Journal of e-Collaboration*, *4*(4), 1–10. doi:10.4018/jec.2008100101

Fornacciari, P., Mordonini, M., Poggi, A., & Tomaiuolo, M. (2017) Software actors for continuous social media analysis. In *18th Workshop on Objects to Agents, WOA 2017* (pp. 84-89). CEUR.

Foster, I., Kesselman, C., & Tuecke, S. (2001). The anatomy of the grid: Enabling scalable virtual organizations. *International Journal of High Performance Computing Applications*, *15*(3), 200–222. doi:10.1177/109434200101500302

Franchi, E., & Poggi, A. (2011). *Multi-agent systems and social networks. Business social networking: Organizational, managerial, and technological dimensions.* Academic Press.

Franchi, E., Poggi, A., & Tomaiuolo, M. (2013). Open social networking for online collaboration. *International Journal of e-Collaboration*, *9*(3), 50–68. doi:10.4018/jec.2013070104

Franchi, E., Poggi, A., & Tomaiuolo, M. (2015). Information and Password Attacks on Social Networks: An Argument for Cryptography. *Journal of Information Technology Research*, *8*(1), 25–42. doi:10.4018/JITR.2015010103

Franchi, E., Poggi, A., & Tomaiuolo, M. (2016a). Social media for online collaboration in firms and organizations. *International Journal of Information System Modeling and Design*, *7*(1), 18–31. doi:10.4018/IJISMD.2016010102

Franchi, E., Poggi, A., & Tomaiuolo, M. (2016b). Blogracy: A peer-to-peer social network. *International Journal of Distributed Systems and Technologies*, *7*(2), 37–56. doi:10.4018/IJDST.2016040103

Fukuyama, F. (1995). *Trust: The social virtues and the creation of prosperity.* Free Press.

Fulk, J., Heino, R., Flanagin, A. J., Monge, P. R., & Bar, F. (2004). A test of the individual action model for organizational information commons. *Organization Science*, *15*(5), 569–585. doi:10.1287/orsc.1040.0081

Goldschlag, D., Reed, M., & Syverson, P. (1999). Onion routing. *Communications of the ACM*, *42*(2), 39–41. doi:10.1145/293411.293443

Granovetter, M. S. (1973). The strength of weak ties. *American Journal of Sociology*, *78*(6), 1360–1380. doi:10.1086/225469

Hayne, S. C., & Smith, C. (2005). The Relationship Between e-Collaboration and Cognition. *International Journal of e-Collaboration*, *1*(3), 17–34. doi:10.4018/jec.2005070102

Hoang, H., & Antoncic, B. (2003). Network-based research in entrepreneurship: A critical review. *Journal of Business Venturing*, *18*(2), 165–187. doi:10.1016/S0883-9026(02)00081-2

Holland, P., & Leinhardt, S. (1974). The Statistical Analysis of Local Structure in Social Networks. *National Bureau of Economic Research Working Paper Series, 44.*

Hollingshead, A. B., Fulk, J., & Monge, P. (2002). Fostering intranet knowledge sharing: An integration of transactive memory and public goods approaches. *Distributed Work*, 335-355.

Houghton, L., & Kerr, D. V. (2006). A study into the creation of feral information systems as a response to an ERP implementation within the supply chain of a large government-owned corporation. *International Journal of Internet and Enterprise Management*, 4(2), 135–147. doi:10.1504/IJIEM.2006.010239

IBM Institute for Business Value. (2011). *From social media to Social CRM*. Retrieved 2012-10-20 from http://public.dhe.ibm.com/common/ssi/ecm/en/gbe03391usen/GBE03391USEN.PDF

Isari, D., Pontiggia, A., & Virili, F. (2011). *Working Together in Organizations Using Social Network Sites: A Laboratory Experiment on Microblog Use for Problem-Solving*. Available at SSRN 1875924.

Jacobs, J. (1961). *The death and life of great American cities*. Vintage.

Jones, B. F., Wuchty, S., & Uzzi, B. (2008). Multi-university research teams: Shifting impact, geography, and stratification in science. *Science*, 322(5905), 1259–1262. doi:10.1126cience.1158357 PMID:18845711

Lin, N. (2017). Building a network theory of social capital. In *Social capital* (pp. 3–28). Routledge.

Lipnack, J., & Stamps, J. (2008). *Virtual teams: People working across boundaries with technology*. John Wiley & Sons.

Loury, G. C. (1987). Why should we care about group inequality? *Social Philosophy & Policy*, 5(1), 249–271. doi:10.1017/S0265052500001345

Malone, T. W., & Crowstone, K. (1994). The Interdisciplinary Study of Coordination. *ACM Computing Surveys*, 26(1), 87–119. doi:10.1145/174666.174668

Maskell, P. (2000). Social capital, innovation, and competitiveness. In *Social capital* (pp. 111–123). Oxford University Press.

McPherson, M., Smith-Lovin, L., & Cook, J. M. (2001). Birds of a Feather: Homophily in Social Networks. *Annual Review of Sociology*, 27(1), 415–444. doi:10.1146/annurev.soc.27.1.415

Millen, D. R., Feinberg, J., Kerr, B., Rogers, O., & Cambridge, S. (2006). *Dogear : Social Bookmarking in the Enterprise*. Academic Press.

Monge, P. R., & Contractor, N. (2003). *Theories of communication networks*. Oxford University Press.

Mordonini, M., Poggi, A., & Tomaiuolo, M. (2016). Preserving Privacy in a P2P *Social Network. In International Conference on Smart Objects and Technologies for Social Good* (pp. 203-212). Springer.

Mowshowitz, A. (1994). Virtual organization: A vision of management in the information age. *The Information Society*, 10(4), 267–288. doi:10.1080/01972243.1994.9960172

Murphy, J., Kim, A., Hagood, H., Richards, A., Augustine, C., Kroutil, L., & Sage, A. (2011). Twitter Feeds and Google Search Query Surveillance: Can They Supplement Survey Data Collection? *Shifting the Boundaries of Research*, 228.

Nahapiet, J., & Ghoshal, S. (1998). Social capital, intellectual capital, and the organizational advantage. *Academy of Management Review, 23*(2), 242–266. doi:10.5465/amr.1998.533225

Parkhe, A., Wasserman, S., & Ralston, D. A. (2006). New frontiers in network theory development. *Academy of Management Review, 31*(3), 560–568. doi:10.5465/amr.2006.21318917

Powell, A., Piccoli, G., & Ives, B. (2004). Virtual Teams: A Review of Current Literature and Directions for Future Research. *The Data Base for Advances in Information Systems, 35*(1), 7. doi:10.1145/968464.968467

Putnam, R. D. (1995). Bowling alone: America's declining social capital. *Journal of Democracy, 6*(1), 65–78. doi:10.1353/jod.1995.0002

Roy, S. R. (2012). Digital Mastery: The Skills Needed for Effective Virtual Leadership. *International Journal of e-Collaboration, 8*(3), 56–66. doi:10.4018/jec.2012070104

Stavrakantonakis, I., Gagiu, A. E., Kasper, H., Toma, I., & Thalhammer, A. (2012). An approach for evaluation of social media monitoring tools. *Common Value Management, 52*.

Su, C., & Contractor, N. (2011). A multidimensional network approach to studying team members' information seeking from human and digital knowledge sources in consulting firms. *Journal of the American Society for Information Science and Technology, 62*(7), 1257–1275. doi:10.1002/asi.21526

Teigland, R. (2004). Extending richness with reach: Participation and knowledge exchange in electronic networks of practice. In *Knowledge networks: Innovation through communities of practice* (pp. 230–242). IGI Global. doi:10.4018/978-1-59140-200-8.ch019

Tomaiuolo, M. (2013). dDelega: Trust Management for Web Services. *International Journal of Information Security and Privacy, 7*(3), 53–67. doi:10.4018/jisp.2013070104

Van de Ven, A., Delbecq, A., & Koenig, R. (1976). Determinants of coordination modes within organizations. *American Sociological Review, 41*(2), 322–338. doi:10.2307/2094477

Vlaar, P. W., van Fenema, P. C., & Tiwari, V. (2008). Cocreating understanding and value in distributed work: How members of onsite and offshore vendor teams give, make, demand, and break sense. *Management Information Systems Quarterly, 32*(2), 227–255. doi:10.2307/25148839

Wasko, M. M., & Faraj, S. (2005). Why should i share? examining social capital and knowledge contribution in electronic networks of practice. *Management Information Systems Quarterly, 29*(1), 35–57. doi:10.2307/25148667

Wasserman, S., & Faust, K. (1994). *Social network analysis: Methods and applications* (Vol. 8). Cambridge University Press. doi:10.1017/CBO9780511815478

Wheatley, M., & Frieze, D. (2006). Using emergence to take social innovation to scale. The Berkana Institute.

Williamson, O. E. (1991). Comparative Economic Organization: The Analysis of Discrete Structural Alternatives. *Administrative Science Quarterly, 36*(2), 219–244. doi:10.2307/2393356

Wuchty, S., Jones, B. F., & Uzzi, B. (2007). The increasing dominance of teams in production of knowledge. *Science*, *316*(5827), 1036–1039. doi:10.1126cience.1136099 PMID:17431139

ADDITIONAL READING

Ardichvili, A., Page, V., & Wentling, T. (2003). Motivation and barriers to participation in virtual knowledge-sharing communities of practice. *Journal of Knowledge Management*, *7*(1), 64–77. doi:10.1108/13673270310463626

Chang, H. H., & Chuang, S. S. (2011). Social capital and individual motivations on knowledge sharing: Participant involvement as a moderator. *Information & Management*, *48*(1), 9–18. doi:10.1016/j.im.2010.11.001

Chiu, C. M., Hsu, M. H., & Wang, E. T. (2006). Understanding knowledge sharing in virtual communities: An integration of social capital and social cognitive theories. *Decision Support Systems*, *42*(3), 1872–1888. doi:10.1016/j.dss.2006.04.001

Coleman, J. S. (1988). Social capital in the creation of human capital. *American Journal of Sociology*, *94*, S95–S120. doi:10.1086/228943

Dubos, R. (2017). *Social capital: Theory and research*. Routledge.

Li, C. (2010). Groundswell. Winning in a world transformed by social technologies. Strategic Direction, *26*(8).

Valenzuela, S., Park, N., & Kee, K. F. (2009). Is there social capital in a social network site? Facebook use and college students' life satisfaction, trust, and participation. *Journal of Computer-Mediated Communication*, *14*(4), 875–901. doi:10.1111/j.1083-6101.2009.01474.x

Wellman, B., Haase, A. Q., Witte, J., & Hampton, K. (2001). Does the Internet increase, decrease, or supplement social capital? Social networks, participation, and community commitment. *The American Behavioral Scientist*, *45*(3), 436–455. doi:10.1177/00027640121957286

KEY TERMS AND DEFINITIONS

Online Network of Practice: A group of people who share a profession or an interest, whose main interactions occur through communication networks and tools.

Privacy: The right to be secluded from the presence or view of others.

Social Capital: Is a form of economic and cultural capital derived from interpersonal relationships, institutions, and other social assets of a society or group of individuals.

Social Network: Social structure made by individuals and organizations that are connected by relationships; relationships that may represent various kinds of ties between member and that can be either symmetrical or asymmetrical.

Social Networking System: A software system that allows users to manipulate a representation of their online social networks and to interact with the other users in the system, especially collaboratively discussing user-produced resources.

Virtual Organization: A network of autonomous organizations and individuals, typically with the main aim of sharing resources in a coordinated fashion.

Virtual Team: A group of workers connected mainly through information and communication technologies that is often temporary and exists only until the achievement of a specific goal.

Section 3
Models and Technology Issues in Business Applications

Organizational information systems support organizations' business processes. This section covers models and technology issues in business supporting applications. The first chapter proposes an approach to enable the robust handling of single process activities on mobile devices based on a mobile process model. The second chapter builds on the idea that business process models already include much of the organization's knowledge or information needed to build the business processes' supporting software systems and proposes two approaches that use that information to derive a set of integrated software models, although it focuses on generating a data model. The SOA and REST application integration approaches are used in this section's third chapter as a starting point for conceiving a new architectural style, structural services, which allows to tune applications' integration between pure service-based and pure resource-based, or an intermediate mix. The fourth chapter provides a comparative review of reference schemes in different modeling languages. The fifth chapter addresses data warehouse support for policy enforcement rule formulation. The last chapter presents a variability management workflow aimed at supporting different developer roles in an ecosystem context. Two kinds of variability are addressed: in-system operation and associated with quality of service.

Chapter 7
Context–Based Handling of Mobile Process Activities

Rüdiger Pryss
Ulm University, Germany

Manfred Reichert
Ulm University, Germany

ABSTRACT

Process technology constitutes a crucial component of information systems. In this context, high flexibility is required as business functions must be quickly adaptable to cope with dynamic business changes. As recent developments allow for the use of mobile devices in knowledge-intensive areas, it is often demanded to enhance process-aware information systems with mobile activity support. In general, the technical integration of this activity type with existing process management technology is challenging. For example, protocols governing the communication between mobile devices and process management systems must be adapted. If a mobile context shall be additionally considered, the integration gets even more complex. However, the use of a mobile context offers advantages. For example, the mobile activity execution time may be decreased if mobile activities are only assigned to those users whose location is beneficial. This chapter proposes an approach to enable the robust handling of single process activities on mobile devices based on a mobile process model.

INTRODUCTION

Daily business routines more and more require mobile access to Information Systems. However, the integration of mobile devices into existing infrastructures is laborious and error-prone. In particular, the infrastructure must cope with ad hoc events, various types of exceptions (e.g., connectivity problems), physical limitations of mobile devices (e.g., limited battery capacity), misbehavior of users (e.g., instant shutdowns), and the evaluation of data collected by mobile sensors (Schobel et al., 2013). In general, proper exception handling constitutes a prerequisite for any mobile activity support. In this context, adaptive and flexible process management technology offers promising perspectives based on a wide range of techniques (Reichert & Weber, 2012; Reichert & Weber, 2013). In particular, it allows for the

DOI: 10.4018/978-1-5225-7271-8.ch007

proper handling of run time exceptions. However, execution of process activities on mobile devices in the same way as on stationary computers is not appropriate when the specific challenges of mobile environments are not taken into account.

A service-oriented environment should allow for mobile activity support during business process execution. This paper presents an approach developed in the MARPLE (Managing Robust Mobile Processes in a Complex World) project. This approach enables the robust execution of single process activities on mobile devices and is based on two services, a service that assigns mobile users to mobile activities and an exception handling service for mobile activities. These services ensure that mobile activities are (a) only assigned to those mobile users that are particularly appropriate based on a mobile context and (b) do not harm the overall process execution when activity exceptions occur. In this context, a service-oriented architecture was realized that integrates the services with existing process management technology. To be more precise, the architecture allows for the instantiation, activation, and exception handling of mobile activities.

This paper presents the support of *mobile activities* and the handling of exceptions during run time without need for manually involving mobile users. Note that this is crucial with respect to higher user acceptance of mobile business processes. Generally, the provisioning of self-healing techniques is crucial for executing mobile activities in the large scale as well as for achieving higher user acceptance.

We firstly discuss fundamental issues arising in the context of mobile environments. Their understanding is crucial for developing the two fundamental services as well as for designing the overall system architecture. In this context, the challenges (e.g., device failures) are considered which must be tackled to ensure robust execution of mobile activities. In detail, challenges are addressed that are related to the mobile environment itself (e.g., a mobile device loses its connectivity), related to the business process execution (e.g., missing data caused by activity exceptions), and related to the behavior of the mobile users (e.g., instant shutdowns).

BACKGROUND

Many domains crave for the integration of mobile devices into business process execution (Lenz & Reichert, 2007; Pryss et al., 2016(a)). Figure 1 shows a simplified healthcare example illustrating this. It depicts a ward round process for which mobile assistance is required (Pryss et al., 2015). For instance, *Prepare Ward Round* constitutes an activity whose mobile support would ease daily work of healthcare professionals.

The use of mobile devices during process execution raises several challenges with respect to mobile activity support. For example, if the mobile device running the activity *Determine Vital Signs* (see Figure 1) encounters physical problems, overall process execution might be harmed; or if activities succeeding a mobile activity in the flow of control have to access data that is usually provided by this mobile activity, standard exception handling strategies (e.g., to skip the mobile activity) are not appropriate when the mobile activity fails. As shown in Figure 1, activity *Finish Ward Round* is data-dependent on mobile activity *Determine Vital Signs*. In turn, this might cause problems when activity exceptions occur, i.e., if *Determine Vital Signs* fails, the process cannot terminate properly, since activity *Finish Ward Round* cannot be properly executed due to the missing value of data element *D1*.

Figure 1. Adding mobile devices to process execution (mobile activities are indicated with an icon)

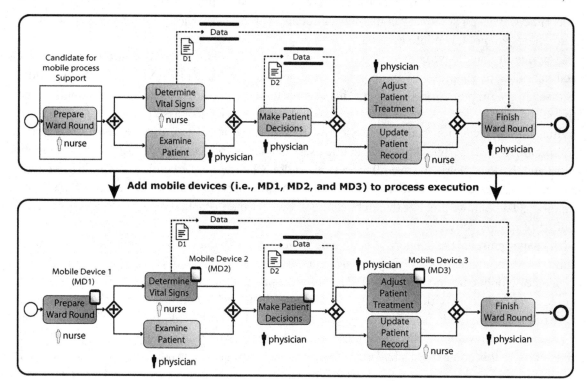

Challenges for Executing Processes With Mobile Activities

To be able to run selected activities on mobile devices during process execution, the challenges imposed by mobile environments need to be properly addressed. These challenges relate to the state of mobile devices as well as the behavior of mobile users. In addition, the specific challenges relating to process execution must be considered as well; e.g., dealing with missing process data due to failed mobile activities at run time. This section presents backgrounds on the elicitation of challenges in this context, discusses relevant and challenges addressed, and categorizes them into process-, mobile environment- and user- related.

In the following, three advanced mobile application scenarios will be discussed. These scenarios (case studies) base the considerations on relevant challenges when executing mobile activities in the context of business processes. Thereby, only one scenario is relevant in the context of business process execution. The remaining two scenarios are not concerned with business process execution, but also constitute demanding scenarios for mobile application development in general. As a result, they revealed similar challenges as have been identified for mobile activity execution. The first mobile application scenario stems from the healthcare domain, whereas the second from the field of augmented reality, and the last one from the psychological domain.

Supporting Medical Ward Rounds With Mobile Task and Process Management

In hospitals, ward rounds are crucial for decision-making in the context of patient treatment processes. In the course of a ward round, new activities are defined and allocated to healthcare professionals. In clinical practice, however, these activities are not properly addressed. During ward rounds, they are jotted down using pen and paper, and their later processing is prone to errors. Furthermore, healthcare professionals must keep track of the processing status of their activities (e.g., medical orders). To relieve healthcare professionals from such a manual activity management, the MEDo (MedicalDo) approach (Pryss et al., 2015) supports ward rounds by transforming the pen and paper worksheet to a mobile user interface on a tablet integrating process support, mobile activity management, and access to the electronic patient record. Based on the lessons learned from this case study, requirements have been derived for mobile activity support in the context of medical ward rounds. As a particular challenge, the following has been identified: if mobile assisted activities will be interrupted and not properly continued later, exceptions like missing data frequently occur. Altogether, Table 1 summarizes which challenges in terms of parameters for executing processes with mobile activities have been identified from this mobile application scenario.

Location-Based Mobile Augmented Reality Applications

In the AREA (Augmented Reality Engine Application) project (Pryss et al., 2016(a); Geiger et al., 2013), an advanced mobile application, which enables location-based mobile augmented reality on three different mobile operating systems (i.e., iOS, Android, and Windows Phone) has been designed and implemented. This kind of mobile application is characterized by high resource demands since various sensors must be queried at run time and numerous virtual objects may have to be drawn in real time on the screen of the mobile device. Therefore, the lessons learned when implementing real world mobile business applications with the mobile augmented reality engine, have revealed profound insights into challenges of mobile application development in general. Table 1 summarizes again which challenges in terms of parameters for executing processes with mobile activities have been identified from this mobile application scenario.

Applying Mobile Technology to Psychological Questionnaires

Many psychological studies are performed with specifically tailored "paper & pencil"- questionnaires. Such a paper-based approach usually results in a massive workload for evaluating and analyzing the collected data afterwards, e.g., to transfer data to electronic worksheets or any statistics software. To relieve researchers from such manual tasks and to improve the efficiency of data collection processes, mobile device applications have been developed in the context of the QuestionSys[1] project for existing psychological questionnaires (e.g., Schobel et al., 2016(c)). Based on these applications, the usefulness of mobile devices for mobile data collection in the context of psychological questionnaires has been demonstrated. Although the implemented applications already have shown several advantages in respect to data collection and analysis, they have not been suitable for psychological studies in the large scale yet. Consequently, new challenges emerged when using the mobile applications in such demanding scenarios. Table 1 summarizes which challenges in terms of parameters for executing processes with mobile activities have been identified from this mobile application scenario as well.

Considered Context for Executing Processes With Mobile Activities

The mobile context is represented by a parameter catalogue. The parameters were identified in the discussed real-world scenarios. In addition, the catalogue is based on a comprehensive literature study. For several reasons, we assign parameters to four categories: First, parameters related to the mobile device of a mobile user (SMD parameters) are managed. For example, a battery status is managed for mobile devices. Second, all parameters associated with mobile activities (MA parameters) are managed. For example, the execution location of the mobile activity is captured. Third, parameters that can be related to the overall process execution are managed. This category became necessary to cope with the complexity of managing a multitude of parameters. For several parameters, it would be costly to manage them separately for each mobile activity. Therefore, a parameter applying to all mobile process activities is used, e.g., to manage a generally demanded battery status for the activation of all mobile activities of a process. Finally, parameters associated with mobile users (MU parameters) are managed, e.g., the usual location of a mobile user. The entire parameter catalogue is presented in Table 1. In addition, Table 1 presents in which real world scenarios a parameter was crucial. Column *T* of Table 1 further indicates whether a parameter is of type symbolic or measured. From the considered application scenarios, we revealed that such differentiation is useful. Symbolic parameters are used in related work to define parameters on an abstract level (Becker & Dürr, 2005). For example, regarding the location of a mobile activity, the symbolic parameter emergency room might be used. First, symbolic parameters are considered as they can already be evaluated before starting a process. For example, consider the following scenario: Symbolic parameters are managed for mobile users and mobile activities. Hence, it can be indicated before the execution of a mobile activity takes places how many mobile users are closely located to the location of the mobile activity that shall be performed based on a simple comparison of the symbolic parameters. Apparently, it is just an indication, but has shown its advantages in practice. Second, for the assignment of mobile users to mobile activities symbolic parameters can be advantageous as well. For example, if precise location information (e.g., GPS) cannot be obtained for a user location due to a connection loss, the symbolic parameter may be used instead. Conversely, measured parameters are automatically determined after starting the process instance. For example, if a mobile activity shall be executed, the battery status of all mobile users is gathered.

Selected parameters require a brief discussion. The form factor parameter is used to indicate the mobile device type (i.e., tablet or smartphone). Geometric coordinates, in turn, are measured and correspond to GPS coordinates in an outdoor scenario and WLAN coordinates in an indoor scenario. Parameter location range refers to the location of a mobile activity defining a radius around its geometric coordinates. Mobile users located inside this radius are considered for executing this mobile activity. Urgency value defines a period (or point in time) during which the mobile activity shall be executed. Furthermore, response frequency is a value that determines the frequency with which the mobile device of a particular user must report its online status to the process management system. If the mobile device does not obey this reporting frequency, an exception handling is triggered. Related to response frequency is parameter offline mode. If the latter is set to *true* for any mobile activity, the mobile device may ignore the response frequency to enable offline execution of this mobile activity. In practice, this was frequently demanded. Finally, network type is used to capture the network connection of a mobile device (e.g., WLAN or UMTS).

In addition, the parameter catalogue contains two threshold parameters. User threshold indicates the number of users that need to be available to activate a mobile activity. In turn, the instant shutdowns parameter captures the behavior of mobile users. Note that in practice users may instantly shutdown their mobile device without reflecting on the consequences of this shutdown. Usually, this constitutes a short-term problem and the device can be restarted soon in most cases. If a user exhibits many instant shutdowns, however, this misbehavior should be considered in the context of mobile activity assignments.

To cope with such careless shutdowns, a mobile device sends a message to a service that an instant shutdown will take place soon. In this context, several mobile development frameworks were evaluated (i.e., Google Android, Apple iOS, Microsoft Windows Mobile) and it could be demonstrated that this solution for detecting instant shutdowns is feasible for all of them. Finally, to assess user behavior over time (e.g., whether or not a user performs many instant shutdowns), parameter instant shutdowns is managed. Related to it, a general process parameter instant shutdown threshold is managed for all mobile activities that is compared with the parameter managed for a particular mobile user. If the parameter value of a mobile user is above the instant shutdown threshold parameter, he or she will be particularly considered for the execution of the mobile activity.

Regarding the presented parameter catalogue, we do not claim that it captures all possible or required parameters. It rather reflects insights we gathered from our analysis of real-world scenarios. Furthermore, the application of the parameters identified in other practical scenarios was promising. More specifically, domain experts were able to determine useful parameter values.

Table 1. Excerpt of considered real world projects revealing parameters for executing processes with mobile activities

	Parameter	*Description*	*Type*	*MEDo*	*AREA*	*QuestionSys*
	Category I: Mobile device (SMD)					
Mobile Environment	SMD_{BS}	Battery Status	M	x	x	x
	SMD_{FF}	Form Factor	S	x	x	-
	SMD_{NT}	Network Type	M	x	x	x
	SMD_{GC}	Geometric Coordinate	M	x	x	-
	Category II: Mobile Activity (MA)					
Process	MA_{SC}	Symbolic Coordinate(s)	S	x	-	-
	MA_{GC}	Geometric Coordinate	M	x	x	-
	MA_{LR}	Location Range	S	x	x	-
	MA_{BS}	Battery Status	M	x	x	x
	MA_{U}	Urgency Value	S	x	-	-
	MA_{OFF}	Offline Mode	S	x	x	x
	MA_{FF}	Form Factor	S	x	x	x
	MA_{RF}	Response Frequency	S	x	x	x
	MA_{UT}	User Threshold	S	x	-	-
	Category III: Process (P)					
	P_{IST}	Instant Shutdown Threshold	S	x	-	-
User Behavior	Category IV: Mobile User (MU)					
	MU_{SC}	Symbolic Coordinate(s)	S	x	-	-
	MU_{IS}	Instant Shutdowns	S	x	-	-
	| Type: M=Measured, S=Symbolic | (x): relevant | (-): not relevant |					

Mobile Process Execution Approaches

Next, we will discuss alternatives for realizing processes that comprise mobile activities and describe corresponding process models. For realizing processes with mobile activities, three different approaches exist (see Figure 2):

Approach 1 (Physical Process Fragmentation aka Process Partitioning)

A process (i.e., process schema) is physically partitioned during design time. The resulting process fragments and their activities are then assigned to a number of mobile devices before run time (and on an instance-per-instance basis, see Approach 1 in Figure 2). Consequently, the execution of process fragments must be synchronized during run time. This is a complex task to accomplish. For example, if the same data element is written by different process fragments, sophisticated synchronization techniques become necessary to ensure data consistency. Another challenge emerges if a device encounters physical problems (e.g., a lost connection).

Approach 2 (Logical Process Fragmentation aka Migrating Processes)

A process schema is partitioned logically. In this case, the resulting process fragments and their activities are executed on different mobile devices. Contrary to the first approach, the original process schema will be preserved during run time when executing the process fragments (Approach 2 in Figure 2). Usually, migration techniques are applied in this context (Zaplata et al., 2010). More precisely, based on the original process schema, it can be determined how the migration between logical process fragments shall be accomplished at run time. Accordingly, it is dynamically determined which device shall execute which process fragments. In particular, this allows for dynamic exchanges of devices already assigned to a fragment. Another challenge emerging in this context is synchronization of the execution of parallel process branches concurrently executed on different mobile devices, i.e., a synchronization method is required to cope with data inconsistencies when joining the execution of the different branches.

Approach 3 (Single Mobile Activity Handling)

Single process activities are executed on mobile devices. For this purpose, a mobile device must cover a subset of the functionality of a stationary process client, e.g., a worklist component that is continuously updated by the process engine (see Approach 3 in Figure 2).

Discussing the Approaches and Related Work

In the following, only a brief discussion about Approaches 3 will be given. Approaches 1 and 2 are predominant in research on distributed processes in general and for distributed mobile processes in particular. However, the robust execution of mobile activities (i.e., Approach *3*) has not been researched extensively. As this paper deals with *Approach 3*, only this approach is discussed in more detail. More information to the other approaches can be found in (Pryss & Reichert, 2016). In general, by following Approach 3, our focus is on the robust execution of mobile activities, while at the same time not burdening mobile users when exceptions occur. Note that *Approach 1* is generally not considered in MARPLE as it reveals too many drawbacks. Approach 2 is considered in MARPLE, but not subject to this paper. Figure 2 finally summarizes all presented approaches.

Approach 3 and Related Work

Note that Approach 3 only focuses on single mobile activities of a business process. Therefore, only related work is important which focuses on the challenges to perform single activities on mobile devices properly. In (Alonso et al., 1995), the challenges of disconnected clients in the context of business process execution have been early discussed with no mobile context. Since disconnections of a device performing an activity constitute the most important aspects for mobile activity execution, (Alonso et al., 1995) can be regarded as first work dealing with challenges relevant for mobile activities in the context of business processes. In sequel to that early research work, less work (e.g., (Tuysuz et al., 2013)) on how to properly execute mobile activities on mobile devices exist. In particular, many characteristic challenges imposed by mobile environments are less considered. Only the aspect of missing or inconsistent data is predominant subject to many research works in this context (Hahn & Schweppe, 2009). For example, (Hahn & Schweppe, 2009) proposed the apply transaction techniques to mobile processes. To deal with failures of mobile devices (e.g., a disconnected device) mobile activities are executed within transactions. Furthermore, transactional properties are defined to determine in what cases a transaction has to be cancelled. Used techniques in this and similar work do not deal with exceptions like presented in this paper. In particular, they do not focus on how to compensate exceptions while ensuring same execution semantics as originally intended. Another research work relevant in this context is proposed by (Pryss et al., 2015). The presented MEDo approach deals with mobile task handling in the context of medical ward rounds. In turn, MEDo does not deal with fine-grained considerations on mobile activities, i.e., user-, process-, and environment challenges, as constituted by the above presented seven challenges.

Furthermore, recent related works address exception handling in the context of mobile services (Chen, Cardozo, & Clarke, 2016; Marinescu, et al., 2015). However, they do not focus on human-centric mobile activities. Furthermore, preventing exceptions in a mobile context is not explicitly considered. For example, approaches dealing with mobile agents (Marinescu, et al., 2015) focus on exception prevention. Again, they do not specifically consider human-centric mobile services as the presented framework does. Finally, existing commercial process management systems supporting the integration of mobile activities do also not provide a particular exception handling concept (IBM, 2018).

Defining Processes With Mobile Activities

This section introduces the notion of our developed process meta-model that is crucial for the matchmaking model (i.e., assigning mobile activities to concrete mobile users) of the mobile activities (see Fig. 3, 1). The meta-model, in turn, is based on an extensive literature review (e.g., (Zaplata et al., 2010; WFMC, 2018)). Consider that Fig. 3 also illustrates mobile worklist management in the context of the meta-model (see Fig. 3, 6; (Pryss et al., 2016(b))). Note that all entities concerned with worklist management are marked accordingly. As can be seen, fundamental adaptations were required to enable worklist management for mobile activities. The meta-model is denoted as *mobile process meta-model*. In the context of worklist changes, two algorithms were developed (see Fig. 3, 2&3). The first algorithm manages user assignments and the execution of mobile activities (see Fig. 3, 2). It is denoted as *Selection Algorithm*, meaning that all mobile users determined by the algorithm are qualified to execute the mobile activity. The qualification, in turn, is based on three concepts: authorization (e.g., roles (Sandhu et al., 1996)), constraints; e.g., to ensure two activities will be executed by the same user (Pryss, Musiol, & Reichert, 2013), and a mobile context (see Fig. 3, 4). As frequently changing circumstances and limited resources

Figure 2. Approaches for realizing mobile processes

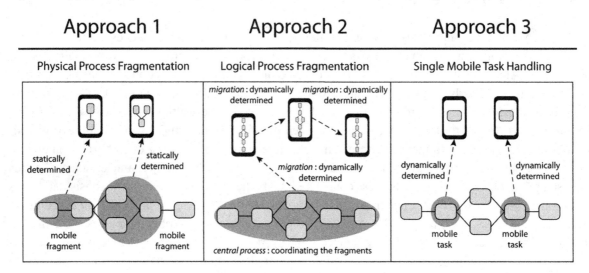

have to be properly addressed in mobile environments, the goal should be to find those mobile users with appropriate capacities (e.g., being closely located to the place the mobile activity shall be enacted) on one hand. On the other, the determined mobile users shall minimize the occurrence of exceptions. In this context, the *Selection Algorithm* evaluates the resource situation of all qualified mobile users as well as the best environment matching (e.g., the user is closely located to the mobile activity.). Note that a good matching in these aspects revealed quicker execution times of mobile activities and hence reduces exceptions. The second algorithm, the *Ranking Algorithm*, handles exceptions (e.g., mobile device crashes) during the execution of mobile activities (see Fig. 3, 3). To enable a proper exception handling, changes in respect to the state model of mobile activities (see Fig. 3, 5) became necessary, i.e., compared to non-mobile activities, the behavior of specific state transitions had to be changed and new states had to be added.

MOBILE PROCESS ACTIVITY INTEGRATION ARCHITECTURE

This section presents the proposed architecture in terms of the delegation and backup concept and discusses the management of user lists for the delegation service. First of all, the run time architecture is sketched, in which delegation and backup services are applied.

Mobile Activity Run Time Architecture

The delegation and backup services allow for the robust execution of mobile activities. Furthermore, their design allows for the use of existing service-driven business process engines. Implementing a specific process engine which provides all functions for creating and executing mobile activities constitutes another possible direction. However, if a process management system is already in use, the introduction of a new process engine is usually a complex endeavor due to high efforts for transferring process models to the new engine. Therefore, the presented architecture provides an engine-independent interface

Figure 3. Mobile Process Meta-Model

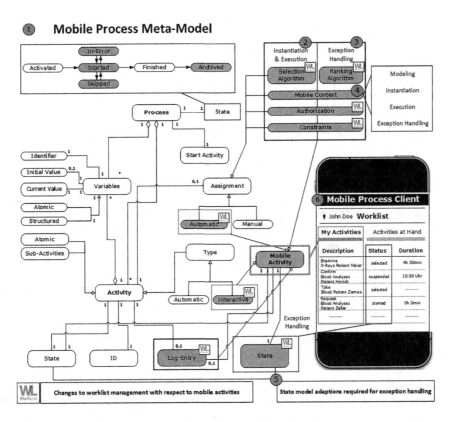

for executing mobile activities. Since communication with Web services constitutes a core feature of any modern process engine, a service-driven approach has been realized (see Figure 4). The core of the run time architecture for executing mobile activities is denoted as mobile execution environment (see Figure 4). Note that the mobile execution environment extends existing business process environments without any mobile support. It provides components to manage mobile users (list management), to handle delegations, to perform the backup service, and the Interfaces 1 and 2. The list management component, in turn, maintains user lists to enable delegation management. Interface 1 is the connection to a business process management environment. Its purpose is to communicate with the business process engine. It is designed and implemented to allow for the integration of a wide range of existing business process environments (e.g., Intalio (Ghalimi, 2006) or Activiti (Meister, 2011)). Finally, Interface 2 is used to integrate mobile devices with the mobile activity execution. Its purpose is to communicate with the mobile devices. Furthermore, a mobile service client has been implemented which is deployed to mobile devices. This client is used to push the following information via Interface 2 to the mobile execution environment: battery status, connection status, user location, and instant shutdowns. Thereby, the mobile device periodically sends status of user location, connectivity, and battery charge level to the mobile execution environment. Note that instant shutdowns are determined as follows: if a mobile device gets offline and recovers, it will be determined whether an instant shutdown has been the reason for getting offline. For example, regarding Android devices, the "<action android:name="android.intent. action.ACTION_SHUTDOWN"/>" will be determined. If an instant shutdown has been identified, the shutdown counter for the respective device will be increased.

Figure 4. Mobile activity run time architecture (simplified)

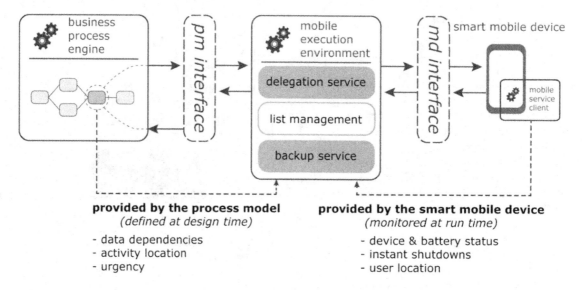

(pm interface: interface to integrate existing **p**rocess **m**anagement engine # md interface: interface to integrate smart **m**obile **d**evices)

Delegation

We introduce the notion of *delegation* during process execution as well as a corresponding approach (see Figure 5).

Approach 1 (Transfer Rights)

Delegation permits a user to assign all or a subset of their authorization rights to other users not possessing these rights at the moment (see the *functionality of Approach 1* in Figure 5). Thereby, they may either assign these rights in the context of a particular process instance or for all process instances. (Schaad, 2003; Crampton & Khambhammettu, 2008; Gaaloul & Charoy, 2009) provide various reasons for delegating respective rights; e.g., a user may not possess required documents, or an entailment constraint like separation of duties must be enforced (Pryss, Musiol, & Reichert, 2013). In this context, delegation may be accomplished based on two techniques: First, delegation may be applied based on user-defined rules stored in a repository. Second, users may delegate their rights dynamically during run time. The two techniques can be summarized as *user-to-user* interaction pattern: A user determines the context in which a delegation may be applied. Finally, delegations only take place when an activity is in a desired state. Note that *Approach 1* constitutes the common notion for delegation in the context of business processes.

Approach 2 (Exception Handling)

Delegation may be further applied in the context of exception handling. It will then be performed when mobile users and their devices encounter problems. This pattern is applied in the proposed architecture. Note that a delegation may be only performed to another mobile user possessing the same rights as the

Figure 5. Delegation mechanisms

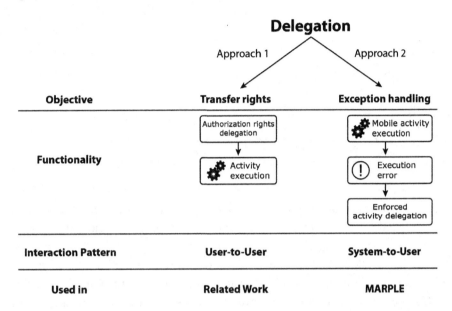

mobile user who has caused the problem. The delegation will then be performed in a *system-to-user* interaction pattern.

User List Management for Delegation and Backup

To foster robust execution of mobile activities, three different user lists are maintained: an initial user list ul_{init}, a user list ul_{mob} comprising appropriate mobile users, and a delegation list dl_{mob}. Note that all lists except ul_{init} are maintained by the mobile execution environment. ul_{init} is provided by a process engine and contains all mobile users u_{mob} authorized to perform a mobile activity t_{mob}. Furthermore, ul_{init} constitutes the basis for determining the two other lists, which are determined based on an analysis of ul_{init}. Thereby, ul_{init} is created by considering the following properties:

As soon as mobile activity t_{mob} becomes activated, ul_{mob} will be calculated by the *delegation service* as follows (see Table 3):

Table 2. Properties for determining ul_{init}

Property	Description
Connectivity	Indicates whether a user u_{mob} is online or offline.
Low Battery Status	Indicates whether the user's device has a low battery status.
User Location vs. Activity Location	The user's current location will be compared to the activity location. For example, if the *location* attribute of a mobile activity has value *emergency unit* and a mobile user is currently staying at another ward, he/she will not be considered for ul_{init}. Moreover, during this phase both the symbolic as well as the geometric coordinates are used (see Table 1)
Pre-filter	Indicates if u_{mob} has been excluded by a *pre-filter*.
Instant Shutdowns	The user's current number of instant shutdowns will be compared to the generally defined threshold for instant shutdowns of a mobile activity.

Table 3. Ranking algorithm

$ul_{mob} \leftarrow \{\}$
FOREACH u_{mob} **IN** ul_{init}
 IF $(u_{mob}.connectivity)$ **AND** $(\neg u_{mob}.pre\text{-}filter)$
IF $(u_{mob}.location = t_{mob}.location)$ or $(u_{mob}.location = \{\}$ and $t_{mob}.location=0)$
 THEN
 $ul_{mob}.append(u_{mob})$
FOREACH u_{mob} **IN** ul_{mob}
$u_{mob}.determine.ranking.value(u_{mob}.resource.behavior^{1})$
$ul_{mob}.sort()$ based on ranking.value and in descending order
$^{1}=$ resource.behavior is a complex procedure not shown here due to space limitations. It evaluates the resource behaviour of a mobile user (based on connection losses, performed instant shutdowns, failed delegations, and low battery times)

According to this procedure, all mobile users from ul_{init} being online, not being pre-filtered (i.e., not being manually excluded for the process or an instance of the process), and are located closely to the required location of the activity (again, both the symbolic and geometric coordinates are evaluated), will be appended to ul_{mob}. Then, ul_{mob} will be sorted in descending order based on a ranking value. The ranking value is determined for each mobile user and determines his resource behaviour. The latter is calculated based on the connection losses, performed instant shutdowns, failed delegations, and low battery times of a mobile user. Thereby, a ranking with high value indicates good resource behaviour for a mobile user; i.e., he has exhibited less connection losses, performed less instant shutdowns, caused less failed delegations, and showed less times a low battery status than other mobile users with a lower ranking value. Finally, the mobile user in ul_{mob} with highest ranking value will be notified about the mobile activity being ready for execution. As a result, he will see this activity in his work list on the mobile device. After the mobile user has claimed the activity, the delegation can be started. If he declines the execution, ul_{mob} will be used to identifiy the mobile user next in line with respect to the ranking value. Then, this identified mobile user will be notified about the mobile activity being ready for execution. The procedure is repeated until a mobile user accepts the delegation request or he constitutes the one in ul_{mob} with the lowest ranking value (i.e., the final mobile user in ul_{mob}). If the latter is the case, the mobile user cannot decline the delegation request.

User Assignment and Race Conditions

The different lists maintained and presented above for delegation and backup service prevent race conditions with respect to user assignments. As a result, only one mobile is responsible for performing a mobile activity at any point in time. This will be enabled due to the following reasons:

- Delegation ensures that a mobile user performing a mobile activity is distracted from the respective mobile activity execution before delegation to another user is performed.
- User list management ensures that work lists on the mobile devices are synchronized and only one user can claim a mobile activity.
- Delegation management only prioritizes mobile users according to the presented aspects (e.g., battery status). As a result, the assignment of users is an atomic operation since it is performed similar to user list management in existing business process engines (e.g., Reichert et al., 2009).

Protocol Management for Delegation

In a process management system that realizes that mobile process meta-model we developed, the delegation concept needs a protocol definition between the mobile device and the process management system. Therefore, the protocol coordinating the interactions between the mobile process client and the process management system is presented (see Fig. 6). First, we present required components (see Fig. 6), which were implemented as a service-oriented middleware that interacts between an existing process management system and the mobile process client. The basic components of the middleware include a service-centric play application and a MySQL database connected to it. The delegation concept presented in this work is realized by the *mobile activity handler*. Processes, in turn, are coordinated by the adaptive process management system

AristaFlow BPM Suite. The realized mobile process client consists of two components that manage the entire communication: the worklist client and the execution client. Thereby, the worklist client manages the worklist, whereas the execution client manages the communication between the worklist client, an invoked mobile application, and the developed service-oriented middleware. The invoked mobile applications, in turn, actually perform the mobile activity (e.g., invoking Mobile Microsoft Excel). Based on this, the delegation protocol was realized. It governs the interactions between the mobile process client and the service-oriented middleware in case of a delegation. The protocol steps are depicted in Fig. 6. Thereby, steps within the *In-Delegation* box are crucial for handling delegations. In particular, they constitute the steps performed after a delegation. Two scenarios must be distinguished. First, the mobile device might no longer work after the occurrence of the exception. Second, it might still work, but no longer be connected to the process management system. In the first case, all steps shown for the mobile process client are not performed. In the second case, all shown steps are performed. After starting the delegation, the process management system performs the following steps. First, it withdraws the mobile activity running on the mobile device by updating its status (see Steps 10'-11'). Second, after updating the status it determines whether the mobile device has reconnected in case the connection loss was only a short-term problem (see Step 12'). Third, depending on the result of Step 12', it may start the delegation. The mobile process client, in turn, applies the following steps. First, the running activity is stopped and the data created is locally cached (see Steps 10-13). Second, after the mobile device reconnects to the process management system, it requests the status of the delegation (see Step 14) and sends its cached data to the process management system. Two additional scenarios need to be distinguished (see Fig. 6, 6) after a reconnection. First, if a delegation has not been accomplished yet, the reconnecting mobile device gets the activity execution back. Second, if the delegation is still running, the cached data is transferred to the mobile device currently performing the delegation. This way it can be ensured that no data is lost. In addition, a feature was realized that enables recipients to manually decide whether or not to use cached data before it will be actually transferred. Furthermore, we identified the protocol points at which the mobile context parameters shall be exchanged between the mobile process client and the service-oriented middleware. Fig. 6 (2,4) depicts two protocol points at which the service-oriented middleware requests parameter values from the mobile process client. In turn, Fig. 6 (1,3,5) shows the points in time at which the mobile process client sends parameter values to the service-oriented middleware.

Figure 6. Delegation protocol

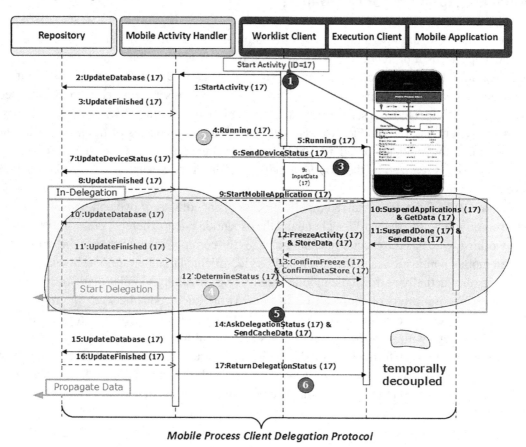

Mobile Process Client Delegation Protocol

Adding Mobile Activities to Process Execution

For adding a mobile activity to a process model and hence integrating it with process execution, two fundamental solutions exist. These will be presented in this section. In particular, it will be shown how the challenges summarized in Table 4 are addressed by these solution approaches:

First, a backup service will be introduced, which adds a backup activity to ensure a robust execution of mobile activities. Second, a delegation service will be defined that automatically delegates the execution of mobile activities among available mobile users, if required. Before presenting these two services in detail, this section illustrates the basic steps required to add a mobile activity to process execution. Overall, the procedure encompasses four phases. Figure 8 shows in which of these phases manual steps (i.e., user interaction) and automated operations (i.e., delegation and backup service executions) are performed. Note that after creating an instance of a process model comprised of mobile activities, mobile users are not burdened with making decisions with regard to exceptions of a mobile activity. This behavior will be ensured since delegation and backup services as well as the user list management are performed automatically.

Table 4. Parameters for processes with mobile activities

	Parameter	Description	Type	Design Time	Instantiation Time	Activation Time	Delegation Time
	— Category I: Mobile device (SMD)						
Mobile Environment	SMD_{BS}	Battery Status	M	x	-	x	x
	SMD_{FF}	Form Factor	S	x	-	x	x
	SMD_{NT}	Network Type	M	-	-	x	x
	SMD_{GC}	Geometric Coordinate	M	-	-	x	x
	Category II: Mobile Activity (MA)						
Process	MA_{SC}	Symbolic Coordinate(s)	S	x	-	x	x
	MA_{GC}	Geometric Coordinate	M	-	-	x	x
	MA_{LR}	Location Range	S	x	-	x	x
	MA_{BS}	Battery Status	M	-	-	x	x
	MA_{U}	Urgency Value	S	x	-	x	x
	MA_{OFF}	Offline Mode	S	x	-	x	x
	MA_{FF}	Form Factor	S	x	-	x	x
	MA_{RF}	Response Frequency	S	x	-	x	x
	MA_{UT}	User Threshold	S	x	-	x	x
	Category III: Process (P)						
	P_{IST}	Instant Shutdown Threshold	S	x	-	x	x
	Category IV: Mobile User (MU)						
User Behavior	MU_{SC}	Symbolic Coordinate(s)	S	x	-	x	x
	MU_{IS}	Instant Shutdowns	S	-	-	x	x
	| Type: M=Measured, S=Symbolic | (x): relevant | (-): not relevant |						

Design Time

The design of a process model which comprises mobile activities consists of two phases. During the first one, which is called *mobile process transformation phase (see Figure 7(1))*, a process designer flags selected activities of the given process model as *mobile*, i.e., these activities shall be executed by mobile users on their respective mobile devices during run time. In this context, the process designer determines parameters to each mobile activity *(see Figure 7(1))* that are presented in Table 4 relevant for the design time. In addition, a mobile activity threshold may be created. The latter defines the minimum number of users that shall be available at run time in order to execute this activity, i.e., the threshold allows controlling the assignment depending on the specific needs of the respective mobile processes. For all mobile activities, for which such a threshold is defined during this phase, the list of users who may perform the mobile activity is determined *(Figure 7(1), validateThreshold)* based on information

Figure 7. Procedure for integrating mobile activities into process execution

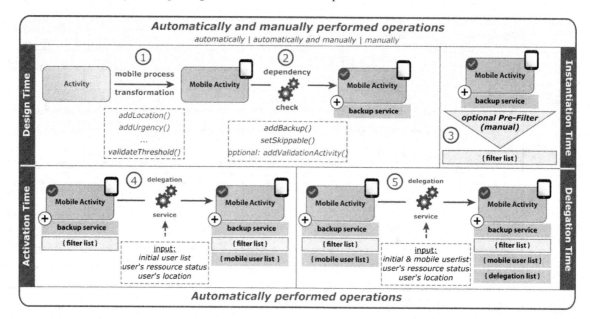

stored in the user repository. Finally, activities whose chosen threshold value lies beyond the number of currently available users are highlighted to the process designer who may then alter this value.

The second design time phase is the *dependency check (see Figure 7(2))*. In this phase, it is determined for which mobile activities the backup service can be provided. While the *mobile process transformation* is done manually (except the validation of the threshold), the *dependency check* can be performed automatically. In this context, scenario specific dependency checks can be used. For example, a dependency check for mobile activities that write data elements, the following check will be automatically accomplished: First, all mobile activities are analyzed with respect to the data elements they provide for subsequent process activities. If a mobile activity writes such data, the backup service will be added for this mobile activity *(see Figure 7(2), addBackup)*. If this does not apply, the mobile activity may be skipped during run time without need for additional exception handling, i.e., operation *setSkippable* may be applied to such a mobile activity (see *Figure 7(2))*. Accordingly, attribute *IS_SKIPPABLE* of this mobile activity is set to *true*. While the backup service (or *setSkippable* operation) is automatically added to a mobile activity, the third operation of this phase (*Figure (2), addValidationActivity)* is performed manually, i.e., the process designer must decide whether or not the execution of backup activities must be manually confirmed during run time. In order to enforce this behavior, the process designer activates the validation activities set by the backup service, i.e., the sync flag read by the validation activities will be set to *true*.

To understand the next three phases with respect to design and run time, Figure 8 summarizes the lifecycle of a mobile activity. Thereby, it relates all phases shown in Figure 7 with the lifecycle (see *1-4 in* Figure 8).

Instantiation Time

When creating a process instance, a service is provided to change the run time configuration of this instance *(see Figure 7(3), addFilterList)*. This service aims to cope with the dynamics of mobile envi-

Figure 8. Mobile activity lifecycle

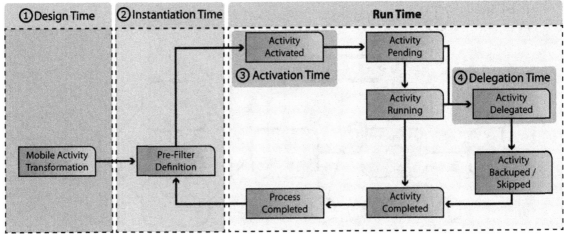

ronments. To perform such a change, the following steps are applied. First, for all mobile activities, user lists are computed. Thereby, only currently online users are considered. Second, for each mobile activity it must be decided whether to change its location or urgency. In addition, users authorized to execute other *activities* may be removed. The latter option allows covering different kinds of mobile business scenarios properly. For example, the mobile device of a physician who needs to cope with an emergency should not be the target for upcoming mobile activities.

Delegation Time

When delegating a mobile activity at run time, it is automatically delegated to another user possessing same rights. Further, for each mobile activity, a delegation list is managed. This list will be created after the first delegation becomes necessary. It also stores a history of all delegations for this mobile activity.

Generally, the following issues are crucial with respect to mobile activity execution (see Figure 11):

- An execution exception of a mobile activity that produces data that is consumed by subsequent process steps may cause severe run time exceptions (Reichert et al., 1999; Reichert & Weber, 2012) (see *missing data in Figure 9*).
- An execution exception of a mobile activity might cause a deadlock (see *deadlock in Figure 9*), i.e., if a mobile activity cannot be properly completed, succeeding activities might not be activated.
- Regarding mobile activity execution, usually, a time period is specified indicating the maximum duration of this activity. For example, it might be required that a blood test is finished within 5 minutes. Accordingly, any execution exception of a mobile activity should be handled in time in order to meet respective temporal constraints.

Figure 9. Mobile activity execution challenges

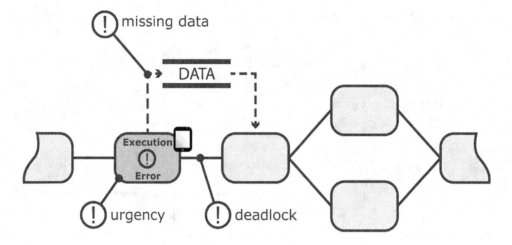

Service-Oriented Solution Approach

The solution approach towards the robust execution of mobile activities, which is presented in this section, tackles the challenges introduced before. Table 5 gives an overview of the main challenges by showing which service, i.e., mobile process transformation (*MPT*), backup service (*BS*), list management (*LM*), and mobile delegation service (*MDS*) addresses which of these challenges.

Delegation Service

During mobile activity execution, the *mobile delegation service* (MDS) ensures that already assigned mobile activities are automatically re-delegated to another authorized mobile user in case of exceptions. Since this delegation service maintains several user lists, the latter are first summarized before presenting the MDS.

User List Management

To enable a flexible delegation and hence to foster robust execution of a mobile activity t, three user lists are maintained for it: ul_{init}, ul_{mob}, and dl_{mob}. User list ul_{init} contains all mobile users that are, in principle, authorized to perform mobile activity t. Based on ul_{init}, the mobile user list ul_{mob} is determined. Thereby, a mobile user from ul_{init} is only added to ul_{mob}, if the user is currently online, user's location complies with the one of t, and the user is not excluded by any filter defined at instantiation time. Based on ul_{mob}, t *is assigned to available* mobile users. Furthermore, if t shall be delegated, a mobile delegation list dl_{mob} is determined. First of all, all users contained in ul_{mob} are added to dl_{mob}. Then, dl_{mob} is ordered by taking the resource behavior of mobile users into account. A low priority is assigned to a mobile user if his resource behavior is inappropriate. Both lists ul_{mob} and dl_{mob} are re-calculated when the connectivity status of a user from list ul_{init} changes.

Table 5. Parameters and solution components of mobile activities

Challenge	Component	Description
Connectivity	LMMDS	Only connected devices will be added to the user and delegation lists. The MDS refreshes these lists continuously and accomplishes any delegation required when a mobile device loses its connection.
Resource Behavior	LMMDS	Only mobile users having a sufficient resource behavior will be added to the user and delegation lists.
User Location	LM	If a location X is explicitly assigned to m*obile activity*, only users whose current location matches X are added to the respective user lists.
Data Dependencies	BS	The backup service ensures that exceptions during the execution of a m*obile activity* do not harm overall process execution, e.g., if subsequent activities are data-dependent on the failed mobile activity, the latter will be replaced by a respective backup activity added to the process model.
Location	MPT	A m*obile activity* may require a certain location for its execution.
Urgency	MPT MDS BS	The urgency of an activity may be set at design time. In turn, the MDS then utilizes this information as trigger for delegating the mobile activity, i.e., a backup service ensures that the mobile activity will be always executed within the specified time frame.

Overall, when considering these three lists, the mobile delegation service may enter six different states (see Figure 10). The latter are denoted as $t(<STATE>)$ and respective state transitions as T_i. Note that the delegation service starts when a mobile activity t becomes activated. The delegation service will be activated before executing the respective activity only if the mobile activity has a value set for *urgency* and no authorized mobile user will promptly execute the activity, then it will be delegated to an authorized mobile user, i.e., delegation is used for changing activity state to running.

The scenarios shown in Table 6 are relevant when taking urgency (specified period of time when the activity must be finished) to_u ($to_u = 0$ denotes a timeout), user list threshold th_{mul}, and the ability to skip a mobile activity t into account.

Figure 10. Mobile delegation service flow during run time

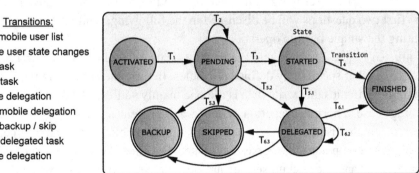

Transitions:

T_1 build mobile user list
T_2 handle user state changes
T_3 start task
T_4 finish task
$T_{5.1}$ mobile delegation
$T_{5.2}$ force mobile delegation
$T_{5.3}$ force backup / skip
$T_{6.1}$ finish delegated task
$T_{6.2}$ mobile delegation

Table 6. Scenarios in which mobile delegation service is applied

Scenario	Description	State Chain
Normal activity execution	$user_a \in ul_{mob}$ starts mobile activity t and performs it.	$t(PENDING) \rightarrow T_3 \rightarrow t(STARTED) \rightarrow T_4 \rightarrow t(FINISHED)$
Delegated activity execution	$user_a \in ul_{mob}$ starts mobile activity t. Then user state changes to offline or $to_u = 0$ holds, such that t will be automatically delegated to another $user_b \in ul_{mob}$ who finishes the mobile activity.	$T_3 \rightarrow t(STARTED) \rightarrow T_{5.1} \rightarrow t(DELEGATED) \rightarrow T_{6.1} \rightarrow t(FINISHED)$
Forced delegation	A forced delegation becomes necessary if the following holds: $t(PENDING) \wedge (|ul_{mob}| < th_{mul} \vee to_u = 0) \vee t(DELEGATED) \wedge (to_u = 0 \vee State(user_b)$ changes to offline) $\rightarrow$ t must be delegated to another $user_n \in ul_{mob}$.	$T_{5.2} \rightarrow t(DELEGATED) \vee T_{6.2} \rightarrow t(DELEGATED)$
Skip or Backup	Skip or backup will be performed if the following holds: If $t(PENDING) \wedge to_u = 0 \wedge |ul_{mob}| = 0) \vee (t(DELEGATED) \wedge to_u = 0 \wedge |dl_{mob}| = 0)$. Furthermore, if IS_SKIPPABLE(T)=true, t will transit to SKIP, otherwise to BACKUP	$t(PENDING) \rightarrow T_{5.3} \rightarrow t(SKIP) \vee t(BACKUP)/ t(DELEGATED) \rightarrow T_{6.3} \rightarrow t(SKIP) \vee t(BACKUP)$

Backup Service

A particular challenge arises if no mobile user is available for processing an activated mobile activity that produces data during run time, i.e., if no delegation is possible anymore. In order to ensure that these mobile activities can still be processed, a backup service is provided. Basically, it consists of two operations, which are added to a process fragment replacing the mobile activity in case of exceptional situations. The first one is called *simple backup operation*, while the second is called *complex backup operation*. Before presenting the backup service in detail, three questions have to be briefly discussed with respect to the backup service: (1) Since the backup operation is performed on a stationary computer and hence failures are more unlikely than using a mobile device, the question arise why performing the activity on a mobile device at first? One can argue that in this case the mobile device is not necessary and affects overall robustness. (2) How are skipping of mobile activities and the backup service relate to each other? (3) Does it make sense to provide the validation activity with the backup service since it may block execution and resulting in the same exceptional situation as caused before by the mobile device? The first two questions will be discussed in the following, while the third one will be discussed after presenting the simple backup operation.

First of all, see Figure 11. Note that the backup service is only applied to mobile activities which write data or have other specifically defined attributes. In turn, the case using the backup service in the context of mobile activities that write data is the one mainly addressed. As depicted in Figure 11, in the best and average case, a normal execution or delegation prevents using the backup service. Note that in case no more delegation is possible, i.e., no more suitable mobile user is able to perform this activity. Only then, the backup operation becomes necessary. Question 2 can now be answered based on this. Skipping an activity and the backup service are not related. Activities to which the backup service is applied can only be delegated or finalized based on the backup service. In general, skipping an activity is only possible for those activities that do not write data. Regarding Question 1, a mobile activity is intended to be performed in a mobile manner. Since the backup operation constitutes a very final alternative, originally intended behavior is preserved more properly. For example, assume the following situation: Two physicians work on urgent mobile activities with their mobile devices. Then, both devices run out of battery (frequently observed in the context of the above presented MEDo project). Further, no other physicians are able to perform these mobile activities (frequently observed as well). In this case, using stationary computers to complete the activities are highly welcome. For this purpose, the backup service will be used. Due to the lack of space, the way how mobile activities are adjusted to be executed on stationary computer can be obtained from (Pryss & Reichert, 2016).

CURRENT RESEARCH

Among others, our current research on mobile activity support deals with the following issues. In general, certain constraints may have to be obeyed when executing mobile activities. As example, consider entailment constraints that may exist between different mobile activities. When executing a mobile process, for example, it might be desirable that two mobile activities are executed by the same user. Related research on integrating such constraints with business processes has received growing attention recently. However, realizing entailment constraints in the context of mobile processes and activities raises additional issues, which must be integrated with our backup and delegation services. Furthermore, a way to specify rules for enhancing the delegation service must be developed; e.g., users should be allowed to specify their own delegation rules.

CONCLUSION

This paper presented an approach for enabling business processes with mobile activity support. The backup service as well as the mobile delegation service allow for a robust process execution. For this purpose, four fundamental issues need to be considered. First, the specific challenges of executing process activities in a mobile environment must be well understood. Second, these challenges must be properly addressed at both design and run time. Third, mobile activities must be executed in a robust way, the backup service and mobile delegation services foster such robustness with respect to mobile activity execution. Fourth, user acceptance is crucial in the context of mobile activity support. Accordingly, the presented services do not involve mobile users in exception handling directly. Finally, a sophisticated architecture has been described showing how the presented approach can be realized in a service-oriented environment.

Figure 11. Use case of backup operation

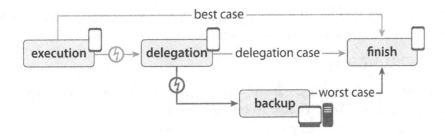

REFERENCES

Alonso, G., Agrawal, D., El Abbadi, A., Kamath, M., Gunthor, R., & Mohan, C. (1996, February). Advanced transaction models in workflow contexts. In *Data Engineering, 1996. Proceedings of the Twelfth International Conference on* (pp. 574-581). IEEE.

Alonso, G., & Gunthor, R., & Agrawal, D., & El Abbadi, A. (1995). *Exotica/FMDC: Handling disconnected clients in a workflow management system*. Academic Press.

Alonso, G., & Schek, H. J. (1996). Research issues in large workflow management systems. *Proceedings of NSF Workshop on Workflow and Process Automation in Information Science*.

Ayora, C., Torres, V., Reichert, M., Weber, B., & Pelechano, V. (2013). Towards run-time flexibility for process families: open issues and research challenges. *Proc. Business Process Management Workshops*. doi:10.1007/978-3-642-36285-9_49

Barros, A., Dumas, M., & Oaks, P. (2005). A critical overview of the web services choreography description language. *BPTrends Newsletter*, *3*, 1–24.

Battista, D., Leoni, M., Gaetanis, A., Mecella, M., Pezzullo, A., Russo, A., & Saponaro, C. (2008). ROME4EU: A Web service-based process-aware system for smart devices. *Proc. ICSOC'08*, 726-727. 10.1007/978-3-540-89652-4_65

Bauer, T., Reichert, M., & Dadam, P. (2003). Intra-subnet load balancing in distributed workflow management systems. *International Journal of Cooperative Information Systems*, *12*(03), 205–223. doi:10.1142/S0218843003000760

Becker, C., & Dürr, F. (2005). On location models for ubiquitous computing. *Personal and Ubiquitous Computing*, *9*(1), 20–31. doi:10.100700779-004-0270-2

Chen, N., Cardozo, N., & Clarke, S. (2016). Goal-driven service composition in mobile and pervasive computing. *IEEE Transactions on Services Computing*.

Cichocki, A., & Rusinkiewicz, M. (1998). Migrating workflows. In *Workflow Management Systems and Interoperability* (pp. 339–355). Springer Berlin Heidelberg. doi:10.1007/978-3-642-58908-9_15

Crampton, J., & Khambhammettu, H. (2008). Delegation and satisfiability in workflow systems. *Proc. of the 13th ACM symposium on Access control models and technologies*, 31-40.

Gaaloul, K., & Charoy, F. (2009). Task delegation based access control models for workflow systems. In Software Services for e-Business and e-Society (pp. 400-414). Academic Press. doi:10.1007/978-3-642-04280-5_31

Geiger, P., Pryss, R., Schickler, M., & Reichert, M. (2013). *Engineering an Advanced Location-Based Augmented Reality Engine for Mobile devices. Technical Report*. University of Ulm.

Ghalimi, I. C., & CEO, I. (2006). *BPM 2.0*.

Hackmann, G., Haitjema, M., & Gill, C. (2006). Sliver: A BPEL workflow process execution engine for mobile devices. *Proc. ICSOC'06*, 503-508. 10.1007/11948148_47

Hahn, K., & Schweppe, H. (2009). Exploring transactional service properties for mobile service composition. *Proc. MMS'09*, 39-52.

IBM Mobile Business Process Management. (2014). Retrieved from http://www.redbooks.ibm.com/abstracts/sg248240.html?Open

Jones, V. M., van Halteren, A. T., Dokovski, N. T., Koprinkov, G. T., Peuscher, J., Bults, R. G. A., . . . Herzog, R. (2006). *Mobihealth: mobile services for health professionals*. Technical Report TR-CTIT-06-38.

Kunze, C. P. (2005). Demac: A distributed environment for mobility-aware computing. In *Adjunct Proc. of the Third International Conference on Pervasive Computing* (pp. 115-121). Academic Press.

Lenz, R., & Reichert, M. (2007). IT Support for Healthcare Processes -Premises, Challenges, Perspectives. *Data & Knowledge Engineering, 61*(1), 39–58. doi:10.1016/j.datak.2006.04.007

Marinescu, A., Dusparic, I., Taylor, A., Cahill, V., & Clarke, S. (2015, May). P-marl: Prediction-based multi-agent reinforcement learning for non-stationary environments. In *Proceedings of the 2015 International Conference on Autonomous Agents and Multiagent Systems* (pp. 1897-1898). International Foundation for Autonomous Agents and Multiagent Systems.

Martin, D., Wutke, D., & Leymann, F. (2008, September). A novel approach to decentralized workflow enactment. In *Enterprise Distributed Object Computing Conference, 2008. EDOC'08. 12th International IEEE* (pp. 127-136). IEEE. 10.1109/EDOC.2008.22

Meister, V.G. (2011). Geschäftsregelbasierte Ansteuerung betrieblicher Anwendungssysteme am Beispiel der Open Source Process Engine Activiti. *Betriebliche Anwendungssysteme*, 65.

Philips, E., Van Der Straeten, R., & Jonckers, V. (2011). NOW: Orchestrating services in a nomadic network using a dedicated workflow language. *Science of Computer Programming*.

Pryss, R., Geiger, P., Schickler, M., Schobel, J., & Reichert, M. (2016). Advanced Algorithms for Location-Based Smart Mobile Augmented Reality Applications. *Procedia Computer Science, 94*, 97–104. doi:10.1016/j.procs.2016.08.017

Pryss, R., Mundbrod, N., Langer, D., & Reichert, M. (2015). Supporting medical ward rounds through mobile task and process management. *Information Systems and e-Business Management, 13*(1), 107–146. doi:10.100710257-014-0244-5

Pryss, R., Musiol, S., & Reichert, M. (2013). Collaboration Support Through Mobile Processes and Entailment Constraints. *Proc. 9th IEEE Int. Conf. on Collaborative Computing: Networking, Applications and Worksharing*. 10.4108/icst.collaboratecom.2013.254063

Pryss, R., & Reichert, M. (2016). Robust execution of mobile activities in process-aware information systems. *International Journal of Information System Modeling and Design, 7*(4), 50–82. doi:10.4018/IJISMD.2016100104

Pryss, R., Reichert, M., Schickler, M., & Bauer, T. (2016). Context-Based Assignment and Execution of Human-centric Mobile Services. In *Mobile Services (MS), 2016 IEEE International Conference on* (pp. 119-126). IEEE. 10.1109/MobServ.2016.12

Pryss, R., Tiedeken, J., Kreher, U., & Reichert, M. (2010). Towards Flexible Process Support on Mobile Devices. *Proc. CAiSE'10 Forum*, 150–165.

Pryss, R., Tiedeken, J., & Reichert, M. (2010). Managing Processes on Mobile Devices: The MARPLE Approach. *Proc. CAiSE'10 Demos*.

Reichert, M., Bauer, T., & Dadam, P. (2009). *Flexibility for distributed workflows*. Academic Press.

Reichert, M., Dadam, P., Rinderle-Ma, S., Lanz, A., Pryss, R., Predeschly, M., ... Goeser, K. (2009). *Enabling Poka-Yoke workflows with the AristaFlow BPM Suite*. Academic Press.

Reichert, M., & Weber, B. (2012). *Enabling Flexibility in Process-Aware Information Systems: Challenges, Methods, Technologies*. Springer. doi:10.1007/978-3-642-30409-5

Reichert, M., & Weber, B. (2013). Process Change Patterns: Recent Research, Use Cases, Research Directions. In Seminal Contributions to Information Systems Engineering - 25 Years of CAiSE (pp. 398–404). Academic Press.

Sandhu, R. S., Coyne, E. J., Feinstein, H. L., & Youman, C. E. (1996). Role-based access control models. *Computer*, *29*(2), 38–47. doi:10.1109/2.485845

Schaad, A. (2003). *A Framework for Organisational Control Principles* (PhD thesis). The University of York, York, UK.

Schmidt, H., & Hauck, F. J. (2007). SAMPROC: middleware for self-adaptive mobile processes in heterogeneous ubiquitous environments. In *Proc. 4th Middleware Doctoral Symposium* (pp. 1-6). Academic Press. 10.1145/1377934.1377935

Schmidt, H., Kapitza, R., & Hauck, F. J. (2007). Mobile-process-based ubiquitous computing platform: a blueprint. In *Proc. 1st Workshop on Middleware-application interaction* (pp. 25-30). Academic Press.

Schobel, J., Pryss, R., Schickler, M., & Reichert, M. (2016). A Lightweight Process Engine for Enabling Advanced Mobile Applications. In *OTM Confederated International Conferences On the Move to Meaningful Internet Systems* (pp. 552-569). Springer International Publishing. 10.1007/978-3-319-48472-3_33

Schobel, J., Pryss, R., Schickler, M., Ruf-Leuschner, M., Elbert, T., & Reichert, M. (2016, June). End-user programming of mobile services: empowering domain experts to implement mobile data collection applications. In *IEEE 5th International Conference on Mobile Services* (pp. 1-8). IEEE. 10.1109/MobServ.2016.11

Schobel, J., Pryss, R., Wipp, W., Schickler, M., & Reichert, M. (2016). A Mobile Service Engine Enabling Complex Data Collection Applications. In *International Conference on Service-Oriented Computing* (pp. 626-633). Springer International Publishing. 10.1007/978-3-319-46295-0_42

Schobel, J., Schickler, M., Pryss, R., Nienhaus, H., & Reichert, M. (2013). Using Vital Sensors in Mobile Healthcare Business Applications: challenges, Examples, Lessons Learned. In *Proc. 9 Int'l Conference on Web Information Systems and Technologies* (pp. 509–518). Academic Press.

Stürmer, G., Mangler, J., & Schikuta, E. (2009). Building a modular service oriented workflow engine. In *Proc. Service-Oriented Computing and Applications (SOCA), 2009 IEEE International Conference on* (pp. 1-4). IEEE. 10.1109/SOCA.2009.5410270

Tuysuz, G., Avenoglu, B., & Eren, P. E. (2013, September). A Workflow-Based Mobile Guidance Framework for Managing Personal Activities. In *Next Generation Mobile Apps, Services and Technologies (NGMAST), 2013 Seventh International Conference on* (pp. 13-18). IEEE. 10.1109/NGMAST.2013.12

van der Aalst, W. M., & Weske, M. (2001, January). The P2P approach to interorganizational workflows. In Advanced Information Systems Engineering (pp. 140-156). Springer Berlin Heidelberg.

Wakholi, P. K., & Chen, W. (2012). *Workflow Partitioning for Offline Distributed Execution on Mobile Devices. Process Aware Mobile Systems. Applied to mobile-phone based data collection.* Academic Press.

Wodtke, D., & Weikum, G. (1997). A formal foundation for distributed workflow execution based on state charts. In Database Theory—ICDT'97 (pp. 230-246). Springer Berlin Heidelberg. doi:10.1007/3-540-62222-5_48

Workflow Management Coalition (WFMC). (2014). Retrieved from http://www.wfmc.org/

Zaplata, S., Dreiling, V., & Lamersdorf, W. (2009). Realizing mobile Web services for dynamic applications. In Proc. I3E'09 (pp. 240-254). Academic Press. doi:10.1007/978-3-642-04280-5_20

Zaplata, S., Hamann, K., Kottke, K., & Lamersdorf, W. (2010). Flexible execution of distributed business processes based on process instance migration. *Journal of Systems Integration, 1*(3), 3–16.

Zaplata, S., Kottke, K., Meiners, M., & Lamersdorf, W. (2010). Towards run time migration of WS-BPEL processes. *Proc. WESOA'09.*

ENDNOTE

[1]   Further information to the project can be found at: http://www.dbis.info/questionsys

Chapter 8
On the Rim Between Business Processes and Software Systems

Maria Estrela Ferreira da Cruz
Polytechnic Institute of Viana do Castelo, Portugal

Ricardo J. Machado
Universidade do Minho, Portugal

Maribel Yasmina Santos
Universidade do Minho, Portugal

ABSTRACT

The constant change and rising complexity of organizations, mainly due to the transforming nature of their business processes, has driven the increase of interest in business process management by organizations. It is recognized that knowing business processes can help to ensure that the software under development will meet the business needs. Some of software development processes (like unified process) already refer to business process modeling as a first effort in the software development process. A business process model usually is created under the supervision, clarification, approval, and validation of the business stakeholders. Thus, a business process model is a proper representation of the reality (as is or to be), having lots of useful information that can be used in the development of the software system that will support the business. The chapter uses the information existing in business process models to derive software models specially focused in generating a data model.

INTRODUCTION

Organizations are constantly being challenged with new demands imposed by markets and must respond to new requirements imposed by governments. Organizations need to have a clear notion of their internal processes to increase their efficiency and the quality of their products or services, enhancing the benefits for their stakeholders (Schmiedel & vom Brocke, 2015; van der Aalst, 2015). Business Process Management allows organizations to know themselves and to be prepared to fight new challenges and easily adapt to new situations (Batoulis et al., 2015).

DOI: 10.4018/978-1-5225-7271-8.ch008

BPM is considered key for innovation helping companies and organizations in the simulation of possible scenarios (Schmiedel & vom Brocke, 2015). For this and other reasons, business process management and modeling is being increasingly used by organizations (Batoulis et al., 2015).

A business process (BP) is a set of activities, their logical ordering, data, and organizational responsibilities, executed to achieve a business goal. BP models allow organizations to improve, control, automatize, and measure their processes (Weske, 2012). There are several languages that can be used to model the BPs. The Business Process Model and Notation (BPMN) language is being used in this research because it is an increasingly used and disclosed standard among companies and is already considered the default language used in business process modeling (Weske, 2012), besides it is a complete language, easy to learn and to use (Kocbek et al., 2015).

One of the main software quality objectives is to assure that a software product meets the business needs (Jalote, 2008). For that, the software product requirements need to be aligned with the business needs, both in terms of business processes (BPs) and in terms of the informational entities those processes deal with. This drives us to the question: Why not use this information, which is already modeled in business process models, to get the software models to the supporting software system? That is the main objective of the work being presented here.

Usually an organization (or company) deals with many BPs, so a supporting software system, typically, supports many BPs. Consequently, to generate complete and useful software design models for the development of software that will support the business, it is necessary to work and aggregate all the information existent in the set of processes that comprise a business.

This work presents and discusses two approaches to derive a data model from a set of business process models: a direct approach, which generates a data model by piecing together information from a set of business process models; and an indirect approach, which generates a data model by adapting the 4SRS (Four Step Rule Set) (Machado et al., 2006) method to generate a logical software architecture from business process models and extending it to derive the data model from the logical software architecture. Thus, the indirect approach generates several software models considering different software perspectives, namely the data model, use case model (including use case descriptions) and software logical architecture. The research steps are presented in Figure 1, where the solid arrows represent new steps created during the present research work, and the dashed arrows represent existing steps that are adapted in this research work.

An approach to obtain the data model directly from a set of interrelated business process models (arrow 1 in Figure 1) has been previously published in (Cruz et al., 2015b) and is revisited in chapter "Deriving a Data Model Directly from a Set of Business Process Models". An approach to obtain a complete use case model, aggregating a set of business process models (arrow 2 in Figure 1), has been published in (Cruz et al., 2014a, Cruz et al., 2015a). The approach is summarized in chapter "From Business Process Models to Use Case Models". An approach to generate the data model based on the previously obtained complete use case model (arrows 3 in Figure 1) has been published in (Cruz et al., 2016) and is briefly described in chapter "Deriving A Data Model from Logical Software Architecture". This approach, adapts and extends 4SRS. The 4SRS is an iterative method that incrementally verifies and validates the elicited requirements modeled as use cases, and creates a logical software architectural model (Machado et al., 2006).

The 4SRS has proved to be able to deal with complexity (Ferreira et al., 2012) and allows detecting and completing lacking information. The main contribution of this article is to present all the steps together, polishing some of the defined rules, and integrating them to capture the big picture of deriving the data model from an organization's BP models, compare the approaches and identify scenarios in which each of the approaches is more suitable than the other to apply.

The remainder of this article is structured as follows. The next section describes the direct approach for data model creation based on a set of BPs. The application of the presented approach is then illustrated through a demonstration case. The approach for generating a use case model aggregating a set of BPs is presented in the subsequent section. The following section describes how the 4SRS has been extended to be able to generate a data model based on the previously generated use case model, and then the approach is applied to a demonstration case. After that, the results are compared and analyzed, and related work is presented. Finally, some conclusions are drawn.

DERIVING A DATA MODEL DIRECTLY FROM A SET OF BUSINESS PROCESS MODELS

This section presents an approach to get the data model based on a set of interrelated BPs, modeled in the BPMN language.

During a business process execution, resources and/or data are used and produced. In fact, the information about the data that flows through the process is very important to the software development. The data received, send, created or used during a process execution can be represented by it message flows or data associations as shown in Table represented in Figure 2. Data that flows through a process are represented by *data objects*. Persistent data are represented by *data stores*. Persistent data are the ones

Figure 1. Main research phases

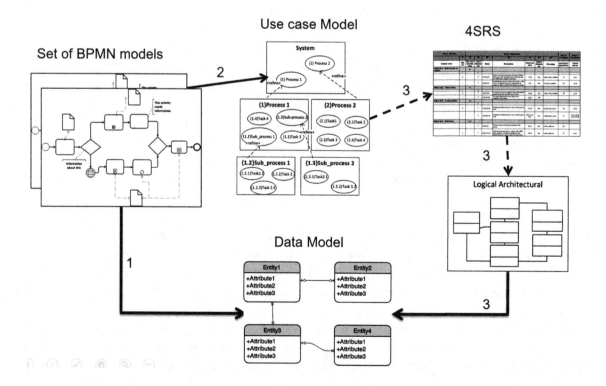

Figure 2. The data handling

Graphical representation	Description
Data store · · · Activity	The activity reads information from the data store.
Activity · · · Data store	The activity writes information in the data store.
· · · Activity	The activity receives a data object.
Activity · · ·	The activity sends a data object.
Partc 1 [Activity] / Prt Ext	The participant, during the activity execution, sends a message to an external participant.
Partc 1 [Activity] / Prt ext	The participant, during the activity execution, receives a message from an external participant.

that remain beyond the process life cycle, or after the process execution ends (OMG, 2011). The transfer of data, received, created or used during a process execution can be represented by *message flows* or *data associations*. A *message flow* connects two pools, representing the message exchange between two participants (OMG, 2011). *Data associations* connect activities to *data objects* or *data stores* (OMG, 2011).

In software development different models are usually used to represent different perspectives. The data model is one of the most important models for designing software applications, representing and organizing data, how it is stored and accessed, and the relationships among different entities.

To generate a data model, it is necessary to identify the entities, the relationship between entities and the entities attributes. An entity is something identifiable, or a concept in the real world that is important to the modeling purpose (Weske, 2012). The information, or the properties, about an entity are expressed through a set of attributes (Weske, 2012). A relationship between two entities is represented through an association between those entities (Chen, 1976). A relationship between two entities can be characterized according to two aspects, Cardinality and Optionality. Both terms are used to denote the number of attributes in a relation. Cardinality represents the maximum number of instances (one or many) of an entity in relation to another entity. Relationship optionality represents the minimum number of elements that exist on that side of the relationship. It may be 1 (the relation is mandatory) or 0 (the relation is not mandatory). In what concerns to cardinality, three types of relationships can be identified (Chen, 1976): mappings (1:n), (m:n) and (1:1).

A set of fourteen rules, summarized next, has been defined to systematically generate a data model from a set of business process models (Cruz et al., 2015b). The first group, constituted by five rules, identifies the data model entities:

R1: A data store, belonging to one of the selected business process models, is represented by an entity (with the same name) in the data model.

R2: Data stores with the same name, involved in several BPs, are represented by the same entity in the data model.

R3: Each participant involved in one of the selected business process models originates an entity in the data model.

R4: Participants with the same name will be represented by the same entity in the data model.

R5: Participants with the same name as data stores will be represented by the same entity in the data model.

Three rules have been created to identify the entities attributes. One to identify the attributes of the entities that represent the participants and another to identify the attributes of the entities that represent the data stores:

R6: A data store is an "*Item-Aware element*", so the data structure definition of these elements could be specified as a XML file (OMG, 2011). The definition of the structure will be used to identify each item that belongs to the data store. Each item identifies an attribute of the entity that represents the data store.

R7: The initial attributes of an entity that represents a participant (involved in one, or several BPs) are *id* and *name*.

R8: When an entity represents a participant and a data store, the entity will aggregate all the attributes.

The last group, constituted by six rules, identifies the relationships between entities. The relationships between entities are derived from the information exchanged between participants and the activities that store information in data stores and from the information that flows through the process. The rules are summarized next:

R9: When a participant is responsible for carrying out an activity that stores information in a data store, the entity that represents the participant must be related with the entity that represents the data store. Each participant can perform the same process (and the same activity) several times, so the relationship between the entity that represents the participant and the entity that represents the data store, by default, will be (1:n).

R10: When an activity that handles a data store, exchanges information with an External Participant (represented in another pool), the entity that represents the data store is related with the entity that represents the participant in the following situations:

- The activity receives information from the participant and writes information in a data store (see Figure 3 a)). In this case, it is assumed that the information stored is provided by the participant.
- The activity reads information from a data store and sends the information to an external participant (see Figure 3 b)). It is assumed that the read information is provided to the participant.
- The activity writes information in a data store and sends information to the participants. It is assumed that the same information is stored and sent to the participant (as for example a receipt or a certificate).

Figure 3. Exchanging information with external participants

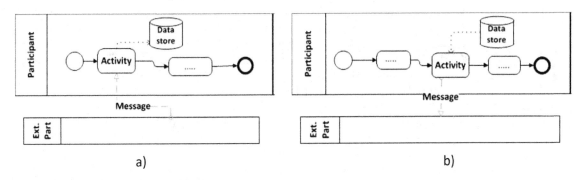

a)   b)

By default, the relationship type is (1:n) from the entity that represents the participant to the entity that represents the data store. The relationship is mandatory on the side of the entity that represents the participant because the activity always interacts with someone playing that role. On the side of the entity that represents the data store it is not mandatory, because this process may never be executed by a specific participant.

R11: When, during a process, an activity writes information in a data store and, in a same process, a previous activity (or the same activity) reads information from another data store (see Figure 4), it is assumed that the read and the written information are related. Consequently, the two entities (representing the two data stores) are related.

By default, the relationship type is (1:n) from the entity that represents the read data store to the entity that represents the written data store. By default, the relationship is mandatory on both sides. But, if the activity that writes information is performed after a merging gateway (not a parallel join) (Figure 5 a)), then the relationship is not mandatory on the side of the entity representing the read data store because the activity that reads the data store may not be executed. If the execution of the activity that writes the information depends on a condition, for example an exclusive decision gateway (see example in Figure 5 b)), then the relationship is not mandatory on the side of the entity representing the written data store.

R12: All relationships derived from the several business processes must be preserved in the data model.

Figure 4. Relating two data stores

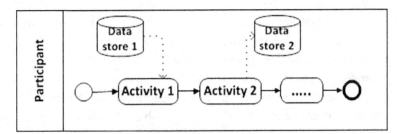

Figure 5. Exclusive gateway example

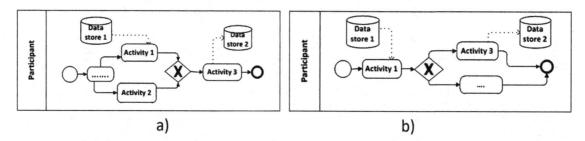

a)   b)

A data store may be manipulated by several activities belonging to distinct (or to the same) business processes, giving origin to different relationships. To prevent the loss of information all the relationships must be represented in the generated data model (for further evaluation).

R13: If, between two entities, there are different relationship types, the relationship type with higher cardinality prevails.

R14: If, between two entities, there are relationships with different mandatory types, the not mandatory type prevails.

Some of the derived relations are redundant, so the generated domain model needs to be analyzed by a software engineer to detect and eliminate redundant relations. The complete set of rules, details and explanations can be found in (Cruz, 2016).

Demonstration Case: Direct Approach

In this section, a well-known example of a School Library System is used as a demonstration case, where a group of five related business process models have been selected to be presented here. The selected BPs are: Register User (represented in Figure 5), Lend a Book (Figure 6), Reserve a Book (Figure 7), Renew a Loan (Figure 8) and Return a Book (Figure 9). The Return a Book business process model includes a sub-process, Penalty treatment, represented in Figure 10.

Analyzing the five BPs selected, it can be seen that the participants involved in all BPs are the same: Borrower and Attendant. The two corresponding entities, with the same name, must be represented in the resulting data model.

The data stores involved in the selected BPs are: Borrower, Book, Loan, Reservation and Receipt.

All identified entities (originated by participants and data stores) and the relationships identified in each process are presented in Table 1.

The resulting data model is shown in Figure 11. In this model the relations are represented according to Chen (1976) terminology. Focusing in one side of a relationship, and considering the optionality and cardinality together, there are the following combinations: 0 or 1 (represented as ⊶), 1 (represented as ⊣⊢), 0 to many (represented as ⊸⋖) and 1 to many (represented as ⊢⋖).

Analyzing the generated data model, it may be said that from a group of interrelated business process models, it is possible to generate a complete data model identifying all the entities involved, attributes and all the relationships between the entities. However, to obtain a complete data model, the business

Figure 6. Register User business process model

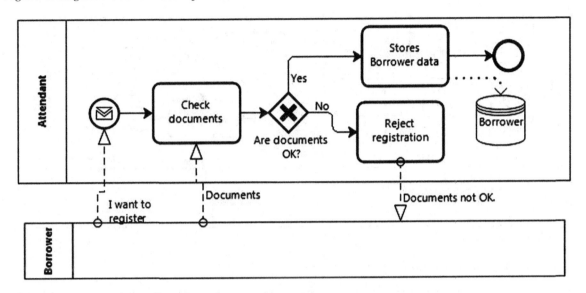

Figure 7. Lend a Book business process model

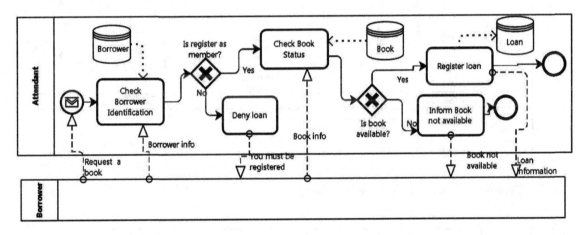

Figure 8. Reserve a Book business process model

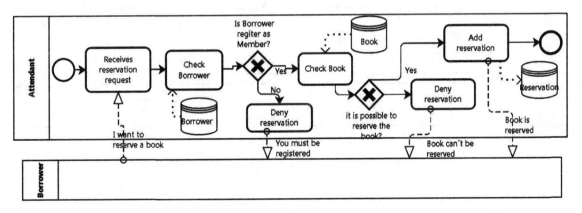

Figure 9. Renew a Loan business process model

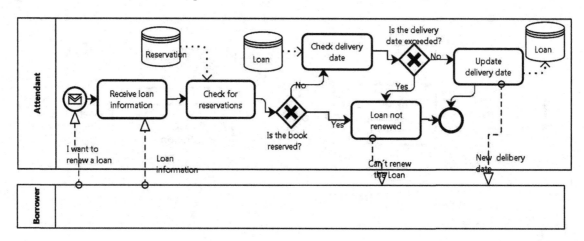

Figure 10. Return a Book business process model

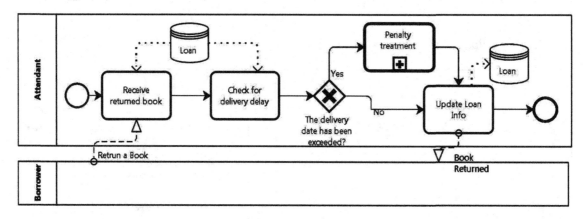

Figure 11. Penalty treatment business process model

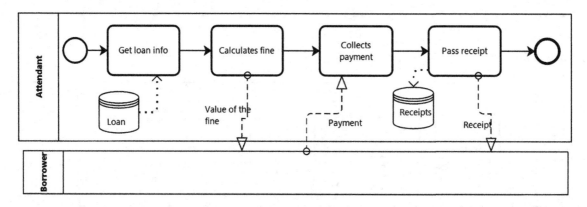

Table 1. Entities and relationships

Business Process	Entities	Relationship
Register User	Attendant, by R1 Borrower, by R5	Attendant-Borrower(1:n), by R9
Lend a Book	Attendant, by R1 Borrower, by R5 Book, by R2 Loan, by R3	Attendant-Loan(1:n), by R9 Borrower-Loan(1:n), by R10 Book-Loan(1:n), by R11
Reserve a Book	Attendant, by R1 Borrower, by R5 Book, by R3 Reservation, by R3	Attendant-Reservation(1:n), by R9 Borrower-Reservation(1:n), by R10 Book-Reservation(1:n), by R11
Renew a Loan	Attendant, by R1 Borrower, by R5 Loan, by R3 Reservation, by R3	Attendant-Loan(1:n), by R9 Borrower-Loan(1:n), by R10
Return a Book + Penalty treatment	Attendant, by R1 Borrower, by R5 Loan, by R3 Receipt, by R3	Attendant-Loan(1:n), by R9 Attendant-Receipt(1:n), by R9 Borrower-Receipt(1:n), by R10 Loan-Receipt(1:n), by R10

Figure 12. The resulting data model

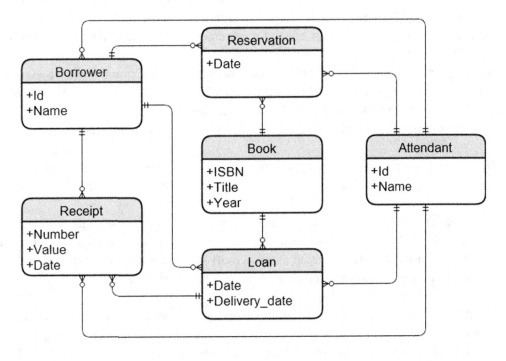

process model must contain all relevant information about data involved in the BPs including the identification of the persistent data.

The approach presented in this section allows getting a complete data model aggregating all the information about persistent data that can be extracted from a set of business process models, serving as a basis for the development of the software that will support the business.

The set of business processes internal to an organization usually complemented each other, meaning that the information written by one process is, most of the times, used in the same, or in another business processes. Consequently, joining all the existent information in the set of business processes it is possible to get a complete data model. However, to enable the ulterior obtainment of the data model, it is necessary that the business process modeling is made taking data into account, i.e. the modeler must monitor the data throughout the process. Moreover, it is necessary to identify the activities that write or make use of the information stored in the data store, and ensure that the roles responsible for performing those activities are identified.

The indirect approach, presented in the next section, starts by generating a use case model aggregating the information that exists in a set of BP models.

FROM BUSINESS PROCESS MODELS TO USE CASE MODELS

One of the most difficult, and crucial, activities in software development is the identification of system functional requirements. A popular way to capture and describe those requirements is through UML use case models. During system analysis, most of requirements information must be incorporated into use case descriptions.

This section proposes an approach to support the construction of use case models based on business process models emphasizing use cases descriptions, which are created using a set of predefined Natural Language (NL) sentences mapped from BPMN model elements.

The basic rules to obtain a use case diagram based in one business process model are:

- A BP activity gives rise to a use case (with the same name) in the use case diagram.
- A participant (represented by a pool) gives rise to an actor in the use case diagram, with the same name.
- The subdivision of a Pool (or Lane) into several lanes gives rise to a hierarchy of actors.
- The relationship between actors and use cases is derived from the participants (represented by the actor) responsible for the execution of the activity (represented by the use case) and from the exchange of information between an external participant and the activity.

Graphically a use case diagram is very simple, involving only actors and use cases (stickman's and ellipses with a brief description). A BPMN diagram is graphically more complex involving lots of graphical elements (activities, events, data stores, gateways, data objects, pools, messages, etc.). However, a use case model can represent as much information as a BPMN model, but most of the information must be embodied in use case descriptions. So, next subsection is specially focused on the generation of use case descriptions from the existent information in business process models.

Obtaining Use Case Descriptions

To describe a use case, a template, which is a simplification of the template presented by Cockburn in (Cockburn, 2001), has been defined. The proposed template is composed by six fields, which are named and described in Table 2.

The main elements involved in a process are participants (pools and lanes), activities, gateways, events, messages, data objects, data stores and artifacts (OMG, 2011). These elements are connected by connecting objects (sequence flow, message flow, associations and data associations). The approach being presented intends to transform business process elements, and their associated information, in a controlled set of sentences in NL.

Based on the existing information in a business process model it is possible to identify the use case name, the related actors and, depending on the incoming and outgoing connections, it is also possible to identify use case's pre-conditions, post-conditions, trigger and the main scenario.

To obtain the descriptions of a use case one will focus on the activity that is represented by the use case, and all incoming and outgoing connections must be reflected in the descriptions of the use case by creating a sentence that describes the connection main purpose. In BPMN, there are different connecting

Table 2. The template for describing use cases

Use case name	The use case name identifies the goal as a short active verb phrase.
Actors	List of actors involved in the use case.
Pre-Conditions	Conditions that must hold or represent things that happened before the use case starts.
Post-Conditions	Conditions that must hold at the conclusion of the use case.
Trigger	Event that starts the use case.
Scenario	Sequence of interactions describing what the system must do to move the process forward.

Figure 13. Incoming and outgoing connections of an activity

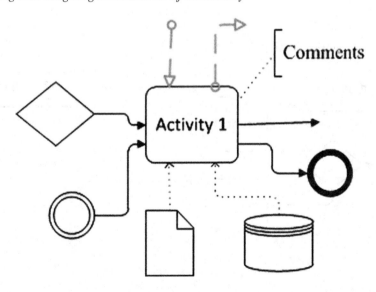

objects (see Figure 12), each one connects different objects, so it will originate different sentences in the use case descriptions (Cruz et al., 2014a).

Very briefly, the use case name is the name of the activity represented by the use case. The actors related to the use case are obtained from the participants involved in the activity represented by the use case. Preconditions are obtained from incoming connections from activity flows and from gateways. Post-conditions are obtained from the outgoing connections from the end or throwing events. Triggers are obtained from the connections coming from start and catching events. All other incoming connections give rise to a phrase that will be included in the use case scenario. As a consequence, several sentences may be included in the use case scenario. The sentences to be appended to the use case scenario must follow the next order: first, all incoming connections representing messages, associations, etc. received by the activity. Then all incoming data associations, representing data read by the activity. After that, all outgoing data associations, representing data written or sent by the activity. Finally, all outgoing connections representing messages, etc. sent by the activity.

Gateways are used to control how the process flows, by diverging (splitting gateways) and converging (merging gateways) sequence flows (see Figure 13). Splitting gateways have one incoming sequence flow and two or more outgoing sequence flows. Merging gateways have two or more incoming sequence flows and one outgoing sequence flow (OMG, 2011).

The gateway's outgoing sequence flows may have a Condition that allows to select alternative paths. Each outgoing sequence flow originates a sentence represented as a pre-condition in the use case description of the sequence flow target activity. The generated sentences are represented in Table represented in Figure 15.

Data associations are used to move data between data objects (or data stores) and activities (OMG, 2011). The sentences generated by data associations and associated data objects, or data stores, are represented in Table represented in Figure 16. The sentences will be appended to the scenario of the use case description of the use case representing the activity.

An event is something that happens during the course of a process and affects the process's flow (OMG, 2011). These events usually have a cause or produce an impact (OMG, 2011). In BPMN 2.0 there is a large number of event types, a general overview of the generic sentences originated in the use case template by the different events categories are presented in Table 3.

Figure 14. Splitting and merging gateways

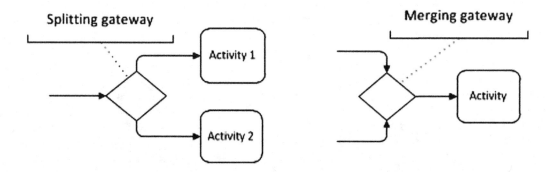

Figure 15. The use case pre-condition originated by gateways

Gateway	Graphical representation	Originated **Pre-condition.**
Exclusive Decision		The <gateway condition> is <sequence flow condition>.
Parallel splitting		The <source name> has been completed.
Inclusive Splitting		The <sequence flow condition> is true.
Complex Splitting		The <sequence flow condition> is true.
Exclusive merging		The <source name> [exclusive or <source2 name>] has been completed.
Parallel join		The <source name> [and < source2 name>] has been completed.
Inclusive merging		The <source name> [or <source2 name>] has been completed.
Complex merging		The <source name> [or <source2 name>] has been completed.

The events affect the sequence or the timing of the process's activities. There are three types of events: Start, Intermediate and End. Start events indicate where a process (or a sub-process) will start. End events indicate where a path of a process will end. Intermediate events indicate where something happens somewhere between the start and end of a process (OMG, 2011). Some events are prepared to catch triggers. These events are classified as catching events. Events that throw a result are classified as throwing *events* (OMG, 2011). All start events and some intermediate events are catching events (OMG, 2011). The sentence originated by a catching event is included as a trigger in the description of the use case that represents the activity that is started by the event. Catching events are represented as triggers because these events cause the start of the activity.

All End events and some Intermediate events are Throwing events (OMG, 2011). The sentences originated by the End and Throwing events are included as a post-condition in the description of the use case that represents the activity that throws the event. Throwing events are represented as a post-condition because the event is a consequence (or a result) of the activity execution.

Some events can also be classified as interrupting or non-interrupting events. Interrupting events stop its containing process whenever the event occurs. When Non-Interrupting events occur, its containing process is not interrupted (OMG, 2011). The sentences generated by Intermediate Interrupting events, are included in the use case scenario.

Figure 16. The use case sentences originated by Data Associations

Data	Graphical representation	Originated sentence in use case scenario.
Data Object as data association source	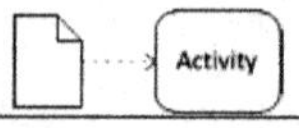	Receives <data object name>.
Data Object as data association target	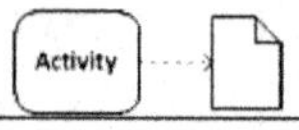	Sends <data object name>.
Data Input	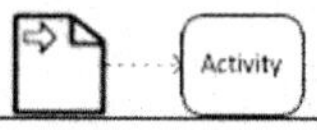	Receives <data object name>.
Data Input Collection (Input set)	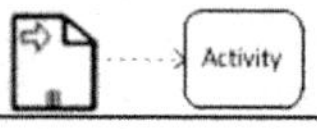	Receives a collection of <data object name>.
Data Output	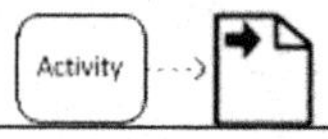	Sends <data object name>.
Data Output Collection (Output set)	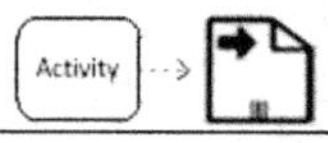	Sends a collection of <data object name>.
Data Store as data association source	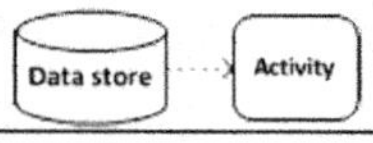	Reads information from <data store name>
Data Store as data association target	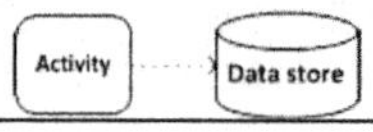	Writes information on <data store name>

Table 3. Generic sentences originated by events

Event type category	Generic sentence originated in use case template
Start	**Trigger:** The <event name - event definition > occurred.
Start (Sub-Process) Interrupting	**Trigger:** The event <event name – event definition > occurred.
Start (Sub-Process) Non-Interrupting	**Trigger:** The event <event name – event definition> occurred.
Intermediate Catching	**Trigger:** The <event name - event definition > is received.
Intermediate Boundary Interrupting	**Scenario:** If the <event name - event definition > occurs, the <activity name> is interrupted.
Intermediate Boundary Non-Interrupting	**Scenario:** The <event name - event definition > occurred.
Intermediate Throwing	**Post-condition:** The <event name – event definition > is created.
End	**Post-condition:** The <event name – event definition > is created. The process ends.

The identified categories are grouped in four tables to address differences that can exist between sentences generated by the events of these groups of categories. These tables, and others not presented in this document, can be found in (Cruz, 2016).

Next subsection presents an approach to aggregate in one use case model the information derived from a set of business process models.

Joining a Set of Business Process Models in One Use Case Model

The set of BPs, belonging to an organization, being supported by the software under development must be grouped in a single use case model because a software development team needs to understand the system context and scope before starting to plan and design a solution. For this reason, first it is needed to identify and specify which BPs are to be supported by the software under development.

A use case model can be created with a high abstraction level or low abstraction level (Cockburn, 2001). A use case model with a very detailed level can be much more useful to software development teams but, at the same time, it may become very complex and hard to understand.

The approach being presented in this section starts with high abstraction level use cases and ends with lower abstraction level use cases. To do that, the decomposition triangle approach, presented in (Cruz et al., 2014b), is being used. The decomposition triangle is an iterative and incremental approach that adopts a refinement mechanism to detail use cases, in a controlled way, to obtain a functional requirements model of the system to be designed. It is organized in several abstraction levels, starting with high abstraction level use cases and ending with lower abstraction level use cases (Cruz et al., 2014b).

When refining a use case, the use case is being decomposed in another use case model, decreasing the use cases abstraction level and, consequently, their ambiguity, by adding more details to them. The abstraction level decreases in every use case decomposition. When the abstraction level decreases, the use case description is enriched with details that may become useful for software development.

The approach starts by grouping all processes that will be supported by the software under development in one use case diagram, where each process is represented as a use case. Each use case is then refined and decomposed in a use case model (Cruz et al., 2015a). All identified use cases are numbered using the *tag=value* UML mechanism.

A generic scheme of applying the decomposition triangle is shown in Figure 14.

The approach organizes the use case models in different abstraction levels:

- **Level 0:** At this level, the system scope and frontier must be identified as well as all the actors involved, so the set of BPs that will be supported by the software under development must be identified. At this level all participants involved in the set of BPs are represented, as actors, in the actor's diagram (see Figure 17, level 0).
- **Level 1:** At this level, the first use case model is created with the highest abstraction level where each top level BP is transformed into a use case, in the use case model (a business use case) (see Figure 17, level 1). Each use case, representing a BP, is related with the corresponding actors representing the participants involved in the process. The use cases are numbered sequentially. The use case description is a general overview of the process it addresses.

Figure 17. A generic decomposition scheme

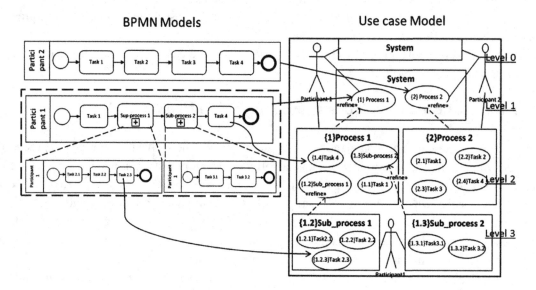

- **Level 2:** At this level, each process (represented as a use case in level 1) is mapped to a use case model. Basically, one activity from a BP is transformed into a use case and each participant is transformed into an actor. All incoming and outgoing connection flows from the activity originate a NL sentence in the description of the use case that represents the activity. Each generated use case model in level 2 refines and decomposes a corresponding use case in level 1 (see Figure 17, level 2).

- **Level (i+1), (i>=2):** At this level, each use case that represents a sub process in *level i* is decomposed and refined in a use case model in *level (i+1)* (see Figure 17, level 3). BPMN has two types of activities: a task (atomic activity) and a sub-process (OMG, 2011). A sub-process is a process, consequently the use case that represents the activity can be decomposed and mapped to another use case model. The decomposition ends when all use cases representing processes or sub-processes are decomposed and refined. In the presented approach, refining a use case means detailing all activities involved in the corresponding BP, including all resources and/or data that are consumed and produced, messages exchanged, decisions that must be taken, events that can occur, etc.

The decomposition results in a tree structure where the leaf nodes represent the tasks and the non-leaf nodes represent the processes and sub-processes. The decomposition tree has high abstraction level use cases at level 1. The abstraction level decreases in every use case decomposition. The approach allows to relate use cases belonging to different abstraction levels allowing to drill down and roll up between different abstraction levels. This way, the approach allows tracing back from requirements to the BP and from the BPs to the corresponding requirements.

This approach helps to ensure the alignment between business and software, and enables traceability between BPs and the corresponding elements in software models.

Demonstration Case: Getting Use Case Model From a Set of BPs

As a demonstration case, the same set of five interrelated BP models presented previously, is being used. The final use case decomposition tree, derived from those five BP from the Library Demonstration Case, is represented in Figure 18.

Looking the selected BPs one may see that *Borrower* and *Attendant* participants are involved in all BPs, each one giving origin to an actor in the use case model. So, the use case diagram level 0 (actors diagram) only has two actors represented (*Borrower* and *Attendant*), each one representing a participant.

In the use case diagram level 1, each of the selected BPs is represented as a use case connected with the actors that represent the corresponding participants. A set of five BPs has been selected, thus, five use cases are presented in use case diagram level 1. Each of these use cases, is then detailed in a use case model at level 2.

Analyzing, for instance, the Return a Book business process model (refer to Figure 10), one can see that the BP comprises five activities: Receive returned book, Search for book's active loan, Check for delivery delay, Update Loan Info and Penalty treatment, each one giving origin to a use case in the use case model that refines the Return a Book use case (level 2). The Penalty Treatment use case represents a sub-process (Figure 11), so it can be represented as a use case model in the next level (level 3), more refined and with greater detail.

Figure 18. A use case diagram of the library demonstration case

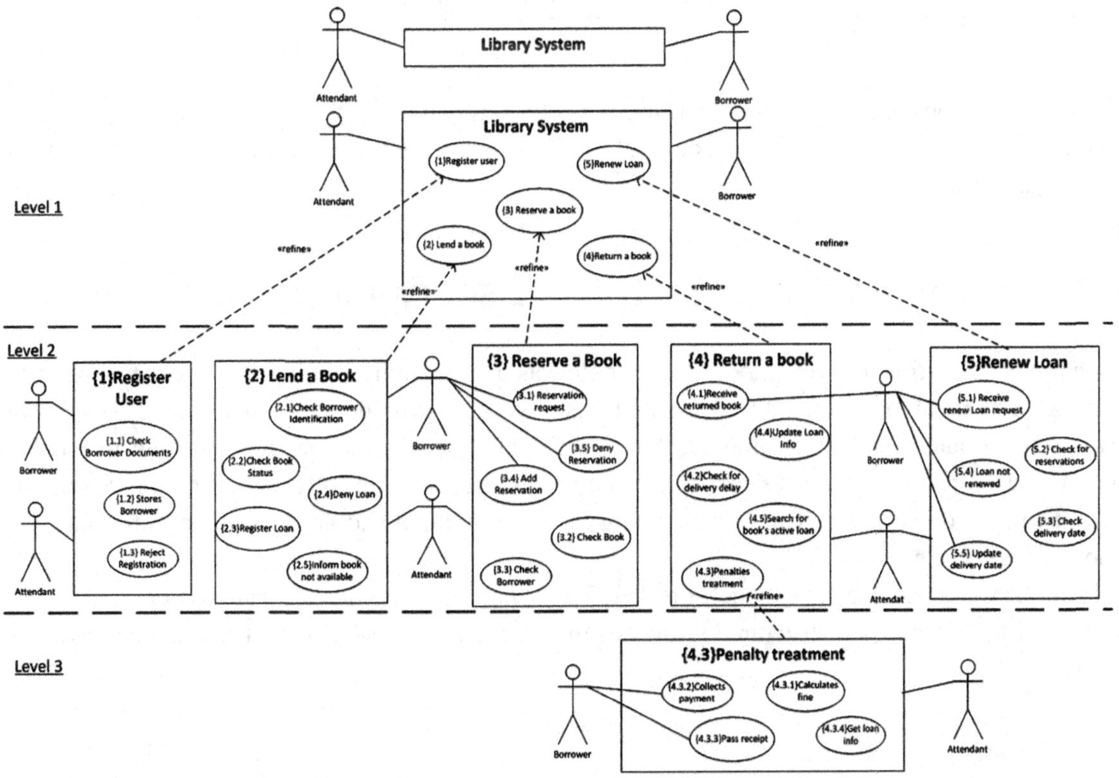

Table 4. Descriptions of the use cases

Use case name	Use case description
{U1.1} Check Borrower Documents	Actors: Borrower, Attendant Trigger: Borrower wants to register Scenario: Receives documents from \<Borrower\>.
{U1.2} Stores Borrower	Actors: Borrower, Attendant Pre-condition: Are Borrower documents OK? Is Yes. Scenario: Writes information on \<Borrower\>. Sends register confirmation to \<Borrower\>.
{U1.3} Reject Registration	Actors: Borrower, Attendant Pre-condition: Are documents OK? Is No. Scenario: Sends message documents not OK to \<Borrower\>.
{U2.1} Check Borrower Identification	Actors: Borrower, Attendant Trigger: The message \<requests a book\> arrives from \<Borrower\>. Scenario: Receives Borrower identification from \<Borrower\>. Reads information from \<Borrower\>.
{U2.2} Check Book status	Actors: Borrower, Attendant Pre-condition: Borrower is register as member? is yes. Scenario: Receives Book information from \<Borrower\>. Reads information from \<Book\>.
{U2.3} Register Loan	Actors: Borrower, Attendant Pre-condition: Is book available? is yes. Scenario: Writes information on \<Loan\>. Sends loan information to \<Borrower\>.
{U.2.4} Deny Loan	Actors: Borrower, Attendant Pre-condition: Borrower is register as member? is No. Scenario: Sends message you must be registered to \<Borrower\>.
{U2.5} Inform book not available	Actors: Borrower, Attendant Pre-condition: Is book available? is no. Scenario: Sends message book not available to \<Borrower\>.

The descriptions of the use cases representing activities belonging to the *Register User* and *Lend a Book* BPs are presented in Table 4, as example. The descriptions of the other use cases may be consulted in (Cruz, 2016).

DERIVING A DATA MODEL FROM LOGICAL SOFTWARE ARCHITECTURE

In the previous section, the decomposition triangle was used to aggregate in one use case model all the information that can be extracted from a set of business process models. The resulting use case model forms a functional requirements model, that is especially prepared to be used as input to the 4SRS approach. This resulting use case model may be represented as a tree structure. The 4SRS selects all leaves from the derived tree structure obtaining the most detailed and non-redundant information that is possible to obtain.

From the obtained use case model, the 4SRS will then generate the software logical architectural. To deal with the generated structured sentences the original 4SRS steps have been adapted as follows (Cruz, 2016):

- **Step 1:** Architectural elements identification - in this step, the original 4SRS method proposes the creation of three types of objects for each use case: interface, data and control (Machado et al., 2006). However, one can distinguish between persistent from non-persistent data, as it happens in the BPMN language (OMG, 2011). Following this idea, the 4SRS is adapted to distinguish persistent data from non-persistent data, by creating two different types of elements involving data: persistent data and volatile data. Each element is labeled with the name of the use case followed by the appropriate type: *i* (interface), *c* (control), *dp* (data persistent) and *dv* (data volatile).

- **Step 2:** Architectural elements elimination - based on the textual description of each use case, it is necessary to decide which ones of the four elements, created in step 1, must be maintained. This step allows detecting and eliminating redundancy in requirements.

- **Step 3:** Architectural elements aggregation and packaging - the architectural elements that remain after the elimination, and those in which it is possible and there is advantage in their unification, are aggregated.

- **Step 4:** Architectural elements association - associations must link the elements resulting from the aggregation based on use cases textual descriptions.

To define a persistent data model, one needs to identify the domain entities, their attributes, and the relationships between entities (Weske, 2012). Therefore, the 4SRS is extended with three additional steps, which are:

- **Step 5:** Entities creation - in this step, the entities involved in each use case are identified. Focusing on the *{-dp} architectural elements*, in the generated logical architecture, each read, written or updated element gives origin to an entity in the resulting data model.

- **Step 6:** Relationships identification - in this step, the relationship between the entities identified in step 5 are identified. When a *{-dp} – persistent data* element that stores information (write or update), is related with a *{-c} - control* element that verifies the information about another entity, one may conclude that the information stored is related with the information checked. Consequently, the entity that represents the written information is related with the entity that represents the checked (and read) information. The relationship is (1:n) from the entity that represents the information checked (previously written information) to the entity that represents the written information because the same information can be read several times and associated to different written information items. On the other hand, the information is stored only once.

- **Step 7:** Entity attributes identification - in this step, the attributes belonging to each entity are identified based on the attachments in BPMN data elements or messages or based on new information provided by stakeholders.

A Demonstration Case: Deriving a Data Model From Logical Software Architecture

Figure 16 illustrates the resulting logical software architecture from applying the 4SRS method to the use case model generated previously (Figure 15 and Table 4 - Descriptions of the use cases) based on the selected five business process models.

Figure 19. The resulting logical software architecture

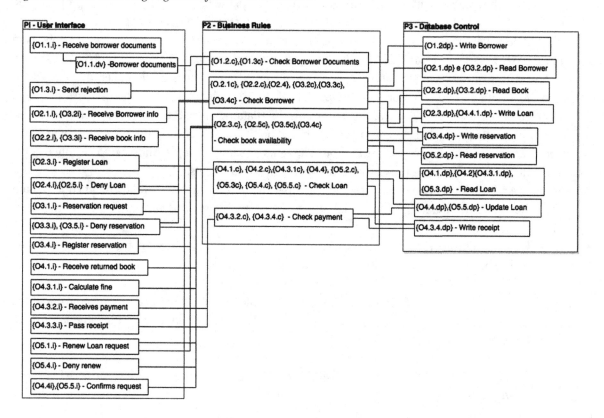

Analyzing the generated logical architecture, one may see that information about *Borrower*, *Book*, *Loan*, *Reservation* and *Receipt* is being written, so, by step 5, each one originates an entity in the data model.

Looking to the logical software architecture (Figure 19) one may see that the *Write Loan* is related with *Check Borrower* architectural element. Thus, by 6, *Loan* entity is related with the *Borrower* and the relationship is (1:n), mandatory on the Borrower side and not mandatory on the Loan side. The same happens with *Write reservation* element and *Check Borrower*, so *Reservation* entity is related with the *Borrower* and the relationship is (1:n), mandatory on the Borrower and not mandatory on the Reservation side.

The resulting data model is presented in Figure 20.

ANALYZING THE RESULTS

The BPMN most recent version has consolidated its importance as a business process modeling language and has become more complete allowing to distinguish persistent from non-persistent data (Aagesen & Krogstie, 2015). This enabled deriving the data model from business process models, which is the main goal of this research work. This has been achieved following two different approaches. A direct approach that derives a data model directly from the existing information in a set of interrelated business process models. And an indirect approach that uses the 4SRS method, which has been adapted to work with a use case model derived from a set of business process models and extended to derive a data model.

Figure 20. The resulting data model

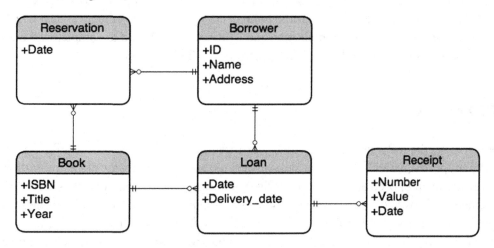

Comparing the data models obtained by applying the two presented approaches (Figure 12 and Figure 20), based on the same set of BPs (Figures from 6 to 11), one can see that they are very similar. Yet, the Attendant entity is only identified in the direct approach where it was identified as an entity because it represents a participant (rule R2). None of the BPs stores information about the Attendant, so it was not identified in the indirect approach (the 4SRS extended approach). It happens because the set of BPs selected to be used in the demonstrations cases is not complete. A BP representing the attendant registration is missing, similarly to what happens with borrower in BP *Register User*.

The two approaches can generate a complete data model including entities, entity attributes and the relationships between those entities, including cardinality and optionality. Still some differences may be pointed out between the two approaches.

Comparing the two presented approaches, one may say that the direct approach is automatable and easier to understand and apply, but it is totally dependent on the existing information in the BPMN models because the BPMN models are the only source of information. Consequently, the direct approach can generate correct and complete data models if the BPMN models are complete and correct. Otherwise, the correctness and completeness of the data model are not assured.

The indirect approach, which extends the 4SRS approach, is only partially automatable mostly because the derived software models need to be analyzed and validated by a software engineer, and the existing information on BPMN models may be complemented with information from other sources. The 4SRS extended approach generates not only the data model but also the use case model and the logical software architecture based on business process models, which can be used to the development of the software that will support the business. The generation of a use case model, including use cases descriptions, based on a set of business process models ensures the implementation of all requirements that come directly from the set of business process models.

Both approaches allow traceability from elements in software models to the BPs and from the BPs to the corresponding elements in software models. Nevertheless, using the 4SRS, the traceability between the software models and business process models may not be direct because of the information that can be provided by other sources.

For the reasons pointed before it may be concluded that the direct approach is suitable to deal with complete business process models, whereas the indirect approach is more suitable to deal with complex systems, being prepared to detect incomplete business process models and to complete the information derived from business process models with information from other sources.

RELATED WORK

It is recognized that the software that supports the business must be aligned with the BPs. Therefore, it is natural to try an approximation between business process modeling and software modeling. Following this idea, several authors proposed approaches to derive software models based in business process models.

The connection between use case models and BPs is studied in several ways. Some authors propose approaches to get use case models from business processes models, as is the case of (Rodríguez et al., 2007; Dijkman & Joosten, 2002). Others try to obtain a business process model from a use case model, as is the case of (Lubke et al., 2008).

Dijkman & Joosten (2002) propose an algorithm to derive a use case diagram from a business process model (using UML Activity Diagram).

Rodríguez et al. (2008) propose a systematic approach for obtaining the use case and class diagrams from the business process models using the UML activity diagram notation. The same authors also suggest an approach for the generation of a use case diagram based in one business process model using BPMN (Rodríguez et al., 2007).

Park et al. (2017) propose an approach to derive UCs representing the software requirements. The approach derives the functional and non-functional requirements (Park et al., 2017).

The importance of data in business process modeling is increasing, motivated by the need of controlling the BPs and the improvement of Business Analytics systems and technical BI (Business Intelligence), whose results are used by organizations to support and planning business (Meyer et al., 2011).

Data are not the focus of business process modelers. However, BPs involve lots of information that must be kept in a persistent manner. Thus, some authors try to obtain the data model based on one business process model. Almost all authors who worked with versions of BPMN prior to version 2.0 ended up proposing an extension to the BPMN to distinguish persistent data from non-persistent data, such as Brambilla et al. (2008) and Magnani & Montesi (2009).

Brdjanin et al. (2011) propose an approach to obtain a database design based on the information existing in a UML activity diagram. The authors propose a direct mapping of all business objects to the respective classes. Each participant is also mapped to a class. Associations between business objects and BP participants are based on the activities performed on those objects (Brdjanin et al., 2011). The same authors also propose an approach for the generation of a database model based on a collaborative BPMN diagram (Brdjanin et al., 2015). To do so, the authors defined a set of formal rules for the generation of the data model.

A. Leshob (2016) proposes an approach that generates a UML domain model from BP models written in BPMN. The approach is based on business patterns from REA (Resources, Events, Agents) ontology.

Most of the approaches cited before, generating software models from business process models, base their analysis in only one business process model. But, as said before, typically, in a real situation, a software product does not support only one process, but a reasonable set of processes. So, to generate useful software models, it is necessary to consider the complete set of business process that will be supported by the software product in development.

Regarding data, usually, interrelated BPs complement each other, meaning that the information written during the execution of one BP is, most of the times, used in another (or the same) BP. Therefore, working with a set of BPs, instead of one, allows to generate a much more complete data model and more resilient to error because if one miss the identification of an entity (or relationship) in one BP it may be identified in another BP.

The two approaches presented in this paper start by identifying the set of BPs that will be supported by the software under development, identifying the system scope. Based on those BPs, the approaches allow to generate the data model, a complete use case model (including use case descriptions) and the logical software architecture.

As mentioned previously, several approaches to obtain a use case diagram based on a business process model have been proposed, but, to our knowledge, there are no proposals to obtaining the use cases description. Nevertheless, the use cases descriptions are one of the most important components of the use case model (Cockburn, 2001). Moreover, without these descriptions most information present in a business process model would be lost when generating the use case diagram from business process models. Besides, none of the presented approaches aggregates in one use case model all information we have in a set of business process models defining this way the system scope and boundaries.

FUTURE RESEARCH DIRECTIONS

As future research, it is intended to create a model-driven approach to obtain a system's complete use case model including relations between use cases, and between these and the structural domain classes. The resulting integrated use case and domain models will then be transformed into the system's default abstract user interface model.

CONCLUSION

It is recognized that knowing business processes can help to ensure that the software under development will meet business needs.

By applying any of the approaches presented, one can collect all the information about persistent data involved in those BPs. The direct approach allows to obtain the data model solely based on existing information in a set of business process models.

Because some business process models have bad quality (incomplete, ambiguous, bad use of BPMN notation, etc.), and to deal with high complex systems, another approach to generate a data model from business process models has been proposed based on the 4SRS method. The 4SRS method has been adapted to deal with a use case model derived from a set of business process models. When necessary the generated use case model may be complemented with information from other sources allowing deriving a more complete data model. At this software development stage, the stakeholders are still involved in the process so they can provide useful information to complement the information provided by business process models.

To use the 4SRS, a use case model is needed. Thus, an approach to generate a use case model from a business process model is presented. The approach is focused on obtaining the descriptions of the use cases and uses a set of predefined sentences in NL.

The 4SRS method needs the intervention of an expert to analyze and validate the information provided by the set of BPMN models and the derived software models. If necessary, the information provided by the BPMN models may be complemented with information provided by other sources. Thus, the derived software models may be more complete and correct than the software models derived directly from a set of BPMN models, but, at the same time, it can involve much more work and it can be more time-consuming in implementing. Both approaches allow traceability from elements in software models to the business processes and from the business processes to the corresponding elements in software models.

The generation of a use case model, including use cases descriptions, based on a set of business process models ensures the implementation of all requirements that come directly from the process models.

The generated models are consistent with each other, meaning that the data entities referred to in the use case model are represented in the data model. This way, business and software modeling efforts can be joined together, reducing the analysis time and avoiding forgetting functional or data requirements.

REFERENCES

Aagesen, G., & Krogstie, J. (2015). BPMN 2.0 for modeling business processes. In Handbook on Business Process Management, International Handbooks on Information Systems (pp. 219-250). Springer Berlin Heidelberg.

Batoulis, K., Meyer, A., Bazhenova, E., Decker, G., & Weske, M. (2015). Extracting decision logic from process models. Advanced Information Systems Engineering, 9097, 349-366. doi:10.1007/978-3-319-19069-3_22

Brambilla, M., Preciado, J. C., Linaje, M., & Sanchez-Figueroa, F. (2008). Business process-based conceptual design of rich internet applications. *Web Engineering, International Conference on*, 155-161.

Brdjanin, D., Banjac, G., & Maric, S. (2015). Automated synthesis of initial conceptual database model based on collaborative business process model. In Bogdanova, A. M. and Gjorgjevikj, D. In I. C. T. Innovations (Ed.), *Advances in Intelligent Systems and Computing* (Vol. 311, pp. 145–156). Springer International Publishing.

Brdjanin, D., Maric, S., & Gunjic, D. (2011). Adbdesign: An approach to automated initial conceptual database design based on business activity diagrams. In Advances in Databases and Information Systems (pp. 117-131). Springer.

Chen, P. P.-S. (1976). The entity-relationship model toward a unified view of data. *ACM Transactions on Database Systems*, *1*(1), 9–36. doi:10.1145/320434.320440

Cockburn, A. (2001). *Writing Effective Use Cases*. Addison Wesley.

Cruz, E. F. (2016). *Derivation of data-driven software models from business process representations* (PhD Thesis). Universidade do Minho, Portugal.

Cruz, E. F., Machado, R. J., & Santos, M. Y. (2014a). From business process models to use case models: A systematic approach. Advances in Enterprise Engineering VIII, 174, 167-181. doi:10.1007/978-3-319-06505-2_12

Cruz, E. F., Machado, R. J., & Santos, M. Y. (2014b). On the decomposition of use cases for the refinement of software requirements. In *Computational Science and Its Applications (ICCSA), 2014 14th International Conference on* (pp. 237-240). IEEE Computer Society. 10.1109/ICCSA.2014.54

Cruz, E. F., Machado, R. J., & Santos, M. Y. (2015a). Bridging the Gap between a Set of Interrelated Business Process Models and Software Models. *Proceedings of the 17th International Conference on Enterprise Information Systems,* 338-345. 10.5220/0005378103380345

Cruz, E. F., Machado, R. J., & Santos, M. Y. (2015b). Deriving a Data Model from a Set of Interrelated Business Process Models. *Proceedings of the 17th International Conference on Enterprise Information Systems,* 49-59. 10.5220/0005366100490059

Cruz, E. F., Machado, R. J., & Santos, M. Y. (2016). Deriving software design models from a set of business processes. *4th International Conference on Model-Driven Engineering and Software Development,* 489-496. 10.5220/0005657204890496

Dijkman, R. M., & Joosten, S. M. (2002). An algorithm to derive use cases from business processes. In 6th ICSEA (pp. 679–684). Academic Press.

Ferreira, N., Santos, N., Machado, R. J., & Gasevic, D. (2012). Derivation of process-oriented logical architectures: An elicitation approach for cloud design. In *PROFES'2012*. Berlin: Springer-Verlag. doi:10.1007/978-3-642-31063-8_5

Jalote, P. (2008). *A concise Introduction to Software Engineering*. Springer Science & Business Media. doi:10.1007/978-1-84800-302-6

Kocbek, M., Jost, G., Hericko, M., & Polancic, G. (2015). Business process model and notation: The current state of affairs. *Computer Science and Information Systems, 1*(00), 1–35.

Leshob, A. (2016). Towards a business-pattern approach for UML models derivation from business process models. *13th IEEE International Conference on e-Business Engineering,* 244-249. 10.1109/ICEBE.2016.049

Lubke, D., Schneider, K., & Weidlich, M. (2008). Visualizing use case sets as BPMN processes. In *Requirements Engineering Visualization* (pp. 21–25). IEEE. doi:10.1109/REV.2008.8

Machado, R., Fernandes, J. a., Monteiro, P., & Rodrigues, H. (2006). Refinement of software architectures by recursive model transformations. In Product-Focused Software Process Improvement (pp. 422-428). Springer Berlin Heidelberg. doi:10.1007/11767718_38

Magnani, M. & Montesi, D. (2009). *BPDMN: A conservative extension of BPMN with enhanced data representation capabilities.* arXiv preprintarXiv:0907.1978

Meyer, A., Smirnov, S., & Weske, M. (2011). *Data in business processes*. Universitatsverlag Potsdam.

OMG. (2011). *Business process model and notation (BPMN), version 2.0. Technical report.* Object Management Group.

Park, G., Fellir, F., Hong, J.-E., Garrido, J. L., Noguera, M., & Chung, L. (2017). Deriving use cases from business processes: A goal-oriented transformational approach. *Proceedings of the Symposium on Applied Computing, SAC '17*, 1288–1295. 10.1145/3019612.3019789

Rodríguez, A., Fernández-Medina, E., & Piattini, M. (2007). Towards CIM to PIM transformation: From secure business processes defined in BPMN to use-cases. Business Process Management, 408-415.

Rodríguez, A., Fernández-Medina, E., & Piattini, M. (2008). Towards obtaining analysis-level class and use case diagrams from business process models. In *Advances in Conceptual Modeling Challenges and Opportunities* (Vol. 5232, pp. 103–112). Springer Berlin Heidelberg.

Schmiedel, T., & vom Brocke, J. (2015). Business process management: Potentials and challenges of driving innovation. In BPM - Driving Innovation in a Digital World, Management for Professionals (pp. 3-15). Springer International Publishing.

van der Aalst, W. (2015). Business process simulation survival guide. In Handbook on Business Process Management 1, International Handbooks on Information Systems (pp. 337-370). Springer Berlin Heidelberg. doi:10.1007/978-3-642-45100-3_15

Weske, M. (2012). *Business Process Management Concepts, Languages, Architectures.* Springer Science & Business Media.

Chapter 9
Improving Application Integration by Combining Services and Resources

José Carlos Martins Delgado
University of Lisbon, Portugal

ABSTRACT

The main application integration approaches, the service-oriented architecture (SOA) and representational state transfer (REST) architectural styles, are rather different in their modeling paradigm, forcing application developers to choose between one and the other. In addition, both introduce more application coupling than required, since data schemas need to be common, even if not all instantiations of those schemas are used. This chapter contends that it is possible to improve this scenario by conceiving a new architectural style, structural services, which combines services and resources to reduce the semantic gap with the applications, allowing to tune the application integration between pure service-based and pure resource-based, or an intermediate mix. Unlike REST, resources are not constrained to offer a fixed set of operations, and unlike SOA, services are allowed to have structure. In addition, compliance is used to reduce coupling to the bare minimum required by the actually used application features.

INTRODUCTION

The world is increasingly distributed and most real case scenarios involve interaction between distributed applications that need to cooperate to achieve common or complementary goals. Examples of such scenarios include:

- Enterprise-class applications (Romero, & Vernadat, 2016), deployed on either conventional or cloud computing platforms (Ritter, May, & Rinderle-Ma, 2017), most likely including hybrid clouds, integrating the enterprise's owned infrastructure with one or more public clouds.

DOI: 10.4018/978-1-5225-7271-8.ch009

- Mobile cloud computing (Abolfazli, Sanaei, Sanaei, Shojafar, & Gani, 2016), particularly given the ever-increasing pervasiveness of smartphones and tablets that created a surge in the BYOD (Bring Your Own Device) tendency (Weeger, Wang, & Gewald, 2016).
- The Internet of Things (Botta, de Donato, Persico, & Pescapé, 2016), with an explosive development rate that raises the need to integrate software applications with the physical world, including sensor networks (Iyengar & Brooks, 2016). Al-Fuqaha, Guizani, Mohammadi, Aledhari, and Ayyash (2015) provide estimates that indicate that the number of Internet-capable, autonomous devices greatly outnumber human-operated devices, which means that the Internet is no longer dominated by human users, but rather by small computer-based devices that require technologies adequate to them, rather than to full-fledged servers.

The world is also increasingly dependent on computers, generating and exchanging more and more data, either at business, personal, or sensor levels. This raises the integration problem to a completely new level, in which conventional integration technologies (such as HTTP, XML, JSON, Web Services, and RESTful APIs) expose their limitations. These technologies were conceived initially for human interaction, with text as the main format and subsecond time scales, not for heavy-duty, machine-level binary data exchange. These new integration problems need new solutions.

Integration (Panetto & Whitman, 2016) can be broadly defined as the act of instantiating a given method to design or adapt two or more systems, so that they cooperate and accomplish one or more common goals. What these words really mean depends largely on the domain to which the systems belong, although there is a pervasive, underlying notion that these systems are active and reacting upon stimuli sent by others, in order to accomplish higher-level goals than those achievable by each single system.

To interact, applications must be interoperable, i.e., able to meaningfully operate together. *Interoperability* (Agostinho, Ducq, Zacharewicz, Sarraipa, Lampathaki, Poler, & Jardim-Goncalves, 2016) is a characteristic that relates systems with this ability and is defined by the 24765 standard (ISO, 2010) as the ability of two or more systems or components to exchange information and to use the information that has been exchanged. This means that merely exchanging information is not enough. Interacting systems must also be able to understand it and to react according to each other's expectations.

Interoperability is distinct from integration. Interoperability is a necessary but not sufficient condition for integration, which must realize the potential provided by interoperability. This is an inherently hard problem, since system interaction occurs at several levels of detail, from very low level (physical communication) to very high level (such as the purpose of the interacting parties to engage in an interaction).

Another problem is *coupling* (Bidve, & Sarasu, 2016), which provides an indication of how much applications are intertwined.

Interoperability and coupling are two facets of the same problem, application integration, and reflect two unfortunately conflicting goals:

- **Interoperability:** Applications need to interact to accomplish collaboration. This necessarily entails some form of mutual knowledge and understanding, but creates dependencies that may hamper the evolution (changes) of these applications.
- **Decoupling:** Applications should not have dependencies on others, in order to be able to evolve freely and dynamically. Unfortunately, independent applications do not understand each other and are not able to interact, which means that some form of coupling is unavoidable to achieve interoperability.

Therefore, the *fundamental problem of integration* is how to provide (at most) the minimum coupling possible while ensuring (at least) the minimum interoperability requirements (Delgado, 2016). This means that the main goal is to ensure that each interacting application knows just enough about the others to be able to interoperate with them but no more than that, to avoid unnecessary dependencies and constraints. This is an instance of the *principle of least knowledge* (Hendricksen, 2014).

Historically, interoperability has been the main goal in Web-based distributed systems, whereas coupling has been one of the top concerns in software engineering, when developing an application, along with other metrics such as *cohesion* (Candela, Bavota, Russo, & Oliveto, 2016).

Software development methods emphasize decoupling, changeability and agility, which means structuring modules of an application so that a change somewhere affects the remaining modules as little as possible and can be implemented in a very short time. Interoperability between modules of a local application is the easy part. Type names and inheritance are shared and there is usually a single programming language.

The interaction between distributed applications is completely different. Interoperability is hard, since these applications are developed, compiled, and linked independently. Most likely, this means different type names, inheritance hierarchies, programming languages, execution platforms, and data formats. Coupling is of paramount importance but has been treated as a side issue in distributed contexts, a best-effort endeavor after achieving the primary goal, interoperability.

The two most used integration approaches, Software-Oriented Architecture (SOA) (Erl, Merson, & Stoffers, 2017) and Representational State Transfer (REST) (Fielding, Taylor, Erenkrantz, Gorlick, Whitehead, Khare, & Oreizy, 2017) hardly comply with the principle of least knowledge. They achieve interoperability but do not solve the coupling problem, since they require that the messages' data schemas used by the interacting applications are the same.

In addition, they use different modeling paradigms, since SOA is guided by behavior (services), whereas REST is guided by state (resources). SOA defines which application types are used and establishes the set of operations provided by each, whereas REST starts with a state diagram, without relevant concern about distinguishing which state belongs to which application.

This chapter revisits the integration problem with an open mind, without being restricted *a priori* by specific technologies, such as Web Services (Zimmermann, Tomlinson, & Peuser, 2012) for SOA and RESTful APIs (Pautasso, 2014) for REST. The only assumption is that there are applications that need to interact, by using messages. The main goal is to propose and describe a new architectural style, Structural Services, which combines the best characteristics of the SOA and REST styles. On the one hand, services have a user-defined interface that can be published, discovered and used. On the other hand, services are implemented by resources, which have structure (composed of other resources). Operations are first class resources and messages are themselves resources, able to include references to other resources. As a result, applications can be designed purely in SOA or REST styles, or as a tunable mix of the two, according to the needs of the application.

The rest of the chapter is structured as follows. It starts by describing the architectural styles that are most relevant to application integration, analyzing SOA and REST in particular. Then, it discusses how application integration can be improved over existing technologies, namely by reducing the semantic gap (tuning the architectural style to better suit the style of the applications) and by reducing coupling with compliance (requiring compatibility only on the features actually used, instead of having to share data schemas). An architectural style that supports these improvements, Structural Services, is then presented and proposed. An example of a service description language to support this architectural style is also presented. Finally, the chapter lays down the lines of future research and draws some conclusions.

BACKGROUND

Interoperability and low coupling need to be combined to achieve an effective cooperation in the integration of distributed applications. These issues have been studied in many domains, such as enterprise cooperation (Popplewell, 2014; Rezaei, Chiew, & Lee, 2014), e-government services (Sharma & Panigrahi, 2015), military operations (Hussain, Mehmood, Haq, Alnafjan, & Alghamdi, 2014), cloud computing (Zhang, Wu, & Cheung, 2013), healthcare applications (Robkin, Weininger, Preciado, & Goldman, 2015), digital libraries (Agosti, Ferro, & Silvello, 2016) and metadata (Chen, 2015).

The two main technological solutions for distributed interoperability, Web Services (Zimmermann, Tomlinson, & Peuser, 2012) and RESTful APIs (Pautasso, 2014), are based on data description languages such as XML (Fawcett, Ayers, & Quin, 2012) and JSON (Bassett, 2015). Although they have achieved the basic objective of interconnecting independent and heterogeneous systems, supporting distributed application interoperability, they are not effective solutions from the point of view of coupling.

There has been a continuing debate over which architectural style, SOA (Erl, Merson, & Stoffers, 2017) or REST (Fielding, Taylor, Erenkrantz, Gorlick, Whitehead, Khare, & Oreizy, 2017), is more adequate for specific classes of applications. The literature on this subject is vast (Bora & Bezboruah, 2015; Kumari & Rath, 2015), usually with arguments more on technology grounds than on conceptual and modeling issues. There are also several proposals to integrate SOA and RESTful services (Dahiya, & Parmar, 2014; Sungkur, & Daiboo, 2015; Sungkur, & Daiboo, 2016; Thakar, Tiwari, & Varma, 2016).

XML-based interoperability, essential for Web Services, assumes that both interacting applications share the same schema, namely in WSDL documents (Zimmermann, Tomlinson, & Peuser, 2012) and other data schemas. XML Schema and other schema languages are complex enough to award additional coupling concerns. Changing a schema affects all applications that use it, both servers and clients, entailing a significant coupling and reducing changeability.

Applications based on RESTful APIs follow the REST architectural style, developed by Fielding (2000), who claims that this style reduces coupling because the client does not depend on the server's specification, since all it needs to do is to traverse the structured data representation of the server, by following its links (URIs). A change in a server can imply changes in the data structured returned but, as long as the data schema remains the same, the client will still be able to traverse it without modification. However, this decoupling is limited to protocol and data syntax. The interacting applications still depend on the shared knowledge about the data schema, not to mention higher-level semantics and assumed behavior.

Several metrics have been proposed to assess the maintainability of service-based distributed applications, based essentially on structural features, namely for service coupling, cohesion and complexity (Babu, & Darsi, 2013). Other approaches focus on dynamic coupling, rather than static, with metrics for assessing coupling during program execution (Geetika, & Singh, 2014). There are also approaches trying to combine structural coupling and other levels of coupling, such as semantics (Alenezi, & Magel, 2014).

Compliance (Tran, Zdun, Oberortner, Mulo, & Dustdar, 2012) is a concept that can be used as the foundation mechanism to ensure partial interoperability and thus minimize coupling. It has been studied in specific contexts, such as choreography (Capel & Mendoza, 2014), modeling (Brandt & Hermann, 2013), programming (Preidel & Borrmann, 2016), and standards (Graydon, Habli, Hawkins, Kelly, & Knight, 2012).

ARCHITECTURAL STYLES FOR APPLICATION INTEGRATION

The Most Relevant Architectural Styles

An architectural style can be defined as a collection of design patterns, guidelines, and best practices to design the architecture of a system (Sharma, Kumar, & Agarwal, 2015), introducing specific characteristics and constraints. Each architectural style has an underlying modeling paradigm, which serves as a guiding tenet.

Table 1 illustrates the main characteristics of several of the most relevant architectural styles for application integration scenarios.

SOA is essentially the extension of the object-oriented paradigm to the distributed application world, whereas REST extends the WWW paradigm (e.g., client-server stateless interaction, fixed set of server operations) to generic distributed application integration. The Process architectural style models behavior as processes, which orchestrate the invocation of services (implemented using either SOA or REST), typically using Business Process Modeling Notation (BPMN) (Chinosi & Trombetta, 2012).

SOA is easy to grasp, since it constitutes a natural evolution of the object-oriented style, with which analysts and programmers are already familiar. However, its Web Services instantiation, with WSDL, XML Schema and SOAP, is complex to use, especially without adequate tools that usually automate and hide most of the development process.

Table 1. Main characteristics of the most relevant architectural styles for application integration

Style	Brief Description	Examples of Characteristics or Constraints
Object-Oriented	• Applications follow the Object-Oriented paradigm.	• Application modules are modeled as classes. • References are pointers. • Reactions discretized into operations. • Polymorphism based on inheritance.
Distributed	• Interacting applications have independent lifecycles.	• References are global links, not local pointers. • Type checking cannot be name-based. • Different applications may use different technologies.
SOA	• Style similar to Object-Oriented, but with distributed constraints.	• Services (interfaces of applications) have no structure. • Each application has its own interface. • No polymorphism. • Integration based on common schemas and ontologies.
Process	• Behavior modeled as orchestrations and choreographies.	• Services are the units of behavior. • A process is an orchestration of services. • Processes must obey the rules of choreographies.
REST	• Resources have structure but a fixed service.	• Clear distinction of the client and server roles. • Resources have a common set of operations. • Stateless interactions.

REST can be comparatively harder to master at first, in particular for people with an object-oriented mindset, who tend to slide to the probably more familiar RPC (Remote Procedure Call) style (Kukreja & Garg, 2014), with operation parameters instead of dynamic resource references, something long criticized by Fielding (2008), the original proponent of REST. On the other hand, its instantiation with HTTP is relatively straightforward to use, even without elaborate tools, since what is involved is essentially plain HTTP messaging.

The motivations behind the appearance of each style can be described in the following way:

- SOA appeared in the context of enterprise integration, with the main goal of achieving interoperability between existing enterprise applications with the then emerging XML-based technologies, more universal than those used in previous attempts, such as CORBA (Common Object Request Broker Architecture) (Henning, 2008) and RPC (Kukreja & Garg, 2014). It was a natural evolution of the object-oriented style, now in a distributed environment and with large-grained resources to integrate. Therefore, the emphasis was put on modeling applications as black boxes, exposing their external functionality with an interface composed of an application-dependent set of operations. Internal structure was avoided, as a measure to reduce coupling by applying the information hiding principle.

- REST appeared in the context of Web applications, as a systematization of the underlying model of the Web and with scalability as the most relevant goal, since interoperability had already been solved by XML (and, later, JSON) and HTTP. As originally proposed by Fielding (2000), REST is based on six constraints. The most relevant are stateless interactions (only the client maintains the interaction state) and uniform interface (all resources have a service with the same set of operations, with variability on structure rather than on service interface). These constraints have decoupling as their main motivation, to support scalability. When potentially thousands of clients connect to a server, server applications need to scale and to evolve as needed and as independently as possible from the clients.

SOA is guided by behavior and REST by representation of state. In the Unified Modeling Language (UML) terminology (Dennis, Wixom, & Tegarden, 2015), modeling with SOA favors a static class diagram, to specify which services are used and the set of operations provided by each, and a sequence diagram to specify their interactions along time. On the other hand, REST interactions can be modeled by a state diagram, without relevant concern about distinguishing which state belongs to which resource.

SOA hides service structure, considering it part of the implementation, whereas REST hides resource behavior (its service) by converting it into resource structure, since each operation is modeled as a resource.

SOA tries to minimize the semantic gap (Sikos, 2017) by modeling services as close as possible to real world entities. Since these are different from each other, offering a specific set of functionalities, the result is a set of services with different sets of operations. The client must know the specific interface of the server. This entails coupling and may only be acceptable if the number of clients for a given server is usually reasonably small and the system evolves slowly, in order to limit the maintenance effort.

The interface coupling is precisely what REST tries to avoid, with a simple guideline: to decompose complex resources into smaller ones (with links to other resources), until they are so primitive and/or atomic that they can all be treated in the same way, with a common interface. The initial complexity is transferred to the richness of the structure of the links between resources. The most distinguishing feature of REST is this uniform interface for all resources, with a common set of operations. This corresponds to separating the mechanism of traversing a graph (the links between resources) from the treatment of each node (resource). The overall idea is that a universal link follow-up mechanism coupled with a universal resource interface leads to decoupling between clients and servers, allowing servers to change what they send back to the clients because they will adapt automatically, by just navigating the structure and following the links to progress in the interaction process.

Unfortunately, both SOA and REST have fallacies and limitations (Delgado, 2016):

- SOA assumes that all services are at the same level and that exposing services is just providing some interface and the respective endpoint. The fallacy is to assert that structure is unimportant. This may be true when integrating very large-grained resources, but not in many applications that include lists of resources that need to expose their services individually. The limitation is in changeability. Changing the interface of the server will most likely require changes in the clients as well.
- REST imposes a uniform interface, which allows treating all the resources in the same way. The fallacy is to consider only a syntactic interface, or even semantic (Verborgh, Harth, Maleshkova, Stadtmüller, Steiner, Taheriyan, & Van de Walle, 2014), but forgetting about the behavior abstraction level. The reaction of resources need to be considered, which means that following a link cannot be done blindly. The client needs to know which kind of reaction the server is going to have and which kind (or type) of answer it may expect. In the same way, traversing a structured resource implies knowing the type of that resource, otherwise which link should be followed next may not be known. Since there is no declaration of resource types, all types of resources to be used must be known in advance, either standardized or previously agreed upon (with custom media types). This is a relevant limitation of REST. However, developers are more than happy to agree on simple resource structures and on an aligned API to match. REST advocates contend that an API should be represented simply by its initial link (an URI – Universal Resource Identifier, for example) and all the functionality should be dynamically discovered by the client by exploring links. This can only be done with a set of fixed resource types (predefined or previously agreed upon). A good advantage of REST is that resource structure can vary, but only within the boundaries of resource types known in advance.

SOA is a good option for large-grained, slowly evolving complex services. REST is a good option for small-grained, structured resources that are relatively simple. In search for simplicity and maintainability, many companies have stopped using SOA APIs in favor of REST, by modeling operations as resources, using naturally occurring lists of resources as structured resources with links, and dynamically building URIs instead of resorting to operation parameters. However, decoupling in REST is not as good as its structure dynamicity seems to indicate. All the resource types (media types) must be known in advance and the client may break if a new media type unknown to the client is returned by the server. In addition, even when the type is known, the client cannot invent what to do and which link to choose when it receives a resource representation of a given type. Collaboration requires that both server and client implement behavior and deal with its effects, which means that they cannot be completely agnostic of each other. Data schema coupling is still there.

Figure 1. An example of business-level distributed interactions

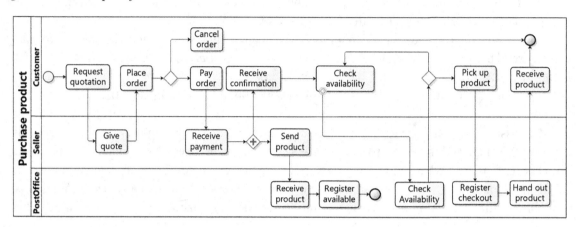

An Example of the SOA-REST Dichotomy

To illustrate the basic dichotomy between SOA and REST, Figure 1 describes a typical online product purchase scenario, using BPMN (Chinosi & Trombetta, 2012) to show the interactions between a customer, a seller, and a post office, which delivers the product.

In this example, a customer wants to buy a product from a seller company, which delivers it by post. To obtain a cheaper transportation cost, the customer chooses to pick up the parcel with the product at the local post office instead of having it delivered at home. The customer first requests a quotation, then places an order and pays it, with the option of canceling that order. The customer then polls the mailbox periodically to check for a notification of arrival and, when it happens, picks up the parcel from the post office.

The interactions between these three actors is illustrated by Figure 2, which depicts the UML sequence diagram corresponding to Figure 1.

This simple example can be modeled both in SOA and REST style, as depicted by Figure 3a and 3b, respectively. For simplicity, only the customer is illustrated in Figure 3b. Essentially, SOA is a behavior-first approach (by designing classes and methods), with state as a byproduct of the execution of a given behavior. REST is a state-first approach, in which activities consist basically of determining to which state the system should transition next.

SOA is guided by behavior and REST by state. In UML terminology, SOA uses a class diagram (Figure 3a) as a first approach, to specify which resource types are used and to establish the set of operations provided by each, whereas REST starts with a state diagram (Figure 3b), without relevant concern about distinguishing which state belongs to which resource. In the end, they perform the same activities and go through the same states. This should not be a surprise since, after all, the original problem described by Figures 1 and 2 is the same in both approaches.

REST may seem more flexible, in the sense that if the server changes the links it sends in the responses, the client will follow this change automatically by using the new links. The problem, however, is that this is not as general as it may seem, since the client must be able to understand the structure of the responses. It is not merely a question of following all the links in a response. To achieve this, REST imposes the constraint that returned representations use standardized or pre-agreed media types. More-

Figure 2. A sequence diagram illustrating the interactions between the actors

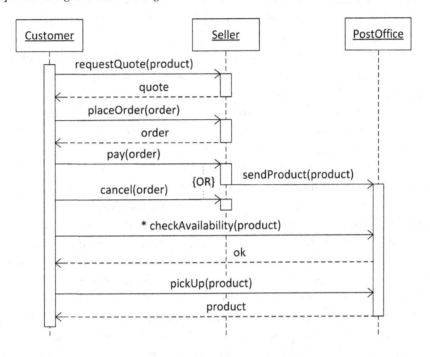

Figure 3. Modeling this example in SOA (a) and REST (b) styles

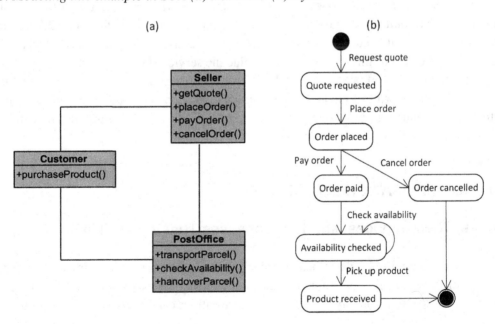

over, just stating the data syntax (using languages such as XML or JSON) is not enough. The semantics and the actual set of names used (the schema, in fact) must be known by both client and server. This is why REST does not entail less coupling than SOA.

What REST indeed does is to trade interface variability for structure variability, something that SOA lacks. REST cleanly separates the mechanism of traversing a graph from the processing of individual node graphs (Meyer, 2000). Therefore, varying the structure allows changing the overall behavior without affecting the traversal mechanism. However, this requires that all nodes are treated alike, which means that all nodes must have the same interface. This implies decomposing the SOA-style objects into its most elementary components and treat them all as first-class resources, which in turn leads to a state diagram programming style, such as the one in Figure 3b.

The main problem with this is that the model is no longer guided by the static entities of the problem, in an object-oriented fashion, but rather by state, as an automaton. Most people will find it harder to model state transitions than static entities (classes). This is not a problem for simpler applications that can be organized in a CRUD (Create, Read, Update, Delete) approach, a natural method when structured state is the guiding concept. However, for more complex applications, in which behavior and information hiding (including state) are the most relevant factors, it is a different issue.

It turns out that many applications are simple and the technologies typically used to implement REST are simpler, lighter, and in many cases cheaper than those used to implement SOA (namely, SOAP Web Services), which justifies the growing popularity of RESTful applications and their APIs. The level of resource coupling in REST, however, is not lower than that of service coupling in SOA, since both require that the schemas (media types) used are known by both interacting parties.

It should also be noted that SOA lacks support for structured resources. Services (the set of operations supported by a resource) have just one level, offering operations but hiding any internal structured state. Structure is a natural occurrence in most problem domains and in this respect REST is a better match. Therefore, the goal of this chapter is to combine the service flexibility of SOA (which provides a low semantic gap in terms of behavior modeling) and the structural flexibility of REST (which leads to a low semantic gap in terms of modeling structural composition and state). This chapter proposes to achieve this goal by unifying the service and resource concepts in the Structural Services architectural style, described below.

IMPROVING APPLICATION INTEGRATION

Resources, Their Services, and the Processes That Invoke Them

The last three architectural styles described by Table 1 embody the basic entities involved in application interaction, namely resources (applications and their components), services (the functionality they offer), and processes (flows of functionality invocations). These entities can be described in the following way:

- A *resource* is an entity that embodies a meaningful, complete, and discrete concept, makes sense by itself and can be distinguished from, although able to interact with, other entities. Resources are the main modeling entities and should express, as closely as possible, the entities in the problem domain. In this context, resources correspond to software applications and their components, as long as they can be addressed and receive messages.

- Resources are discrete and distinct entities, atomic (indivisible whole) or structured (recursively composed of other resources, its components, with respect to which it performs the role of container). Each component can only have one direct container, yielding a strong composition model, in a tree shaped resource structure. Resources can also exhibit a weak composition model, by referring to each other by references (links).
- Each resource implements a *service*, the set of operations supported by that resource and that together define its behavior (the set of reactions to messages that the resource exhibits). The basic interaction pattern (service invocation) constitutes a transaction.
- A *process* is a graph of all the transactions that are allowed to occur, starting with a transaction initiated at some resource and ending with a transaction that neither provides a response nor initiates new transactions. A process corresponds to a use case of a resource and usually involves other resources as transactions flow (including loops and recursion, eventually).
- In summary, the three topmost entities of this model can therefore be characterized as:
  - Resources entail structure, state, and behavior.
  - Services refer only to behavior, without implying a specific implementation.
  - Processes are a view of the behavior sequencing and flow along services, which are implemented by resources.

This simple model subsumes SOA, by considering only atomic resources (no structure) and REST, by constraining all resources to exhibit services with a common service interface at syntax level (fixed set of operations), although with a variable semantics (the same operation can behave differently in different resources).

Improving the Semantic Gap by Tuning Architectural Styles

These concepts (resource, service, and process) lead to the three main architectural styles grasped by the market and industry (the last three in Table 1), according to which is the main concept that guides system modeling:

- Process-oriented architectures (Käster, Heßler, & Albayrak, 2016). This is the classical approach to isolated or loosely integrated information systems, before the advent of XML-based electronic services.
- Service-oriented architectures, or SOA (Erl, Merson, & Stoffers, 2017). Albeit not necessarily, current implementations of SOA usually resort to Web Services and do not follow a pure service-oriented style, since basic functionality is modeled by services but these need to be orchestrated and choreographed by processes (Barros, 2015), using a language such as WS-BPEL (Juric & Weerasiri, 2014). Nevertheless, services are the innovative factor.
- Resource-oriented architectures, or ROA (Baker, Ugljanin, Faci, Sellami, Maamar, & Kajan, 2018). In this style, everything is modeled as a resource, including behavior components (operations). Structure (including URIs) and state become the dominant factors and each resource's service is reduced to a CRUD style (create, read, update and delete), following the REST principles enunciated by Fielding (2000). The behavior complexity of SOA is traded for structure and state complexity. Lower level than SOA, has some significant advantages for client-server web applica-

tions with many clients. Services and processes are secondary concepts, used mainly as modeling, intermediate steps.

It is important to acknowledge that any active system (involving some form of activity execution) includes all these concepts. The emphasis given to each of them and to what degree they are combined yields the architectural style of the system. Figure 4 shows the relationship between them and Table 2 describes the limits of the corresponding variability.

To exercise this variability, this chapter considers the two seemingly most relevant styles in interacting applications:

- **Client-Server:** Many clients are expected for each server. Scalability and performance are the most important issues, given the high number of client requests that a server must support, concurrently. This style is typical of many Web applications;
- **Peer to Peer:** This has nothing to do with file sharing systems and only reflects that interacting applications are peers in similar terms and none has a clear dominance role regarding the others. This style is typical of enterprise applications, usually in the area of enterprise integration, and the number of interacting parties is usually small.

The semantic gap (Sikos, 2017) gives an indication of how close applications based on a given architectural style models real world entities and their interactions. The modeling effort benefits from using

Figure 4. The service, resource, and process triangle

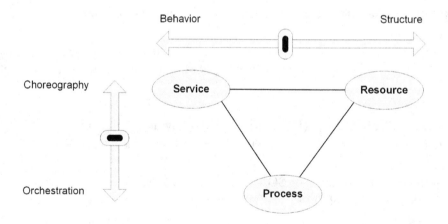

Table 2. Limits of architectural variability

	Pure Behavior	**Pure Structure**
Pure choreography	There are only services (with one resource per service, just for implementation). One service starts and invokes others. Each service coordinates the services it invokes, in a decentralized fashion.	There are only resources (each implementing the same set of operations). One resource starts by invoking operations on its links. Each resource manages its links, in a decentralized fashion.
Pure orchestration	All services are primitive (black box). All the programmable behavior is defined at processes.	One resource has links to all others that are relevant and implements the entire functionality.

the architectural style that best matches the applications in question. Since applications can vary widely in specifications and architecture, having the possibility of tuning the architectural style to suit the needs of the applications can be of great value, in design, implementation and maintenance. This would solve the restriction of having to choose between SOA and REST, for example, and use the combination of the two styles that is best suited for the applications to integrate.

Considering again the three main concepts (resource, service, and process) and the relevance given to each in system modeling and design, the full range of architectural styles and their adequacy to support application styles can be exploited, as illustrated by Table 3.

The classification used in the rightmost columns is only qualitative and is based essentially on scalability and modeling alignment (ease of expressing the application semantics) between the application styles and the architectural styles used to implement them.

Pure architectural styles are hard to find in practice. Even RESTful applications have frequently several variations and violations of the model. Pure RESTful resources usually implement different services because the semantics of the operations are different. Only the interface (not the semantics) must be uniform. Mixed styles, in which two of the main concepts are combined, is the most common case.

Table 3. Architectural styles and a qualitative assessment of their adequacy to two application styles

Main Concepts Supported	Architectural Style	Application Style	
		Client-Server	Peer to Peer
Process	Pure process-based architectures (everything is a process), stateless. Useful for pipeline type of applications (such as production processes), in which a process produces an output from an input, without side effects.	− −	+
Service	Pure-service oriented (everything is a service), with no implementation (resources missing). Can be useful for abstract system modeling or documentation, but not for execution.	+	+
Resource	Pure resource-oriented (everything is a resource). One example is REST. In the general case, REST constraints (such as interaction statelessness) need not be imposed.	+ +	− −
Process + Service	Services serve as functionality primitives and are orchestrated by processes. Typical implementations of SOA fall into this case. Alternatively, a large service's operations can be implemented with processes (a department modeled as a service, for example).	+	+ +
Process + Resource	Classical process-based architectures with state (database), used either to implement a classical stand-alone information system or in enterprise integration.	+	+
Service + Resource	Classical distributed system architecture, in which each resource offers an arbitrary service and is responsible for maintaining its internal data and for choreographing its own behavior. There are no central, orchestrating processes. Resource granularity is medium-low. Historically this corresponds to RPC style architectures, but interoperability today is at the level of a data description language (such as XML).	+	+ +
Process + Service + Resource	This architectural style supports all combinations of architectural styles and therefore should be the most flexible and a good fit for most application styles. There are currently no market single solutions at this level, although there are academic efforts towards integrating the service and resource orientations and WS-BPEL has been shown to work under the resource-oriented approach. This chapter makes a proposal for this architectural style, designated Structural Services.	+ +	+ +

The basic idea is that processes and general services have a good matching to peer style applications, because scalability is not a requirement as important as in the client-server style applications and their flexibility allows a good match between application concepts and architecture entities. Services receive a top grade because service-oriented modeling leads to a better match to real world systems than process-based modeling (for the same reason that object-oriented programming leads to a better modeling match than classic structured programming).

The resource-oriented style shines in the client-server style of application, in which it is the best match (good scalability and performance, allied to a small functional variability), but entails a semantic model rather different from the distributed object-oriented view that is typical of applications built out of a set of interacting peers.

The last architectural style (Process + Service + Resource) is the most flexible, as long as it supports the various styles, but does not exist as a single implementation (Delgado, 2016), motivating the proposal for the Structural Services architectural style made by this chapter. In simple terms, it can be seen as a SOA with structure and state, or as a ROA in which resources can have any type of service, with a process modeled as an operation of a large-grained service.

Improving Decoupling With Compliance

Conventionally, searching for an interoperable application is done by schema matching with similarity algorithms (Elshwimy, Algergawy, Sarhan, & Sallam, 2014) and ontology matching and mapping (Anam, Kim, Kang, & Liu, 2016). This may find similar server schemas, but does not ensure interoperability and manual adaptations are usually unavoidable.

Compliance (Tran, Zdun, Oberortner, Mulo, & Dustdar, 2012), a concept expressed in Figure 5, allows exact, not just approximate, interoperability even if the client and server schemas are not identical, as long as compliance requirements are verified.

Figure 5. Compliance-based interoperability. Only the request message validation is shown

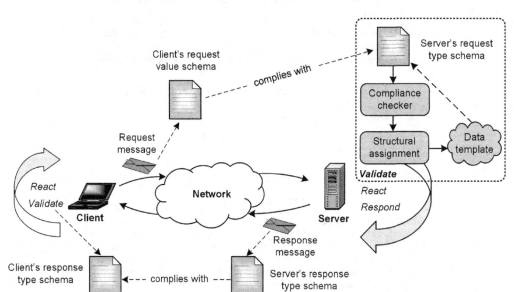

The compliance-based interoperability mechanism of Figure 5 can be described in the following way:

- The server publishes a request *type schema*, which describes the type of request message values that the server can accept.
- The actual request message, sent by the client, is described by a *value schema*. This is simply a self-description and, unlike type schemas, includes no variability (range of structured values).
- When the request message arrives at the server, the message's value schema is validated by checking it for satisfaction of, or compliance with, the type schema of the server, in the *compliance checker*. If compliance holds, the request message is one of those that satisfy the server's request type schema and is accepted.
- The request message's value is structurally assigned to the *data template*, which is a data structure that satisfies the server's type schema and includes default values for the components in the type schema that are optional (minimum number of occurrences specified as zero).
- Structural assignment involves mapping the request message to the server's request type schema, by assigning the message to the data template, component by component, according to the following basic rules:
  - Components in the message that do not comply with any component in the data template are not assigned but simply ignored.
  - Components in the data template that are also present in the message have their values set to the corresponding message's component values, otherwise maintain their default values.
  - Structured components are assigned by recursive application of these rules.

After this, the data template is completely populated and ready to be accessed by the server. Each request message populates a new instance of the data template. Note that this mechanism is different from the usual data binding of existing technologies, since the server deals only with its own request message schema. It does not know the actual schema of the request message and there is no need for a data binding stub to deal with it. The mapping between the request message and the data template is done in a universal manner and does not depend on the schemas used by either the client or the server. As long as compliance holds, the structural assignment rules can be applied.

This inherently asymmetric interoperability can be characterized in the following way:

- A server should accept any request message with a schema that satisfies the mandatory items of the server's schema. Optional items need not be present in the request message, with default values provided by the server's schema, and any item in the request message not contemplated by the server's schema should be ignored.
- The same applies to the response message and the client's schema, now reversing the roles of the client and server as sender and receiver of the message (details in this direction omitted in figure 5, for simplicity).
- Both client and server deal only with their own message schema. The translation between them, both in structural and semantic terms, should be done by a universal mechanism. There should be no stubs to adapt the client or the server to a common message schema.

This means that coupling is reduced in comparison with classical interoperability technologies, since:

- Coupling is limited to the actually used features of a schema and not to the full set of features of that schema.
- A client is more likely to find suitable servers based on a smaller set of features, rather than on a full schema.
- A server will be able to serve a broader base of clients, since it will impose fewer restrictions on them.

THE STRUCTURAL SERVICES ARCHITECTURAL STYLE

Main Characteristics

In a single, non-distributed application, the object-oriented paradigm is probably the best, with its low semantic gap, information reuse (inheritance), polymorphism and ability to expose both behavior and structure. In a distributed application environment, however, simple pointers to objects can no longer be used and inheritance stops working, since the lifecycles of the objects are not synchronized (they can be modified, recompiled and linked independently).

Remote Procedure Call (Kukreja & Garg, 2014) was an early attempt to transport the object-oriented paradigm to the distributed world, but failed due to a very poor interoperability model, language specific. SOA was a much better interoperability solution, thanks to the characteristics of XML. It still embodied the object-oriented spirit, but could not provide the mechanisms by which classes could expose structure or benefit from polymorphism.

REST abandoned the object-oriented modeling, exposing only structure and even converting operations into resources, or behavior into structure. In any case, it also does not provide a solution for polymorphism (media types need to be previously known).

These architectural styles are the main application integration solutions today, but application designers are forced to choose one or the other. This dichotomy is the basic motivation for the proposal of the Structural Services architectural style. The goal is to combine the best features of SOA and REST, by allowing a resource:

- To refer to other resources through distributed references (e.g., URIs).
- To expose a universal set of common operations such as returning a description of itself, under request.
- To expose an additional, application-specific set of operations (service), as required for a low semantic gap in complex resource modeling.
- To expose structure, to easily model resources that are naturally structured.
- To base data interoperability on compliance, rather than of shared schemas. This allows using structural (rather than inheritance-based) polymorphism, for increased interoperability, adaptability and changeability, without the need to have resource types (schemas) necessarily shared or known beforehand.

In a sense, the ideal would be to have the object-oriented paradigm back, but now with distributed references, structural polymorphism and self-description, by designing an architectural style, Structural Services, with the following main characteristics:

- The main modeling concept is the resource, which can be structured and is able to expose that structure. A resource can be identified by a globally accessible path, starting at a directory root or at some other previously known resource.
- Operations are first class resources but do not expose structure, only behavior. Data resources can be structured but expose state only (apart from basic getters and setters). Other resources are typically composed of operations and data resources.
- Resources are active and can respond to a message sent to it, by automatically choosing an operation adequate to process that message. If the receiver itself is an operation, that is the one invoked.
- Messages are themselves resources and can include operations.
- A service is the exposed interface of a resource. This is the equivalent to a WSDL document, but also including component resources (structure), not just operations.
- Resources are described by a distributed programming language, designed to be compiled and executed by a platform (server handler and an interpreter). Since resources are active (not passive data documents) and exhibit a service, an interface description language such as WSDL is not enough.
- Interoperability is based on structural compliance, not on schema sharing or predefined media types. This means that two interacting resources need to be interoperable only in the operations and/or data actually accessed (partial interoperability) and not on the entire definition of their services. This is a way of reducing coupling.

Table 4 summarizes the intended main differences and advantages of the Structural Services architectural style regarding SOA and REST, in the light of the discussion already made in section "An Example of the SOA-REST Dichotomy".

One of the advantages of the Structural Services style is the ability to lean more towards SOA or towards REST, according to modeling convenience, and mix several approaches and patterns in the same problem (Figure 4). In particular, it should be noted that, in the object-oriented style, inheritance-based polymorphism is based on the assumption that objects belonging to classes inheriting from a common base class share a common set of features (variables and operations of the base class). In Structural Services, resources do not belong to any class and there is no inheritance, but polymorphism still works on similar grounds, thanks to compliance. The server never deals with request messages, only with the data template (Figure 5). All the request messages that can be morphed into the data template (all for which compliance holds) will be seen as having a common set of features (those of the data template) and will be treated in the same way, exactly as in inheritance-based polymorphism, but now with the added advantage of supporting application distribution.

It is also important to acknowledge that the REST style requires a fixed set of operations, without stating which operations should be in that set. The HTTP implementations use some of the HTTP verbs, but this is just one possibility. The Structural Services style allows a further step in flexibility, by opening the possibility of using several fixed set of operations in the same problem. Now not only both extremes are possible (one different set for each resource, SOA style, or one common set for all resources, REST style), but also any intermediate combination can be used, with different sets of operations for different

Table 4. Comparison between SOA, REST and Structural Services

	SOA	REST	Goals of Structural Services
Basic tenet	Behavior.	Hypermedia (structure + links).	Tunable between pure behavior and pure hypermedia.
Distinguishing features	• Resource-specific interface. • Operations are entry points to a service. • Design-time service declaration.	• Uniform interface. • Operations are resources. • Clients react to structure received (do not invoke resource interfaces).	• Variable resource interface. • Resources are structured. • Operations are resources. • Links are resources. • Resource types need not be known at design time.
Best applicability	Large-grained resources (application integration).	Small-grained resources (CRUD-oriented APIs).	Wide range (small to large, behavior to structured-oriented).
Interoperability based on	Schema sharing.	Predefined media types.	Structural polymorphism (compliance).
Self-description	Repository (e.g., WSDL document).	Content type declaration in resource representations.	Included in each resource, message or application resource.
Main advantages	Low semantic gap (resources model closely real world entities).	Structured resources, with links to other resources (hypermedia).	• Low semantic gap. • Structured resources with links. • Polymorphism. • Self-description.
Main fallacy	Resource structure is unimportant.	Hypermedia increases decoupling.	None identified.
Main limitation	No polymorphism (coupling higher than needed).	Fixed interface (semantic gap higher than needed).	None identified.

sets of resources. This includes the distributed polymorphism mechanism based on compliance. Each server's type schema in Figure 5 specifies, in practice, a set of features common to all the resources that comply with that type schema.

Implementing the Structural Services Style

The basis for current integration technologies lies in data description languages such as XML (Fawcett, Ayers, & Quin, 2012) and JSON (Bassett, 2015), which merely describe data and their structure. JSON is much simpler than XML and, as a result, its popularity has been constantly increasing.

SOA is usually implemented by Web Services, with WSDL (a set of conventions on XML usage) to describe services at the interface level and SOAP as the message protocol (again, based on XML). The verbosity and complexity of WSDL and SOAP have progressively turned away developers in favor of the much simpler REST, which is usually implemented by messages directly on HTTP, using its main verbs as its fixed set of operations.

Since XML and JSON can only describe data, behavior is usually implemented by some generic programming language, which will not provide universal interoperability. At a higher level, WS-BPEL (Juric & Weerasiri, 2014) is platform agnostic, but it entails an unwieldy XML-based syntax that forces programmers to use visual programming tools that generate WS-BPEL and increase the complexity stack. For example, a simple variable assignment, which in most programming languages would be represented as x=y, requires the following in WS-BPEL:

```
<assign>
    <copy>
        <from variable="y" />
        <to variable="x" />
    </copy>
 </assign>
```

The evolution of the dynamic nature of the Web, as shown by JavaScript and HTML5 (Lubbers, Albers, & Salim, 2010), hints that data description is not enough anymore and distributed programming is a basic requirement. Current Web-level interoperability technologies are greatly constrained by the initial decision of basing Web interoperability on data (not services) and text markup as the main description and representation mechanism. This has had profound consequences in the way technologies have evolved, with disadvantages such as textual parsing overheads, full interoperability (based on schema sharing), and cumbersome syntax (e.g., WSDL, WS-BPEL) because everything must be described as data.

The Structural Services style could be implemented using current technologies. For example, WSDL documents could be extended with a structural section to support structured resources, or a variable set of operations could be emulated on top of HTTP verbs. However, these technologies and the corresponding set of tools were not conceived for this purpose and compliance checks would just be too slow. The simplicity of REST would be lost and the complexity of SOA would be reinforced.

Therefore, this chapter followed a different approach, by placing basic interoperability at the resource and service description levels, instead of merely at the data level. A distributed programming language, SIL (Service Interoperability Language), was defined and implemented, with a classic syntax style and an object-oriented look and feel. The goal is to provide native support for both data components and operations, as well as structural interoperability based on structural compliance (Delgado, 2016).

The following section presents an example. This is the only way in which the new features of Structural Services can be assessed without the limitations of current technologies. The intent is to provide a proof of concept and not to compete with established technologies or tools.

Each resource in SIL is represented by a SPID (SIL Public Interface Descriptor), which corresponds to a Web Service's WSDL but is much more compact and able to describe both structure and operations. It is automatically obtained from the resource description itself by including only the public parts (public component resources and operation headings). Unlike XML or even JSON, there is no separate schema document to describe a resource.

A compiler for SIL has been developed, based on ANTLR (Parr, 2013), which is able to produce the SPID automatically and to convert source to instructions and data in a binary format, using TLV (Tag, Length, and Value) binary markup (Dubuisson, 2000). An interpreter then executes the binary code (silcodes, similar to Java's bytecodes). The current implementation, in pure Java, is optimized for flexibility rather than performance and is roughly 50 to 100 times slower than a Java Virtual Machine (JVM). Much of that time is spent just on method dispatch, the mechanism used to execute the various silcodes. A C/C++ based interpreter would be faster but less portable and harder to develop and to maintain. Given the need for flexibility and control of implementation, JVM was not used as a compilation target.

A Jetty web server was used to support distribution, although any other server will do. The Jetty server connects to a SIL server (to handle SIL's own message level protocol) that hosts a resource directory for service discovery. This is a regular service, just like any other, which contains references to the SPIDs of the resources registered in it. This directory can be searched for a suitable service by supplying keywords and/or a SPID as required by the client. The directory then searches for these keywords in the registered SPIDs and performs a structural compliance check to ensure that the returned references to SPIDs are adequate to the SPID used in the search.

SIL: A Language to Implement the Structural Services Style

This section illustrates the distributed programming language that has been developed to implement the Structural Services style. Listing 1 shows a simple example of resources described in SIL, involving sensors in the context of the Internet of Things (Want, Schilit, & Jenson, 2015). It includes a temperature controller (tempController), with a list of references to temperature sensors with history (tempSensorStats). Each of these has a reference to a remote temperature sensor (tempSensor). The lines at the bottom illustrate how these resources can be used and should be included in some resource that uses them.

Listing 1 can be described in the following way:

Listing 1. Describing and Using Resources Using SIL

```
tempSensor: spid {  // descriptor of a temperature sensor
   getTemp: operation (-> [-50.0 .. +60.0]);
};


tempSensorStats: { // temperature sensor with statistics
   sensor: @tempSensor;    // reference to sensor (can be remote)
   temp: list float;       // temperature history
   startStats<||;          // spawn temperature measurements
   getTemp: operation (-> float) {
      reply sensor@getTemp<--; // forward request to sensor
   };
   getAverageTemp: operation ([1 .. 24] -> float) {
      for (j: [temp.size .. temp.size-(in-1)])
         out += temp[j];
      reply out/in; // in = number of hours
   };
   private startStats: operation () {  // private operation
      while (true) {
         temp.add<-- (getTemp<--); // register temperature
         wait 3600;   // wait 1 hour and measure again
      }
   }
};


tempController: { // controller of several temperature sensors
   sensors: list @tempSensorStats;   //list of references to sensors
```

continued on following page

Listing 1. Continued

```
addSensor: operation (@tempSensor) {
   t: tempSensorStats;    // creates a tempSensorStats resource
   t.sensor = in;         // register link to tempSensor
   sensors.add<-- @t;     // add sensor to list
};
getStats: operation (-> {min: float; max: float; average: float})
{
   out.min = sensors[0]@getTemp<--;
   out.max = out.min;
   total: float:= out.min;   // initial value
   for (i: [1 .. sensors.length-1) {   // sensor 0 is done
      t: sensors[i]@getTemp<--; // dereference sensor i
      if (t <out.min) out.min = t;
      if (t >out.max) out.max = t;
      total += t;
   };
   out.average = total/sensors.length;
   reply;   // nothing specified, returns out
}
};


// How to use the resources
// tc contains a reference to tempController
tc@addSensor<-- ts1; // reference to a tempSensor resource
tc@addSensor<-- ts2; // reference to a tempSensor resource
x: tc@sensors[0]@getAverageTemp<-- 10;   // average last 10 hours
```

- The temperature sensor (tempSensor) is remote and all that is available is its SPID, the equivalent to a Web Service's WSDL. For example, the SPID of tempSensorStats can be expressed by the following lines:

```
tempSensorStats: spid { // temperature sensor with statistics
   sensor: @tempSensor; // reference to sensor (can be remote)
   temp: list float;    // temperature history
   getTemp: operation (-> float);
   getAverageTemp: operation ([1 .. 24] -> float);
}
```

- Resources and their components are declared by a name, a colon and a resource type, which can be primitive, such as integer, a range (e.g., [1..24]), float or user defined (enclosed in braces, i.e., "{...}"). There are some resemblances to JSON, but component names are not strings and operations are supported as first class resources.

- The definition of a resource is similar to a constructor. It is executed only once, when the resource is created, and can include statements. This is illustrated by the statement "startStats<||" in temp-SensorStats. Actually, this is an asynchronous invocation ("<||") of private operation startStats, which is an infinite loop registering temperature measurements every hour. Asynchronous invocations return a future (Schippers, 2009), which will be later replaced by the returned value (in this example, the returned future is ignored). Synchronous invocation of operations is done with "<--", followed by the argument, if any.

- Operations have at most one argument, which can be structured (with "{...}"). The same happens with the operation's reply value, as illustrated by operation getStats. Inside operations, the default names of the argument and the value to return are in and out, respectively. The heading of operations specifies the type of the argument and of the reply value (inside parentheses, separated by "->").

- References to resources (indicated by the symbol "@") are not necessarily URIs, not even strings. They can also be structured and include several addresses, so that a resource in a network (e.g., the Internet) can reference another in a different network, with a different protocol (e.g., a sensor network). It is up to the nodes and gateways of the network supporting these protocols, to interpret these addresses so that transparent routing can be achieved, if needed.

- Resource paths, to access resource components, use dot notation, except if the path traverses a reference, in which case a "@" is used. For example, the path used in the last line of Listing 1 computes the average temperature, along the last 10 hours, in sensor 0 of the controller.

Listing 2 illustrates the compliance concept, by providing two additional temperature sensors (weatherSensor and airSensor) in relation to Listing 1. Only the additional and relevant parts are included here.

In Listing 2, weatherSensor and airSensor conform to tempSensor, since they offer the same operation and the result is within the expected variability. This means that they can be used wherever a tempSensor is expected (client compliance will be maintained), which is illustrated by adding all these types of sensors to tempController (through tc, a reference to it) as if they were of type tempSensor. Non-relevant operations are ignored.

The result of invoking the operation getStats on tempController is a resource with three components (as indicated in Listing 1), whereas "s" has only two. However, the assignment is still possible. Structural compliance ignores the extra component.

The last statement triggers a compliance check by the compiler, which issues an error. The cause is that the variability of the value returned by operation getTemp in tempSensor (referenced by ts1) is outside the variability range declared for component temp.

FUTURE RESEARCH DIRECTIONS

The main goal of the Structural Services architectural style is to benefit from the best characteristics of SOA and REST, by being able to tune the modeling approach to the applications and by reducing the coupling to the minimum required by interoperability. It has the potential to improve substantially the current application integration landscape, although much remains to be done before the architectural style is realistically tested and its capabilities demonstrated.

Listing 2. Example of Partial Interoperability with Structural Compliance

```
tempSensor: spid {
   getTemp: operation (->[-50.0 .. +60.0]);
};

weatherSensor: spid {
   getTemp: operation (->[-40.0 .. +50.0]);
   getPrecipitation: operation (-> integer);
};

airSensor: spid {
   getTemp: operation (->[-40.0 .. +45.0]);
   getHumidity: operation (-> [10 .. 90]);
};

// tc contains a reference to tempController
tc@addSensor<-- ts1; // reference to a tempSensor resource
tc@addSensor<-- ts2; // reference to a tempSensor resource
tc@addSensor<-- as1; // reference to an airSensor resource
tc@addSensor<-- ws1; // reference to an weatherSensor resource
tc@addSensor<-- ws2; // reference to an weatherSensor resource
tc@addSensor<-- as2; // reference to an airSensor resource

x: tc@sensors[0]@getAverageTemp<-- 10;   // average last 10 hours
s: {max: float; average: float};
s = tc@getStats<--;   // only max and average are assigned to s

temp: [-50.0 .. +50.0];
temp = ws1@getTemp <--;   // complies. Variability ok
temp = ts1@getTemp <--;   // does not comply. Variability mismatch
```

A comparative study needs to be carried out, including qualitative and quantitative assessment, between the Structural Services architectural style, SOA, and REST, with their instantiations (Web Services and RESTful APIs, respectively).

The implementation of SIL needs to be completed. For example, it supports concurrency and asynchronous communication, based on futures and delegation, but these features are not implemented yet. Semantics is another aspect to complete.

Compliance is a basic concept in interoperability and can be applied to all domains and levels of abstraction and complexity. Although work exists on its formal treatment in specific areas, such as choreographies (Yang, Ma, Deng, Liao, Yan, & Zhang, 2013), an encompassing and systematic study needs to be conducted to formalize the meaning of compliance.

Cloud interoperability (Kostoska, Gusev, & Ristov, 2016) is also a huge problem with increasingly importance, in which compliance can play a role. Cloud providers favor standardization but not homogeneity, since they need differentiation as a marketing argument. A study needs to be carried out on the suitability of compliance as a partial interoperability solution in cloud computing, including the possibility of defining APIs at the resource level.

Non-functional interoperability and coupling are also important, namely in context-aware applications and in those involving the design and management of SLR (Service Level Requirements). Detailing how compliance can be applied in these cases requires additional research.

CONCLUSION

This chapter has described and proposed an architectural style for application integration, Structural Services, which combines the behavior flexibility of SOA, the structural hypermedia capabilities of REST, and structural interoperability based on compliance.

These features are essential to the solution of the fundamental integration problem, resulting in a low modeling semantic gap (resources closely model real world entities, both in structure and behavior), while minimizing coupling for high adaptability, changeability and reliability. This is made possible by combining both the resource and service concepts in the same architectural style.

This is in contrast with the SOA and REST dichotomy over the modeling principle, forcing application developers to choose between flat (unstructured) services, primarily oriented towards behavior (SOA), and structured resources, primarily oriented towards state (REST). Many applications would be better modeled with a mixed approach, supporting both services and resources, so that complex functionality could use high-level service descriptions and application structure could be translated into structured resources. This constitutes the argument of the Structural Services style to reduce the semantic gap in application modeling (Sikos, 2017).

Coupling remains an unsolved problem in both SOA and REST, since data schemas must be shared by the interacting applications. SOA-based technologies usually provide a link to the schema, shared by the consumer and by the provider, whereas REST-based technologies usually agree on a given schema prior to the application interaction. If an application changes the schema it uses, those interacting with it must follow suit, to avoid breaking the interaction.

The fundamental problem of application integration is how to achieve the minimum possible coupling, so that dependencies between applications that hinder changeability are kept to a minimum, while ensuring the minimum interoperability requirements, so that applications are able to effectively interact. The solution preconized by the Structural Services architectural style is to use structural compliance (Tran, Zdun, Oberortner, Mulo, & Dustdar, 2012), relaxing the constraint of having to share message schemas. Two applications that share at least the characteristics actually required for interoperability can interoperate, independently of knowing the rest of the characteristics, thereby minimizing coupling.

The Structural Services architectural style was conceived to solve these problems and limitations. The intent is not to replace SOA or REST, but rather to evaluate what can be gained by using a technology that natively supports characteristics such as those of the Structural Services architectural style, geared for improved application integration, instead of compensating the limitations of existing architectural styles with additional layers of complexity.

REFERENCES

Abolfazli, S., Sanaei, Z., Sanaei, M. H., Shojafar, M., & Gani, A. (2016). Mobile Cloud Computing. In S. Murugesan & I. Bojanova (Eds.), *Encyclopedia of Cloud Computing* (pp. 29–40). Chichester, UK: John Wiley & Sons, Ltd. doi:10.1002/9781118821930.ch3

Agosti, M., Ferro, N., & Silvello, G. (2016). Digital library interoperability at high level of abstraction. *Future Generation Computer Systems*, *55*, 129–146. doi:10.1016/j.future.2015.09.020

Agostinho, C., Ducq, Y., Zacharewicz, G., Sarraipa, J., Lampathaki, F., Poler, R., & Jardim-Goncalves, R. (2016). Towards a sustainable interoperability in networked enterprise information systems: Trends of knowledge and model-driven technology. *Computers in Industry*, *79*, 64–76. doi:10.1016/j.compind.2015.07.001

Al-Fuqaha, A., Guizani, M., Mohammadi, M., Aledhari, M., & Ayyash, M. (2015). Internet of things: A survey on enabling technologies, protocols, and applications. *IEEE Communications Surveys and Tutorials*, *17*(4), 2347–2376. doi:10.1109/COMST.2015.2444095

Alenezi, M., & Magel, K. (2014). Empirical evaluation of a new coupling metric: Combining structural and semantic coupling. *International Journal of Computers and Applications*, *36*(1). doi:10.2316/Journal.202.2014.1.202-3902

Anam, S., Kim, Y., Kang, B., & Liu, Q. (2016). Adapting a knowledge-based schema matching system for ontology mapping. In *Proceedings of the Australasian Computer Science Week Multiconference* (p. 27). New York, NY: ACM Press. 10.1145/2843043.2843048

Babu, D., & Darsi, M. (2013). A Survey on Service Oriented Architecture and Metrics to Measure Coupling. *International Journal on Computer Science and Engineering*, *5*(8), 726–733.

Baker, T., Ugljanin, E., Faci, N., Sellami, M., Maamar, Z., & Kajan, E. (2018). Everything as a resource: Foundations and illustration through Internet-of-things. *Computers in Industry*, *94*, 62–74. doi:10.1016/j.compind.2017.10.001

Barros, A. (2015). Process Choreography Modelling. In J. vom Brocke & M. Rosemann (Eds.), Handbook on Business Process Management (pp. 279-300). Berlin, Germany: Springer. doi:10.1007/978-3-642-45100-3_12

Bassett, L. (2015). *Introduction to JavaScript Object Notation: A to-the-point Guide to JSON*. Sebastopol, CA: O'Reilly Media, Inc.

Bidve, V. S., & Sarasu, P. (2016). Tool for measuring coupling in object-oriented java software. *IACSIT International Journal of Engineering and Technology*, *8*(2), 812–820.

Bora, A., & Bezboruah, T. (2015). A Comparative Investigation on Implementation of RESTful versus SOAP based Web Services. *International Journal of Database Theory and Application*, *8*(3), 297–312. doi:10.14257/ijdta.2015.8.3.26

Botta, A., de Donato, W., Persico, V., & Pescapé, A. (2016). Integration of cloud computing and internet of things: A survey. *Future Generation Computer Systems*, *56*, 684–700. doi:10.1016/j.future.2015.09.021

Brandt, C., & Hermann, F. (2013). Conformance analysis of organizational models: A new enterprise modeling framework using algebraic graph transformation. *International Journal of Information System Modeling and Design*, *4*(1), 42–78. doi:10.4018/jismd.2013010103

Candela, I., Bavota, G., Russo, B., & Oliveto, R. (2016). Using cohesion and coupling for software remodularization: Is it enough? *ACM Transactions on Software Engineering and Methodology*, *25*(3), 24. doi:10.1145/2928268

Capel, M., & Mendoza, L. (2014). Choreography Modeling Compliance for Timed Business Models. In *Proceedings of the Workshop on Enterprise and Organizational Modeling and Simulation* (pp. 202-218). Berlin, Germany: Springer. 10.1007/978-3-662-44860-1_12

Chen, Y. (2015). A RDF-based approach to metadata crosswalk for semantic interoperability at the data element level. *Library Hi Tech*, *33*(2), 175–194. doi:10.1108/LHT-08-2014-0078

Chinosi, M., & Trombetta, A. (2012). BPMN: An introduction to the standard. *Computer Standards & Interfaces*, *34*(1), 124–134. doi:10.1016/j.csi.2011.06.002

Dahiya, N., & Parmar, N. (2014). SOA AND REST Synergistic Approach. *International Journal of Computer Science and Information Technologies*, *5*(6), 7045–7049.

Delgado, J. (2016). Bridging Services and Resources with Structural Services. *International Journal of Information System Modeling and Design*, *7*(4), 83–110. doi:10.4018/IJISMD.2016100105

Dennis, A., Wixom, B., & Tegarden, D. (2015). *Systems analysis and design: An object-oriented approach with UML*. John Wiley & Sons.

Dubuisson, O. (2000). *ASN.1 Communication Between Heterogeneous Systems*. San Diego, CA: Academic Press.

Elshwimy, F., Algergawy, A., Sarhan, A., & Sallam, E. (2014). Aggregation of similarity measures in schema matching based on generalized mean. *Proceedings of the IEEE International Conference on Data Engineering Workshops* (pp. 74-79). Piscataway, NJ: IEEE Computer Society Press. 10.1109/ICDEW.2014.6818306

Erl, T., Merson, P., & Stoffers, R. (2017). *Service-oriented Architecture: Analysis and Design for Services and Microservices*. Upper Saddle River, NJ: Prentice Hall PTR.

Fawcett, J., Ayers, D., & Quin, L. (2012). *Beginning XML*. Indianapolis, IN: John Wiley & Sons.

Fielding, R. (2000). *Architectural Styles and the Design of Network-based Software Architectures* (Doctoral dissertation). University of California, Irvine, CA.

Fielding, R. (2008). REST APIs must be hypertext-driven. *Roy Fielding's blog: Untangled*. Retrieved May 2, 2018, from http://roy.gbiv.com/untangled/2008/rest-apis-must-be-hypertext-driven

Fielding, R., Taylor, R., Erenkrantz, J., Gorlick, M., Whitehead, J., Khare, R., & Oreizy, P. (2017). Reflections on the REST architectural style and principled design of the modern web architecture. In *Proceedings of the 2017 11th Joint Meeting on Foundations of Software Engineering* (pp. 4-14). New York, NY: ACM Press. 10.1145/3106237.3121282

Geetika, R., & Singh, P. (2014). Dynamic coupling metrics for object oriented software systems: A survey. *Software Engineering Notes, 39*(2), 1–8. doi:10.1145/2579281.2579296

Graydon, P., Habli, I., Hawkins, R., Kelly, T., & Knight, J. (2012). Arguing Conformance. *IEEE Software, 29*(3), 50–57. doi:10.1109/MS.2012.26

Hendricksen, D. (2014). *12 More Essential Skills for Software Architects.* Upper Saddle River, NJ: Addison-Wesley Professional.

Henning, M. (2008). The rise and fall of CORBA. *Communications of the ACM, 51*(8), 52–57. doi:10.1145/1378704.1378718

Hussain, T., Mehmood, R., Haq, A., Alnafjan, K., & Alghamdi, A. (2014). Designing framework for the interoperability of C4I systems. In *International Conference on Computational Science and Computational Intelligence* (102–106). Piscataway, NJ: IEEE Computer Society Press. 10.1109/CSCI.2014.102

ISO. (2010). *Systems and software engineering – Vocabulary. In ISO/IEC/IEEE 24765:2010(E) International Standard* (p. 186). Geneva, Switzerland: International Organization for Standardization.

Iyengar, S., & Brooks, R. (Eds.). (2016). *Distributed sensor networks: sensor networking and applications.* Boca Raton, FL: CRC Press.

Juric, M., & Weerasiri, D. (2014). *WS-BPEL 2.0 beginner's guide.* Birmingham, UK: Packt Publishing Ltd.

Käster, T., Heßler, A., & Albayrak, S. (2016). Process-oriented modelling, creation, and interpretation of multi-agent systems. *International Journal of Agent-Oriented Software Engineering, 5*(2-3), 108–133. doi:10.1504/IJAOSE.2016.080892

Kostoska, M., Gusev, M., & Ristov, S. (2016). An overview of cloud interoperability. In *Federated Conference on Computer Science and Information Systems* (pp. 873-876). Piscataway, NJ: IEEE Computer Society Press. 10.15439/2016F463

Kukreja, R., & Garg, N. (2014). Remote Procedure Call: Limitations and Drawbacks. *International Journal of Research, 1*(10), 914–917.

Kumari, S., & Rath, S. (2015). Performance comparison of SOAP and REST based Web Services for Enterprise Application Integration. In *International Conference on Advances in Computing, Communications and Informatics* (pp. 1656–1660). Piscataway, NJ: IEEE Computer Society Press. 10.1109/ICACCI.2015.7275851

Lubbers, P., Albers, B., & Salim, F. (2010). *Pro HTML5 Programming: Powerful APIs for Richer Internet Application Development.* New York, NY: Apress. doi:10.1007/978-1-4302-2791-5

Meyer, B. (2000). *Object-Oriented Software Construction.* Upper Saddle River, NJ: Prentice Hall.

Panetto, H., & Whitman, L. (2016). Knowledge engineering for enterprise integration, interoperability and networking: Theory and applications. *Data & Knowledge Engineering, 105,* 1–4. doi:10.1016/j.datak.2016.05.001

Parr, T. (2013). *The Definitive ANTLR 4 Reference.* Raleigh, NC: Pragmatic Bookshelf.

Pautasso, C. (2014). RESTful web services: principles, patterns, emerging technologies. In Web Services Foundations (pp. 31-51). New York, NY: Springer. doi:10.1007/978-1-4614-7518-7_2

Popplewell, K. (2014). Enterprise interoperability science base structure. In K. Mertins, F. Bénaben, R. Poler, & J. Bourrières (Eds.), *Enterprise Interoperability VI: Interoperability for Agility, Resilience and Plasticity of Collaborations* (pp. 417–427). Cham, Switzerland: Springer International Publishing. doi:10.1007/978-3-319-04948-9_35

Preidel, C., & Borrmann, A. (2016). Towards code compliance checking on the basis of a visual programming language. *Journal of Information Technology in Construction, 21*(25), 402–421.

Rezaei, R., Chiew, T., & Lee, S. (2014). A review on E-business interoperability frameworks. *Journal of Systems and Software, 93*, 199–216. doi:10.1016/j.jss.2014.02.004

Ritter, D., May, N., & Rinderle-Ma, S. (2017). Patterns for emerging application integration scenarios: A survey. *Information Systems, 67*, 36–57. doi:10.1016/j.is.2017.03.003

Robkin, M., Weininger, S., Preciado, B., & Goldman, J. (2015). Levels of conceptual interoperability model for healthcare framework for safe medical device interoperability. In *Symposium on Product Compliance Engineering* (pp. 1–8). Piscataway, NJ: IEEE Computer Society Press. 10.1109/ISPCE.2015.7138703

Romero, D., & Vernadat, F. (2016). Enterprise information systems state of the art: Past, present and future trends. *Computers in Industry, 79*, 3–13. doi:10.1016/j.compind.2016.03.001

Schippers, H. (2009). Towards an Actor-based Concurrent Machine Model. In I. Rogers (Ed.), *Proceedings of the 4th workshop on the Implementation, Compilation, Optimization of Object-Oriented Languages and Programming Systems* (4-9). New York, NY: ACM Press.

Sharma, A., Kumar, M., & Agarwal, S. (2015). A Complete Survey on Software Architectural Styles and Patterns. *Procedia Computer Science, 70*, 16–28. doi:10.1016/j.procs.2015.10.019

Sharma, R., & Panigrahi, P. (2015). Developing a roadmap for planning and implementation of interoperability capability in e-government. *Transforming Government: People. Process and Policy, 9*(4), 426–447.

Sikos, L. (2017). The Semantic Gap. In *Description Logics in Multimedia Reasoning* (pp. 51–66). Cham, Switzerland: Springer. doi:10.1007/978-3-319-54066-5_3

Sungkur, R., & Daiboo, S. (2015). SOREST, A Novel Framework Combining SOAP and REST for Implementing Web Services. In *Proceedings of the Second International Conference on Data Mining, Internet Computing, and Big Data* (pp. 22-34). Red Hook, NY: Curran Associates, Inc.

Sungkur, R., & Daiboo, S. (2016). Combining the Best Features of SOAP and REST for the Implementation of Web Services. *International Journal of Digital Information and Wireless Communications, 6*(1), 21–33. doi:10.17781/P001923

Thakar, U., Tiwari, A., & Varma, S. (2016). On Composition of SOAP Based and RESTful Services. In *Proceedings of the 6th International Conference on Advanced Computing* (pp. 500-505). Piscataway, NJ: IEEE Computer Society Press. 10.1109/IACC.2016.99

Tran, H., Zdun, U., Oberortner, E., Mulo, E., & Dustdar, S. (2012). Compliance in service-oriented architectures: A model-driven and view-based approach. *Information and Software Technology*, *54*(6), 531–552. doi:10.1016/j.infsof.2012.01.001

Verborgh, R., Harth, A., Maleshkova, M., Stadtmüller, S., Steiner, T., Taheriyan, M., & Van de Walle, R. (2014). Survey of semantic description of REST APIs. In C. Pautasso, E. Wilde, & R. Alarcon (Eds.), *REST: Advanced Research Topics and Practical Applications* (pp. 69–89). New York, NY: Springer. doi:10.1007/978-1-4614-9299-3_5

Want, R., Schilit, B., & Jenson, S. (2015). Enabling the Internet of Things. *IEEE Computer*, *48*(1), 28–35. doi:10.1109/MC.2015.12

Weeger, A., Wang, X., & Gewald, H. (2016). IT consumerization: BYOD-program acceptance and its impact on employer attractiveness. *Journal of Computer Information Systems*, *56*(1), 1–10. doi:10.108 0/08874417.2015.11645795

Yang, H., Ma, K., Deng, C., Liao, H., Yan, J., & Zhang, J. (2013). Towards conformance testing of choreography based on scenario. In *Proceedings of the International Symposium on Theoretical Aspects of Software Engineering* (pp. 59-62). Piscataway, NJ: IEEE Computer Society Press. 10.1109/TASE.2013.23

Zhang, Z., Wu, C., & Cheung, D. (2013). A survey on cloud interoperability: Taxonomies, standards, and practice. *Performance Evaluation Review*, *40*(4), 13–22. doi:10.1145/2479942.2479945

Zimmermann, O., Tomlinson, M., & Peuser, S. (2012). *Perspectives on Web Services: Applying SOAP, WSDL and UDDI to Real-World Projects*. Berlin: Springer-Verlag.

ADDITIONAL READING

Amundsen, M. (2014). APIs to Affordances: A New Paradigm for Services on the Web. In C. Pautasso, E. Wilde, & R. Alarcon (Eds.), *REST: Advanced Research Topics and Practical Applications* (pp. 91–106). New York, NY: Springer. doi:10.1007/978-1-4614-9299-3_6

Baghdadi, Y. (2014). Modelling business process with services: Towards agile enterprises. *International Journal of Business Information Systems*, *15*(4), 410–433. doi:10.1504/IJBIS.2014.060377

Bloomberg, J., & Schmelzer, R. (2013). *Deep Interoperability: Getting REST Right (Finally!). The Agile Architecture Revolution: How Cloud Computing, Rest-Based SOA, and Mobile Computing are Changing Enterprise IT* (pp. 147–176). Hoboken, NY: John Wiley & Sons, Inc.

Charalabidis, Y., Lampathaki, F., & Jardim-Goncalves, R. (2014). On the scientific foundations of enterprise interoperability: The ENSEMBLE Project and Beyond. In Y. Charalabidis, F. Lampathaki, & R. Jardim-Goncalves (Eds.), *Revolutionizing Enterprise Interoperability through Scientific Foundations* (pp. 336–355). Hershey, PA: IGI Global. doi:10.4018/978-1-4666-5142-5.ch014

Díaz, M., Martín, C., & Rubio, B. (2016). State-of-the-art, challenges, and open issues in the integration of Internet of things and cloud computing. *Journal of Network and Computer Applications*, *67*, 99–117. doi:10.1016/j.jnca.2016.01.010

Erl, T., Carlyle, B., Pautasso, C., & Balasubramanian, R. (2012). *SOA with REST: Principles, Patterns & Constraints for Building Enterprise Solutions with REST*. Upper Saddle River, NJ: Prentice Hall Press.

Khalfallah, M., Figay, N., Barhamgi, M., & Ghodous, P. (2014). Model driven conformance testing for standardized services. In *IEEE International Conference on Services Computing* (pp. 400–407). Piscataway, NJ: IEEE Computer Society Press. 10.1109/SCC.2014.60

Mezgár, I., & Rauschecker, U. (2014). The challenge of networked enterprises for cloud computing interoperability. *Computers in Industry*, *65*(4), 657–674. doi:10.1016/j.compind.2014.01.017

Panetto, H., Zdravkovic, M., Jardim-Goncalves, R., Romero, D., Cecil, J., & Mezgár, I. (2016). New perspectives for the future interoperable enterprise systems. *Computers in Industry*, *79*, 47–63. doi:10.1016/j.compind.2015.08.001

Pautasso, C., Wilde, E., & Alarcon, R. (Eds.). (2014). *REST: advanced research topics and practical applications*. New York, NY: Springer. doi:10.1007/978-1-4614-9299-3

Saxena, V., & Kumar, S. (2012). Impact of Coupling and Cohesion in Object-Oriented Technology. *Journal of Software Engineering and Applications*, *5*(9), 671–676. doi:10.4236/jsea.2012.59079

KEY TERMS AND DEFINITIONS

Architectural Style: A set of constraints on the concepts of an architecture and on their relationships.

Compliance: Asymmetric property between a consumer C and a provider P (C is compliant with P) that indicates that C satisfies all the requirements of P in terms of accepting requests.

Consumer: A role performed by a resource A in an interaction with another B, which involves making a request to B and typically waiting for a response.

Coupling: A measurement of how much an application is dependent on the interface of another application.

Integration: The act of instantiating a given method to design or to adapt two or more resources, so that they become interoperable as a requisite to be able to cooperate and to accomplish one or more common goals.

Interoperability: Asymmetric property between a consumer C and a provider P (C is compatible with P) that holds if C is compliant with P.

Provider: A role performed by a resource B in an interaction with another A, which involves waiting for a request from A, honoring it and typically sending a response to A.

Resource: An entity of any nature (material, virtual, conceptual, noun, action, and so on) that embodies a meaningful, complete and discrete concept, makes sense by itself and can be distinguished from, although able to interact with, other entities.

Service: The set of operations supported by a resource and that together define its behavior (the set of reactions to messages that the resource exhibits).

Chapter 10
Reference Scheme Modeling

Terry Halpin
INTI International University, Malaysia

ABSTRACT

In natural language, individual things are typically referenced by proper names or definite descriptions. Data modeling languages differ considerably in their support for such linguistic reference schemes. Understanding these differences is important both for modeling reference schemes within such languages and for transforming models from one language to another. This chapter provides a comparative review of reference scheme modeling within the Unified Modeling Language (version 2.5.1), the Barker dialect of entity relationship modeling, Object-Role Modeling (version 2), relational database modeling, the Web Ontology Language (version 2.0), and LogiQL (an extended form of datalog). The authors identify which kinds of reference schemes can be captured within these languages as well as those reference schemes that cannot be captured. The analysis covers simple reference schemes, compound reference schemes, disjunctive reference, and context-dependent reference schemes.

INTRODUCTION

In this article, the term "object" means any individual thing. If an object is currently in our view, we may refer to that object simply by ostension (pointing at the object). Whether or not an object is in view, we may refer to it by using a linguistic expression. This allows us to reference concrete objects from the past (e.g. Einstein), the present (e.g. this article), or the future (e.g. the next solar eclipse), as well as intangible objects (e.g. a specific course in logic).

An information system models a specific *universe of discourse* (UoD), also known as a business domain (a world about which users wish to discourse within the business). For example, one UoD might concern a company's product sales, while another UoD might deal with flight bookings. In natural language, linguistic expressions used to reference objects within a given UoD are typically *proper names* (e.g. "Donald Trump") or *definite descriptions* (e.g. "the president of the USA") (Allen, 1995).

DOI: 10.4018/978-1-5225-7271-8.ch010

In philosophy, many proposals exist regarding the precise nature of proper names (e.g. see http://plato.stanford.edu/entries/names/) and definite descriptions (e.g. see http://plato.stanford.edu/entries/descriptions/). One popular account treats proper names as rigid designators, where "A rigid designator designates the same object in all possible worlds in which that object exists and never designates anything else" (http://plato.stanford.edu/entries/rigid-designators/). The term "possible world" may be assigned different meanings. In this article, a *possible world is treated as a state of the UoD being modeled by an information system*, and proper names are treated as rigid identifiers within the UoD of interest. Definite descriptions are often characterized as non-rigid, since some of them may refer to different objects in different possible worlds. For example, if we take "the president of the USA" as shorthand for "the current president of the USA", then uttering this expression in 2016 refers to Barack Obama, while uttering the same expression in 2018 refers to Donald Trump—a simple example of deixis where the denotation of a term depends on its context (in this case, the time of utterance). However, given our sense of possible world, some definite descriptions are rigid designators (within a given UoD). For example, if we restrict the UoD to our world history, the definite description "the 45th president of the USA" always refers to Donald Trump. Moreover, if we further restrict the UoD to the year 2018 then "the president of the USA" is a rigid designator within that UoD.

The information models discussed in this article use both proper names and definite descriptions for identification, so each usage refers to just one object within the given UoD. However, the same object may take on different preferred identifiers in different contexts. As noted by Guizzardi (2005, ch. 4), for the same identifier to apply to an object throughout its lifetime, the object must belong to a *rigid type*. We define a type to be rigid if and only if each instance of that type must belong to that type for its whole lifetime *in the business domain being modeled*. Consider a UoD in which a person is identified by a student number while at a given university and is later identified by an employee number while working for a given company. Here, the type Person is rigid, but the types Student and Employee are not. To model this situation, we use a global, rigid identifier based on Person (e.g. PersonNr) that always applies, then introduce Student and Employee as "role subtypes" of Person, along with their local identifiers (StudentNr and EmployeeNr) for recording facts specific to their context as a student or employee. Setting up a 1:1 correspondence between the global and local identifiers allows history to be maintained about persons who migrate from one role subtype to another. If instead the UoD records facts about persons only while they are students at a given university, then for our purposes of information modeling, the type Student is rigid, even though it is not rigid in the ontological sense (since a person may enter and leave studenthood throughout his/her actual lifetime). Hence information models of business domains can be well formed even if they are not proper ontologies. For further discussion of such cases and temporal aspects of subtyping including mutability see Halpin (2009).

Computerized systems model linguistic reference schemes, either directly or indirectly. However, there are major differences in the way that popular data modeling and semantic web languages support such reference schemes. This article provides a comparative review of how such reference schemes are supported in current versions of the following modeling languages: the Unified Modeling Language (UML) version 2.5.1 (Object Management Group, 2017), the Barker dialect of Entity Relationship modeling (Barker ER) (Barker, 1990), Object-Role Modeling (ORM) version 2 (Halpin, 2005; Halpin, 2015b), relational database (RDB) modeling, the Web Ontology Language (OWL) version 2 (W3C, 2017), and LogiQL, an extended form of datalog (Halpin & Rugaber, 2014). Understanding the significant differences in the way these languages support reference schemes is important for modeling identification schemes within such languages and for transforming models from one language to another. Of these languages, ORM provides the most comprehensive coverage of reference schemes at the conceptual level, so will be used as a basis for comparison when discussing support for reference schemes in the other languages.

Fact-oriented modeling approaches such as ORM, Natural Language Information Analysis Method (NIAM) (Wintraecken, 1990) and Fully Communication Oriented Information Modeling (FCO-IM) (Bakema, Zwart, & van der Lek, 2000) differ from ER, RDB, and class modeling in UML by uniformly modeling atomic facts as unary or longer relationships that are instances of *fact types* (e.g. Person smokes, Person was born in Year, Person joined Company on Date) instead of modeling some facts as relationships and others as instances of attributes (e.g. Person.isSmoker, Person.birthyear). This attribute-free approach enables all facts, constraints, and derivation rules to be verbalized naturally in sentences that are easily understood and validated by nontechnical business users using concrete examples, and promotes semantic stability, since one never needs to remodel existing structures in order to add facts about attributes (Halpin, 2010). Overviews of various fact-oriented modeling approaches may be found in (Halpin, 2007; Halpin, 2011b), and a detailed coverage of ORM in (Halpin & Morgan, 2008). OWL is attribute-free, but in contrast to ORM, OWL facts are restricted to binary relationships (subject-predicate-object triples) whose subjects cannot be literals. Like ORM, datalog based languages such as LogiQL are based directly on predicate logic and model all facts as relationships rather than using attributes.

Earlier work (Halpin, 2013a) provided a basic coverage of reference schemes in common modeling languages. Later work (Halpin, 2015a) discussed related philosophical and logical foundations, and added further examples and explanations, further formalization of reference patterns, and coding of disjunctive reference in OWL. The current article extends our earlier work by updating the discussion in various ways, conforming to the latest versions of the modeling approaches, and adding LogiQL to the modeling languages under consideration.

The rest of the paper is structured as follows. The next section covers simple reference schemes in which an object is identified either by an individual constant or by means of a single attribute or a relationship to another object. We then discuss compound reference schemes, where an entity is identified by combining two or more attributes or relationships. We then consider disjunctive reference schemes, in which some components of the reference scheme are optional, followed by context-dependent reference schemes, where the preferred identifier for an entity varies according to the context. We conclude by summarizing the main contributions via a tabular comparison of the kinds of reference schemes supported in the various modeling languages, identifying areas for future research, and listing the references cited.

SIMPLE REFERENCE SCHEMES

A *simple reference scheme* identifies objects of a given kind either by an individual constant or by means of a single attribute or a relationship to another object. In this article as well as ORM, an *object* is any individual thing of interest, so corresponds to the notion of individual in classical logic. An individual object may be an *entity* (e.g. a country), a *domain value* (i.e. a value used for communication in the business domain, e.g. a country code), or a simple *data value* (e.g. a character string). As discussed shortly, domain values (e.g. the country code 'CH') carry additional semantics determined by their domain type (e.g. Country) over and above data values (e.g. the character string 'CH').

Figure 1(a) displays a simplified ORM metamodel fragment that partitions object types into entity types, domain value types and datatypes. ORM displays object types as named, soft rectangles using solid, dashed or dotted lines respectively for entity types, domain value types and datatypes. Subtyping relationships are depicted by arrows from subtype to supertype. The lifebuoy symbol connected to the subtyping arrows denotes an exclusive-or constraint.

In ORM, a *fact* either asserts the existence of an object, or predicates over one or more objects. A *fact role* (or role for short) is a part played within a fact, and is depicted graphically as a box connected by a line to its object type. An *elementary fact type* is a set of one or more typed, logical predicates for expressing one kind of irreducible fact. A *predicate* is displayed as an ordered set of role boxes, with a predicate reading (read left to right or top-down unless reversed by an arrow tip). A bar beside a role depicts a uniqueness constraint (for each state of the model, each instance playing that role appears only once). A solid dot at an end of a role connector depicts a mandatory role constraint (each instance in the current population of the role's type must play that role). An ORM schema may be *populated* with sample instances of object types and fact types, which may be displayed in fact tables as shown in Figure 1.

In ORM, an entity is an object that typically may change its state and has an explicit reference scheme involving at least one relationship (e.g. the Country that has the CountryCode 'CH'). A domain value is essentially a domain typed constant (e.g. the CountryCode 'CH'), and a data value is an instance of a datatype (e.g. the string 'CH'). Since values (domain values or data values) are typed constants, they cannot change their state. For simplicity, finer aspects of data types such as facets (e.g. assigning country codes a fixed length of 2 characters) and language culture (e.g. en:US) are ignored in this paper.

ORM's distinction between domain values and data values conforms to the Principle of Indiscernibility of Identicals (identical objects necessarily have exactly the same properties). Using Φ as variable ranging over predicates, this may be formalized in second-order logic as follows: $\forall x,y \ [x = y \rightarrow \forall \Phi \ (\Phi x \equiv \Phi y)]$. For example, the country code 'CH' is based on a term in Latin (*Confederatio Helvetica*, the Latin name for Switzerland), but this is not true of the IATA airline code 'CH' (used for Bemidji airlines), so the country code 'CH' and the IATA code 'CH' are not identical, even though they are represented by the same character string 'CH'. Our latest formalization of ORM (Halpin, 2012) reserves the predicate symbol $\approx$ for the representation relationship that provides an injective (mandatory 1:1 into) mapping from domain values of a given type to data values (e.g. Figure 1(b)), so "$x \approx y$" is read "x is represented by y". ORM implicitly transforms between domain and data values as needed.

Figure 1. ORM viewpoint on (a) object types and (b) value representation

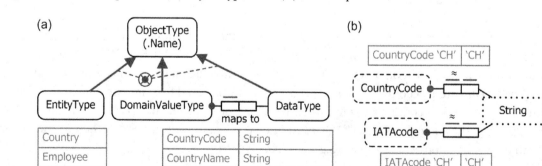

ER, UML, RDB, OWL and LogiQL do not distinguish between domain values and data values, so when mapping ORM to these languages this distinction is typically ignored. ORM and LogiQL allow any kind of object (including a value) to play the role of subject in a fact reading. For example: The CountryCode 'CH' is based on the Language named 'Latin'; The Word 'OK' abbreviates the Word 'Okay'. UML, ER and OWL don't allow values as subjects, so require domain values that are subjects to be artificially remodeled as entities. Domain types have a fixed relationship to their representing datatypes, so such cases cannot be modeled in term of quality individuals (Guizzardi et al., 2006). In ER and UML, if the value was originally modeled as populating an attribute, then one has to remodel the attribute as an entity or relationship, e.g. consider the optional fact type PersonTitle determines Gender (Halpin, 2010). This example is easily extended to cater for cases where the dependency is time-dependent by using temporal modeling patterns (Halpin & Morgan, 2008, sec. 10.3).

Moving on from value reference, the rest of this section focuses on simple reference schemes to identify an entity either by means of a single attribute or relationship to another object, or by an individual constant. Figure 2(a) models some ways to refer to a country using ORM. The reference mode "(.Code)" indicates that countries are primarily identified by their country code, where each country has exactly one country code. For our purposes, we use ISO 3166 alpha-2 codes (e.g. "US" for the United States of America) for country codes, and also use ISO country names.

The constraints on the current name relationship indicate that it is mandatory (each country has a current country name) and one-to-one (each country has at most one current country name, and vice versa). The fact type Country has previous- CountryName is also one-to-one, but is *optional* for Country. Only a few countries have a previous name (e.g. Sri Lanka was called "Ceylon" until 1972, and Myanmar formerly had the ISO country name "Burma"). The circled "X" in the ORM models denotes the exclusion constraint that no country name is both a current and a previous country name. This constraint can't be captured graphically in the other modeling notations. OWL and LogiQL models have no standard graphical notation, and are specified textually.

Figure 2. A schema in (a) ORM, (b) ORM, (c) RDB, (d) Barker ER, and (e) UML notation

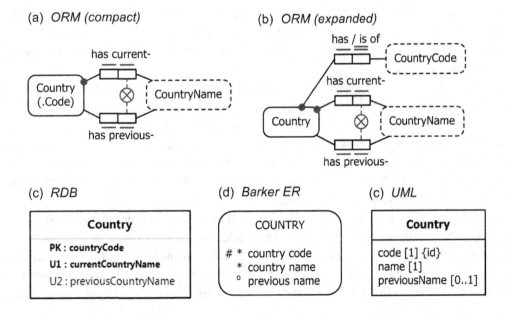

The Country(.code) reference mode notation in Figure 2(a) abbreviates the mandatory 1:1 fact type Country has CountryCode shown in Figure 2(b), where the uniqueness constraint on the role of CountryCode is chosen for the preferred identifier (as indicated by a double bar). In ORM, the simplest kind of entity identification scheme is a mandatory, 1:1 relationship from the entity type to a value type. In this example, each of the country code and current country name relationships provide a simple identification scheme for Country. The previous country name relationship is not an identification scheme, since not all instances of Country have to participate in this relationship. Nevertheless, previous country names are identifiers for some countries.

Figure 2(c) displays the RDB schema diagram generated from the ORM schema using the NORMA tool (Curland & Halpin, 2010), an open source plug-in to Microsoft Visual Studio. The table scheme for Country has three attributes. The countryCode and currentCountryName attributes are in bold type, indicating that they are mandatory (not nullable). The previousCountryName attribute is unbolded, so is optional (nullable). The "PK" marks countryCode as a primary key component for Country. No other columns in Country are marked "PK", so countryCode is the whole primary key of that table. The "U1" on currentCountryName marks it as a component of another uniqueness constraint (named U1 in the scope of this table). No other attributes in the table are marked "U1", so entries in the currentCountryName column are unique (no duplicates). Since currentCountryName is also mandatory, it is an alternate key for Country. The "U2" applied just to the previousCountryName column indicates that its non-null entries are unique, so those countries with a previous name can also be identified by that previous name.

Suppose we populate the Country table in Figure 2(c) with the tuple ('MM', 'Myanmar', 'Burma'). The facts intended by this row entry may be verbalized as: The country that has the country code 'MM' has the current country name 'Myanmar'; The country that has the country code 'MM' has the previous country name 'Burma'. These verbalizations use definite descriptions ("The country that has the country code 'MM'", "the country code 'MM'", etc.) to refer to objects. Various ways to formalize definite descriptions and address related problems (e.g. how to make sense of statements such as "The country named 'Utopia' does not exist") have been debated by logicians since the time of Bertrand Russell (Russell, 1905) till the present day, e.g. System !S in (Garson, 2006).

Like Russell's theory of descriptions, ORM rewrites such definite expressions in terms of classical predicate logic, but it differs by formalizing the underlying reference schemes, and then completing the fact instances by adding simple existential assertions within the context of the reference scheme (Halpin, 1989; Halpin, 2012). A similar approach could be used to formalize definite descriptions within other data modeling approaches.

Figure 2(d) depicts the example schema in Barker ER notation (Barker, 1990), arguably the best industrial ER notation. The "#" on the country code attribute marks it as a component of the primary identifier for the Country entity type. In this case, it is the whole primary identifier. An asterisk "*" before an attribute indicates that it is mandatory for its entity type, and a small "o" indicates the attribute is optional. Graphically, the only identifier that Barker ER can depict is the primary identifier, so it cannot mark the country name attribute as an alternate key. Nor can it display the uniqueness constraint on the non-null entries for the previous name attribute.

Figure 2(e) depicts the example as a UML class diagram. Attribute multiplicities appear in square brackets after the attribute name. A multiplicity of 1 indicates that the attribute is mandatory and single valued, and a multiplicity of "0..1" means the attribute is optional and single-valued, so each country has exactly one code, exactly one (current) name, and at most one previous name. UML recently introduced the capability to declare a class property (attribute or association end owned by the class) to be a component of a value-based identifier for the class. On a class diagram, the class property is annotated with an {id} modifier (Object Management Group, 2017). In Figure 2(e) only the code attribute is marked with {id} so this declares it as the natural identifier for the Country class. While UML does not require value-based identifiers to be declared, for successful communication with humans such identifiers are essential.

UML allows at most one identification scheme per class to be depicted with the {id} modifier, so cannot graphically depict the name attribute as an alternate identifier for Country. Even if Country had no other identification schemes, we cannot use the {id} modifier to depict the previousName attribute as unique for its non-null entries, since UML does not allow the components of an {id} scheme to all be optional.

OWL has no standard graphical notation, but has five textual languages for declaring ontologies: RDF/XML (Resource Description Framework/eXtensible Markup Language); OWL/XML; Manchester syntax; Turtle (Terse RDF Triple Language); and Functional syntax. Of these, Manchester syntax (W3C, 2012c) is by far the most readable, so is used for OWL code samples in this article. Turtle syntax for these examples may be found (Halpin, 2015a).

To use the OWL code supplied in this article, relevant prefix abbreviations are needed at the start of the file. In Manchester syntax you can use the following:

```
Prefix:: <http://eg.org#>
Prefix: dc: <http://purl.org/dc/elements/1.1/>
Prefix: owl: <http://www.w3.org/2002/07/owl#>
Prefix: rdf: <http://www.w3.org/1999/02/22-rdf-syntax-ns#>
Prefix: xml: <http://www.w3.org/XML/1998/namespace>
Prefix: xsd: <http://www.w3.org/2001/XMLSchema#>
Prefix: rdfs: <http://www.w3.org/2000/01/rdf-schema#>
```

To save space, these prefix declarations are omitted from OWL code listings in the rest of this article.

In OWL models, entities (in the sense given earlier) are typically identified by Internationalized Resource Identifiers (IRIs), such as www.eg.org#Czech_Republic, which function like individual constants in logic. Many country names contain embedded spaces, so can't be used directly as IRIs. Use of IRIs to identify all countries of interest is not reflected in the Figure 2 data models, which are designed for database applications where country codes are standardly used to identify countries.

Some OWL ontologies use meaningless, automatically generated identifiers as IRIs just as some relational database designers prefer artificial, surrogate keys for their table schemes. Human-readable labels can be associated with IRIs using rdfs:label annotation properties, and many OWL software tools can be configured to display labels instead of IRIs to make ontologies more readable. Assuming IRIs are provided, the Figure 2 model (ignoring the exclusion constraint) may be coded in OWL using Manchester syntax basically as shown below.

```
DataProperty: hasCountryCode
  Domain: Country
  Range: xsd:string
  Characteristics: Functional
DataProperty: hasCurrentCountryName
```

```
    Domain: Country
    Range: xsd:string
    Characteristics: Functional
DataProperty: hasPreviousCountryName
    Domain: Country
    Range: xsd:string
    Characteristics: Functional
Class: Country
    SubClassOf:  hasCountryCode min 1
    HasKey:   hasCountryCode
    SubClassOf:  hasCurrentCountryName min 1
    HasKey:   hasCurrentCountryName
    HasKey:   hasPreviousCountryName
```

In OWL, declaring a predicate as a *HasKey* property is similar to saying that it is inverse functional. For example, "HasKey: hasCountryCode" declares that each character string is the country code of at most one named country. The HasKey feature must be used for this constraint, since OWL forbids data properties (that relate individuals to literals) to be directly declared as inverse functional properties (W3C, 2012b).

Because of their formal foundation on description logics, semantic web languages such as OWL may be used to perform logical inferences, thus enabling some facts to be derived from other facts. To cater for the possibility that the data for the web fact structures of interest might be incomplete, these languages adopt the *open world assumption* (OWA). This entails that if a given proposition of interest (e.g.:Phobos:orbits:Mars) is neither asserted nor inferable from other facts, its truth value taken to be unknown, rather than false.

Logic programming languages are also formally based on logic, and have very strong inferencing capabilities, but unlike OWL, they adopt the *closed world assumption* (CWA), so assume that all the relevant facts are known. Hence a proposition of interest is assumed to be false unless it is either asserted or derivable from other facts. This CWA approach is also typically used when querying relational databases. The two most popular logic programming languages are Prolog and datalog.

The term "datalog", coined by David Maier to combine "data" and "logic", is appropriate for an executable, logic-based language designed for modeling and querying databases. Both Prolog and datalog enable recursive rules and queries to be simply and elegantly expressed, and efficiently executed. Unlike Prolog however, datalog is purely declarative, and its syntax conforms to safety rules that guarantee that any syntactically well formed datalog program will terminate. For a classical, technical reference on datalog see (Abiteboul, Hull, & Vianu, 1995).

Of the many datalog and datalog-based systems used in practice, *LogiQL* (*Log*ical *Q*uery *L*anguage, pronounced "logical") is a good example of the state of the art, with a successful track record in industrial business optimization, especially for predictive and control analytics involving large data sets. LogiQL extends traditional datalog in several ways, supporting blocks for modularity, many built-in functions (including aggregate functions), and other advanced features. While retaining much of datalog's traditional notation, LogiQL provides additional syntax to distinguish between constraints and derivation rules, and to simplify the formulation of various aspects (e.g. declaring a predicate to be functional).

Although a commercial version of LogiQL is available from LogicBlox, this article focuses on the free REPL (Read-Eval-Print-Loop) tool available on the cloud-based version of LogiQL that is accessible at https://developer.logicblox.com/playground/. For details on using the REPL tool to enter and query a wide range of LogiQL models, see our series of articles on Logical Data Modeling accessible at www. BRcommunity.com as well as www.orm.net.

LogiQL is a typed datalog, so each of its predicates is constrained to apply to a sequence of zero or more types. Object types are modeled as unary predicates. Entity types are directly supported, but value types are currently handled as implicit subtypes of the associated data type. Type declarations are specified as constraints, or "right-arrow" formulas, using "->" (read as "implies") for the material implication operator "→" of logic. Entity types that are identified using reference modes are declared along with their reference modes, using a colon ":" in the variable list of the reference predicate. The ORM schema in Figure 2(a) may be coded in LogiQL as follows.

```
Country(c), hasCountryCode(c:cc)  ->  string(cc).
currentCountryNameOf[c] = cn  ->  Country(c), string(cn).
previousCountryNameOf[c] = cn  ->  Country(c), string(cn).
currentCountryNameOf[c1] = cn, currentCountryNameOf[c2] = cn  ->  c1 = c2.
previousCountryNameOf[c1] = cn, previousCountryNameOf[c2] = cn  ->  c1 = c2.
Country(c)  ->  currentCountryNameOf[c] = _.
currentCountryNameOf[c] = cn  ->  ! previousCountryNameOf[c] = cn.
```

The first line of LogiQL code declares the entity type Country as well as its country code reference scheme. A comma "," stands for the logical conjunction operator (read as "and"). Here Country is a unary *predicate* for the entity type Country, string is a unary predicate for the character string datatype, and hasCountryCode is a binary predicate for the reference relationship that relates countries to their country codes (or more correctly, the data values representing those country codes). Predicates are written in prefix notation, with their arguments appended in parentheses. In this case, the arguments c and cc are *individual variables*.

The colon ":" in hasCountryCode(c:cc) distinguishes hasCountryCode as a *refmode predicate* (and hence injective), so there is no need to write further code to enforce the mandatory and uniqueness constraints on that predicate. LogiQL *formulae must always end with a period*, and are *case-sensitive*, so letters entered in lowercase are considered different from letters entered in uppercase.

The formula "Country(c), hasCountryCode(c:cc) -> string(cc)." is treated as an abbreviation for the following four formulae in predicate logic. The first formula declares that Country is an entity type of interest—for each individual c, if c is a country then c is an entity. To avoid typing "∀", LogiQL formulae assume that *variables that occur on both sides of an arrow are implicitly universally quantified*.

$$\forall c \; (\text{Country } c \rightarrow \text{Entity } c)$$
$$\forall c, cc \; [\; c \text{ hasCountryCode } cc \rightarrow (\text{Country } c \; \& \; \text{string } cc) \;]$$
$$\forall c \; [\; \text{Country } c \rightarrow \exists^1 cc \; c \text{ hasCountryCode } cc) \;]$$
$$\forall cc \; \exists^{0..1} c \; c \text{ hasCountryCode } cc$$

The second logical formula is a *typing constraint* to declare the types of the arguments of the has-CountryCode predicate. LogiQL requires all its predicates to be strongly typed. The third formula is an integrity constraint to ensure that each country has exactly one (i.e. at least one and at most one) country code. The fourth formula constrains each country code to refer to at most one country.

If an n-ary predicate has a uniqueness constraint spanning just its first n-1 roles, a square-bracket notation is used to indicate the functional nature of the predicate. The second line of the LogiQL code "currentCountryNameOf[c] = cn -> Country(c), string(cn)." constrains the types of the current country name predicate, and uses functional notation to constrain the predicate to be functional (so each country has at most one current country name). Similarly, the third line of LogiQL code types the previous country name predicate, and constrains it to be functional.

The fourth line of LogiQL code "currentCountryNameOf[c1] = cn, currentCountryNameOf[c2] = cn -> c1 = c2." declares the uniqueness constraint on the righthand role of the current country name predicate (so each country name is a current name of at most one country). Similarly, the fifth line of LogiQL code ensures that each country name is a previous name of at most one country.

An *anonymous variable* (denoted by an underscore "_" and read as "something") is used to existentially quantify a variable not referenced elsewhere in the formula. The sixth line of LogiQL code "Country(c) -> currentCountryNameOf[c] = _." uses the anonymous variable to declare the mandatory role constraint that each country has a current country name (if c is a country then its current country name equals something).

The last line of LogiQL code "currentCountryNameOf[c] = cn -> ! previousCountryNameOf[c] = cn." uses an exclamation mark "!" for the logical negation operator, and captures the exclusion constraint that no current country name is a previous country name (if cn is a current country name then it is not a previous country name).

In Figure 2, country entities are referenced by relating them to a value. Our next example, shown in Figure 3, identifies top politician entities by relating them to an entity. Here, a top politician (e.g. a president or prime minister) is identified by the country that he or she heads (as chief politician). This example assumes assume that if a country has both a president and a prime minister, only one of them is a top politician.

Figure 3. Identifying top politicians by country: (a) ORM; (b), (c) RDB; (d) UML notation

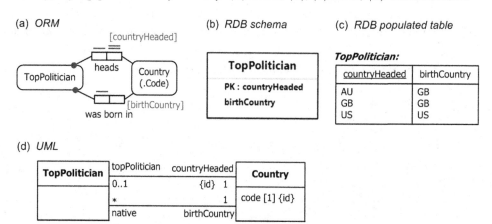

The ORM schema in Figure 3(a) models the reference scheme for TopPolitician using the mandatory 1:1 fact type TopPolitician heads Country, with the double-bar indicating the uniqueness constraint for the preferred identifier. Names for the roles played by instances of Country appear in square brackets beside their role. Figure 3(b) shows the RDB schema generated from the ORM schema using the NORMA tool. Here the countryHeaded primary key is used to identify the top politicians. Figure 3(c) includes a sample fact population for this table entered in an earlier year when Julia Gillard (who was born in the United Kingdom) was prime minister of Australia. The first row of this table records the fact that the top politician who heads Australia (country code 'AU') was born in the United Kingdom (country code 'GB') without knowing the name of that politician (Julia Gillard).

Figure 3(d) shows a UML class diagram for this example. The {id} modifier marks the association end TopPolitician.countryHeaded as identifying instances of the TopPolitician class. Although Barker ER allows relationships as components of a composite primary identifier, it does not cater for cases where a single relationship provides the whole identifier (Barker, 1990, p. 3-13), so does not support this kind of reference scheme.

OWL allows object properties (that relate individuals to individuals) to be directly declared inverse functional. In OWL an individual may be named (identified by an IRI) or unnamed (represented by a blank node). This allows OWL to capture identification schemes that identify individuals by relating them directly to other individuals.

The Figure 3 schema may be coded in OWL using Manchester syntax as shown below. The identification scheme for TopPolitician is captured by specifying the object property headsCountry as an injective (i.e. mandatory, one-to-one) relationship from TopPolitician to Country by declaring its minCardinality to be 1 and characterizing the predicate as both functional and inverse functional.

```
ObjectProperty: wasBornInCountry
  Domain: Politician
  Range: Country
  Characteristics: Functional
  InverseOf:  isBirthCountryOf
ObjectProperty: headsCountry
  Domain: TopPolitician
  Range: Country
  Characteristics: Functional, InverseFunctional
DataProperty: hasCountryCode
  Domain: Country
  Range: xsd:string
  Characteristics: Functional
Class: Country
  SubClassOf:  hasCountryCode min 1
  HasKey:  hasCountryCode
Class: TopPolitician
  SubClassOf:  headsCountry min 1
  SubClassOf:  wasBornInCountry min 1
```

The fact corresponding to the ('AU', 'GB') relational tuple entry may be coded by using blank nodes (represented by Skolem constants starting with an underscore) for the politician and country. In Manchester syntax, this may be declared thus:

```
Individual:  _:p1
  Facts: headsCountry  _:c1,  wasBornInCountry  _:c2
Individual:  _:c1
  Facts: hasCountryCode  "AU"
Individual:  _:c2
  Facts: hasCountryCode  "GB"
```

Although the OWL code discussed emulates the data models in Figure 2 and Figure 3, the semantics are not precisely the same. Constraints specified in data models are not translated into actual constraints in OWL, but rather logical propositions that are understood in terms of *open world semantics* where some individuals may be unnamed (Krötzsch, Simancik, & Horrocks, 2012). For example, declaring the subclass restriction "wasBornInCountry min 1" for top politicians simply says that each top politician was born in a country—it doesn't require the system to know which country that is. So OWL's support for unnamed individuals differs from what might be intuitively expected by users of typical database systems.

The subjects of OWL object properties and data properties may be named individuals (i.e. individuals explicitly named by an IRI) or anonymous individuals (denoted by blank node ids). They may also be other things (e.g. classes or properties) but such possibilities are irrelevant to the concerns of this article. For discussion purposes, Figure 4 expands the ORM schema in Figure 3(a) by explicitly depicting IRI reference relationships and the country code relationship. As the constraints indicate, each IRI identifies at most one entity (in this case, a top politician or a country), but any given entity may have more than one IRI (by default, OWL does not apply the Unique Name Assumption). For example, if we add the following facts to the previous OWL schema, an OWL reasoner will correctly infer that Myanmar and Burma are the same country.

```
Individual:  Myanmar
  Facts: hasCountryCode  "MM"
Individual:  Burma
  Facts: hasCountryCode  "MM"
```

In OWL, an InverseFunctional characteristic may be applied only to an object property, whereas both object properties and data properties can be declared as HasKey properties. Moreover, the uniqueness aspect of *HasKey applies only to named individuals*. In contrast, InverseFunctional declarations apply to any kind of individual (named individuals, anonymous individuals, and individuals whose existence is implied by existential quantification) (W3C, 2012c, sec. 9.5).

Given our current OWL schema for top politicians, we can assert that Julia Gillard was born in some country that has country code "GB" as follows, without knowing which country has that country code.

```
Individual:  JuliaGillard
  Facts: wasBornInCountry _:c1
```

Figure 4. A simplified view of adding IRI references to the ORM schema in Figure 3(a)

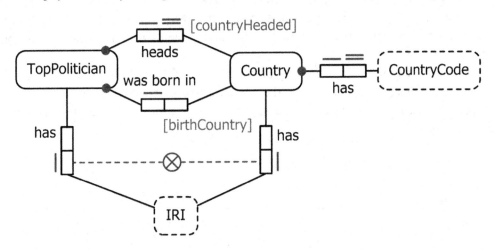

```
Individual:   _:c1
    Facts:   hasCountryCode "GB"
```

Now suppose we discover that the United Kingdom has the country code "GB", and we choose "TheUK" (in the scope of the current document) as an IRI for the United Kingdom. We can now add the following code to assert that the UK has the country code "GB".

```
Individual:   TheUK
    Facts:   hasCountryCode "GB"
```

One might now expect that it is correct to infer the following fact that Julia Gillard was born in the United Kingdom:

```
Individual:   JuliaGillard
    Facts:   wasBornInCountry   TheUK
```

However, this fact does not follow! HasKey declarations apply only to named individuals (with IRIs explicitly asserted). So declaring hasCountryCode as a HasKey property for Country says that at most one named individual has a given country code, while allowing that there could be many unnamed individuals with that same country code. Our assertion that Julia Gillard was born in some (i.e. at least one) country (which might be named or unnamed) that has the country code "GB" does not imply that this is the same as the named country (TheUK) that has that country code. This restriction of HasKey semantics to named individuals is designed to help ensure that inference rules using HasKey properties are "DL-safe" (W3C, 2012a, sec. 9.5), so they will execute in a finite time. The choice of the OWL term "HasKey" is unfortunate, as this notion is weaker than key declarations in data modeling approaches.

Since typical database users often assume closed world semantics for most of their data, and expect constraints to be enforced accordingly, considerable care is required when transforming to or from OWL ontologies that typically adopt open world semantics and use logical conditionals instead of constraints.

To address this issue, some recent proposals have been made to extend OWL with the ability to classify Tbox propositions as either derivation rules or as constraints (Motik, Horrocks, & Sattler, 2009), or to classify selected types and properties as complete by making them DBox predicates (Patel-Schneider & Franconi, 2012).

The ORM schema in Figure 3(a) may easily be coded in LogiQL as follows. The second line of code declares that TopPolitician is an entity type, the next two lines declare the functional predicates, the next line constrains the country headed predicate to be inverse functional, and the final line adds the mandatory role constraints.

```
Country(c), hasCountryCode(c:cc) -> string(cc).
TopPolitician(p) -> .
countryHeadedBy[p] = c -> TopPolitician(p), Country(c).
birthCountryOf[p] = c -> TopPolitician(p), Country(c).
countryHeadedBy[p1] = c, countryHeadedBy[p2] = c -> p1 = p2.
TopPolitician(p) -> countryHeadedBy[p] = _, birthCountryOf[p] = _.
```

COMPOUND REFERENCE SCHEMES

This section considers *compound reference schemes* (also known as composite reference schemes), where an entity may be identified by means of a combination of two or more attributes or relationships. Figure 5 displays some examples.

In the ORM schema in Figure 5(a), the circled double bar denotes an external uniqueness constraint underlying a compound, preferred reference scheme for Room (each room is identified by combining its building with its local room number). This corresponds identifying rooms by compound definite descriptions (e.g. the Room that has RoomNr 205 and is in the Building with BuildingNr 3). The circled single bar depicts an external uniqueness constraint for a compound, alternate reference scheme for buildings based on a combination of their x and y coordinates. Buildings also have a simple, preferred reference scheme (based on building number). The unary fact type Room is windowed records which rooms have a window, and has closed world semantics (rooms not recorded to play the is-windowed role are assumed to have no window).

Figure 5(b) shows the RDB schema generated by NORMA from the ORM schema. The preferred reference schemes for Room and Building are indicated by their primary key attributes, and the alternate reference scheme for Building is captured by marking the coordinate pair as unique and mandatory. To save space, display of data types is suppressed (the isWindowed attribute is Boolean).

Figure 5(c) shows a Barker ER schema for the same example. The composite reference scheme for Room is indicated by the # on the room nr attribute and the vertical stroke "|" through Room's role in its containment relationship with Building. This use of the stroke to declare a relationship as part of a reference scheme differs from many other versions of ER for which the stroke in this context would instead indicate a minimum cardinality of one. The simple reference scheme for Building is captured by the # on the building nr attribute, but Barker ER has no way to indicate that the building coordinate pair provides an alternate reference scheme for Building.

Figure 5. Compound reference in (a) ORM, (b) RDB, (c) Barker ER, (d) UML notation

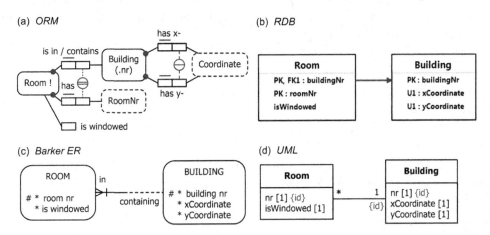

Figure 5(d) shows a UML class diagram for the same example. The composite reference scheme for Room is captured by marking the attribute Room.nr and the association end Room.building with the {id} qualifier. The simple reference scheme for Building is indicated by the {id} modifier on Building. nr, but UML cannot graphically depict that the coordinate combination is also unique for buildings.

In OWL, most of the example may be coded in a similar way to that discussed earlier. The isWindowed predicate may be declared as a functional data property with domain Room and range xsd:boolean, with individual facts using true or false as appropriate. For the external uniqueness constraints in Figure 5(a), composite HasKey properties are declared as shown below assuming the relevant properties are defined.

```
Class:  Building
   HasKey:  hasBuildingNr
   HasKey:  hasXcoordinate, hasYcoordinate
Class:  Room
  HasKey: isInBuilding, hasRoomNr
```

However, these HasKey declarations have no effect on specific room or building instances unless an IRI is also explicitly declared for those instances. In this case, one could invent meaningful IRIs, for example Building3 for the building with building number 3, and Room3-205 for room 205 in building 3. In this case, we can assert the existence of room 3-205 and the fact that it has no windows thus:

```
Individual: Room3-205
  Types: Room
  Facts: isInBuilding Building3, hasRoomNr 205, isWindowed  false
```

In cases where meaningful IRIs are impractical (e.g. IRIs for street addresses), we can use surrogate identifiers (e.g. address_1, address_2, etc.) or instead simply abandon any attempt to capture the uniqueness semantics in the OWL ontology.

The ORM schema in Figure 4(a) is easily coded in LogiQL as follows. The integer type is denoted by "int". Comments (prepended by "//") precede the code for the external uniqueness constraints in the reference schemes for Room and Building.

```
Room(r)  ->  .
Building(b), hasBuildingNr(b:bn)  ->  int(bn).
buildingContaining[r] = b  ->  Room(r), Building(b).
roomNrOf[r] = rn  ->  Room(r), string(rn).
// external uniqueness constraint for Room
buildingContaining[r1] = b, roomNrOf[r1] = rn,
   buildingContaining[r2] = b, roomNrOf[r2] = rn  ->  r1 = r2.
Room(r)  ->  buildingContaining[r] = _, roomNrOf[r] = _.
isWindowed(r)  ->  Room(r).
xCoordinateOf[b] = x  ->  Building(b), int(x).
yCoordinateOf[b] = y  ->  Building(b), int(y).
// external uniqueness constraint for building
xCoordinateOf[b1] = x,  yCoordinateOf[b1] = y,
   xCoordinateOf[b2] = x,  yCoordinateOf[b2] = y  ->  b1 = b2.
Building(b)  ->  xCoordinateOf[b] = _,  yCoordinateOf[b] = _.
```

DISJUNCTIVE REFERENCE SCHEMES

In a *disjunctive reference scheme*, entities are identified by a logical disjunction of attributes or relationships, at least one of which is optional for the entity type, while the disjunction itself is mandatory for the entity type. Such schemes violate entity integrity (where all primary key components must be non-null), so cannot be implemented as primary keys in a pure relational model, but may be implemented in SQL systems since they do not require primary keys to be declared. To our knowledge, disjunctive reference was first investigated at the relational level by Thalheim (1989). Our initial research on disjunctive reference at the conceptual level is discussed in (Halpin & Ritson, 1992). The treatment in this section introduces extensions to our earlier work.

Figure 6(a) shows a tiny fragment of the ORM metamodel. The external uniqueness constraint ensures that if a role has a name then that name is unique within its predicate. The constraint has *inner join semantics*, so the relation scheme Role(roleId, predicateId, [rolename]) formed by inner-joining the two relation schemes has a uniqueness constraint over the attribute-pair (predicateId, roleName). This allows many unnamed roles within an ORM predicate.

The external uniqueness constraint shape in Figure 6(b) has an added "o", indicating *outer join semantics*. The relation scheme Course(courseCode, courseTitle, [departmentCode]) formed by outer-joining the two relation schemes has a uniqueness constraint over the attribute-pair (courseTitle, departmentCode), where nulls are treated as actual values for this constraint. So in this UoD the same course title applies to at most one course with no department, but may also apply to many courses in different departments.

Figure 6. Disjunctive reference in ORM: (a) inner join semantics; (b), (c) outer join semantics

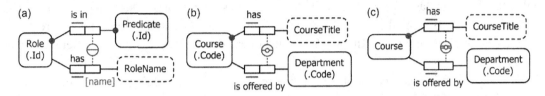

The schema in Figure 6(c) also has outer join semantics, but the double-bar in the external uniqueness constraint shape indicates that this is used for the preferred reference scheme for Course (course codes are not used). When the uniqueness constraint involves an optional relationship, inner join semantics can't be used for the preferred reference scheme. For example, if we remove the RoleId reference scheme from Figure 6(a), then a predicate with two unnamed roles has no way to identify its roles.

Figure 7(a) shows the weakest pattern that can be used in ORM to reference all instances of an entity type A. This involves a set of n functional binary relationships (n > 1) whose first roles are disjunctively mandatory (depicted by the circled dot) and whose second roles are restricted by an external uniqueness constraint with outer join semantics. The object types B1 to Bn are not necessarily distinct. Figure 7(b) formalizes the external uniqueness constraint, with the first conjunct covering the inner join part and the later conjuncts dealing with the outer join part by covering all cases where at least one component of the reference scheme is absent. For example, consider a minimalist model for storing the location of labeled points on a Cartesian plane excluding the origin, where points on the x-axis may also be identified simply by their x-coordinate, points on the y-axis may be identified simply by their y-coordinate, and non-axis points may be identified by the combination of their x and y coordinates. For graphical depiction of this model in ORM and RDB notation, see Halpin (2015a).

In practice, additional constraints often apply that allow more compact formalizations. For example, the external uniqueness constraint in Figure 6(b) may be formalized as follows, where the first conjunct captures the inner join semantics and the second conjunct captures the extra semantics for the outer join:

$\forall ct$:CourseTitle, d:Department $\exists^{0..1}c$:Course (c hasCourseTitle ct & c isOfferedBy d)

& $\forall ct$:CourseTitle $\exists^{0..1}c$:Course [c hasCourseTitle ct & $\sim\exists d$:Department c isOfferedBy d]

Figure 7. Weakest pattern for disjunctive reference in ORM

(a)

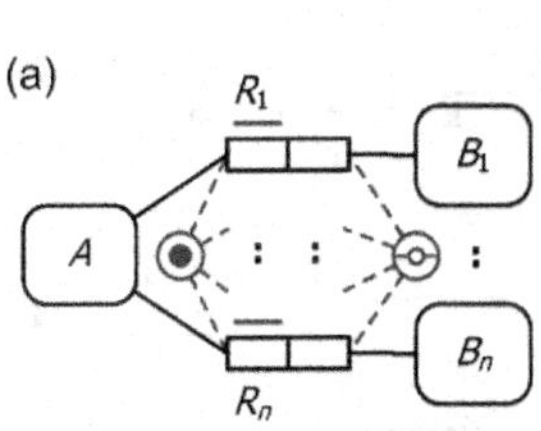

(b)
$$\forall y_1..y_n \exists^{0..1}x \,(xR_1y_1 \,\&\, ... \,\&\, xR_ny_n)$$
$$\&$$
$$\forall y \,\exists^{0..1}x \,[xR_1y \,\&\, \sim\exists z(xR_2z \,... \,\vee\, xR_nz)]$$
$$\& ...$$
$$\&\, \forall y_1..y_{n-1} \exists^{0..1}x \,(xR_1y_1 \,\&\, ... \,\&\, xR_{n-1}y_{n-1} \,\&\, \sim\exists z \,xR_nz)$$

Our original work on disjunctive reference was motivated by the need to handle such cases in industrial modeling, such as botanical classification schemes or complex addressing schemes. Halpin (2015a) discusses the botanical classification case using the new ORM notation. The full treatment of the botanical classification model (Ritson, 1994) illustrates how complex disjunctive reference schemes can be in practice.

Figure 8 shows two further cases of disjunctive reference. These use a construct recently added to ORM. A uniqueness bar with a dotted line over it indicates that its constrained role provides a preferred way to *reference just some instances* of the relevant entity type. In Figure 8(a), a top politician is identified by the country of which he/she is president or prime minister. Unlike our earlier top politician example, this allows a country with a president and a prime minister to treat both as top politicians.

The exclusive-or constraint in Figure 8(a) ensures that exactly one of these relationships applies to any given top politician. This model allows us to assert facts about the gender of top politicians without knowing their name. For example, the current president of the USA (country code = "US") is male, but the current president of Malta (country code = "MT") is not male.

Figure 8(b) models a situation where some famous persons may be identified by their popular name (e.g. 'Confucius' instead of 'Kong Qiu'), others simply by their family name (e.g. 'Einstein' and 'Newton' denote Albert Einstein and Isaac Newton), while others may be identified by a combination of their family name and a specific given name (e.g. Marie Curie, Pierre Curie). The circled subsethood operator depicts the subset constraint that each famous person with a given name also has a family name.

To implement disjunctive reference in a relational database, it is usually best to introduce a simple identifier for the primary key, moving the disjunctive reference to an alternate key. The simple identifier can be either a surrogate or a meaningful identifier obtained via a derivation rule to concatenate the components (type casting data types to string where needed). For basic discussion of mapping alternatives see Halpin and Morgan (2008, pp. 524-525), which discusses multiple ways of mapping the disjunctive reference scheme for botanical classification. Disjunctive reference is not supported in the graphical notation of Barker ER or UML.

In OWL, HasKey properties have inner join semantics, so cases like that of Figure 6(a) can easily be coded, along with the usual limitations discussed earlier for HasKey properties. Capturing external uniqueness constraints with outer join semantics in OWL requires more work. Typically, this involves *introducing a class for the instances that don't play the relevant optional role, then declaring a HasKey property for that class.* To ensure that the HasKey declarations are effective, *IRIs must be included for the referenced instances.* For example, for the Figure 6(b) model, the class for courses offered by no department may be introduced in Manchester syntax as follows:

Figure 8. Further cases of disjunctive reference in ORM

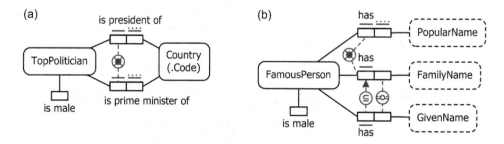

```
Class: NonDepartmentalCourse
    EquivalentTo: Course and (isOfferedBy max 0 Department)
    HasKey: hasCourseTitle
```

Disjunctive reference schemes cannot be used as primary reference schemes in OWL, since Has-Key properties are enforceable only on named individuals. However, once an IRI reference scheme is introduced, disjunctive reference may be supported as a secondary reference scheme. For example, for implementation in OWL the model in Figure 6(c) should be replaced by the model in Figure 6(b). Basic work on mapping ORM to OWL or description logic has been carried out by others (e.g. Keet, 2007; Franconi, Mosca, & Solomakhin, 2012).

We now show one way in which the additional disjunctive reference cases discussed in Figure 8 may be modeled in OWL. To cater for the exclusive-or constraint in Figure 8(a), we partition the TopPolitician class into President and PrimeMinister classes as shown in Figure 9. Each subclass then has a mandatory, one-to-one relationship to Country which may be used for identification. As these relationships are object properties their inverse functional nature may be declared simply as an inverse functional characteristic.

The following OWL code implements this schema in Manchester syntax and populates it with facts to declare that the president of the USA and the prime minister of Australia are male, while the president of Malta is female (i.e. isMale is false).

```
DisjointClasses: TopPolitician, Country
DisjointClasses: President, PrimeMinister
Class: TopPolitician
    EquivalentTo: President or PrimeMinister
DataProperty: hasCountryCode
    Characteristics: Functional
    Domain: Country
    Range: xsd:string
DataProperty: isMale
    Domain: TopPolitician
    Range: xsd:boolean
    Characteristics: Functional
Class: Country
    SubClassOf: hasCountryCode min 1 xsd:string
    HasKey: hasCountryCode
```

Figure 9. Remodeling the ORM schema in Figure 8(a) for coding in OWL

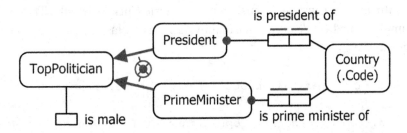

```
ObjectProperty: isPresidentOf
    Domain: President
    Range:  Country
    Characteristics: Functional, InverseFunctional
ObjectProperty: isPrimeMinisterOf
    Domain: PrimeMinister
    Range:  Country
    Characteristics: Functional, InverseFunctional
Class: President
    SubClassOf: isPresidentOf min 1 Country
Class: PrimeMinister
    SubClassOf: isPrimeMinisterOf min 1 Country
Individual: _:c1
    Facts: hasCountryCode  "US"
Individual: _:c2
    Facts: hasCountryCode  "AU"
Individual: _:c3
    Facts: hasCountryCode  "MT"
Individual: _:p1
    Facts: isPresidentOf _:c1, isMale true
Individual: _:p2
    Facts: isPrimeMinisterOf  _:c2, isMale true
Individual: _:p3
    Facts: isPresidentOf _:c1, isMale false
```

Figure 10 shows one way to remodel the disjunctive reference model in Figure 8(b) for coding in OWL. As the relationships to the names are data properties, their inverse functional nature needs to be captured by HasKey properties. This entails that the referenced individuals are *named*. Currently, ORM requires this to be provided by an explicit naming scheme, so we introduce a new naming scheme for famous persons (here, we have chosen to use person numbers). As with the previous example, two partitioned subtypes are introduced to cater for the exclusive-or constraint.

The external uniqueness constraint with inner join semantics ensures that each (FamilyName, Given-Name) pair refers to at most one famous person with a normal name (not a popular name). A derived subtype for normally named persons with no given name is introduced using the FORML derivation rule shown. The FORML constraint in footnote 1 then ensures that family names are identifying for instances of the derived subtype.

The following OWL code implements this schema in Manchester syntax and populates it with facts to declare that Confucius and Einstein are male and that Marie Curie is female. The footnote constraint in Figure 10 is implemented by declaring hasFamilyName as a HasKey property for FamousPerson-WithOnlyFamilyName.

```
DisjointClasses: FamousPersonWithPopularName, FamousPersonWithNormalName
Class: FamousPerson
    EquivalentTo: FamousPersonWithPopularName or FamousPersonWithNormalName
```

Figure 10. Remodeling the ORM schema in Figure 8(b) for coding in OWL

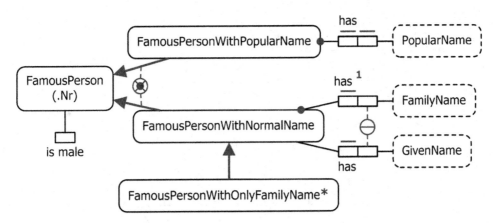

* **Each** FamousPersonWithOnlyFamilyName **is defined as
   some** FamousPersonWithNormalName **who** has **no** GivenName.

[1] **For each** FamilyName,
   at most one FamousPersonWithOnlyFamilyName has **that** FamilyName.

```
     SubClassOf: hasPersonNr min 1 xsd:string
     HasKey: hasPersonNr
DataProperty: hasPersonNr
     Domain: FamousPerson
     Range: xsd:string
     Characteristics: Functional
DataProperty: isMale
     Domain: FamousPerson
     Range: xsd:boolean
     Characteristics: Functional
DataProperty: hasPopularName
     Characteristics: Functional
     Domain: FamousPersonWithPopularName
     Range: xsd:string
Class: FamousPersonWithPopularName
     SubClassOf: hasPopularName min 1 xsd:string
     HasKey: hasPopularName
DataProperty: hasFamilyName
     Characteristics: Functional
     Domain: FamousPersonWithNormalName
     Range: xsd:string
DataProperty: hasGivenName
     Characteristics: Functional
     Domain: FamousPersonWithNormalName
     Range: xsd:string
```

```
Class: FamousPersonWithNormalName
    SubClassOf: hasFamilyName min 1 xsd:string
    HasKey: hasPopularName, hasGivenName
Class: FamousPersonWithOnlyFamilyName
    SubClassOf: FamousPersonWithNormalName and (hasGivenName max 0 xsd:string)
    HasKey: hasFamilyName
Individual: person1
    Types: FamousPersonWithPopularName
    Facts: hasPersonNr "p1", hasPopularName "Confucius",       isMale true
Individual: person2
    Types: FamousPersonWithOnlyFamilyName
    Facts: hasPersonNr "p2", hasFamilyName "Einstein", isMale true
Individual: person3
    Types: FamousPersonWithNormalName
    Facts: hasPersonNr "p3", hasFamilyName "Curie",       hasGivenName "Marie",
            isMale false
```

The use of person numbers in this example is artificial and is not really required in OWL since the user may provide his/her own IRIs for the named persons, and for readability may even choose identifiers that are intuitively meaningful (e.g. Confucius, Einstein, MarieCurie). For example, if all mention of the hasPersonNr predicate is removed from the above code, the facts about Marie Curie may be entered thus:

```
Individual: MarieCurie
    Types: FamousPersonWithNormalName
    Facts: hasFamilyName "Curie", hasGivenName "Marie", isMale false
```

Classifying uniqueness constraints as preferred is a pragmatic rather than a logical issue. Apart from this preferred reference aspect, LogiQL's deep support for formal logic allows it to model all of the disjunctive reference cases discussed. For example, the ORM schema in Figure 8(b) may be specified in LogiQL as follows. LogiQL uses a semicolon ";" for the inclusive-or operator. An ORM exclusive-or constraint combines inclusive-or and exclusion constraints.

```
FamousPerson(p)  ->  .
isMale(p)  ->  FamousPerson(p).
popularNameOf[p] = pn  ->  FamousPerson(p), string(pn).
familyNameOf[p] = pn  ->  FamousPerson(p), string(pn).
givenNameOf[p] = pn  ->  FamousPerson(p), string(pn).
popularNameOf[p1] = pn, popularNameOf[p2] = pn  ->  p1 = p2.
// inner join aspect of external uniqueness constraint
familyNameOf[p1] = pn, givenNameOf[p1] = gn,
  familyNameOf[p2] = pn, givenNameOf[p2] = gn  ->  p1 = p2.
// outer join aspect of external uniqueness constraint
familyNameOf[p1] = pn, !givenNameOf[p1] = _,
```

```
   familyNameOf[p2] = pn, !givenNameOf[p2] = _  ->  p1 = p2.
givenNameOf[p1] = pn, !familyNameOf[p1] = _,
   givenNameOf[p2] = pn, !familyNameOf[p2] = _  ->  p1 = p2.
// inclusive or constraint
FamousPerson(p)  ->  popularNameOf[p] = _; familyNameOf[p] = _.
//exclusion constraint
popularNameOf[p] = _  ->  ! familyNameOf[p] = _.
// subset constraint
givenNameOf[p] = _  ->  familyNameOf[p] = _.
```

CONTEXT-DEPENDENT REFERENCE SCHEMES

In a *context-dependent reference scheme*, the preferred identifier for an entity varies according to the context. ORM supports this notion by allowing subtypes to introduce new preferred reference schemes used within the scope of their immediate fact types. For example, in the schema shown in Figure 11 student employees have a global person number, but are identified by their student number for degree enrolment facts, and by their employee number for employment and tutoring facts (a solid subtyping arrow implies inheritance of preferred reference scheme). For further discussion of this topic, along with relational mapping options, see (Halpin & Morgan, 2008, pp. 519-521).

Barker ER and UML have no direct support for this notion, but UML's implicit use of oids to identify members of classes provides built-in support for global identifiers. While OWL does not formalize the notion of preferred reference, its allowance of multiple IRIs for the same entity and use of the owl:sameAs predicate to equate individuals provides one way to emulate such context-dependent reference.

Ignoring the preferred aspect of uniqueness constraints, the top two subtyping relationships in Figure 11 may be coded in LogiQL as follows. The lang:entity construct is used to classify Student and Employee as entity types (rather than property predicates hosted by a type, such as isaStudent and isanEmployee).

Figure 11. An ORM schema with context-dependent reference schemes

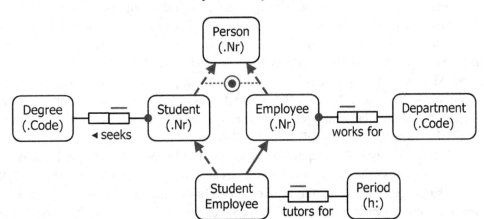

```
Person(p), hasPersonNr(p:pn)  ->  int(pn).
Student(s)  ->  Person(s).
lang:entity(`Student).
Employee(e)  ->  Person(e).
lang:entity(`Employee).
Person(p)  ->  Student(p); Employee(p).
```

The predicates for Student and Employee (e.g. hasStudentNr, seeks, hasEmployeeNr, worksFor) may be declared and constrained in the usual way. Currently however, LogiQL does not properly support multiple inheritance, so the further subtyping of StudentEmployee cannot be modeled in LogiQL.

ORM currently requires a preferred reference scheme to be declared for all entity types. This enables concrete examples of relevant facts to be verbalized in language used in the business domain, which is important for validating the information model with business users. Populating the model with real data also allows generation of a populated, sample database for further testing by users. Use of artificial identifiers for validation purposes is far less effective. For relational mapping, distinguishing between preferred and alternate reference schemes is essential for automatically generating relational database schemes with distinguished primary and secondary keys.

When multiple reference schemes are available for the same entity type (e.g. country codes and country names for countries), selecting one reference scheme as preferred is not always a conceptual issue, since in some situations any of the identifiers could be used for model creation and validation. However, in some cases it really is a business decision to choose one scheme as preferred for a given context (e.g. using student numbers to identify students when recording facts about the roles they play as students). For such cases, the choice of preferred reference is arguably a conceptual issue. However, ontological modeling using semantic web languages such as OWL does not distinguish a reference scheme as preferred for a class when multiple reference schemes are available for that class. While choosing a preferred reference scheme has pragmatic value for information modeling, we are considering relaxing this requirement to facilitate use of ORM for ontological modeling.

CONCLUSION

Popular languages for data modeling and ontology modeling differ substantially in their support for reference schemes, so an understanding of these differences is important for transforming models from one language to another. This article provided a comparative review of how reference schemes may be modeled in ORM, Relational databases, Barker ER, UML, OWL and LogiQL.

Halpin and Morgan (2018) provides further detailed comparisons between the expressibility of the graphical notations for ORM, Barker ER, and UML class models in general (not just for reference schemes). A detailed discussion of mapping a wide range of ORM models to OWL is provided in our series of 15 articles on ontological modeling for the Business Rules Journal. For example, see (Halpin, 2013b). For a detailed discussion of mapping most kinds of ORM models to LogiQL see our series of articles on logical data modeling for the Business Rules Journal. For example, see (Halpin, 2017).

While all six languages discussed in this article provide basic support for some simple and compound reference scheme patterns, various limitations in the latter four languages were identified with respect to their support for other reference scheme patterns, as summarized in Table 1.

Table 1. Summary of reference scheme support in various modeling languages

Reference scheme support	ORM	RDB	Barker ER	UML	OWL	LogiQL
simple primary	*Yes*	*Yes*	*Mostly*	*Yes*	*Mostly*	*Yes*
simple secondary	*Yes*	*Yes*	*No*	*No*	*Mostly*	*Yes*
compound primary	*Yes*	*Yes*	*Yes*	*Yes*	*Mostly*	*Yes*
compound secondary	*Yes*	*Yes*	*No*	*No*	*Mostly*	*Yes*
disjunctive	*Yes*	*Yes*	*No*	*No*	*Mostly*	*Yes*
context-dependent	*Yes*	*Yes*	*No*	*Partly*	*Partly*	*Partly*

For example, Barker ER and UML do not graphically support secondary (i.e. alternate) reference schemes, Barker ER does not support simply entity-to-entity reference, Barker ER and UML have no intrinsic support for disjunctive reference, and OWL's use of HasKey properties is restricted to inner join semantics and named individuals, thus relegating disjunctive reference support to secondary reference schemes, and LogiQL does not support context dependent reference schemes involving multiple inheritance.

In this table, the RDB column indicates a relational database system in which tables without primary keys are allowed, as in the SQL standard and most commercial SQL systems. Although not conformant with relational model theory, this allowance is needed to implement a preferred reference scheme that is disjunctive.

The new ORM constraint symbols introduced to distinguish the ways in which internal and external uniqueness constraints underlie different kinds of reference schemes have been adopted in ORM, and are supported for diagramming purposes in the latest Visio stencil for ORM. However, they are not yet fully supported in the NORMA tool (e.g. with distinguished automated verbalizations and relational mapping options). Such implementation support for NORMA is planned for the future. Further research and development work is encouraged to extend support for modeling reference schemes in other languages used in practice to model information systems.

Subsequent to, and initially unaware of, our previously published research in this regard, Bordiga, Toman and Weddell (2016a; 2016b) specified a variant of description logic as well as an idealized SQL-like syntax that can be used to capture most of the reference schemes discussed in this article.

ACKNOWLEDGMENT

This research was partially supported by an Erasmus Mundus Scholarship funded by the European Master's Program in Computational Logic. We also thank Enrico Franconi for sharing his insights into some finer points on the formal foundations of OWL.

REFERENCES

Abiteboul, S., Hull, R., & Vianu, V. (1995). *Foundations of Databases*. Reading, MA: Addison-Wesley.

Allen, J. (1995). *Natural Language Understanding* (2nd ed.). Redwood City, WA: Benjamin/Cummings.

Bakema, G., Zwart, J., & van der Lek, H. (2000). *Fully Communication Oriented Information Modelling*. Ten Hagen Stam.

Barker, R. (1990). *CASE*Method: Entity Relationship Modelling*. Wokingham: Addison-Wesley.

Borgida, A., Toman, D., & Weddell, G. (2016a). On Referring Expressions in Query Answering over First Order Knowledge Bases. In *Proc. KR 2016* (pp. 319-328). Assoc. for Advancement of Artificial Intelligence.

Borgida, A., Toman, D., & Weddell, G. (2016b). On Referring Expressions in Information Systems Derived from Conceptual Modelling. In *Proc. ER 2016* (pp. 183-197). Heidelberg, Germany: Springer. 10.1007/978-3-319-46397-1_14

Chen, P. P. (1976). The entity-relationship model—towards a unified view of data. *ACM Transactions on Database Systems*, *1*(1), 9–36. doi:10.1145/320434.320440

Curland, M., & Halpin, T. (2010). The NORMA Software Tool for ORM 2. In *CAiSE Forum 2010* (pp. 190-204). Berlin: Springer-Verlag.

Franconi, E., Mosca, A., & Solomakhin, D. (2012). ORM2: Formalisation and Encoding in OWL2. In OTM 2012 Workshops (pp. 368-378). Heidelberg, Germany: Springer.

Garson, J. (2006). *Modal Logic for Philosophers*. Cambridge, UK: Cambridge University Press. doi:10.1017/CBO9780511617737

Guizzardi, G. (2005). *Ontological Foundations for Structured Conceptual Models* (PhD thesis). University of Twente.

Guizzardi, G., Masolo, C., & Borgo, S. (2006). In the Defense of a Trope-Based Ontology for Conceptual Modeling: An Example with the Foundations of Attributes, Weak Entities and Datatypes. In *Proc. 25th Int. Conf. on Conceptual Modeling (ER'2006)* (pp. 112-125). Berlin: Springer-Verlag.

Halpin, T. (1989). *A Logical Analysis of Information Systems: static aspects of the data-oriented perspective* (Doctoral dissertation). University of Queensland. Retrieved from http://www.orm.net/Halpin_PhDthesis.pdf

Halpin, T. (2005). ORM 2. In OTM 2005 Workshops (pp. 676-87). Heidelberg, Germany: Springer.

Halpin, T. (2007). Fact-Oriented Modeling: Past, Present and Future. In J. Krogstie & ... (Eds.), *Conceptual Modelling in Information Systems Engineering* (pp. 19–38). Berlin: Springer. doi:10.1007/978-3-540-72677-7_2

Halpin, T. (2009). Enriched Conceptualization of Subtyping. In T. Halpin, J. Krogstie, & H. Proper (Eds.), *Innovations in Information Systems Modeling: Methods and Best Practices* (pp. 1–16). Hershey, PA: IGI Global. doi:10.4018/978-1-60566-278-7.ch001

Halpin, T. (2010). Object-Role Modeling: Principles and Benefits. *International Journal of Information System Modeling and Design, 1*(1), 32–54. doi:10.4018/jismd.2010092302

Halpin, T. (2011). Structural Aspects of Data Modeling Languages. In BPMDS 2011 and EMMSAD 2011 (pp. 428-442). Berlin: Springer-Verlag. doi:10.1007/978-3-642-21759-3_31

Halpin, T. (2011). Fact-Orientation and Conceptual Logic. In *Proc. 15th International EDOC Conference* (pp. 14-19). Helsinki: IEEE Computer Society.

Halpin, T. (2012). Formalization of ORM Revisited. In OTM 2012 Workshops (pp. 348-357). Heidelberg, Germany: Springer. doi:10.1007/978-3-642-33618-8_49

Halpin, T. (2013a). Modeling of Reference Schemes. In BPMDS 2013 and EMMSAD 2013 (pp. 308-323). Berlin: Springer. doi:10.1007/978-3-642-38484-4_22

Halpin, T. (2013b). Ontological Modeling: Part 15. *Business Rules Journal, 14*(2). Retrieved from http://www.BRCommunity.com/a2013/b734.html

Halpin, T. (2015a). Modeling of Linguistic Reference Schemes. *International Journal of Information System Modeling and Design, 6*(4), 1–23. doi:10.4018/IJISMD.2015100101

Halpin, T. (2015b). *Object-Role Modeling Fundamentals*. Technics Publications.

Halpin, T. (2016). *Object-Role Modeling Workbook*. Technics Publications.

Halpin, T. (2017). Logical Data Modeling: Part 10. *Business Rules Journal, 18*(11). Retrieved from http://www.brcommunity.com/a2017/b929.html

Halpin, T., Curland, M., Stirewalt, K., Viswanath, N., McGill, M., & Beck, S. (2010). Mapping ORM to Datalog: An Overview. In OTM 2010 Workshops (pp. 504-513). Heidelberg, Germany: Springer.

Halpin, T., & Morgan, T. (2008). *Information Modeling and Relational Databases* (2nd ed.). San Francisco: Morgan Kaufmann.

Halpin, T., & Ritson, R. (1992). Fact-Oriented Modelling and Null Values. In B. Srinivasan & J. Zeleznikov (Eds.), *Research and Practical Issues in Databases*. Singapore: World Scientific.

Halpin, T., & Rugaber, S. (2014). *LogiQL: A Query Language for Smart Databases*. Boca Raton, FL: CRC Press. doi:10.1201/b17711

Keet, C. (2007). Prospects for and issues with mapping the Object-Role Modeling language into DLRifd. In *20th Int. Workshop on Description Logics (DL'07)* (pp. 331-338). CEUR-WS.

Krötzsch, M., Simancik, F., & Horrocks, I. (2012). *A Description Logic Primer*. Retrieved from http://arxiv.org/abs/1201.4089

Motik, B., Horrocks, I., & Sattler, U. (2009). Bridging the Gap Between OWL and Relational Databases. *Journal of Web Semantics, 7*(2), 74–89. doi:10.1016/j.websem.2009.02.001

Object Management Group. (2017). *OMG Unified Modeling Language (OMG UML), version 2.5.1*. Retrieved from http://www.omg.org/spec/UML/2.5.1/

Patel-Schneider, P., & Franconi, E. (2012). Ontology Constraints in Incomplete and Complete Data. *Proc. 11th International Semantic Web Conference*. 10.1007/978-3-642-35176-1_28

Ritson, P. (1994). *Use of Conceptual Schemas for Relational Implementation* (Doctoral dissertation). University of Queensland.

Russell, B. (1905). On Denoting. *Mind, 14*(4), 479–493. doi:10.1093/mind/XIV.4.479

Thalheim, B. (1989). On Semantic Issues Connected with Keys in Relational Databases. *J. Inf. Process. Cybern., 1*(2), 11–20.

W3C. (2011). *Turtle – Terse RDF Triple Language*. Retrieved from http://www.w3.org/TeamSubmission/turtle/

W3C. (2012a). *OWL 2 Web Ontology Language: Primer* (2nd ed.). Retrieved from http://www.w3.org/TR/owl2-primer/

W3C. (2012b). *OWL 2 Web Ontology Language: Direct Semantics* (2nd ed.). Retrieved from http://www.w3.org/TR/owl2-direct-semantics/

W3C. (2012c). *OWL 2 Web Ontology Language Manchester Syntax* (2nd ed.). Retrieved from http://www.w3.org/TR/owl2-manchester-syntax/

W3C. (2012d). *OWL 2 Web Ontology Language Structural Specification and Functional-Style Syntax* (2nd ed.). Retrieved from http://www.w3.org/TR/owl2-syntax/

W3C. (2017). *OWL Web Ontology Language Current Status*. Retrieved from https://www.w3.org/standards/techs/owl#w3c_all

Wintraecken, J. (1990). *The NIAM Information Analysis Method: Theory and Practice*. Deventer: Kluwer. doi:10.1007/978-94-009-0451-4

Chapter 11
Data Warehouse Support for Policy Enforcement Rule Formulation

Deepika Prakash
NIIT University, India

ABSTRACT

It is believed that a data warehouse is for operational decision making. Recently, a proposal was made to support decision making for formulating policy enforcement rules that enforce policies. These rules are expressed in the WHEN-IF-THEN form. Guidelines are proposed to elicit two types of actions, triggering actions that cause the policy violation and the corresponding correcting actions. The decision-making problem is that of selecting the most appropriate correcting action in the event of a policy violation. This selection requires information. The elicited information is unstructured and is "early." This work is extended by proposing a method to directly convert early information into its multi-dimensional form. For this, an early information mode is proposed. The proposed conversion process is a fully automated one. Further, the tool support is extended to accommodate the conversion process. The authors also apply the method to a health domain.

INTRODUCTION

Traditionally a data warehouse (DW) supports operational work related decision-making (Inmon, 2005). Recent proposals address the full range of corporate decision making. (Prakash and Prakash, 2015) address the issue of providing support for policy formulation decisions. (Prakash and Gupta, 2014) support decision making for formulating policy enforcement rules (PER).

(Prakash, 2010) showed that there is in fact a decision continuum that exists in the decision making environment of an organization. The outer most layer of the continuum is where policy formulation decisions are taken. Once policies have been formulated, policy enforcement rules are formulated. PER formulation decisions form the next inner layer. PERs enforce policies in the organization. Once the policy enforcement rules are formulated, operational decisions are taken. Operational decision form

DOI: 10.4018/978-1-5225-7271-8.ch011

the inner most layer of the continuum. It is possible to move from the policy decision layer to the PER layer and from the PER layer to the operational layer. A DW is required to support the three layers of decision making.

Based on this view, the data warehouse requirements engineering (DWRE) process has three main steps (a) identifying the set of decisions, (b) eliciting information to support the decisions, and (c) converting information into multi-dimensional structure.

A number of techniques exist to convert information to multi-dimensional structure. They can be classified based on the number of steps required to complete this conversion. The one-step approach identifies facts and dimensions as a one shot activity. The two and the three step approaches break the requirements engineering task into smaller pieces and therefore techniques are developed for each piece.

Techniques of (Giorgini, 2005; Giorgini, 2009; Salinesi and Gam, 2006; Mazon, 2007) follow the one step approach where the moment information is determined, by the stakeholder, facts and dimensions are identified. This process of identification is unguided and completely based on the experience of the requirements engineer/developer.

Two-step approaches have been proposed by (Boehnlein, 1999; Boehnlein, 2000; Bonifati, 2001; Corr and Stagnitto, 2012). The first step in the two-steps is usually a generic representation of information. (Boehnlein, 1999; Boehnlein, 2000) map service measures, from stakeholders, to SERM. In the next step multi-dimensional structures are obtained from SERM diagram. In the case of (Bonifati, 2001), abstraction sheets capture quality, variation factors among others. This is treated as information which is converted to the MD structure in the second step. (Corr and Stagnitto, 2012) obtains MD structure from tables. It is in the tables that information is captured. In all the three techniques, the intermediate step can be used to guide the process of identifying the MD structure.

Three-step processes include (Prakash and Gupta, 2014). Here the identified information is 'early', which is defined as unstructured information. In the second step, early information is converted to ER diagram which in the third step is converted into the multi-dimensional form. For the third step the authors rely on the work by (Golfarelli, 1998; Moody, 2000).

Broadly speaking, the number of steps is an indication of the complexity of the process. Therefore, it is good to reduce the number of steps. The difficulty with reducing the number of steps is that the properties of information like aggregation required, historical period is lost.

We propose to solve this problem by first introducing an early information model. This model gives us the flexibility to explore further properties of information. Subsequently we propose an algorithmic approach to directly move from early information to multi-dimensional model.

Our technique can be applied to a three-step proposal thereby converting the three step process into a two-step process. It can also be applied to a two-step process where, while the number of steps remains the same, properties of information are explored.

Further, since our conversion process is algorithmic, it is fully automated, systematic and does not require intervention by the requirements engineer. Thus, our process is much faster than the other processes with manual intervention. This process was first outlined in (Prakash, 2018) and is fully detailed here. Additionally, a tool has been developed in this paper that uses this algorithm.

The layout of this paper is as follows. In the next section, we present an overview of the approach of (Prakash and Gupta, 2014). Here policy enforcement rules are formulated, and the set of decisions are identified. Thereafter, we discuss our early information model. Subsequently, we discuss the early information elicitation techniques. This is followed by our algorithmic approach to convert early information into multi-dimensional form. Subsequently, we discuss our tool support for the same. We apply our methodology to the same case study as (Prakash and Gupta, 2014) and present the lessons learnt. Finally, we state the conclusion.

POLICY ENFORCEMENT RULE FORMULATION DECISIONS

In order to formulate policy enforcement rules the set of policies of an organization must already be formulated. Formulated policies are expressed in extended first order logic form which is discussed below.

Representing Policies

There are two kinds of variables, those that denote a single value, SV, and others that denote a set of values, CV.

- A simple *term, ST,* can either be
  ◦ A constant
  ◦ an SV
  ◦ an *n*-adic function symbol applied to *n* SVs
- A *collective term, CT,* is
  ◦ a CV
  ◦ an *n*-adic function symbol applied to *n* CVs
- An *atom* is P(x1....xn) where P is a predicate and xi is either ST or CT. There are standard predicates for the six relational operators named EQ (x, y), NEQ (x, y), GEQ (x, y), LEQ (x, y), GQ (x, y), LQ (x, y)
- Every atom is a formula
- If F1, F2 are formulae then F1 AND F2, F1 OR F2 and Not F1 are formulae
- If F1, F2 are formulae then F1 → F2 is also a formula
- If F1 is a formula then ∃ sF1 and ∀ sF1 are formulae. Here s is a variable.
- Parenthesis may be placed around formulae as needed
- Nothing else is a formula.

The precedence while evaluating the formulae is as follows:

- Universal and existential quantifiers, ∀, ∃

Logical AND, OR, NOT
As an example consider the policy "the number of beds in a semi-private ward must be at-least one but not greater than 3"
This is represented as:

S(x): x is a semi private ward
LEQ(x,c1): x is less than or equal to to c1 where c1 is a constant
GT(x,c1): x is greater than c1 where c1 is a constant
b is a set of beds

∀x∃b[S(x)→ LEQ(count(b),3) AND GT(count(b),1)]

Now, there can be several ways to represent a natural language statement in first order logic. (Prakash and N, 2018) have proposed metrics that measure the structural complexity of policies. Lower the value of the metrics higher is the understand-ability. Thus, here we assume that these metrics have been applied to the policies and suitable ones selected. The selected policies form the set of formulated policies.

Representing Policy Enforcement Rules

Once the policies have been formulated, the next issue is to ensure their compliance. This is done by formulating policy enforcement rules (PER).

Let us re-examine the structure of any formulated policy. Notice the general form of a policy is left hand side formula-implication-right hand side formula. The formulae can be of two types. A complex formula is one that has one of the following:

- Conjunctions, or
- Disjunctions, or
- n-adic functions.

All other formulae are simple.

Based on the nature of the formulae on either side of the implication, we divide policies into four categories namely,

1. Simple-Simple or SS: Consider the policy every lecturer must have a Ph.D degree represented as ∀x∃b [Lecturer(x)→ Degree(x, Ph.D)]. Here both the LHS and the RHS are simple and so the policy is of type SS.
2. Simple-Complex or SC: As an example of SC policy, consider every undergraduate class can have a maximum of 60 students and a minimum of 10 students. This policy can be represented as ∀x∃s [UG(x)→ LEQ (s, 60) AND GEQ (s,10)] where x is an undergraduate class and s is a set of students. Here, while the LHS is simple, the RHS is complex due to the conjunction AND.
3. Complex-Simple or CS: The policy ∀x [lecturer(x) AND GEQ(experience(x), 8)→ designation(x, Assoc_Prof)] has the LHS as complex and RHS as simple and so is CS type.
4. Complex-Complex or CC: Consider the policy every student who has less than 70% attendance or whose has got an E grade has to repeat the course wither in summer or during the next semester. This is represented as ∀x[LEQ (attendance(x), 70) OR grade(x, E)→repeat(x, summer) OR repeat (x, sem)]. Clearly, due to OR on both the LHS and RHS side, the policy is a complex one.

An organization is compliant with its policy if both the LHS and the RHS of the implication are True. Now, a policy violation occurs when an action causes either the LHS to be False when the RHS is True or RHS to be False when LHS is True. Such an action is called a triggering action. The task naturally, is to find the necessary correcting actions so that the organization is brought back into being policy compliant.

A PER is expressed in the following format:

WHEN triggering action IF condition THEN correcting action

This brings us to the structure of the triggering action and correcting action. An action takes on the form of <verb><range variable>. The range variable represents a single instance of a noun. A range variable can be defined as: <noun><range variable>. A noun can be a simple noun or can be a noun-noun modification. For example, ward is a simple noun whereas private ward is formed by a noun-noun modification.

In other words, a PER is of the form:

WHEN <verb><range variable> IF condition THEN <verb><range variable>

The remaining question is to determine guidelines to elicit correcting actions.

Eliciting Actions

We elicit correcting actions using two guidelines as mentioned below:

- **Guideline I:** We suggest to the requirements engineer to define one or more triggering actions to make LHS true. Now, policy violation occurs when the RHS becomes false. Therefore, we have to elicit correcting actions that cause RHS to become *true*.
- **Guideline II:** We suggest to the requirements engineer to define one or more triggering actions to make RHS false. Policy violation can occur if the LHS of the policy is true. To avoid this, correcting action to make the LHS false has to be elicited.

These guidelines are applied to each of the policy types namely SS, SC, CS and CC. Once the necessary triggering and correcting actions are elicited, the PER is constructed by filling in the actions in the WHEN-IF-THEN format.

We consider the same example as in (Prakash and Gupta, 2014) for the sake of continuity. For the policy

$$\forall x[S(x) \rightarrow LEQ(count(b),3) \text{ AND } GT(count(b),1)]$$

We define range variables:

<Semi-private ward> <*spw*>

<bed> <*b*>

Guideline I

When a new semi private ward is started, then since count(b) is zero, the correcting action has to increase the number of beds to at-least one. We can elicit actions as follows:

1. Purchase bed
2. Transfer bed

Thus, we obtain two policy enforcement rules for the triggering action start semi-private ward. These are:

- WHEN start *spw* IF !GT(count(*b*),1) THEN Purchase *b*
- WHEN start *spw* IF !GT(count(*b*),1) THEN Transfer *b*

Guideline II

If bed is removed from the ward then it may happen that there is no bed left in the ward, i.e., GT(count(*b*),1) is false. In this case correcting action to falsify the LHS is to be elicited. The elicited action may be 'Relocate semi-private ward'. This gives us the policy enforcement rule

- WHEN remove *b* IF !(GT(count(*b*),1)) THEN Relocate *spw*

ELISPE

Policy enforcement rule formulation was implemented using an in-house tool, ELiciting Information Support for Policy Enforcement (ELISPE). The front end part of the tool deals with action elicitation and policy enforcement rule formulation. We, in this paper, reuse the front end architecture of ELISPE. The user interfaces are also kept the same. The back end part is looked at in the subsequent sections.

Organizational policies are present in the policy base (Figure 1). These policies are presented one at a time in textual form to the requirements engineer to the Action Elicitor. For each policy, the Action Elicitor applies the guidelines stated above. The elicited actions are stored in the Action base (see Figure 1).

The actions in the Action base are now input in the policy enforcement rule maker and the policy enforcement rules are stored in the policy enforcement base. The actions are divided depending upon whether they play a triggering or correcting role. The tool constructs the rule in the WHEN IF THEN format.

Figure 1. The front end architecture of ELISPE

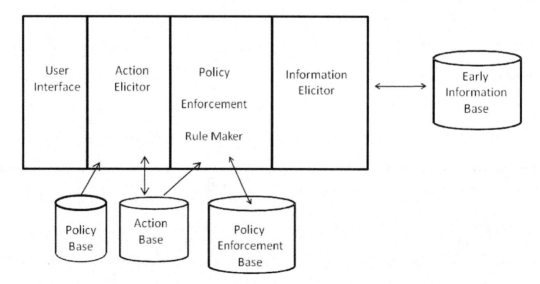

DW support has to be provided to decide on which correcting action is to be implemented in the event of a policy violation. Suppose an action 'start semi-private ward' is performed in the organization. This is a triggering action for the policy '$\forall x[S(x) \rightarrow LEQ(count(b),3)$ AND $GT(count(b),1)]$'. The decision making task is to determine which correcting action is to be taken. In other words, we have to choose one from the choice set {select 'transfer bed', select 'purchase bed'}.

In order to choose one from the choice set, information is required. While (Prakash and Gupta, 2014) gave the components of early information, we formally develop a model. We present the same in the next section.

EARLY INFORMATION MODEL

The early information model is shown in Figure 2 below.

As can be seen, early information is of the following types:

1. Detailed early information: Information here is at the lowest grain. For example, suppose a university wants to increase its presence at conferences by funding the professors. Detailed information will therefore reflect the amount allocated to *each* professor of the university.
2. Aggregate early information: This type of information is summarized. It is obtained from detailed information or from previously aggregated information. An example is *total* amount of funds given by the university. Notice, that there is no mention any particular professor. Generally, aggregations come to us in many forms, for example, as functions like sum, count, min, max etc. The relationship 'function-of' between aggregate information and information captures this.

Information can be historical and has two properties. Duration indicates the time for which this information needs to be maintained in the DW to-be and Time unit tells us the temporal unit of capturing this information namely daily, monthly, yearly etc.

Information can be computed from other information. For example, sales revenue per product is calculated from the number of units sold multiplied by the sales price per unit. Both number of units sold and sales price are detailed information, there is no aggregate function used here. This relationship is captured as 'computed from' between information and information.

Figure 2. The early information model

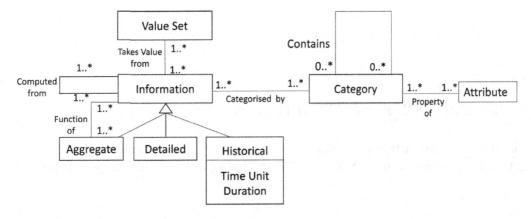

Information is related to Value Set by a relationship. For example, number of units of beds purchased is information that takes values from the set of integers. Similarly, value in rupees of beds purchased is a piece of information that is related to the set of real numbers.

Information can be categorized by category as shown by the information-category relationship in Figure 2. Using this relationship, information can be categorized in different ways. Consider the example of university conference funding. The funding given can be categorized professor wise and department wise where department and professor become categories for information 'university funding'. Figure 2 also shows that categories have attributes associated with them. This tells us the descriptive properties of category. So for category department, the name of the department is one of the attributes.

A category may 'contain' other categories. For example, in the example considered above, there are two categories, department and professor. In a typical university set up, two or more departments come make an Area. So, for example, the departments of electronics and computer science come under Engineering while departments of biology and chemistry come under Sciences. In other words, a department is contained in an Area or an Area 'contains' department.

Now, after the set of decisions have been identified, the elicited early information is modelled by instantiating Figure 2. Let us consider an example. A hospital keeps information about the average time the patient spends in the hospital before s/he gets to visit a doctor. Let us refer to this as the waiting time of patients. Waiting time is calculated as the time between registration and consultation. Here average time spent for consultation per doctor and department is needed and the average is to be taken over a month. A history if 5 years is to be maintained.

Clearly, this is aggregate information with the function average. The aggregate function, Average, is applied after calculating the difference between Time of registration and Time of consultation. Thus, we obtain:

Information

```
Average waiting time of patient
Function: Average
Computed from: Time of registration; Time of consultation;
Category: Department, Doctor
Categorized by:
        < waiting time, department>
        < waiting time, doctor>
Attributes:
1. Department Attributes: Name
2. Doctor Attributes: Name, Designation, Specialization, Experience in years
History Time Unit and Duration: Monthly; 5 years
```

EARLY INFORMATION ELICITATION TECHNIQUES

Now that the early information model has been presented, we require techniques for eliciting early information. In addition to CSFI, ENDSI and MEANSI analysis techniques described in (Prakash and

Gupta, 2014), in this paper, we enhance the suit of elicitation techniques by adding a fourth technique called the Outcome feedback information (OFI).

All the four techniques provide the necessary focal points that guide the information elicitation process. Let us look at the four techniques.

Critical Success Factor Information (CSFI): here the focal point is the factors a manager considers as critical to his/her success. These factors are called critical success factors (CSF). For example, for the decision to 'start a new private ward', one of the CSF can be the availability and non-availability of the ward.

CSFI analysis is a two-step process, (a) identify CSF, and (b) for each CSF identified in step (a) elicit early information. Early information is required to assess the factors. In our example, the number of times a private ward has been requested and not been available to patients is one piece of early information. Let us say that for this information the time unit is daily and the information has to be kept for one year. Instantiating our early information model above with this information we get,

Information 1

```
Requests for private ward
Category: Private Ward
Computed from: Allocated status (Boolean valued: yes or no)
Categorized by:
          < requests, private ward>
Attributes: (1) Private ward: Room number
History Time Unit and Duration: daily; 1
```

Ends Information (ENDSI)

The focus is on identifying the end that is to be achieved by taking the decision. For the same decision to "start a new private ward", one end can be to provide treatment to various patients.

ENDSI analysis is a three step process, (a) identify ends, (b) for each end, identify its effectiveness factor, and (c) for each effectiveness factor elicit early information. In our example, one of the effectiveness factors can be facilities provided. Information required to access the facilities provided is to know the number of equipment, furniture per private ward. Again instantiating the early information model, we get:

Information 2

```
Facilities provided
Function: Sum
Category: private ward, equipment, furniture
Categorized by:
          <Facilities, private ward>
          < Facilities, lab equipment >
          < Facilities, furniture>
Attributes:
```

```
(1) Equipment: Name, Type, IDNumber, Price
(2) Furniture: Name, Type, IDNumber, Price
(3) Private ward: Room number
```
History Time Unit and Duration: quarterly; 1

Means Information (MEANSI): The focus is to identify early information to measure the efficiency of the means adopted to achieve the end. For the same decision to "start a new private ward", one mean can be to construct a new ward.

MEANSI analysis is a three step process, (a) identify means, (b) for each mean, identify its efficiency factor, and (c) for each efficiency factor elicit early information. One of the efficiency factors for the mean construct new private ward is the resources needed. Information to measure this efficiency factor is space required, cost per square metre etc. Thus, we obtain:

Information 3

```
Construction details
```
Computed from: Space in m², cost per m²
Category: private ward
Categorized by:
```
        <Facilities, private ward>
```
Attributes: (1) Private ward: Room number
History Time Unit and Duration: yearly; 5

Outcome feedback information (OFI): The effect a decision has on its environment is considered. This is in accordance with Sterman (Sterman, 1989) who states that when a decision causes a change in its environment, the changed environment in turn alters the conditions of the choice. This change in the choice feeds back into the decision thus forming a cycle. For example, let us say that the decision to start a private ward is taken. Now, this may result in an increase in the number of patients. An increase in the number of patients will mean that another private ward may have to be started forming a cycle.

OFI is a two-step process (a) Identification of outcome variable (b) elicitation of information for each variable. In our example, the feedback variable is increase in the number of patients. Information is the yearly count of patients for each department of the hospital. In other words,

Information 4

```
Patients Admitted
```
Function: Count
Computed from: Date of admission
Category: patient, private ward wise
Categorized by:
```
        < patients admitted, private ward>
        < patients admitted, patient>
```
Attributes:
```
        (1) Private ward: Room number
```

```
        (2) Patient: Registration Number, Name, Age, Gender
History Time Unit and Duration: daily; 1
```

Now the remaining question is to directly convert the information elicited into a multi-dimensional model.

EARLY INFORMATION TO MULTI-DIMENSIONAL MODEL

The entire information obtained by applying the four elicitation techniques above is converted into a multi-dimensional schema. We, in this section, propose a set of rules to derive the multidimensional schema from early information.

Rule 1: Early information is the FACT.
Rule 2: The 'computed-from' fields are the measures.
Rule 3: Categories form the Dimensions and their attributes become dimensional attributes.
Rule 4: Each 'Contains' indicates a dimensional hierarchy.
Rule 5: If history is to be maintained then the fact created is augmented to include a time stamp. Further, a Date dimension is added to the schema.

These rules have been formalized as an algorithm which is presented below.
Algorithm: Conversion of early information to multi-dimensional schema

```
Input: Early Information, I
Output: Snowflake schema for I
1:  for Each early information, I do
2:       F:= createfact(I)
3:       for Each computed-from,M, associated with I do
4:            addMeasure(M,I);
5:       for Each category, C associated with I do
6:            D:= createDimension(C);
7:            if D does not exist then
8:                 for Each attribute, A, linked to category C do
9:                      Add A to D as a Dimensional attribute
10:                end for
11:                Link D to F;
12:           end if
13:           else Link already existing D to F and discard current D
14:           for Each category, cc, contained in C do
15:                SD = createSubDimension(cc)
16:                if SD does not exist then
17:                     for Each attribute, A, linked to cc do
18:                          Add A to SD as a Dimensional attribute
19:                     end for
20:                     Link SD to D
```

```
21:              end if
22:              else Link already existing SD to D and discard current SD
23:         end for
24:    end for
25:    if History is to be maintained then
26:         for Each D, linked to F, for which history is required do
27:              Augment(D, timestamp)
28:         end for
29:         Add Dimension Date and link to F
30:    end if
31: end for
```

For each piece of early information, I, the function *createfact* (step 2) takes I as the argument and creates a fact of the multidimensional schema. Each element of the 'computed from' field of the early information, I, becomes measures of the Fact. Steps 3 and 4 show the same.

Now, the remaining task is to identify the dimensions. For this the *createdimension* function takes each 'category' of I and makes it into a dimension. Internally, this function generates a surrogate key field for the dimension. Attributes of the category become attributes of the dimension. The dimensions are then connected to the Fact (steps 5-13). Further, if any category has a 'contains' property then *createSubDimension* creates a sub-dimension between the category and its contained category. The attributes of the sub-dimension are obtained in a manner similar to the one for obtaining attributes for dimensions (steps 14-24).

If history is to be maintained then the fact created is augmented to include a time stamp, TS, by the Augment function (steps 25-31). Further, a Date dimension is added to the schema.

A special mention of step 7 of the algorithm: Suppose one piece of early information has a category c. When we apply algorithm 3 we will obtain dimension D. Let another piece of information also have category c. Recall, that early information has already been integrated and conflicts have been resolved. Thus, the attributes of category c will be the same across all pieces of information categorized by category c. In other words, once a dimension has been created, there is no need to create it again and we can simply link the old dimension to the new fact. This has been taken care of in steps 7 and 13 of the algorithm. This has also been done in the case of sub-category (steps 16 and 22).

Notice that due to the 'contains' relationship between categories, the resulting multi-dimensional schema is a snowflake schema. Naturally, if there is no contains relationship we obtain a star schema.

Let us apply our algorithm to the elicited early information in the previous section. Let us say that the first information to be processed is Information 1. Request for private ward becomes the Fact. It is computed from allocated status and thus 'allocated status becomes the measure. The information is to be categorized private ward wise. This gives us the dimension private ward. Since this is the first piece of early information being processed, dimension private ward does not already exist. Each attribute of category private ward is added as dimensional attributes to the dimension private ward. Now the dimension private ward is linked to the Fact Request for private ward. Since information is to be captured on a daily basis as indicated by the field History, data in dimensions Patient is time-stamped and a date dimension is added and linked to the fact.

Subsequently this process is repeated for information 2, 3 and 4 of the previous section. Notice the dimension private ward and date were already created while processing information 1 and therefore need not be created again. The existing dimensions are simply linked to the new facts created. The full schema obtained is shown in Figure 3.

IMPLEMENTATION

We enhanced the back end of ELISPE to include the concepts introduced in this paper. This is shown in Figure 4. The Information Elicitor of Figure 2 has been expanded here. Actions in the Action base are the input to the information elicitation section of the tool. The four information elicitation techniques are applied and early information relevant for an action is elicited. This early information is stored in the early information base.

The early information from the early information base is input into the MD Structure Generator. Here early information is converted into the multi-dimensional structure by implementing the algorithm.

As before, we reuse the user interface for CSFI, ENDSI and MEANSI analysis. Figure 5 shows the user interface for OFI analysis.

The user interface for OFI analysis is shown in Figure 5. The top left hand side of the screen shows the action for which the analysis is being done. The requirements engineer can either choose an existing outcome or add a new outcome. When the former is chosen a list of the existing outcomes are displayed. Along with this, the option of updating this outcome is also given. As seen in the figure the outcome that already exists is 'Increase in patient admissions'. For a new outcome to be inserted, the 'add new outcome' radio button is clicked. Figure 5 shows a new outcome 'additional equipment required' being inserted.

Let us look at the structure of the early information base. Each piece of elicited information is associated with the decision it is elicited for. It may happen that the same piece of information is elicited for more than one decision. In this case, the information will be associated with each decision separately.

The repository supporting the tool is in three parts as shown in Figure 6. The action base contains the actions; CSF, effectiveness factor, efficiency factor and outcome factor base contains the factors and variables; early information base contains information resulting from the population of the early information model. These three parts are related to one another as shown in the figure.

Figure 3. Multi-dimensional schema obtained after applying algorithm

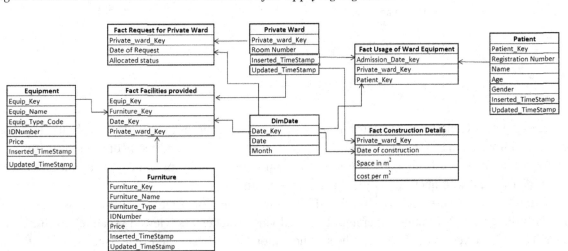

Figure 4. Architecture of enhanced ELISPE

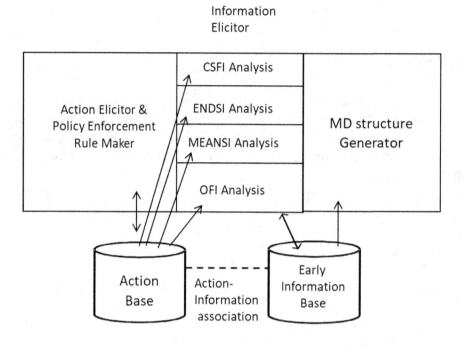

Figure 5. User interface for OFI analysis

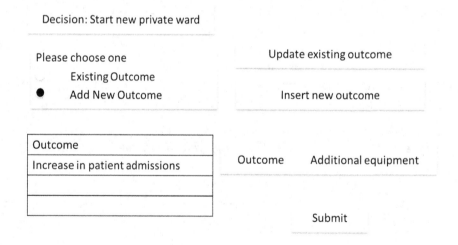

The repository exploits the relationship between the different bases to provide traceability. Information in the information base can be traced back to its source action either directly or transitively through factors and variables. It is also possible to retrieve information relevant to given action as well as to factors and variables. A query facility exists to support this.

Figure 7 shows the user interface for the MD structure generator. There are two options for viewing the multi-dimensional structure generated. Each individual fact can be viewed separately or the entire schema can be viewed. As can be seen, the second option has been selected. The panel at the bottom of

Figure 6. The structure of the repository

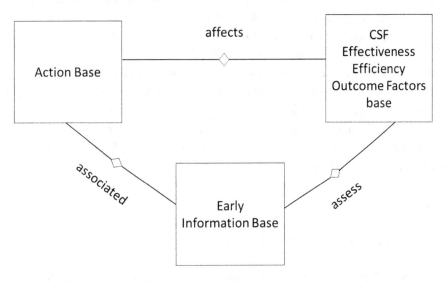

Figure 7. The generated multi-dimensional model

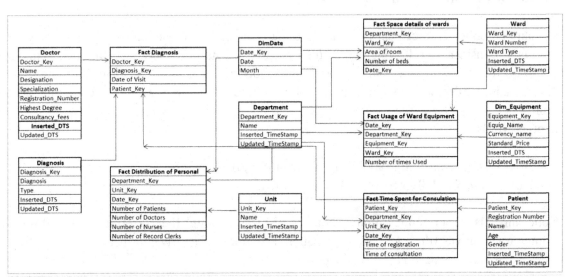

the screen displays the entire schema. The linking of the facts with the dimensions is done based on the dimensional key column name and an arrow appears automatically.

We applied our technique to the same medical system of (Prakash and Gupta, 2014). This is a traditional system offering treatments in Ayurvedic medicine, Yoga, Unani and Naturopathy. The policy base of the tool was populated with policies of the hospital.

As stated there are a total of 151 policies. The action elicitor of ELISPE elicited a total of 1624 actions. This included both triggering and correcting actions. The actions are stored in the Action base. These are then input to the policy enforcement rule maker. Total number of policies enforcement rules obtained from guideline 1 was 492 and from guideline 2 was 320. This gives us the total number of policy enforcement rules to be 812. These are stored in the policy enforcement base.

1134 actions were found to be common actions and as reported in (Prakash and Gupta, 2014). We only consider 524 unique actions for early information elicitation. These 524 actions are taken through the four techniques of information elicitation. The elicited early information is stored in the early information base. Finally, the elicited early information in input to the MD structure generator and the multi-dimensional structure is obtained.

Lessons Learned

(Prakash and Gupta, 2014) discussed the lesson learned as

1. Actions that are both triggering and correcting are considered only once for information elicitation.
2. MEANSI, and ENDSI is applicable to almost all the actions.
3. CSFI is applicable to only a more limited number of actions.

In addition to the above observations, other lessons learnt by us are as follows:

Effect of Common Correcting Actions

More than one policy enforcement rule can have the same correcting action for different triggering action. Let us consider the following two. In the first case, the start of a new speciality means that the patient to doctor ratio is not met and the correcting action for this is to hire a doctor d. In the second PER, resignation of doctors causes the number of doctors to fall below 3 and so the correcting action is to hire a doctor d.

In other words,

1. WHEN *start speciality* IF !(ratio(count(p),count(d),1,6) THEN *hire d*.
2. WHEN *resign d* IF !GEQ(count(d),3) THEN *hire d*.

Notice hire d is the correcting action for both the PERs even though the triggering action is different.

Common actions yield the same early information. Therefore, once early information has been elicited for a particular action, it need not be done again.

Effect of OFI Analysis

Inclusion of OFI analysis provided a new focal point for identifying information. We found two effects of this:

- The major effect was that it led to more triggering actions being generated. More triggering actions meant new correcting actions and this in turn led to formulation of new policy enforcement rules.
- It was applicable to almost all the actions.

A further analysis of the effect of OFI analysis could have to be carried out.

Effect of the Direct Conversion of Early Information to Multi-Dimensional Model

Our conversion is an algorithmic process that is implemented as part of the ELISPE tool. Being automatic it removes any intervention by the requirements engineer.

When we compare this to the three-step process we find:

- Early information to ER conversion requires intervention of the requirements engineer. In fact while the entities and attributes are relatively easily identified, for the ER diagram to be completed, the relationships between entities and cardinalities also have to be worked out. This process is a completely manual and often requires a domain expert.
- The conversion of ER diagram to its multi-dimensional form is a semi-automated process. The disadvantages of this have been highlighted in (Prakash and Prakash, 2009).

Finally, we conclude that this direct conversion shifts the focus from conversion to decision discovery and structuring information.

CONCLUSION

DWRE for policy enforcement rule formulation involves (a) identifying the set of decisions (b) eliciting information to support these decisions, and (c) converting information to facts and dimensions.

For (b), we have proposed an early information model. This model helps us explore properties of information like categorization, aggregation etc. We have also introduced a fourth analysis technique called the outcome feedback information, OFI analysis. This is in addition to CSFI, ENDSI and MEANSI. The information elicited is in accordance with the model developed.

For (c), we have developed an algorithmic approach to convert early information to multi-dimensional model. The benefits of this are that it being fully automated approach makes it faster than other manual approaches and also no manual intervention is required in the process.

We enhance the ELISPE tool to include our extensions.

REFERENCES

Boehnlein, M., & Ulbrich vom Ende, A. (1999). Deriving initial Data Warehouse Structures from the Conceptual Data Models of the Underlying Operational Information Systems. In *Proc. Of Workshop on Data Warehousing and OLAP* (pp. 15-21). ACM 10.1145/319757.319780

Boehnlein, M., & Ulbrich vom Ende, A. (2000). Business Process Oriented Development of Data Warehouse Structures. In Proceedings of Data Warehousing 2000 (pp. 3- 21). PhysicaVerlag HD. doi:10.1007/978-3-642-57681-2_1

Bonifati A. Cattaneo, F., Ceri, S., Fuggetta, A., & Paraboschi, S. (2001). Designing Data Marts for Data Warehouses. *ACM Transactions on Software Engineering and Methodology*, *10*(4), 452–483. doi:10.1145/384189.384190

Corr, L., & Stagnitto, J. (2012). *Agile Data Warehouse Design*. DecisionOne Press.

Giorgini, P., Rizzi, S., & Garzetti, M. (2005). Goal-oriented requirement analysis for data warehouse design. In *Proceedings of the 8th ACM international workshop on Data warehousing and OLAP* (pp. 47-56). ACM 10.1145/1097002.1097011

Giorgini, P., Rizzi, S., & Garzetti, M. (2008). GRAnD: A goal-oriented approach to requirement analysis in data warehouses. *Decision Support Systems*, *45*(1), 4–21. doi:10.1016/j.dss.2006.12.001

Golfarelli, M., Maio, D., & Rizzi, S. (1998). Conceptual Design of Data Warehouses from E/R schemes. In *System Sciences, 1998, Proceedings of the Thirty-First Hawaii International Conference on* (*Vol. 7*, pp. 334-343). IEEE.

Inmon, B. (2005). *Building the data warehouse* (4th ed.). New York: John Wiley & Sons.

Leal, C. A., Mazón, J. N., & Trujillo, J. (2013). A business-oriented approach to data warehouse development. *Ingenieria e Investigacion*, *33*(1), 59–65.

Mazón, J. N., Pardillo, J., & Trujillo, J. (2007). A model-driven goal-oriented requirement engineering approach for data warehouses. In *Advances in Conceptual Modeling–Foundations and Applications* (pp. 255–264). Springer Berlin Heidelberg. doi:10.1007/978-3-540-76292-8_31

Nasiri, A., Wrembel, R., & Zimányi, E. (2015) Model-Based Requirements Engineering for Data Warehouses: From Multidimensional Modelling to KPI Monitoring. In *International Conference on Conceptual Modeling* (pp. 198-209). Springer. 10.1007/978-3-319-25747-1_20

Prakash, D., (2018). Direct Conversion of Early Information to Multi-dimensional model. *ENASE 2018*.

Prakash, D., & Gupta, D. (2014). Eliciting data warehouse contents for policy enforcement rules. *International Journal of Information System Modeling and Design*, *5*(2), 41–69. doi:10.4018/ijismd.2014040103

Prakash, D., & Prakash, N. (2015, November). Towards DW support for formulating policies. In *IFIP Working Conference on The Practice of Enterprise Modeling* (pp. 374-388). Springer. 10.1007/978-3-319-25897-3_24

Prakash, N., Prakash, D., & Gupta, D. (2010, June). Decisions and decision requirements for data warehouse systems. In *Forum at the Conference on Advanced Information Systems Engineering (CAiSE)* (pp. 92-107). Springer.

Prakash, N., Prakash, D., & Sharma, Y. K. (2009). Towards Better Fitting Data Warehouse Systems. In The Practice of Enterprise Modeling (pp. 130-144). Springer Berlin Heidelberg. doi:10.1007/978-3-642-05352-8_11

Prakash, N. (2018). Measuring Understandability of Organizational Policies: A Metric Based Approach. *International Journal of Cooperative Information Systems, 27*(2).

Salinesi, C., & Gam, I. (2006, June). A requirement-driven approach for designing data warehouses. In Requirements Engineering: Foundations for Software Quality (REFSQ'06) (p. 1). Academic Press.

Sterman, J. D. (1989). Modeling managerial behavior: Misperceptions of feedback in a dynamic decision making experiment. *Management Science, 35*(3), 321–339. doi:10.1287/mnsc.35.3.321

Chapter 12
Managing Variability as a Means to Promote Composability:
A Robotics Perspective

Matthias Lutz
Ulm University of Applied Sciences, Germany

Juan F. Inglés-Romero
Biometric Vox, S.L., Spain

Dennis Stampfer
Ulm University of Applied Sciences, Germany

Alex Lotz
Ulm University of Applied Sciences, Germany

Cristina Vicente-Chicote
Universidad de Extremadura, Spain

Christian Schlegel
Ulm University of Applied Sciences, Germany

ABSTRACT

Complex systems usually have to deal with a huge number of potential situations and contingencies. Therefore, a mechanism is required that enables the expression of variability at design-time so that it can be efficiently resolved at run-time. As composability plays an increasingly relevant role in building systems in an economic way, variability management should also contribute to and be taken into account in terms of composability. This chapter presents a variability management workflow aimed at supporting different developer roles in an ecosystem context. Two kinds of variability are addressed: in system operation and associated with quality of service. The former provides robustness to contingencies, while the latter focuses on the quality of the application (in terms of non-functional properties) under changing situations and limited resources. The concepts introduced in this chapter conform to the structures and principles of the H2020 European Project RobMoSys, which consolidates composability in the robotics domain.

DOI: 10.4018/978-1-5225-7271-8.ch012

INTRODUCTION

With more and more mature robotic technology available (e.g. real-world capable localization systems, cheap and safe robotic manipulators and mobile platforms, etc.) and an increasing number of robotic systems being visible, the push on the expectations to bring robotic technology into application is getting stronger. However, robotic software development is still challenging and expensive. Actually, the need for systematic software engineering and development approaches in robotics has been recognized by the Strategic Research Agenda for Robotics in Europe (euRobotics aisbl, 2013-2014).

Nowadays, assembling applications out of existing components remains an open challenge. Integrating pre-existing building blocks usually requires extensive adaptations to make them fit together and fulfill the overall user and system requirements. These adaptations are not only costly, but also hinder reusability and maintainability. As a result, a paradigm shift from integration to composability is being increasingly demanded. Composability is the ability to combine and recombine building blocks as-is into different systems for different purposes. Composability requires that (i) the building blocks make their properties explicitly available, and that (ii) the system guaranties that these properties remain invariant under composition.

In this vein, the H2020 European Project RobMoSys (RobMoSys, 2017-2020) aims at providing composable models and software for robotic system development applying model-driven methods and tools. RobMoSys aims at coordinating the whole community's best and consorted efforts to realize a step-change towards an ecosystem for open and sustainable industry-grade robotics software development. Apart from composability, separation of roles and concerns, and "freedom from choice" (Lee 2010) (as an alternative to the more conventional "freedom of choice") are key design principles at the core of RobMoSys. It is worth mentioning that the contributions presented in this chapter conform with the RobMoSys structures and principles.

With these principles in mind, it is worth noting that service robots (e.g., companion, health care, or co-working robots) are expected to robustly and efficiently fulfill different tasks in complex environments. Being able to cope with the inherent complexity of open-ended environments (e.g., domestic, outdoor or crowded public spaces), together with the growing demand of more and more complex and "intelligent" (e.g., adaptive) behaviors, requires taking variability into account from the very beginning, throughout the whole system design and development process and, even beyond, at run-time. In fact, variability modeling and management, spanning from design-time to run-time, across different roles and building blocks in an ecosystem, needs to be faced in order to achieve composability.

Dealing with variability is nothing new neither in robotics nor in other application domains. However, it has been traditionally addressed in an ad-hoc way, that is, trying to predict future execution conditions and implementing specific mechanisms to deal with each particular situation. Among other issues, this approach tends to spread the variability management rationale throughout the application code, leading to increased complexity, poor reuse and difficult maintenance.

In this chapter we deal with variability from two different perspectives. On the one hand, *variability in operation* relates to how robots flexibly plan the sequence of actions they have to perform in order to fulfill their tasks, taking into account changes in the environment, noisy perception and potential execution failures. Managing variability in operation provides the robot with a high degree of robustness and allows it to maintain a high success rate in task fulfillment. On the other hand, *variability in quality* relates to the wide range of alternatives typically available to succeed in a task. Among these possibilities, some might be better than others according to quality criteria defined by the designer (e.g., in terms of resource consumption, safety, performance, etc.). Thus, managing variability in quality aims at improving the overall service robot performance.

This chapter extends our previous works, presented in (Lotz et al., 2013) and in (Lotz et al., 2014), in which two Domain Specific Languages (DSLs) were presented to separately specify *variability in operation* and *variability in quality*. This chapter presents the extensions and improvements contributed to these two DSLs. In addition, it also extends the originally proposed variability management workflow, which now considers important additional roles (e.g. system architect and behavior developer), detailing how they contribute to the robotics ecosystem. This workflow explicates which of the involved stakeholders (roles) is exposed to which variability, and how they are allowed to exploit it. In this sense, variability modeling becomes an essential ingredient for achieving separation of roles and concerns.

As illustrated in Figure 1, the proposed variability management workflow covers the entire development process, promoting separation of roles while enabling stakeholder collaboration towards system composition. Variability is constrained and refined step by step until, at run-time, the robot makes the final decisions according to the then available information, and consistently with the variability purposely left open (decision space) in the previous steps. Overall, this approach optimizes performance and systematically arranges complexity and efforts between design-time and run-time.

The chapter illustrates the proposal in the domain of robotics since robots are particularly complex software systems that naturally have to deal with open-ended environments and, as a consequence, need to manage variability. However, authors believe that the basic ideas introduced in this chapter are interesting and general enough to be considered in other domains.

The rest of this paper is structured as follows. Section 2 introduces the proposed stepwise variability management workflow. Section 3 describes the robotics example, implemented on a service robot fleet, that will be used throughout the paper to illustrate the proposal. Sections 4 and 5 introduce the improvements contributed to SmartTCL and VML, respectively, linking them with the overall development workflow. Section 6 shows how these two DSLs can be consistently executed without interfering in their individual decision spaces. Finally, section 7 presents related works and section 8 draws the conclusions and points out future work.

SEPARATION OF ROLES AND VARIABILITY MANAGEMENT

Successful business ecosystems strongly rely on the idea of *separation of roles* and *concerns* as it promotes the symbiotic coexistence and cooperation among different stakeholders based on their expertise (Figure 2). Besides, it allows to share risks and efforts and to lower costs and time to market, while increasing robustness and overall product quality. In order to support separation of roles and concerns, it becomes essential to be able to compose complex systems out of reusable building blocks defined by different roles. Thereby, our proposal relies on the Component-Based Software Engineering (CBSE) and the Model-Driven Engineering (MDE) paradigms as, together, they allow explicating the vital parts of component-based systems using models that are shared by and handed over between related (i.e., interacting) roles (Schlegel et al., 2013). These models are transformed into tailored representations using individual domain knowledge of the corresponding roles. Overall, this allows a stepwise model refinement where each role, on the one hand, individually contributes to the overall system (according to its concerns) and, on the other hand, explicates those parts in models that need to be further refined in successive development steps or, respectively, by other roles. Thus, variability is gradually reduced,

Figure 1. Proposed variability management workflow

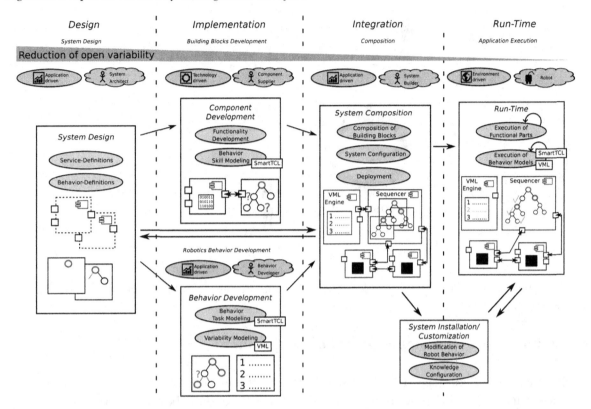

making the overall system more and more concrete until, at some point, at run-time, a final decision on the still open decision spaces is made, according to the then available information.

A key point in this approach is that the system itself is not fixed at design-time, but contains purposefully left open variability that is used at run-time. This feature becomes more and more important not only in robotics, but also in many other application domains. Increasingly, all kinds of complex information systems have to run continuously, are composed by parts of many contributing organizations, and operate in environments where the available resources frequently fluctuate. For such systems, traditional approaches break down since exhaustive verification and testing is not possible, manual reconfiguration does not scale, and offline improvement is not an option. This requires considering variability throughout the whole software development life-cycle (i.e., from design to operation).

With the idea of a robotics ecosystem in mind, and the fact that the different roles involved in robotic system development will interact and exchange artifacts (models, components, binaries, etc.), we propose a basic development workflow. The individual roles are decoupled, their contributions or requirements can be pushed to or fetched from a robotics business ecosystem market. The development of a concrete robotics application introduces a relation between the roles, which can be mapped into a workflow. This workflow is driven by the idea that each role will contribute relevant parts during the overall system development process, which can be divided into four phases, i.e., design, implementation, integration and run-time (see Figure 1). Each role contributing to the system development (or participating within the ecosystem), is somehow involved in either the definition, the realization, or the use of variability to contribute to the development of a flexible and robust robotic system. The next subsection will take

Figure 2. Different stakeholders, playing different roles, collaborate and contribute to the ecosystem

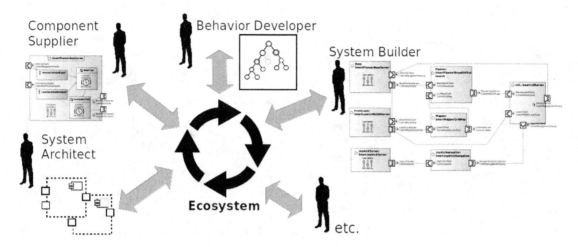

a closer look at some of the pivotal roles involved in the proposed workflow, and how they relate to system variability.

Roles Involved in the Stepwise System Refinement

During the *Design Phase* (see Figure 1, first column from the left) the role of the *System Architect* defines which interfaces will be used by the building blocks the system will be composed of. This role may either define new interfaces or reuse those provided by others in the ecosystem (e.g. using experience from the community or even meeting some common standards). The *System Architect* needs to know the application domain in order to define or select the most appropriate interfaces, i.e., the capabilities required to realize the application. The interfaces comprise several levels, defining the common point of reference for the decoupled roles to work together, e.g. the link between the variability in operation and the variability in quality models, as detailed in the following section. From a variability perspective, the most relevant interfaces are those related to component coordination and behavior coordination modeling. On the one hand, the component coordination interfaces model how components can be coordinated. At this point, the variability is expressed in terms of configuration options (e.g. the different values a parameter can take at run-time). On the other hand, the behavior coordination interfaces model how behavior blocks can be used to compose complex robot behaviors, without binding their implementation. The variability at this point is expressed in terms of behavior variables or parameters that will need to be fixed, at the latest, at run-time. Separating the specification of both component and behavior interfaces from their realization allows to easily replace building blocks based on interface compatibility, enables independent development, and promotes collaboration in the ecosystem.

During the *Implementation phase* (see Figure 1, second column from the left), the functionality within components and the robot behavior coordination is realized. The behavior coordination part includes the modeling of the operational variability. Some of the components or behavior models required for the application may not be implemented from scratch but reused as provided by other ecosystem participants. The *Component Suppliers* and *Behavior Developers*, are able to work independently, using the previously defined interfaces as a common point of reference.

Component Suppliers develop components independently of the applications they will be later composed into. These components encapsulate the functionalities required to realize any application. As these functionalities usually strongly depend on the specific underlying technology, *Component Suppliers* are technology experts in a particular domain. In addition, *Component Suppliers* also provide the skill level behavior models, according to the designed behavior and coordination interfaces. Those models realize the coordination of the components using the defined component coordination interface. Thus, with these models, *Component Providers* lift the level of abstraction and offers the basic behavior building blocks in terms of skills (e.g. move the robot, grasp something, recognize objects), providing the capabilities to realize complex robotics behaviors. The *Component Provider* uses the interface definitions specified by the System Architect during the design phase to realize the functionalities, including the defined variability (configuration options).

Behavior Developers model the required robot behaviors in terms of tasks, independently of the components, providing the functionalities. The tasks use the functionalities, through the skill behavior interfaces, during the integration phase being bound to skill level behavior models and concrete components. The role is driven by the application needs and realizes the variability at a task level, thereby using and fixing some of the variability provided either by the skill level behavior models or by other reused task level behavior models. The *Behavior Developer* may also include additional variability by specifying expansion points, together with the rules that will determine how they will be bound at run-time, using the then available information. This role is also responsible for modeling the operational variability, that is, for defining the rules and policies that will determine how the system can adapt itself in order to optimize the service it provides.

During the *Integration Phase* (see Figure 1, second column from the right) the *System Builder* selects the building blocks that will realize the system according to the interfaces defined during the design phase and composes them to a runnable system. Those building blocks can be taken from those developed during the implementation phase and from those readily available in the ecosystem marketplace. At this point, some of the available variability included both in component and behavior models is bound to meet the application requirements.

At *Run-Time* (see Figure 1, first column from the right), the system uses all the variability left open to cope with the challenges posed by the real-world environment in the best way possible. The variability available within behavior coordination models is used to flexibly orchestrate the system, considering the limited resources and the required quality of service. The left-open extension points are bound considering the operational context.

It is worth noting that some of the open extension points and configuration options may be fixed in a separated system installation or customization step, defined in between the integration and the run-time phases. In this case, the user of the system is the one that fixes (totally or partially) those variabilities according to his or her particular needs. To support this installation/customization process, the user is provided with specific tooling that displays the options and parameters that can be configured.

Domain-Specific Languages for Variability Modeling and Exploitation

This chapter proposed the use of two DSLs to deal with variability at design-time, namely: SmartTCL and VML. Each one allows the different roles to specify, in turn, variability in operation and variability in quality. This encourages the separation of two concerns: one for modeling how to coordinate the actions (e.g., a flexible task plan considering contingencies), and another one for modeling the best way of achieving a task (e.g., in terms of non-functional properties such as safety or power consumption). As later detailed in sections 4 and 5, these two languages describe dynamic variability and its run-time management, independently of the application domain and granularity. Thus, using SmartTCL and VML, together with a CBSE environment (e.g., the SmartSoft MDSD toolchain (Stampfer et al., 2016)) supports the proposed development process outlined in Figure 1. Moreover, the adoption of MDE enables stepwise system modeling and refinement by means of models and model transformations.

At run-time, variability is managed using two orthogonal mechanisms: (i) sequencing the robot's actions to handle variability in operation; and (ii) optimizing the non-functional properties for variability in quality. These two mechanisms enable the robot to decide on proper behavior variations by applying the design-time model information and taking the current situation into account. This approach improves the robustness and the task execution quality, optimizes robot performance, and systematically arranges complexity and efforts between design-time and run-time.

ROBOTICS PRODUCTION LOGISTICS SCENARIO

In this section, the robotic production logistics scenario that will be used throughout the rest of the chapter to illustrate the variability modeling capabilities offered both by SmartTCL and VML is presented (see Figure 3). In this scenario, a fleet of Robotino® robots is used to realize the flexible transportation of goods between production stations. Following the Industry 4.0 idea of flexible factories, the system is not coordinated in a classical top-down (hierarchical) fashion, but rather the individual robots organize and coordinate with each other according to the current tasks to be carried out and to the context and environment they are operating in. The flexibility achieved with the proposed approach focuses on the individual robots, improving the services each robot contributes to the fleet. The coordination among the robots in the fleet is done in a local rule-based approach (Lutz, Verbeek & Schlegel, 2016), and is not in the scope of this chapter. However, the fleet will gain from the improved services offered by the individual robots.

To achieve flexibility in robot operation, SmartTCL allows designers to model possible contingencies appearing during task execution. The sequence of appropriate actions to execute a given task often depends on constraints, such as the robot capabilities (e.g. HW compatibility with docking stations), application-specific properties (e.g. priorities of jobs) or the environment in which the robot is operating (e.g. empty hallways or crowded spaces). In the proposed scenario, the sequence of loading or unloading goods, robot to station and vice versa, may depend, for instance, on the type of station the robot is at, or if a human coworker performs some action or not. Variability is also required in case of deviations from usual execution, for instance, if docking to a station went wrong. How to deal with such situations depends on the current state of the robot and of the environment. For example, if a robot is waiting behind another robot it is not appropriate to reverse to the previous position and try docking again. Both in normal and in deviated cases, it is hard (if not impossible) to define in advance (i.e., at design time) every sequence of actions in response to all possible contingencies. Thus, the approach adopted by SmartTCL is to model rules that specify how to react on situations by finding appropriate sequence of actions to achieve a task. This approach allows realizing flexible robotic systems, while reducing the design-time assumptions developers need to make.

In order to optimize the quality of the transportation service provided by the robots, they will need to trade-off different aspects: (i) goods need to be moved as fast as possible to the stations to avoid unproductive idle times; (ii) however, depending on the environment (e.g. crowded spaces) and of the battery level, the maximal allowed velocity is limited, due to safety constraints or simply to save energy; (iii) nevertheless, fast task execution improves the overall transportation performance and allows coping with punctual workload peaks.

In addition, depending on the job to be executed, the robot can choose from (or to) which station a good is collected (or delivered) as, in the real-world scenario, multiple stations provide the same service. The robot can reach each station using different routes, implying travelling different distances. Some of these routes are more likely to be crowded, implying the need to reduce the velocity. Thus, the robot needs to decide: (i) which station to choose; (ii) how to get there; and (iii) how fast it is allowed to move. This decision can only be made at run-time (e.g., depending on the current robot battery level and on how crowded are the different routes at a given moment) and should be aimed at improving the overall quality of the robot service. Obviously, maximizing performance while simultaneously minimizing power consumption imposes conflicting requirements. At this point, VML enters into action as it allows modeling, at design-time, the existing dependencies among conflicting requirements such that, at run-time, the robot can find the right balance among them.

Although the main functionality of the robots is to provide a transportation service, regardless of how well it is performed, VML can help designers to model, on top of the functionality, QoS policies based on (often conflicting) non-functional properties. As a result, the variability modeled at design-time (e.g. the robot velocity, the station to use, and which route to take) is bound at run-time to optimize these policies according to the current application context (e.g., the robot battery level, the number of jobs to be attended, etc.).

MODELING VARIABILITY WITH SmartTCL

The Task Coordination Language (SmartTCL) (Steck & Schlegel, 2011) is used to model the behavior of robotic systems on a task and skill abstraction level (Figure 4). Task Coordination Blocks (TCB) as the central element in SmartTCL are modeled on both levels, they can be carried out by robots and are

Figure 3. Real-world robotics industry 4.0 production logistics scenario

used to orchestrate the components in a robotics software system to realize the robotic behavior. Task level models are independent of the components realizing those functionalities required to fulfill a task. Skills level models realize the connection between the realization independent tasks level models and the components realizing the functionalities. Skill level models lift the abstraction level from functional and service, realized within the components, to skill level, thereby making the functionalities accessible for robotics behavior coordination. Figure 4 illustrates the different abstraction levels a robotics system can be partitioned into.

The SmartTCL DSL is implemented as internal DSL, using Lisp as host language, the basic grammar of the DSL has been published in (Lotz et. al., 2014). The different roles developing the behavior models using SmartTCL are supported by tailored tooling integrated in the SmartMDSD Toolchain, based on a Xtext editor (Xtext, 2013).

Using the SmartMDSD Toolchain, the different roles can model TCBs (tasks and skills level) hierarchically, composing lower-level TCBs (e.g. "approach location" and "dock to production station") to higher-level TCBs (e.g. deliver good to production station), the refinement is performed during run-time. As skill level models realize the coordination of the components and the functionalities realized within (connection, configuration, activation, results, life-cycle), skill level TCBs typically form the ends and the leaf nodes of a run-time expanded task-tree. At run-time, on the robot, SmartTCL orchestrates the software components of the robot. Thereby, each TCB together with the expanded task tree represents a certain, consistent system state with all the configuration parameters for individual components.

Due to the open-ended environment service robotic system work in, it is very difficult or even impossible to predict and to model all possible situations the application will face in advance, even if the target application is known. SmartTCL, follows a different way defining general action plots for certain tasks together with open expansion points which are first bound at run-time. The expansion points are bound following rules expressed within the behavior models. The task-trees are thereby created and evolve only at run-time, considering the then available run-time information and events such as changes

Figure 4. Robotic software systems partitioned in abstraction levels

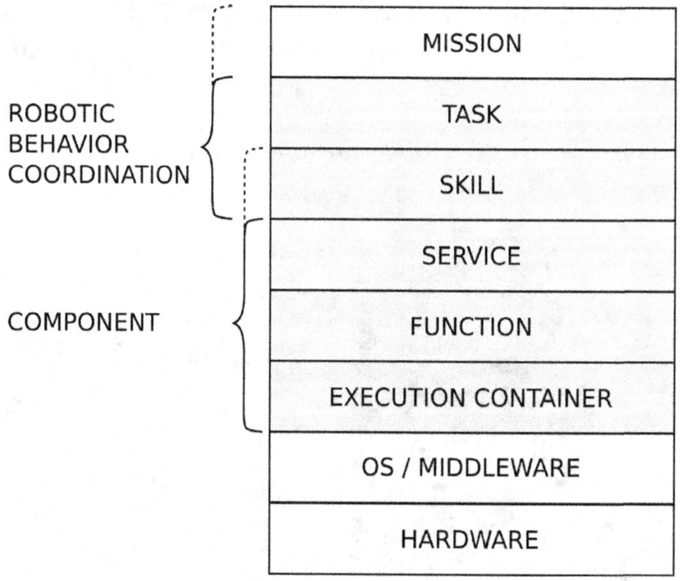

in the environments or execution failures. It is even possible and a regular practice to generate complete (sub)trees by asking a symbolic planner. For instance, if there are parts in action plots which cannot be predicted by the designer due to combinatorial explosion (e.g., the right sequence to move between buildings and levels). These parts can be resolved at run-time by asking an expert component (such as a symbolic planner). In other cases, one wants to model different predefined variants how to archive the same thing, e.g. handing over a production good to an automated station or a human worker. SmartTCL chooses the most appropriate variant based on rules applied during run-time. In addition, SmartTCL allows to express rules which define how a system reacts (or respectively recovers) in case of contingencies in execution. This leads to a much more flexible and robust system behavior. In summary, the main purpose of SmartTCL is twofold, on the one hand to define the tasks (i.e., the action plots) and on the other hand to define variability in operation. Variability at run-time is designed using experts, rules and exploiting the variability of the components. The following sections show how SmartTCL enables the developer to model variability in operation and how the system will use and bind this left open variability at run-time.

Component Coordination: Using Component Variability

As described in the development workflow section 2, the role of the component provider realizes the functionalities and explicates the variability the component as building blocks offers. The role also models the skill level behavior coordination models, which lifts the functionalities provided by the components to a skill abstraction level. Thereby, the components run-time variability (the run-time configuration options) defined at the coordination interface and realized by the components is used within the skill behavior models.

At run-time, those configuration options are bound dependent on the context the component is used in. In many cases the values are bound at run-time to a design time fix value (e.g. driving in large hallways with 2 m/s) however in some cases the valued are run-time constituted, e.g. dependent on information gather from the environment (e.g. driving slower the more densely populated a hallway is). The later proposed VML language and its run-time engine is an example how such data can be used and derived given the then available information about the context and the environment.

Figure 5 shows an example from the scenario how the offered component variability, in form of components parameters is used for behavior coordination. Here as a simple example the traveling speed of the robot is configured. The components providing the functionality to move the robot, realize and offer this configuration option. It is important to understand that configuration modeled in the TCB are applied not until the TCB is instantiated within the task tree at run-time.

SmartTCL: Behavior Coordination Model Variability

Within behavior models, at task or skill abstraction level, variability can be expressed as expansion points. During run-time those points are bound at the selection of the next TCB to instantiate, defining how the task tree will ultimately expand. SmartTCL supports several mechanisms to model variability through task tree expansion:

The developer is able to model specialized variants of tasks, through the usage of the parameters of a TCB. Thereby a general TCB is specialized binding a parameter variable. During run-time the Sequencer will select the matching TCB based on the binding of the used variable. The order how the compatible

Figure 5. Using component variability, to coordinate components in a skill level TCB

```
(define-tcb (tcb-move-robot 'approach-exact ?location)
  (action (
          (format t "tcb-move-robot 'approach-exact ~s ~%" '?location)
          (let* ((pose (get-value (tcl-kb-query :key '(is-a name)
                                                :value '( (is-a location) (name ?location))) 'approach-exact-pose))
                 (velocity-travelling (get-value (tcl-kb-query :key '(is-a) :value '((is-a robot))) 'velocity-travelling)))
            (tcl-activate-event :name 'evt-cdlgoal :handler 'handler-cdl :server 'SmartCdlServer
                                :service 'goalEventServer :mode 'continuous)

            (tcl-param :server 'SmartCdlServer :slot 'TRANSVEL :paramvalue (first velocity-travelling))
            (tcl-param :server 'SmartCdlServer :slot 'ROTVEL :paramvalue (second velocity-travelling))
            (tcl-param :server 'SmartCdlServer :slot 'GOALREGION :paramvalue '(,(first pose) ,(second pose) 0))
            (tcl-param :server 'SmartCdlServer :slot 'COMMIT)

            (tcl-state :server 'SmartCdlServer :state 'moverobot)
            '(SUCCESS ()))))))
```

TCBs are checked for instantiation can be modified using the priority clause of a TCB. Figure 6 shows an example as excerpt of the scenario where the mechanism is used to run-time select which docking approach is applied to access a production station. This mechanism allows to express specialized variants without the need to change other existing TCB variants.

Another mechanism to model the variable expansion of TCBs is the expression of preconditions at TCBs. Each TCB can have a precondition with is checked at run-time before the TCB is instantiated. This mechanism extends the previous selection mechanism via parameter binding, adding the possibilities to express logic that evaluates to a Boolean value deciding whether to instantiate the TCB or not. Figure 7 shows an example use case from the scenario where this mechanism is used to run-time select the navigation strategy how to approach a location. This mechanism enables the easy usage of knowledge (e.g. context or configuration of the robot) to influence the flexible expansion of the task tree, again without the need to modify other variants of the TCB or a using parent TCB.

The last and most flexible mechanism is the modification of tree expansion within the action-clauses in the different TCL elements (task coordination block, event handler, rule). The developer can use the underlying host language to express the logic how the task-tree is further expanded. This is by far the most flexible method to influence the expansion of the task tree. Unlike the preconditions which will evaluate during the expansion of the task tree, this method is modifying the task tree with regard to the

Figure 6. Variable task expansion through task specialization using bound TCB parameters

```
;; docking using vision
(define-tcb (tcb-mps-station-dock 'vision ?stationid)
  (action (
          (format t "tcb-mps-station-dock vision docking~s: ~%" ?stationid)
          ;...
          )))

;; docking using laser
(define-tcb (tcb-mps-station-dock 'laser ?stationid)
  (action (
          (format t "tcb-mps-station-dock laser docking~s: ~%" ?stationid)
          ;...
          )))

;; docking using laser and ir
(define-tcb (tcb-mps-station-dock 'laser-ir ?stationid)
  (action (
          (format t "tcb-mps-station-dock laser-ir docking~s: ~%" ?stationid)
          ;...
          )))
```

Figure 7. Variable task expansion through preconditions

```
;; navigation using grid based planning
(define-tcb (tcb-approach-location ?location)
  (precondition (equal '(region) (get-value (tcl-kb-query :key '(is-a name)
  :value '( (is-a location) (name ?location))) 'approach-type)))
  (priority 99)
  (rules (rule-unknown-location rule-location-success rule-robot-blocked))
  (plan (
        (tcb-move-robot 'approach-region ?location)
        (tcb-move-robot 'orientate-region ?location))))

;; navigation using navigation corridors
(define-tcb (tcb-approach-location ?location)
  (precondition (equal '(path-nav) (get-value (tcl-kb-query :key '(is-a name)
  :value '( (is-a location) (name ?location))) 'approach-type)))
  (priority 99)
  (rules (rule-unknown-location rule-location-success rule-robot-blocked
          rule-path-nav-start-too-far-away rule-path-nav-no-path-found))
  (plan (
        (tcb-check-current-symbolic-pose)
        (tcb-move-robot 'approach-using-path ?location)
        (tcb-move-robot 'orientate-region ?location))))
```

next expansion step. This mechanism is also the way to incorporate expert components to decide how to expand the task tree e.g. calling a symbolic planner or asking the VML-Engine. Figure 8 shows an example from the scenario where the expansion of the task tree is run-time selected within a contingency handling rule. In this example the rule is executed if the loading of a good from a station failed.

To summarize, SmartTCL features several mechanisms to enable the developer to model variability in operation, using the run-time expansion of the task tree as central element and using the variability provided by the components.

MODELING VARIABILITY WITH VML

The first part of this section briefly reviews the Variability Modeling Language (VML), already introduced in (Inglés-Romero et al., 2012), the main modeling concepts it provides, and the mechanisms it leverages to allow expressing variability in quality, that is, how a system should adapt at run-time to maintain or improve the system execution quality under changing conditions. Then, some of the limitations of the original approach are discussed, and the new features contributed to VML to deal with them are introduced in the second part of this section.

Figure 8. Variable task tree expansion in an action clause in case of a contingency handling rule

```
;; acknowledge loading error
(define-rule (rule-mps-load-failed)
  (tcb (tcb-mps-station-load))
  (return-value (ERROR (LOAD LOADING)))
  (action (
        (format t "RULE: ( rule-mps-load-failed (ERROR (LOAD LOADING)) ~%")
        (tcl-push-plan :plan `(
          (tcb-wait-for-error-ack 'SW-ACK)
          (tcb-mps-station-load))))))
```

VML Basics

Although the abstract syntax of VML is formally defined in terms of a meta-model, for the sake of clarity, its main modeling concepts are reviewed next based on the scenario presented in section 3.

In a VML model, *variation points* represent the points in the software where different variants might be chosen to derive the system configuration at run-time. Therefore, variation points determine the decision space of the VML models. As shown in Figure 9, variation points (varpoint) can be defined according to one of the four basic data types supported by VML, i.e., events, enumerators, ranges of numbers and Booleans. For instance, the maxVelocity variation point, aimed at deciding the maximum velocity of the robot, may take values in the range 100 to 600, with a precision of 10 mm/s. Similarly, the station variation point is an enumerator that gathers the available stations from where, or to which a good can be delivered by the robot. Similarly, *context variables* (context) identify the situations in which variation points need to be adapted. Figure 9 includes five context variables: (i) the battery level (an integer in the range 0-100), (ii) the distance to each station (a real number in the range 0-20 with precision 0.1), and (iii) the waiting time at each station (an integer in the range 10-300), taking into account the hand over time of the station (constant time) and the time the robot has to wait because there are other robots waiting for it (variable time).

Figure 9. Excerpt of a simple VML Model for the robotic scenario

```
/* Context variables */
context ctx_battery          : number [0:1:100]
context ctx_distanceStation1 : number [0:0.1:20]
context ctx_distanceStation2 : number [0:0.1:20]
context ctx_waitingStation1  : number [0:0.1:20]
context ctx_waitingStation2  : number [0:0.1:20]

/* Auxiliary variables */
var timeStation1 := ctx_waitingStation1 + ctx_distanceStation1/600
var timeStation2 := ctx_waitingStation2 + ctx_distanceStation2/600

/* ECA rules */
rule lowBattery_NearStation1:
    ctx_battery < 15 and ctx_distanceStation1 < ctx_distanceStation2
    implies station = @station.STATION_1
rule lowBattery_NearStation2:
    ctx_battery < 15 and ctx_distanceStation1 >= ctx_distanceStation2
    implies station = @station.STATION_2
rule lowBattery_NearStation1:
    ctx_battery >= 15 and timeStation1 > timeStation2
    implies station = @station.STATION_1
rule lowBattery_NearStation1:
    c ctx_battery >= 15 and timeStation1 <= timeStation2
    implies station = @station.STATION_2

/* Properties to optimize */
property performance maximizes {
    priority := max(exp(-1*ctx_battery/15), 10sec) - exp(-1*ctx_battery/15)
    definition := maxVelocity
}
property powerConsumption minimizes {
    priority := exp(-1*ctx_battery/15)
    definition := exp(maxVelocity/150)
}

/* Variation points */
varpoint maxVelocity : number [100:10:600]
varpoint station : enum { STATION_1, STATION_2 }
```

Once variation points and context variables have been defined, designers need to model how the former are determined in terms of the later. This is achieved through *properties* (property) and Event-Condition-Action (ECA) rules* (rule). Properties specify the features of the system that need to be optimized, i.e., minimized or maximized. Properties are defined using *priorities* and *definitions*. Definitions characterize the property in terms of the variation points (i.e., definitions are the objective functions to be optimized). For instance, Figure 9 includes the definition of the performance property as a linear function of the maximum velocity variation point (the faster the robot accomplishes its task, the better its performance). Similarly, the power consumption property also depends (in this case, exponentially) on the maximum velocity (the faster the robot moves, the higher its power consumption). On the other hand, priorities describe the importance of each property in terms of one or more context variables (i.e., priorities weight the objective functions). For instance, power consumption becomes more and more relevant as the robot battery decreases. In fact, when the battery is full, power consumption is not considered an issue and, as a consequence, the priority of this property is very small. Regarding the ECA rules, they define direct relationships between context variables and variation points. As shown in Figure 9, the left-hand side of a rule expresses a trigger condition (depending on one or more context variables) and its right-hand side sets the variation point. For example, the decision of which station to select in each situation is modeled using ECA rules. Basically, the first two rules are applied when the battery is low (less than 15%) to select the nearest station (reducing travel distance lowers power consumption when the battery is critical). Conversely, if the battery is high enough, the last two rules select the machine with a shorter waiting time (reducing the delivery time improves performance when the battery is not an issue).

At this point, it is worth mentioning that VML have been developed using a *Model-Driven Engineering* (MDE) approach. Tool support for VML includes a textual model editor, developed using the Xtext framework (Xtext, 2013). This editor provides designers with some advanced features such as syntax checking, coloring and completion. Besides, considering the development process described in Figure 1, it is worth noting that VML is built on top of the variability left open by the component suppliers (e.g., via parameters or services in the components). The behavior developer and the system integrator refine this variability providing adaptation strategies (at the application level) in terms of non-functional properties. Finally, at run-time, the system acts according to these specifications in order to optimize its execution quality.

Dealing With Context Uncertainty

A VML model, like the one shown in Figure 9, specifies a constrained optimization problem, that is, it describes the global weight function that optimizes the variation points to improve the overall system quality. This global function is obtained by aggregating the property definitions (terms to be optimized), weighted by their corresponding priorities. Besides, the ECA rules pose additional constraints that need to be satisfied. However, this approach, adopted as the original optimization process in (Inglés-Romero et al., 2012), has some limitations when dealing with uncertainty.

Changes in the context trigger the re-evaluation of the property priorities. These priorities are defined as functions that assign specific weights to concrete context situations. For instance, according to the priority function defined for power consumption in Figure 9, whenever the battery drops to 5%, the weight of this property will always be 0.7165. However, identifying which weight values adequately represent a context situation is a major difficulty. It is mainly because being able to select these values with absolute certainty implies determinism, i.e., the fact that in the same situation the adaptation should always be the same. Unfortunately, this is not the case in most scenarios, since context variables may provide only a partial view, and the system may never know the real situation for certain or where it will end up after a sequence of actions.

To cope with the inherent uncertainty introduced by the context, VML has included the notion of *QoS metrics*. A QoS metric expresses, as a real number in the range [0,1], the perceived degree of fulfilment of a property. In other words, it is a score of how well the system performs, e.g., with regard to "power consumption", based on the context information received. If the metric is 1, the system is optimal in terms of the property, while 0 indicates the opposite. Besides, this value can change as the behavior of the robot evolves during its operation. Thus, the system will show an improvement if, in a period of time, this metric varies from 0.43 to 0.52, or a deterioration if the variation trend is the opposite. Lastly, QoS metrics should not be taken as accurate and rigorous measures, but as rough context indicators that are estimated from the information available.

Although QoS metrics may seem similar to property priorities, in the sense of being a number in the same range that indicates the importance of a property, QoS metrics are calculated using a non-deterministic approach. That is, now, VML allows users to model relevant context patterns (e.g., "the battery level drops by more than 1% per minute") using a new type of rules (see Figure 10). Detected a pattern, the rule will trigger a positive (or negative) observation that reinforces (or reduces) the belief that the robot is optimal in terms of the considered property (e.g., power consumption). Basically, the corresponding QoS metric is the quantification of this belief after applying probabilistic reasoning. For example, continuing with the "power consumption" example, a value of 0.67 can be understood as the robot probability of showing maximum efficiency in power consumption. At run-time, VML uses a probabilistic reasoning approach based on *Dynamic Bayesian Networks* (Russell & Norvig, 2009). Thus, instead of weighting properties using priority functions, a QoS metric is implicitly defined for each property. At a given point, the resulting estimation of each QoS metric is used to weight the corresponding property in the optimization process.

Figure 10. VML dealing with uncertainty

```
context ctx_battery : number [0:1:100]

/* Negative observation with a medium impact*/
rule "battery drops by more than 1% per minute":
    maxdiff(ctx_battery, 1min) > 1
    reduces powerConsumption

/* Positive observation with a high impact*/
rule "battery over 90%":
    ctx_battery > 90
    reinforces powerConsumption HIGHLY

property powerConsumption minimizes {
    definition := exp(maxVelocity/150)
}
varpoint maxVelocity  : number [100:10:600]
```

RUN-TIME INTEGRATION OF SmartTCL AND VML

To this point, the chapter explained how to use SmartTCL and VML to separately specify the variability in operation and the variability in quality, respectively. This section addresses one of the key issues when using both variability management mechanisms together, i.e., how to integrate them at run-time in a safe and consistent way. As both engines VML and SmartTCL (Sequencer) have an impact on the system configuration, all their actions need to be consistent.

In the robotics domain, the clear definition of a coordination hierarchy is a common pattern, mainly motivated by the fact that the physical entity robot needs to operate as a whole, it cannot decide to go left and right at the same time. It is important to notice that this does not imply a single master controlling everything in the system. In fact, the important part is the orthogonal assignment of decision space. Following the subsidiarity principle, the coordination or control of the robotics system can be distributed and delegated, as proposed with SmartTCL (variability in operation) and VML (variability in quality), delegating the decision space at run-time according to design-time modeled rules.

Earlier work (Lotz et al., 2014) presented two approaches to combine VML and SmartTCL. In particular, the approach enabling the activation or deactivation of similar variants, in practice led to the modelling of many duplicated (very similar) variants of the same TCB, therefore has been dropped. Instead, the systematic explication at design time of interaction points between VML and TCL, using entries in the robot and environment models, maintained at run-time in the knowledge base, has been pursued.

VML can be used together with SmartTCL in two different modes, as a service on demand, VML queried by the Sequencer, and as a continuous service (see Figure 11). In the second case, the Sequencer delegates the decision to the VML engine to continuously select an appropriate value for system configuration within predefined boundaries.

Both mechanisms use contexts and variation points as interface between the Sequencer and the VML engine. A context represents the current situation and the robot state. A variation point is an entry in the robot model, whose boundaries are not static, but can be adjusted at run-time by the Sequencer according to the current functional needs. The remaining variability is then delegated to, and used by the VML engine to decide on concrete values.

For example, asking the VML engine for advice which production station to use (see Figure 11 on the left). The Sequencer will attach the pertinent context information in the query so that the VML engine can make an informed decision. For VML as a continuous service, a different mechanism is used. For example, for the selection of the maximum allowed velocity, an according entry in the knowledge base (in the Robot Model in Figure 11 on the right) is used. Thereby, the Sequencer adjusts this entry according to its functional needs, and the VML engine is only allowed to set this entry within the remaining boundaries. The VML engine is triggered whenever the monitor detects a situation that requires adjusting the maximum allowed velocity (e.g., when the environment is crowded) and updates the entry in the robot model, which is then used by the Sequencer to coordinate the components. The monitoring component can access the components raw data, or use the abstracted information of the robot or environment model in the knowledge base. The use of the robot model or the environment model by other components (not the Sequencer), lead to the design decision to separate the knowledge base from the Sequencer, supporting a subscription/event interaction mechanism.

Figure 11. On the left: VML as service on demand; on the right: VML as a continuous service

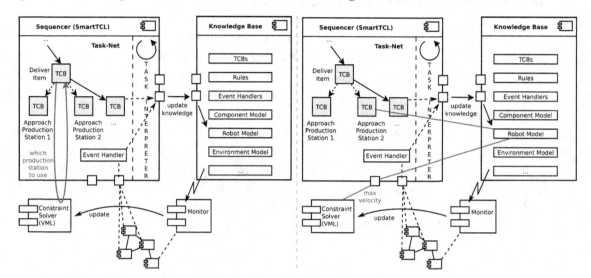

In summary, this approach enables the Sequencer to be aware of VML models, and to ensure consistency (i) either by asking for advice about the possible alternatives, not conflicting with the overall task, or (ii) by propagating an already constrained configuration to VML so that it can further constrain it without conflicting with the operational part.

RELATED WORK

Although the work in this chapter is inspired by the robotics domain, its focus is broader and therefore it does not cover the huge body of relevant robotics references. A more extensive list of works related to service robotics can be found in (Schlegel et al., 2016). Service robotics is a challenging domain that exhibits a clear need for modeling and managing variability: robots should be able to change their behavior in response to changes in their operation or their environment. One step to solve this problem is to introduce mechanisms to model robot tasks independently of the components. In this sense, some work aims to rapidly compose complex robot behaviors based on state machines (Bohren & Cousins, 2010; Dhouib et al., 2012) or statecharts (M. Klotzbücher & Bruyninckx, 2012). These approaches support static composition of behaviors with few capabilities for situation dependent task adjustments. Therefore, designers need to include in the description of the functionality, which contingencies may occur for each situation, with almost no reuse. Conversely, SmartTCL (Steck & Schlegel, 2011) allows to easily model dynamic task trees, which are rearranged at run-time according to the current situation. Recent work on robotic control focuses on expressing reusable skills (Rovida et. al.,SkiROS 2017a), some organized in behavior tree approaches (Rovida, Grossmann & Krüger, 2017b), to be used by symbolic planners. While those address flexibility and reuse, neither systematically connects to encapsulated software components to support a clear separation of roles, as needed for reuse in an ecosystem.

Literature about dynamic variability in software systems is quite extensive, bringing together efforts in different areas, such as, Dynamic Software Product Lines (Bencomo, Hallsteinsen & Santana de Almeida, 2012), Autonomic Computing or Context-awareness (Krupitzer, et al., 2015). In the following, we highlight some approaches for managing variability that have been applied to robotics. The authors in (Iftikhar & Weyns, 2014) present ActivFORMS that promotes the direct execution of verifiable formal models to deal with dynamic variability. A formal model expresses the adaptation logic as a network of timed automata. Whenever the system detects that the model being executed cannot handle the current state of the system, an uppermost layer – the goal management layer – tries to find a different model to satisfy the system goals. The authors show ActivFORMS applied to a set of robots performing transportation tasks in a warehouse environment, where self-adaptation deals with lanes that have to be closed temporally, e.g., to perform maintenance tasks or to solve a problem with a robot. Unlike our work, this approach does not distinguish between variability in operation and in quality, however, the use of formal methods in the variability management process allows verifying the adaptation goals at design-time and guarantee the correct behavior of the system at run-time. DiaSpec (Bertran et al., 2012) is a DSL to specify Sense/Compute/Control (SCC) applications, where the interaction with the physical environment is essential. DiaSpec allows designing applications independently of the underlying architecture, describing entities (e.g., components) and controllers, which execute actions on entities when a context situation is reached. The DiaSpec compiler generates Java code that needs to be completed with the application logic. Like SmartTCL and VML, DiaSpec platform-independence enables specification reuse. However, DiaSpec adaptation mechanisms completely rely on ECA-based rules and do not support any kind of optimization.

The NoMPRoL approach presented in (Sykes et al., 2013) targets unstable and dynamic environments, where uncertainty leads to incomplete and inaccurate models. The authors manage dynamic variability in terms of rules. When these rules do not seem to fit well, due to run-time discrepancies between expected and actual behavior, this approach uses probabilistic learning to update the rules or generate new ones based on context observations. Despite not considering the role of non-functional properties in the variability modeling, the authors recognize the importance of handling uncertainty. In this sense, NoMPRoL is aligned with the probabilistic method that VML uses to estimate QoS metrics. Moreover, like our proposal, this work shows a robotic scenario based on the transport of goods in a factory. Also, related to variability management under uncertainty, the authors in (Paucar & Bencomo, 2017) present ARRoW, a decision-making process supported by conditional probabilities based on Dynamic Decision Networks (DDNs). The process is similar to the one included in VML based on Dynamic Bayesian Networks, i.e., DDNs link context evidences, state of non-functional properties and utilities to make informed decisions. However, ARRoW only focuses on managing variability in quality.

In general, most approaches seem to focus on optimizing a single type of variability, whether it is variability in operation or variability in quality. Hence, there does not seem to be an integrated development process that combines the specificities of each type of variability at design-time and executes them effectively at run-time.

CONCLUSION AND FUTURE RESEARCH

This chapter extends previous works by the authors related to dynamic variability modeling and exploitation in complex systems. The two approaches and DSLs introduced in the previous works, enabling designers to separately specify variability in operation and variability in quality, have been considerably improved and extended in this chapter. The original variability management workflow has also been extended, e.g., to include important additional roles (e.g. system architect and behavior developer), and detailing how these roles contribute to a robotics ecosystem. The new workflow explicates which of the involved stakeholders (roles) is exposed to which variability, and how they are allowed to exploit it.

It is worth noting that individual roles in the proposed workflow are decoupled and their contributions (or requirements) can be pushed (or fetch) from a robotics business ecosystem market. However, although the roles are decoupled, the proposed workflow also represents the relationships that may arise between them when developing concrete applications. Besides, stepwise system refinement, separation of roles and concerns, and systematic variability management, all elements at the core of this proposal, are recognized as key factors towards successful business ecosystems.

The proposal is illustrated in the context of a real-world robotics scenario focused on production logistics. This scenario is used as a conducting example to explicate the proposal, including the new features contributed to the two variability modeling DSLs and the new roles and processes included in the variability management workflow.

Next, some of the open challenges considered pivotal by the authors, are reviewed:

- **Measuring Quality of Service:** The variability management proposal presented here assumes that the system improves its behavior compared to fixed alternatives (not considering dynamic variability). However, although this fact has been empirically demonstrated in several robotic scenarios, it needs further research, i.e., system builders should be able to quantify to what extent managing variability at run-time actually improves system performance. In this sense, RoQME (Robot Quality-of-Service Metrics) (RoQME, 2018), an Integrated Technical Project funded by RobMoSys and led by some of the authors, could help address this question.

- **Integration and Reuse of Non-Functional Properties:** Although non-functional properties can be modeled in VML, some issues remain open. For instance, there is a lack of a generic and systematic process in which quality attributes (associated with non-functional properties) can be specified in individual building blocks to be later integrated when modeling variability in quality for different applications. Thus, a common vocabulary is needed between component suppliers and system integrators. The authors have already made some progress in this direction, e.g., in (Lotz et al., 2016) and (Inglés-Romero et al., 2017). Moreover, one of the goals of RobMoSys is to support this collaboration in the context of the robotics ecosystem.

- **Dealing with Uncertainty When Managing Variability:** As uncertainty is inherent in real-world scenarios, it is important to handle it adequately when managing variability. In this vein, we plan to continue working on improving the probabilistic methods included in VML and to explore how reinforcement learning (Ghosh et al., 2017) can be used to infer the utility functions associated with non-functional properties.

- **Providing Tool Support for the Complete Variability Management Workflow:** Although some of the RobMoSys compliant tool-chains, such as the SmartSoft MDSD (Schlegel et al., 2016), currently support some of the roles included in the proposed workflow (namely: component suppliers, behavior developers, and system integrators), the complete stepwise variability management workflow is not yet fully supported. For instance, the system installation and configuration process, aimed at enabling system users (e.g., logistics workers) to fix certain parameters instead of leaving the robot to deal with them at run-time (e.g. defining the locations of the objects of interest, rather than leaving the robot to look for them) is not yet supported.

ACKNOWLEDGMENT

This research was supported by the European Union's H2020 research and innovation programme under grant agreement No 732410 (both the RobMoSys project and the RoQME Integrated Technical Project funded by RobMoSys), the BMBF (LogiRob 01IS16008B), and the BMWi (SeRoNet 01MA17003D).

REFERENCES

Bauer, A., Botea, V., Brown, M., Gray, M., Harabor, D., & Slaney, J. (2010). An Integrated Modelling, Debugging, and Visualisation Environment for G12. In D. Cohen (Ed.), *Principles and Practice of Constraint Programming (CP 2010)* (Vol. 6308, pp. 522–536). Heidelberg, Germany: Springer. doi:10.1007/978-3-642-15396-9_42

Bencomo, N., Hallsteinsen, S., & Santana de Almeida, E. (2012). A View of the Dynamic Software Product Line Landscape. *Computer*, *45*(10), 36–41. doi:10.1109/MC.2012.292

Bertran, B., Bruneau, J., Cassou, D., Loriant, N., Balland, E., & Consel, C. (2012). DiaSuite: a Tool Suite To Develop Sense/Compute/Control Applications. Science of Computer Programming, Fourth special issue on Experimental Software and Toolkits.

Bohren, J., & Cousins, S. (2010). The smach high-level executive (ros news). *IEEE Robotics & Automation Magazine*, *17*(4), 18–20. doi:10.1109/MRA.2010.938836

Dhouib, S., Kchir, S., Stinckwich, S., Ziadi, T., & Ziane, M. (2012). RobotML, a Domain-Specific Language to Design, Simulate and Deploy Robotic Applications. In I. Noda, N. Ando, D. Brugali, & J. J. Kuffner (Eds.), *SIMPAR 2012* (Vol. 7628, pp. 149–160). Heidelberg, Germany: Springer. doi:10.1007/978-3-642-34327-8_16

euRobotics aisbl. (2013-2014). *Strategic Research Agenda*. Author.

Ghosh, P., Bardhan, M., Chowdhury, N. R., & Phadikar, S. (2017). IDS Using Reinforcement Learning Automata for Preserving Security in Cloud Environment. *International Journal of Information System Modeling and Design*, *8*(4), 21–37. doi:10.4018/IJISMD.2017100102

Iftikhar, M. U., & Weyns, D. (2014). Activforms: Active formal models for self-adaptation. *Proceedings of International Symposium on Software Engineering for Adaptive and Self-Managing Systems*, 125–134.

Inglés-Romero, J. F., Lotz, A., Vicente-Chicote, C., & Schlegel, C. (2012). Dealing with Run-Time Variability in Service Robotics: Towards a DSL for Non-Functional Properties. *3rd International Workshop on Domain-Specific Languages and models for ROBotic systems (DSLRob-12)*.

Inglés-Romero, J. F., Romero-Garces, A., Vicente-Chicote, C., & Martínez, J. (2017). A Model-Driven Approach to Enable Adaptive QoS, In DDS-Based Middleware. *IEEE Transactions on Emerging Topics in Computational Intelligence.*, *1*(3), 176–187. doi:10.1109/TETCI.2017.2669187

Klotzbücher, M., & Bruyninckx, H. (2012). Coordinating Robotic Tasks and Systems with rFSM Statecharts. *Journal of Software Engineering for Robotics, 3*(1).

Krupitzer, C., Roth, F. M., VanSyckel, S., Schiele, G. & Becker, C. (2015). A survey on engineering approaches for self-adaptive systems. *Pervasive and Mobile Computing. 17*, 184-206. doi:10.1016/j.pmcj.2014.09.009

Lee, E. (2010). *Disciplined Heterogeneous Modeling.* In MODELS 2010, Oslo, Norway.

Lotz, A., Hamann, A., Lange, R., Heinzemann, C., Staschulat, J., Kesel, V., ... Schlegel, C. (2016). Combining Robotics Component-Based Model-Driven Development with a Model-Based Performance Analysis. *Proceedings of IEEE International Conference on Simulation, Modeling, and Programming for Autonomous Robots.* 10.1109/SIMPAR.2016.7862392

Lotz, A., Inglés-Romero, J. F., Vicente-Chicote, C., & Schlegel, C. (2013). Managing run-time variability in robotics software by modeling functional and non-functional behavior. In S. Nurcan, H. A. Proper, P. Soffer, J. Krogstie, R. Schmidt, T. Halpin, & I. Bider (Ed.), BPMDS and EMMSAD (pp. 441-455). Springer. doi:10.1007/978-3-642-38484-4_31

Lotz, A., Inglés-Romero, J. F., Vicente-Chicote, C., Stampfer, D., Lutz, M., Vicente-Chicote C., & Schlegel., C. (2014). Towards a Stepwise Variability Management Process for Complex Systems – A Robotics Perspective. *International Journal of Information System Modeling and Design, 5*(3), 55-74.

Lutz, M., Verbeek, C., & Schlegel, C. (2016). Towards a Robot Fleet for Intra-Logistic Tasks: Combining Free Robot Navigation with Multi-Robot Coordination at Bottlenecks. *Proceedings of the 21th IEEE International Conference on Emerging Technologies and Factory Automation (ETFA).* 10.1109/ETFA.2016.7733602

Paucar, L. H. G., Bencomo, N., & Yuen, K. K. F. (2017). Juggling Preferences in a World of Uncertainty. *IEEE 25th International Requirements Engineering Conference (RE),* 430-435. 10.1109/RE.2017.12

RobMoSys Project. (2017-2020). *Composable Models and Software for Robtics Systems, towards an EU Digital Industrial Platform for Robotics.* Available at: http://robmosys.eu/wiki/

RoQME Integrated Technical Project. (2018-2019). *Dealing with non-functional properties through global Robot Quality-of- Service Metrics.* Available at: http://robmosys.eu/roqme/

Rovida, F., Crosby, M., Holz, D., Polydoros, A. S., Großmann, B., Petrick, R. P. A., & Krüger, V. (2017a). SkiROS - A skill-based robot control platform on top of ROS. Robot Operating System (ROS): The Complete Reference (Volume 2). *Studies in Computational Intelligence, 707,* 121–160.

Rovida, F., Grossmann, B., & Krüger, V. (2017b). Extended behavior trees for quick definition of flexible robotic tasks. *Proceedings of 2017 IEEE/RSJ International Conference on Intelligent Robots and Systems (IROS),* 6793-6800. 10.1109/IROS.2017.8206598

Russell, S., & Norvig, P. (2009). *Artificial Intelligence: A Modern Approach* (3rd ed.). Upper Saddle River, NJ: Prentice Hall Press.

Schlegel, C., Lotz, A., Lutz, M., Stampfer, D., Inglés-Romero, J. F., & Vicente-Chicote, C. (2013). Model-Driven Software Systems Engineering in Robotics: Covering the Complete Life-Cycle of a Robot. In Workshop Roboter-Kontrollarchitekturen, Informatik 2013. Springer.

Stampfer, D., Lotz, A., Lutz, M., & Schlegel, C. (2016). The SmartMDSD Toolchain: An Integrated MDSD Workflow and Integrated Development Environment (IDE) for Robotics Software. *Journal of Software Engineering for Robotics, 7*(1), 3-19.

Steck, A., & Schlegel, C. (2011). Managing execution variants in task coordination by exploiting design-time models at run-time. In *Proceedings of 2011 IEEE/RSJ International Conference on Intelligent Robots and Systems (IROS)* (pp. 2064–2069). IEEE. 10.1109/IROS.2011.6094732

Sykes, D., Corapi, D., Magee, J., Kramer, J., & Russoetal, A. (2013). Learning revised models for planning in adaptive systems. *Proceedings of the 2013 International Conference on Software Engineering,* 63-71. 10.1109/ICSE.2013.6606552

Xtext. (2013). *Development of programming languages and Domain Specific Languages*. Available at: http://www.eclipse.org/Xtext/

Compilation of References

Aagesen, G., & Krogstie, J. (2015). BPMN 2.0 for modeling business processes. In Handbook on Business Process Management, International Handbooks on Information Systems (pp. 219-250). Springer Berlin Heidelberg.

Abbott, S. (2015). *The Co+Factor - The Exclusively-For-Everyone, Not-To-Be-Kept-Secret Ingredient/Benefit For Helping You and Your Organization Create, Engage and Prosper.* Retrieved April 2, 2018, from http://bemobileworksocial. com/wp-content/uploads/2015/02/The-Co-Factor-E-Book.pdf

Abiteboul, S., Hull, R., & Vianu, V. (1995). *Foundations of Databases.* Reading, MA: Addison-Wesley.

Abolfazli, S., Sanaei, Z., Sanaei, M. H., Shojafar, M., & Gani, A. (2016). Mobile Cloud Computing. In S. Murugesan & I. Bojanova (Eds.), *Encyclopedia of Cloud Computing* (pp. 29–40). Chichester, UK: John Wiley & Sons, Ltd. doi:10.1002/9781118821930.ch3

Agosti, M., Ferro, N., & Silvello, G. (2016). Digital library interoperability at high level of abstraction. *Future Generation Computer Systems*, 55, 129–146. doi:10.1016/j.future.2015.09.020

Agostinho, C., Ducq, Y., Zacharewicz, G., Sarraipa, J., Lampathaki, F., Poler, R., & Jardim-Goncalves, R. (2016). Towards a sustainable interoperability in networked enterprise information systems: Trends of knowledge and model-driven technology. *Computers in Industry*, 79, 64–76. doi:10.1016/j.compind.2015.07.001

Ale Ebrahim, N., Ahmed, S., & Taha, Z. (2009). Virtual R&D teams in small and medium enterprises: A literature review. *Scientific Research and Essays*, 4(13), 1575–1590.

Alenezi, M., & Magel, K. (2014). Empirical evaluation of a new coupling metric: Combining structural and semantic coupling. *International Journal of Computers and Applications*, 36(1). doi:10.2316/Journal.202.2014.1.202-3902

Alexopoulou, N., Kanellis, P., Nikolaidou, M., & Martakos, D. (2008). A holistic approach for enterprise agility. In *Handbook of research on enterprise systems*. Hershey, PA: IGI Global.

Alexopoulou, N., Nikolaidou, M., Anagnostopoulos, D., & Martakos, D. (2009, September). An event-driven modeling approach for dynamic human-intensive business processes. In *International Conference on Business Process Management* (pp. 393-404). Berlin, Heidelberg: Springer.

Alexopoulou, N., Nikolaidou, M., & Martakos, D. (2013). Exploring the business process agility issue: An experience report. *International Journal of Information System Modeling and Design*, 4(1), 25–41. doi:10.4018/jismd.2013010102

Al-Fuqaha, A., Guizani, M., Mohammadi, M., Aledhari, M., & Ayyash, M. (2015). Internet of things: A survey on enabling technologies, protocols, and applications. *IEEE Communications Surveys and Tutorials*, 17(4), 2347–2376. doi:10.1109/COMST.2015.2444095

Allen, J. (1995). *Natural Language Understanding* (2nd ed.). Redwood City, WA: Benjamin/Cummings.

Alonso, G., & Gunthor, R., & Agrawal, D., & El Abbadi, A. (1995). *Exotica/FMDC: Handling disconnected clients in a workflow management system.* Academic Press.

Alonso, G., Agrawal, D., El Abbadi, A., Kamath, M., Gunthor, R., & Mohan, C. (1996, February). Advanced transaction models in workflow contexts. In *Data Engineering, 1996. Proceedings of the Twelfth International Conference on* (pp. 574-581). IEEE.

Alonso, G., & Schek, H. J. (1996). Research issues in large workflow management systems. *Proceedings of NSF Workshop on Workflow and Process Automation in Information Science.*

Anam, S., Kim, Y., Kang, B., & Liu, Q. (2016). Adapting a knowledge-based schema matching system for ontology mapping. In *Proceedings of the Australasian Computer Science Week Multiconference* (p. 27). New York, NY: ACM Press. 10.1145/2843043.2843048

Anat, A., & Iris, R. B. (2008). A Domain Engineering Approach for Situational Method Engineering. *ER 2008,* 455-468.

Anat, A., & Iris, R. B. (2011). Semi-Automatic Composition of Situational Methods. *Journal of Database Management,* 22(4), 1–29. doi:10.4018/jdm.2011100101

Anklam, P. (2004, May). KM and the Social Network. *Knowledge Management Magazine,* 24-28.

Antunes, G., Bakhshandeh, M., Mayer, R., Borbinha, J., & Caetano, A. (2013). Using Ontologies for Enterprise Architecture Analysis. In *2013 17th IEEE International Enterprise Distributed Object Computing Conference Workshops* (pp. 361–368). IEEE. 10.1109/EDOCW.2013.47

Arowosegbe, A., & Mohamed, S. (2015). A Systematic Change Management Capability Maturity Assessment Framework for Contracting Organizations. *American Scientific Research Journal for Engineering, Technology, and Sciences,* 13(1), 88–96.

AT&T. (2008). *The Business Impacts of Social Networking.* Retrieved 2012-10-20 from http://www.business.att.com/content/whitepaper/WP-soc_17172_v3_11-10-08.pdf

Aydin, M. N. (2007). Examining Key Notions for Method Adaptation. *Situational Method Engineering,* 2007, 49–63.

Ayora, C., Torres, V., Reichert, M., Weber, B., & Pelechano, V. (2013). Towards run-time flexibility for process families: open issues and research challenges. *Proc. Business Process Management Workshops.* doi:10.1007/978-3-642-36285-9_49

Babu, D., & Darsi, M. (2013). A Survey on Service Oriented Architecture and Metrics to Measure Coupling. *International Journal on Computer Science and Engineering,* 5(8), 726–733.

Bakema, G., Zwart, J., & van der Lek, H. (2000). *Fully Communication Oriented Information Modelling.* Ten Hagen Stam.

Baker, T., Ugljanin, E., Faci, N., Sellami, M., Maamar, Z., & Kajan, E. (2018). Everything as a resource: Foundations and illustration through Internet-of-things. *Computers in Industry,* 94, 62–74. doi:10.1016/j.compind.2017.10.001

Baker, W. E. (1990). Market networks and corporate behavior. *American Journal of Sociology,* 96(3), 589–625. doi:10.1086/229573

Balabko, P., Wegmann, A., Ruppen, A., & Clement, N. (2004). *The Value of Roles in Modeling Business Processes.* Paper presented at BPMDS.

Barczyk, C. C., & Duncan, D. G. (2012). Social Networking Media: An Approach for the Teaching of International Business. *Journal of Teaching in International Business,* 23(2), 98–122. doi:10.1080/08975930.2012.718703

Barghouti, N. S., & Rosenblum, D. S. (1994, October). A case study in modeling a human-intensive, corporate software process. In *Software Process, 1994.'Applying the Software Process', Proceedings., Third International Conference on the* (pp. 99-110). IEEE. 10.1109/SPCON.1994.344418

Barker, R. (1990). *CASE*Method: Entity Relationship Modelling.* Wokingham: Addison-Wesley.

Barlow, J. B., & Dennis, A. R. (2016). Not As Smart As We Think: A Study of Collective Intelligence in Virtual Groups. *Journal of Management Information Systems, 33*(3), 684–712. doi:10.1080/07421222.2016.1243944

Barros, A. (2015). Process Choreography Modelling. In J. vom Brocke & M. Rosemann (Eds.), Handbook on Business Process Management (pp. 279-300). Berlin, Germany: Springer. doi:10.1007/978-3-642-45100-3_12

Barros, A., Dumas, M., & Oaks, P. (2005). A critical overview of the web services choreography description language. *BPTrends Newsletter, 3,* 1–24.

Bassett, L. (2015). *Introduction to JavaScript Object Notation: A to-the-point Guide to JSON.* Sebastopol, CA: O'Reilly Media, Inc.

Batoulis, K., Meyer, A., Bazhenova, E., Decker, G., & Weske, M. (2015). Extracting decision logic from process models. Advanced Information Systems Engineering, 9097, 349-366. doi:10.1007/978-3-319-19069-3_22

Battista, D., Leoni, M., Gaetanis, A., Mecella, M., Pezzullo, A., Russo, A., & Saponaro, C. (2008). ROME4EU: A Web service-based process-aware system for smart devices. *Proc. ICSOC'08,* 726-727. 10.1007/978-3-540-89652-4_65

Bauer, A., Botea, V., Brown, M., Gray, M., Harabor, D., & Slaney, J. (2010). An Integrated Modelling, Debugging, and Visualisation Environment for G12. In D. Cohen (Ed.), *Principles and Practice of Constraint Programming (CP 2010)* (Vol. 6308, pp. 522–536). Heidelberg, Germany: Springer. doi:10.1007/978-3-642-15396-9_42

Bauer, T., Reichert, M., & Dadam, P. (2003). Intra-subnet load balancing in distributed workflow management systems. *International Journal of Cooperative Information Systems, 12*(03), 205–223. doi:10.1142/S0218843003000760

Baum, J. A. (1999). Whole-part coevolutionary competition in organizations. *Variations in organization science,* 113-135.

Bear, M. (2015). Survival of the fittest: Using social media to thrive in the 21st century. *Journal Of Brand Strategy, 4*(2), 106–113.

Becker, C., & Dürr, F. (2005). On location models for ubiquitous computing. *Personal and Ubiquitous Computing, 9*(1), 20–31. doi:10.100700779-004-0270-2

Begel, A., DeLine, R., & Zimmermann, T. (2010). Social media for software engineering. In *Proceedings of the FSE/SDP workshop on Future of software engineering research* (pp. 33-38). ACM. 10.1145/1882362.1882370

Bekkers, W., van de Weerd, I., Brinkkemper, S., & Mahieu, A. (2008). The Influence of Situational Factors in Software Product Management: An Empirical Study. *Proceedings of the 21st International Workshop on Product Management,* 41-48. 10.1109/IWSPM.2008.8

Bencomo, N., Hallsteinsen, S., & Santana de Almeida, E. (2012). A View of the Dynamic Software Product Line Landscape. *Computer, 45*(10), 36–41. doi:10.1109/MC.2012.292

Bergenti, F., Poggi, A., & Tomaiuolo, M. (2018). Agent-Based Social Networks. In Encyclopedia of Information Science and Technology, Fourth Edition (pp. 6950-6960). IGI Global. doi:10.4018/978-1-5225-2255-3.ch602

Bergenti, F., Franchi, E., & Poggi, A. (2011). *Agent-based social networks for enterprise collaboration. In 20th IEEE International Workshops on Enabling Technologies: Infrastructure for Collaborative Enterprises* (pp. 25–28). IEEE.

Bergenti, F., Franchi, E., & Poggi, A. (2013). Agent-based interpretations of classic network models. *Computational & Mathematical Organization Theory, 19*(2), 105–127. doi:10.100710588-012-9150-x

Bergenti, F., Poggi, A., & Tomaiuolo, M. (2014). An actor based software framework for scalable applications. In *International Conference on Internet and Distributed Computing Systems* (pp. 26-35). Springer. 10.1007/978-3-319-11692-1_3

Berkman, R. (2014). The social enterprise: where does the information professional fit? *Online Searcher*, (6), 45-48.

Bertran, B., Bruneau, J., Cassou, D., Loriant, N., Balland, E., & Consel, C. (2012). DiaSuite: a Tool Suite To Develop Sense/Compute/Control Applications. Science of Computer Programming, Fourth special issue on Experimental Software and Toolkits.

Bev, G., Campbell, S., Levy, J., & Bounds, J. (2008). *Social media and the federal government: Perceived and real barriers and potential solutions.* Federal Web Managers Council.

Bidve, V. S., & Sarasu, P. (2016). Tool for measuring coupling in object-oriented java software. *IACSIT International Journal of Engineering and Technology, 8*(2), 812–820.

Boehnlein, M., & Ulbrich vom Ende, A. (2000). Business Process Oriented Development of Data Warehouse Structures. In Proceedings of Data Warehousing 2000 (pp. 3- 21). PhysicaVerlag HD. doi:10.1007/978-3-642-57681-2_1

Boehnlein, M., & Ulbrich vom Ende, A. (1999). Deriving initial Data Warehouse Structures from the Conceptual Data Models of the Underlying Operational Information Systems. In *Proc. Of Workshop on Data Warehousing and OLAP* (pp. 15-21). ACM 10.1145/319757.319780

Bohren, J., & Cousins, S. (2010). The smach high-level executive (ros news). *IEEE Robotics & Automation Magazine, 17*(4), 18–20. doi:10.1109/MRA.2010.938836

Bonifati A. Cattaneo, F., Ceri, S., Fuggetta, A., & Paraboschi, S. (2001). Designing Data Marts for Data Warehouses. *ACM Transactions on Software Engineering and Methodology, 10*(4), 452–483. doi:10.1145/384189.384190

Bora, A., & Bezboruah, T. (2015). A Comparative Investigation on Implementation of RESTful versus SOAP based Web Services. *International Journal of Database Theory and Application, 8*(3), 297–312. doi:10.14257/ijdta.2015.8.3.26

Borgatti, S. P., & Foster, P. C. (2003). The network paradigm in organizational research: A review and typology. *Journal of Management, 29*(6), 991–1013. doi:10.1016/S0149-2063(03)00087-4

Borgida, A., Toman, D., & Weddell, G. (2016a). On Referring Expressions in Query Answering over First Order Knowledge Bases. In *Proc. KR 2016* (pp. 319-328). Assoc. for Advancement of Artificial Intelligence.

Borgida, A., Toman, D., & Weddell, G. (2016b). On Referring Expressions in Information Systems Derived from Conceptual Modelling. In *Proc. ER 2016* (pp. 183-197). Heidelberg, Germany: Springer. 10.1007/978-3-319-46397-1_14

Börner, R. (2010). Applying Situational Method Engineering to the Development of Service Identification Methods. *16th Americas Conference on Information Systems*, 1-10.

Borner, R., Goeken, M., Kohlborn, T., & Korthaus, A. (2011). Context Factors for Situational Service Identification Methods; ICIW 2011, *The Sixth International Conference on Internet and Web Applications and Services*, 35-42

Botta, A., de Donato, W., Persico, V., & Pescapé, A. (2016). Integration of cloud computing and internet of things: A survey. *Future Generation Computer Systems, 56*, 684–700. doi:10.1016/j.future.2015.09.021

Boyd, D. (2008). *Taken out of context: American teen sociality in networked publics.* Berkeley, CA: School of Information, University of California-Berkeley.

Boyd, D. M., & Ellison, N. B. (2008). Social network sites: Definition, history, and scholarship. *Journal of Computer-Mediated Communication, 13*(1), 210–230. doi:10.1111/j.1083-6101.2007.00393.x

Brambilla, M., Preciado, J. C., Linaje, M., & Sanchez-Figueroa, F. (2008). Business process-based conceptual design of rich internet applications. *Web Engineering, International Conference on*, 155-161.

Brambilla, M., Fraternali, P., & Vaca Ruiz, C. K. (2012). Combining social web and BPM for improving enterprise performances: the BPM4People approach to social BPM. In *Proceedings of the 21st international conference companion on World Wide Web*. ACM. 10.1145/2187980.2188014

Brandt, C., & Hermann, F. (2013). Conformance analysis of organizational models: A new enterprise modeling framework using algebraic graph transformation. *International Journal of Information System Modeling and Design, 4*(1), 42–78. doi:10.4018/jismd.2013010103

Brdjanin, D., Maric, S., & Gunjic, D. (2011). Adbdesign: An approach to automated initial conceptual database design based on business activity diagrams. In Advances in Databases and Information Systems (pp. 117-131). Springer.

Brdjanin, D., Banjac, G., & Maric, S. (2015). Automated synthesis of initial conceptual database model based on collaborative business process model. In Bogdanova, A. M. and Gjorgjevikj, D. In I. C. T. Innovations (Ed.), *Advances in Intelligent Systems and Computing* (Vol. 311, pp. 145–156). Springer International Publishing.

Brinkkemper, S., Saeki, M., & Harmsen, F. (1998). Assembly Techniques for Method Engineering. *CAiSE 1998*, 381-400.

Brown, J. S. (2012). *Learning in and for the 21st Century*. National Institute of Education.

Bucher, T., Klesse, M., Kurpjuweit, S., & Winter, R. (2007). Situational Method Engineering– On the Differentiation of "Context" and "Project Type". *Situational Method Engineering, 2007*, 33–48.

Bucher, T., & Winter, R. (2008). Dissemination and Importance of the "Method" Artifact in the Context of Design Research for Information Systems. *Third International Conference on Design Science Research in Information Systems and Technology (DESRIST 2008)*, 39-59.

Buckley, S. (2011). IT Change Management. *Internal Auditor*. Retrieved from http://www.theiia.org/intAuditor/itaudit/2011-articles/it-change-management/

Buckl, S., Ernst, A. M., Matthes, F., & Schweda, C. M. (2009). Visual roadmaps for managed enterprise architecture evolution. In *10th ACIS Conference on Software Engineering, Artificial Intelligence, Networking and Parallel/Distributed Computing, SNPD 2009* (pp. 352–357). ACIS. 10.1109/SNPD.2009.99

Burt, R. S. (1987). Social Contagion and Innovation: Cohesion versus Structural Equivalence. *American Journal of Sociology, 92*(6), 1287–1335. doi:10.1086/228667

Burt, R. S. (1995). *Structural holes: The social structure of competition*. Harvard University Press.

Buschle, M., Grunow, S., Matthes, F., Ekstedt, M., Hauder, M., & Roth, S. (2012). Automating Enterprise Architecture Documentation using an Enterprise Service Bus. In *Americas Conference on Information Systems (AMCIS 2012)* (pp. 1–14). AMCIS.

Campbell, J. H. (1985). An organizational interpretation of evolution. *Evolution at a crossroads*, 133.

Candela, I., Bavota, G., Russo, B., & Oliveto, R. (2016). Using cohesion and coupling for software remodularization: Is it enough? *ACM Transactions on Software Engineering and Methodology, 25*(3), 24. doi:10.1145/2928268

Capel, M., & Mendoza, L. (2014). Choreography Modeling Compliance for Timed Business Models. In *Proceedings of the Workshop on Enterprise and Organizational Modeling and Simulation* (pp. 202-218). Berlin, Germany: Springer. 10.1007/978-3-662-44860-1_12

Casati, F., Ceri, S., Pernici, B., & Pozzi, G. (1996). Workflow Evolution. *Proceedings of ER '96*, 438–455.

Cavusoglu, H., Cavusoglu, H., & Zhang, J. (2004). Economics of Security Patch Management. *Annual Workshop on the Economics of Information Security*. Retrieved November 14, 2012, from http://ns2.honlab.dc.hu/~mfelegyhazi/courses/BMEVIHIAV15/readings/06_Cavasoglu2006security_patch.pdf

Chan, J. (2004). *Essentials of Patch Management Policy and Practice*. Retrieved January 20, 2013, from http://www.patchmanagement.org/pmessentials.asp

Charbonnier-Voirin, A. (2011). The development and partial testing of the psychometric properties of a measurement scale of organizational agility. *M@n@gement*, *14*(2), 119-156.

Chen, N., Cardozo, N., & Clarke, S. (2016). Goal-driven service composition in mobile and pervasive computing. *IEEE Transactions on Services Computing*.

Chen, P. P.-S. (1976). The entity-relationship model toward a unified view of data. *ACM Transactions on Database Systems*, *1*(1), 9–36. doi:10.1145/320434.320440

Chen, Y. (2015). A RDF-based approach to metadata crosswalk for semantic interoperability at the data element level. *Library Hi Tech*, *33*(2), 175–194. doi:10.1108/LHT-08-2014-0078

Chinosi, M., & Trombetta, A. (2012). BPMN: An introduction to the standard. *Computer Standards & Interfaces*, *34*(1), 124–134. doi:10.1016/j.csi.2011.06.002

Chow, W. S., & Chan, L. S. (2008). Social network, social trust and shared goals in organizational knowledge sharing. *Information & Management*, *45*(7), 458–465. doi:10.1016/j.im.2008.06.007

Cicchetti, A., Di Ruscio, D., Eramo, R., & Pierantonio, A. (2008a). Automating co-evolution in model-driven engineering. In *Proceedings - 12th IEEE International Enterprise Distributed Object Computing Conference, EDOC 2008* (pp. 222–231). IEEE Computer Society. 10.1109/EDOC.2008.44

Cicchetti, A., Di Ruscio, D., Eramo, R., & Pierantonio, A. (2008b). Meta-model differences for supporting model co-evolution. *Proceedings of the 2nd Workshop on ModelDriven Software Evolution MoDSE'2008*.

Cichocki, A., & Rusinkiewicz, M. (1998). Migrating workflows. In *Workflow Management Systems and Interoperability* (pp. 339–355). Springer Berlin Heidelberg. doi:10.1007/978-3-642-58908-9_15

Cockburn, A. (2001). *Writing Effective Use Cases*. Addison Wesley.

Coleman, J. S. (1988). Social capital in the creation of human capital. *American Journal of Sociology*, *94*, 95–120. doi:10.1086/228943

Cook, K. (1982). Network Structures from an Exchange Perspective. In *Social Structure and Network Analysis*. Sage Publications.

Corr, L., & Stagnitto, J. (2012). *Agile Data Warehouse Design*. DecisionOne Press.

Cortada, J. (2012). *The Business of Social Business: What works and how its done*. IBM Institute for Business Value. Retrieved January 28, 2018, from http://www.ibm.com/midmarket/common/att/pdf/IBV_2012_The_business_of_social_business.pdf

Crampton, J., & Khambhammettu, H. (2008). Delegation and satisfiability in workflow systems. *Proc. of the 13th ACM symposium on Access control models and technologies*, 31-40.

Cruz, E. F. (2016). *Derivation of data-driven software models from business process representations* (PhD Thesis). Universidade do Minho, Portugal.

Cruz, E. F., Machado, R. J., & Santos, M. Y. (2014a). From business process models to use case models: A systematic approach. Advances in Enterprise Engineering VIII, 174, 167-181. doi:10.1007/978-3-319-06505-2_12

Cruz, E. F., Machado, R. J., & Santos, M. Y. (2014b). On the decomposition of use cases for the refinement of software requirements. In *Computational Science and Its Applications (ICCSA), 2014 14th International Conference on* (pp. 237-240). IEEE Computer Society. 10.1109/ICCSA.2014.54

Cruz, E. F., Machado, R. J., & Santos, M. Y. (2015a). Bridging the Gap between a Set of Interrelated Business Process Models and Software Models. *Proceedings of the 17th International Conference on Enterprise Information Systems*, 338-345. 10.5220/0005378103380345

Cruz, E. F., Machado, R. J., & Santos, M. Y. (2015b). Deriving a Data Model from a Set of Interrelated Business Process Models. *Proceedings of the 17th International Conference on Enterprise Information Systems*, 49-59. 10.5220/0005366100490059

Cruz, E. F., Machado, R. J., & Santos, M. Y. (2016). Deriving software design models from a set of business processes. *4th International Conference on Model-Driven Engineering and Software Development*, 489-496. 10.5220/0005657204890496

Curland, M., & Halpin, T. (2010). The NORMA Software Tool for ORM 2. In *CAiSE Forum 2010* (pp. 190-204). Berlin: Springer-Verlag.

Dadam, P., & Reichert, M. (2009). The ADEPT project: A decade of research and development for robust and flexible process support. *Computer Science—Research for Development*, 23(2), 81–97.

Dahiya, N., & Parmar, N. (2014). SOA AND REST Synergistic Approach. *International Journal of Computer Science and Information Technologies*, 5(6), 7045–7049.

Daoudi, F., & Nurcan, S. (2007). A benchmarking framework for methods to design flexible business processes. *Software Process Improvement and Practice*, 12(1), 51–63. doi:10.1002pip.304

Dayal, U., Hsu, M., & Ladin, R. (1990). Organizing Long-Running Activities with Triggers and Transactions. *Proceedings of ACM International Conference on Management of Data*, 204-214. 10.1145/93597.98730

De Boer, F. S., Bonsangue, M. M., Groenewegen, L. P. J., Stam, A. W., Stevens, S., & Van Der Torre, L. (2005). Change impact analysis of enterprise architectures. In *Proceedings of the 2005 IEEE International Conference on Information Reuse and Integration, IRI - 2005* (Vol. 2005, pp. 177–181). IEEE. 10.1109/IRI-05.2005.1506470

Delgado, J. (2016). Bridging Services and Resources with Structural Services. *International Journal of Information System Modeling and Design*, 7(4), 83–110. doi:10.4018/IJISMD.2016100105

Deming, W. E. (1986). *Out of the Crisis*. Cambridge, MA: MIT Press.

Deming, W. E. (1993). *The New Economics*. Cambridge, MA: MIT Press.

Deneckere, R., Adrian, I., Elena, K., & Carine, S. (2009). From Method Fragments to Method Services. *CoRR abs/0911.0428*, 80-96.

Deneckere, R., Elena, K., & Bruno, C. (2010). Contextualization of Method Components. *RCIS*, 10, 235–246.

Dennis, A., Wixom, B., & Tegarden, D. (2015). *Systems analysis and design: An object-oriented approach with UML.* John Wiley & Sons.

Dhouib, S., Kchir, S., Stinckwich, S., Ziadi, T., & Ziane, M. (2012). RobotML, a Domain-Specific Language to Design, Simulate and Deploy Robotic Applications. In I. Noda, N. Ando, D. Brugali, & J. J. Kuffner (Eds.), *SIMPAR 2012* (Vol. 7628, pp. 149–160). Heidelberg, Germany: Springer. doi:10.1007/978-3-642-34327-8_16

Di Stefano, G., Piacentino, B., & Ruvolo, G. (2017). Mentalizing in Organizations: A Psychodynamic Model for an Understanding of Well-Being and Suffering in the Work Contexts. *World Futures, 73*(4-5), 216–223. doi:10.1080/026 04027.2017.1333851

Diakopoulos, N., De Choudhury, M., & Naaman, M. (2012, May). Finding and assessing social media information sources in the context of journalism. In *Proceedings of the 2012 ACM annual conference on Human Factors in Computing Systems* (pp. 2451-2460). ACM. 10.1145/2207676.2208409

Dijkman, R. M., & Joosten, S. M. (2002). An algorithm to derive use cases from business processes. In 6th ICSEA (pp. 679–684). Academic Press.

DiMicco, J. (2007). Identity management: multiple presentations of self in facebook. *6th International Conference on Supporting Group Work (GROUP'07),* 1–4. 10.1145/1316624.1316682

DiMicco, J., Millen, D., & Geyer, W. (2008). Motivations for social networking at work. *Conference on Computer Supported Cooperative Work,* 711–720.

Dodge, R., Daly, A., Huyton, J., & Sanders, L. (2012). The challenge of defining wellbeing. *International Journal of Wellbeing, 2*(3), 222–235. doi:10.5502/ijw.v2i3.4

Dorn, J., Grün, C., Werthner, H., & Zapletal, M. (2007). A Survey of B2B Methodologies and Technologies: From Business Models towards Deployment Artifacts. *Proceedings of 40th Hawaii International Conference on Systems Science.*

Drell, L., & Davis, J. (2014). Getting started with social media success metrics. *Marketing Research, 26*(5), 22–27.

Dubuisson, O. (2000). *ASN.1 Communication Between Heterogeneous Systems.* San Diego, CA: Academic Press.

Dumas, M., Aalst, W., & Hofstede, A. (2005). Process-Aware Information Systems. John Wiley & Sons Inc.

Dwyer, P. (2011). Measuring Collective Cognition in Online Collaboration Venues. *International Journal of e-Collaboration, 7*(1), 47–61. doi:10.4018/jec.2011010104

Ellison, N. B., Gibbs, J. L., & Weber, M. S. (2015). The use of enterprise social network sites for knowledge sharing in distributed organizations: The role of organizational affordances. *The American Behavioral Scientist, 59*(1), 103–123. doi:10.1177/0002764214540510

Elshwimy, F., Algergawy, A., Sarhan, A., & Sallam, E. (2014). Aggregation of similarity measures in schema matching based on generalized mean. *Proceedings of the IEEE International Conference on Data Engineering Workshops* (pp. 74-79). Piscataway, NJ: IEEE Computer Society Press. 10.1109/ICDEW.2014.6818306

Erickson, B. H. (2017). Good networks and good jobs: The value of social capital to employers and employees. In *Social capital* (pp. 127–158). Routledge.

Erl, T., Merson, P., & Stoffers, R. (2017). *Service-oriented Architecture: Analysis and Design for Services and Microservices.* Upper Saddle River, NJ: Prentice Hall PTR.

euRobotics aisbl. (2013-2014). *Strategic Research Agenda.* Author.

Fawcett, J., Ayers, D., & Quin, L. (2012). *Beginning XML*. Indianapolis, IN: John Wiley & Sons.

Fedorowicz, J., Laso-Ballesteros, I., & Padilla-Meléndez, A. (2008). Creativity, Innovation, and E-Collaboration. *International Journal of e-Collaboration, 4*(4), 1–10. doi:10.4018/jec.2008100101

Ferreira, M. J., Moreira, F., & Seruca, I. (2015). Social Business: A Way to Promote Organizational Transformation. *International Journal of Information System Modeling and Design, 6*(4), 57-81. Doi:10.4018/IJISMD.2015100104

Ferreira, M. J., Moreira, F., & Seruca, I. (2017). Organizational training within digital transformation: The ToOW model. *19th International Conference on Enterprise Information Systems (ICEIS)*.

Ferreira, M.J., Moreira, F. & Seruca, I. (2014a). A traditional organization towards a new dimension of labour – social business. In *Information systems and Technology for Organizational Agility, Intelligence, and Resilience* (pp. 180-204). Hershey, PA: Information Science Reference (IGI). doi:10.4018/978-1-4666-5970-4.ch009

Ferreira, M. J., Moreira, F., & Seruca, I. (2014b). Social business – a new dimension for education and training in organizations: The ETOW model. *Proceedings Of 16th International Conference on Enterprise Information Systems (ICEIS)*, 420-427.

Ferreira, N., Santos, N., Machado, R. J., & Gasevic, D. (2012). Derivation of process-oriented logical architectures: An elicitation approach for cloud design. In *PROFES'2012*. Berlin: Springer-Verlag. doi:10.1007/978-3-642-31063-8_5

Fielding, R. (2000). *Architectural Styles and the Design of Network-based Software Architectures* (Doctoral dissertation). University of California, Irvine, CA.

Fielding, R. (2008). REST APIs must be hypertext-driven. *Roy Fielding's blog: Untangled*. Retrieved May 2, 2018, from http://roy.gbiv.com/untangled/2008/rest-apis-must-be-hypertext-driven

Fielding, R., Taylor, R., Erenkrantz, J., Gorlick, M., Whitehead, J., Khare, R., & Oreizy, P. (2017). Reflections on the REST architectural style and principled design of the modern web architecture. In *Proceedings of the 2017 11th Joint Meeting on Foundations of Software Engineering* (pp. 4-14). New York, NY: ACM Press. 10.1145/3106237.3121282

Florez, H., Sánchez, M., Villalobos, J., & Vega, G. (2012). Coevolution assistance for enterprise architecture models. *Proceedings of the 6th International Workshop on Models and Evolution - ME '12*, 27–32. 10.1145/2523599.2523605

Fornacciari, P., Mordonini, M., Poggi, A., & Tomaiuolo, M. (2017) Software actors for continuous social media analysis. In *18th Workshop on Objects to Agents, WOA 2017* (pp. 84-89). CEUR.

Foster, I., Kesselman, C., & Tuecke, S. (2001). The anatomy of the grid: Enabling scalable virtual organizations. *International Journal of High Performance Computing Applications, 15*(3), 200–222. doi:10.1177/109434200101500302

Franchi, E., & Poggi, A. (2011). *Multi-agent systems and social networks. Business social networking: Organizational, managerial, and technological dimensions*. Academic Press.

Franchi, E., Poggi, A., & Tomaiuolo, M. (2013). Open social networking for online collaboration. *International Journal of e-Collaboration, 9*(3), 50–68. doi:10.4018/jec.2013070104

Franchi, E., Poggi, A., & Tomaiuolo, M. (2015). Information and Password Attacks on Social Networks: An Argument for Cryptography. *Journal of Information Technology Research, 8*(1), 25–42. doi:10.4018/JITR.2015010103

Franchi, E., Poggi, A., & Tomaiuolo, M. (2016a). Social media for online collaboration in firms and organizations. *International Journal of Information System Modeling and Design, 7*(1), 18–31. doi:10.4018/IJISMD.2016010102

Franchi, E., Poggi, A., & Tomaiuolo, M. (2016b). Blogracy: A peer-to-peer social network. *International Journal of Distributed Systems and Technologies, 7*(2), 37–56. doi:10.4018/IJDST.2016040103

Franconi, E., Mosca, A., & Solomakhin, D. (2012). ORM2: Formalisation and Encoding in OWL2. In OTM 2012 Workshops (pp. 368-378). Heidelberg, Germany: Springer.

Fukuyama, F. (1995). *Trust: The social virtues and the creation of prosperity.* Free Press.

Fulk, J., Heino, R., Flanagin, A. J., Monge, P. R., & Bar, F. (2004). A test of the individual action model for organizational information commons. *Organization Science, 15*(5), 569–585. doi:10.1287/orsc.1040.0081

Gaaloul, K., & Charoy, F. (2009). Task delegation based access control models for workflow systems. In Software Services for e-Business and e-Society (pp. 400-414). Academic Press. doi:10.1007/978-3-642-04280-5_31

Gaál, Z., Szabó, L., & Obermayer-Kovács, N. (2015). The Power of Social Media in Fostering Knowledge Sharing. *Proceedings of the European Conference on Intellectual Capital*, 114-121.

Garson, J. (2006). *Modal Logic for Philosophers.* Cambridge, UK: Cambridge University Press. doi:10.1017/CBO9780511617737

Geetika, R., & Singh, P. (2014). Dynamic coupling metrics for object oriented software systems: A survey. *Software Engineering Notes, 39*(2), 1–8. doi:10.1145/2579281.2579296

Geiger, P., Pryss, R., Schickler, M., & Reichert, M. (2013). *Engineering an Advanced Location-Based Augmented Reality Engine for Mobile devices. Technical Report.* University of Ulm.

Gerace, T., & Cavusoglu, H. (2009). The Critical Elements of Patch Management. *Communications of the ACM, 52*(8), 117–121. doi:10.1145/1536616.1536646

Gerace, T., & Mouton, J. (2004). The Challenges and Successes of Implementing an Enterprise Patch Management Solution. In *Proceedings of the 32nd Annual ACM SIGUCCS Fall Conference* (pp. 30-33). ACM. 10.1145/1027802.1027810

Ghalimi, I. C., & CEO, I. (2006). *BPM 2.0.*

Ghosh, P., Bardhan, M., Chowdhury, N. R., & Phadikar, S. (2017). IDS Using Reinforcement Learning Automata for Preserving Security in Cloud Environment. *International Journal of Information System Modeling and Design, 8*(4), 21–37. doi:10.4018/IJISMD.2017100102

Giorgini, P., Rizzi, S., & Garzetti, M. (2005). Goal-oriented requirement analysis for data warehouse design. In *Proceedings of the 8th ACM international workshop on Data warehousing and OLAP* (pp. 47-56). ACM 10.1145/1097002.1097011

Giorgini, P., Rizzi, S., & Garzetti, M. (2008). GRAnD: A goal-oriented approach to requirement analysis in data warehouses. *Decision Support Systems, 45*(1), 4–21. doi:10.1016/j.dss.2006.12.001

Global Audit Technology Guide (GTAG) 2 Change and Patch Management Controls Critical for Organizational Success. (2012). (2nd ed.). The Institute of Internal Auditors.

Goldschlag, D., Reed, M., & Syverson, P. (1999). Onion routing. *Communications of the ACM, 42*(2), 39–41. doi:10.1145/293411.293443

Golfarelli, M., Maio, D., & Rizzi, S. (1998). Conceptual Design of Data Warehouses from E/R schemes. In *System Sciences, 1998, Proceedings of the Thirty-First Hawaii International Conference on* (Vol. 7, pp. 334-343). IEEE.

Goyal, S. B. (2012). *From Situational to Functional Method Engineering* (PhD Thesis). Banasthali University, Rajastahn, India.

Goyal, S. B., & Prakash, N. (2008). *From Situational to Functional Method Engineering.* Retrieved on March 17, 2012, from sites.upc.edu/~www-pi/ER2008/PhD/papers /ShyamGoyal.pdf

Goyal, S. B., & Prakash, N. (2013). Functional Method Engineering. *IGI-IJISMD, 4*(1), 79-103.

Granovetter, M. S. (1973). The strength of weak ties. *American Journal of Sociology, 78*(6), 1360–1380. doi:10.1086/225469

Graydon, P., Habli, I., Hawkins, R., Kelly, T., & Knight, J. (2012). Arguing Conformance. *IEEE Software, 29*(3), 50–57. doi:10.1109/MS.2012.26

Grosz, G., Rolland, C., Schwer, S., Souveyet, C., Plihon, V., Si-Said, S., ... Griaho, C. (1997). Modelling and Engineering the Requirements Engineering Process: An Overview of the NATURE Approach. *Requir. Eng., 2*(3), 115–131.

Gruschko, B., Kolovos, D., & Paige, R. (2007). Towards synchronizing models with evolving metamodels. In *Proceedings of the International Workshop on Model-Driven Software Evolution* (p. 3). Academic Press.

Guizzardi, G. (2005). *Ontological Foundations for Structured Conceptual Models* (PhD thesis). University of Twente.

Guizzardi, G., Masolo, C., & Borgo, S. (2006). In the Defense of a Trope-Based Ontology for Conceptual Modeling: An Example with the Foundations of Attributes, Weak Entities and Datatypes. In *Proc. 25th Int. Conf. on Conceptual Modeling (ER'2006)* (pp. 112-125). Berlin: Springer-Verlag.

Gulbahar, M. O., & Yildirim, F. (2015). Marketing Efforts Related to Social Media Channels and Mobile Application Usage in Tourism: Case Study in Istanbul. *Procedia - Social and Behavioral Sciences, 195*, 453-462. doi:10.1016/j.sbspro.2015.06.489

Gustas, R., & Gustiene, P. (2012). A Graphical Method for Conceptual Modelling of Business and Software Scenarios. *Proceedings of 11th International Conference on Intelligent Software Methodologies, Tools and Techniques*, 238-253.

Haar, G. (2015). *What Has KLM Learned From 5 Years of Social Media Service?* Retrieved February 03, 2018, from https://blog.klm.com/what-has-klm-learned-from-5-years-of-social-media-service/

Hackmann, G., Haitjema, M., & Gill, C. (2006). Sliver: A BPEL workflow process execution engine for mobile devices. *Proc. ICSOC'06*, 503-508. 10.1007/11948148_47

Hagel, J., Brown, J. S., & Davison, L. (2010). *The Power of Pull: How Small Moves, Smartly Made, Can Set Big Things in Motion*. New York: Basic Books.

Hahn, K., & Schweppe, H. (2009). Exploring transactional service properties for mobile service composition. *Proc. MMS'09*, 39-52.

Halpin, T. (1989). *A Logical Analysis of Information Systems: static aspects of the data-oriented perspective* (Doctoral dissertation). University of Queensland. Retrieved from http://www.orm.net/Halpin_PhDthesis.pdf

Halpin, T. (2005). ORM 2. In *OTM 2005 Workshops* (pp. 676-87). Heidelberg, Germany: Springer.

Halpin, T. (2011). Structural Aspects of Data Modeling Languages. In *BPMDS 2011 and EMMSAD 2011* (pp. 428-442). Berlin: Springer-Verlag. doi:10.1007/978-3-642-21759-3_31

Halpin, T. (2012). Formalization of ORM Revisited. In *OTM 2012 Workshops* (pp. 348-357). Heidelberg, Germany: Springer. doi:10.1007/978-3-642-33618-8_49

Halpin, T. (2013a). Modeling of Reference Schemes. In *BPMDS 2013 and EMMSAD 2013* (pp. 308-323). Berlin: Springer. doi:10.1007/978-3-642-38484-4_22

Halpin, T. (2013b). Ontological Modeling: Part 15. *Business Rules Journal, 14*(2). Retrieved from http://www.BRCommunity.com/a2013/b734.html

Halpin, T. (2017). Logical Data Modeling: Part 10. *Business Rules Journal, 18*(11). Retrieved from http://www.brcommunity.com/a2017/b929.html

Halpin, T., Curland, M., Stirewalt, K., Viswanath, N., McGill, M., & Beck, S. (2010). Mapping ORM to Datalog: An Overview. In OTM 2010 Workshops (pp. 504-513). Heidelberg, Germany: Springer.

Halpin, T. (2007). Fact-Oriented Modeling: Past, Present and Future. In J. Krogstie & ... (Eds.), *Conceptual Modelling in Information Systems Engineering* (pp. 19–38). Berlin: Springer. doi:10.1007/978-3-540-72677-7_2

Halpin, T. (2009). Enriched Conceptualization of Subtyping. In T. Halpin, J. Krogstie, & H. Proper (Eds.), *Innovations in Information Systems Modeling: Methods and Best Practices* (pp. 1–16). Hershey, PA: IGI Global. doi:10.4018/978-1-60566-278-7.ch001

Halpin, T. (2010). Object-Role Modeling: Principles and Benefits. *International Journal of Information System Modeling and Design, 1*(1), 32–54. doi:10.4018/jismd.2010092302

Halpin, T. (2011). Fact-Orientation and Conceptual Logic. In *Proc. 15th International EDOC Conference* (pp. 14-19). Helsinki: IEEE Computer Society.

Halpin, T. (2015a). Modeling of Linguistic Reference Schemes. *International Journal of Information System Modeling and Design, 6*(4), 1–23. doi:10.4018/IJISMD.2015100101

Halpin, T. (2015b). *Object-Role Modeling Fundamentals*. Technics Publications.

Halpin, T. (2016). *Object-Role Modeling Workbook*. Technics Publications.

Halpin, T., & Morgan, T. (2008). *Information Modeling and Relational Databases* (2nd ed.). San Francisco: Morgan Kaufmann.

Halpin, T., & Ritson, R. (1992). Fact-Oriented Modelling and Null Values. In B. Srinivasan & J. Zeleznikov (Eds.), *Research and Practical Issues in Databases*. Singapore: World Scientific.

Halpin, T., & Rugaber, S. (2014). *LogiQL: A Query Language for Smart Databases*. Boca Raton, FL: CRC Press. doi:10.1201/b17711

Harmsen, A. F. (1997). *Situational Method Engineering*, Retrieved March, 17, 2012, http://eprints.eemcs.utwente.nl/17266/01/af_harmsen%5B1%5D.pdf

Harmsen, F., Brinkkemper, S., & Han Oei, J. L. (1994). Situational method engineering for informational system project approaches. *Methods and Associated Tools for the Information Systems Life Cycle. CRIS, 94*, 169–194.

Harmsen, F., Lubbers, I., & Wijers, G. (1995). Success-driven Selection of Fragments for Situational Methods: The S3 model. *Second International Workshop on Requirements Engineering: Foundations of Software Quality (REFSQ'95)*, 104-115.

Harpham, B. (2018). 8 ways you're failing at change management. *CIO*. Retrieved from http://lib-proxy.jsu.edu/login?url=https://search-proquest-com.lib-proxy.jsu.edu/docview/1983884418?accountid=11662

Hayne, S. C., & Smith, C. (2005). The Relationship Between e-Collaboration and Cognition. *International Journal of e-Collaboration, 1*(3), 17–34. doi:10.4018/jec.2005070102

Hendricksen, D. (2014). *12 More Essential Skills for Software Architects*. Upper Saddle River, NJ: Addison-Wesley Professional.

Henning, M. (2008). The rise and fall of CORBA. *Communications of the ACM, 51*(8), 52–57. doi:10.1145/1378704.1378718

Herrmannsdoerfer, M., Benz, S., & Juergens, E. (2009). COPE - automating coupled evolution of metamodels and models. Lecture Notes in Computer Science, 5653, 52–76.

Herrmannsdoerfer, M., Vermolen, S., & Wachsmuth, G. (2011). An extensive catalog of operators for the coupled evolution of metamodels and models. *Software Language Engineering*, 163–182.

Higby, C., & Bailey, M. (2004). Wireless Security Patch Management System. In *Proceedings of the 5th Conference on Information Technology Education* (pp. 165-168). ACM.

Hiriyappa, B. (2008). *Strategic Management for Chartered Accountants*. New Age International Pvt Ltd Publishers.

Hoang, H., & Antoncic, B. (2003). Network-based research in entrepreneurship: A critical review. *Journal of Business Venturing*, *18*(2), 165–187. doi:10.1016/S0883-9026(02)00081-2

Hoef, R., Rob, L. W., Rolf, E., & Vincent, T. (1997). An Environment for Object-oriented Real-time Systems Design. *SEE, 1997*, 23–33.

Holland, P., & Leinhardt, S. (1974). The Statistical Analysis of Local Structure in Social Networks. *National Bureau of Economic Research Working Paper Series, 44*.

Hollingshead, A. B., Fulk, J., & Monge, P. (2002). Fostering intranet knowledge sharing: An integration of transactive memory and public goods approaches. *Distributed Work*, 335-355.

Houghton, L., & Kerr, D. V. (2006). A study into the creation of feral information systems as a response to an ERP implementation within the supply chain of a large government-owned corporation. *International Journal of Internet and Enterprise Management*, *4*(2), 135–147. doi:10.1504/IJIEM.2006.010239

Hussain, T., Mehmood, R., Haq, A., Alnafjan, K., & Alghamdi, A. (2014). Designing framework for the interoperability of C4I systems. In *International Conference on Computational Science and Computational Intelligence* (102–106). Piscataway, NJ: IEEE Computer Society Press. 10.1109/CSCI.2014.102

Iacovelli, A., Carine, S., & Rolland, C. (2008). Method as a Service (MaaS). *RCIS, 2008*, 371–380.

IBM Institute for Business Value. (2011). *From social media to Social CRM*. Retrieved 2012-10-20 from http://public.dhe.ibm.com/common/ssi/ecm/en/gbe03391usen/GBE03391USEN.PDF

IBM Mobile Business Process Management. (2014). Retrieved from http://www.redbooks.ibm.com/abstracts/sg248240.html?Open

IDC. (2018). *Digital Transformation*. Retrieved march 03, 2018, from https://www.idc.com/promo/thirdplatform/fourpillars

Iftikhar, M. U., & Weyns, D. (2014). Activforms: Active formal models for self-adaptation. *Proceedings of International Symposium on Software Engineering for Adaptive and Self-Managing Systems*, 125–134.

Inglés-Romero, J. F., Lotz, A., Vicente-Chicote, C., & Schlegel, C. (2012). Dealing with Run-Time Variability in Service Robotics: Towards a DSL for Non-Functional Properties. *3rd International Workshop on Domain-Specific Languages and models for ROBotic systems (DSLRob-12)*.

Inglés-Romero, J. F., Romero-Garces, A., Vicente-Chicote, C., & Martínez, J. (2017). A Model-Driven Approach to Enable Adaptive QoS, In DDS-Based Middleware. *IEEE Transactions on Emerging Topics in Computational Intelligence.*, *1*(3), 176–187. doi:10.1109/TETCI.2017.2669187

Inmon, B. (2005). *Building the data warehouse* (4th ed.). New York: John Wiley & Sons.

ISACA. (2012a). *COBIT 5: A Business Framework for the Governance and Management of Enterprise IT*. ISACA.

ISACA. (2012b). *COBIT 5: Enabling Processes*. ISACA.

ISACA. (2013). *Configuration Management Using COBIT 5*. ISACA.

Isari, D., Pontiggia, A., & Virili, F. (2011). *Working Together in Organizations Using Social Network Sites: A Laboratory Experiment on Microblog Use for Problem-Solving*. Available at SSRN 1875924.

ISO. (2010). *Systems and software engineering – Vocabulary. In ISO/IEC/IEEE 24765:2010(E) International Standard* (p. 186). Geneva, Switzerland: International Organization for Standardization.

IT Governance Institute. (2007). COBIT 4.1. Author.

Iyengar, S., & Brooks, R. (Eds.). (2016). *Distributed sensor networks: sensor networking and applications*. Boca Raton, FL: CRC Press.

Jacobs, J. (1961). *The death and life of great American cities*. Vintage.

Jalote, P. (2008). *A concise Introduction to Software Engineering*. Springer Science & Business Media. doi:10.1007/978-1-84800-302-6

Janssen, C. (2014). *Social Media Monitoring*. Retrieved February 03, 2018, from http://www.techopedia.com/definition/29592/social-media-monitoring

Jarrahi, M. H., & Sawyer, S. (2013). Social Technologies, Informal Knowledge Practices, and the Enterprise. *Journal of Organizational Computing and Electronic Commerce, 23*(1-2), 110–137. doi:10.1080/10919392.2013.748613

Jones, V. M., van Halteren, A. T., Dokovski, N. T., Koprinkov, G. T., Peuscher, J., Bults, R. G. A., . . . Herzog, R. (2006). *Mobihealth: mobile services for health professionals*. Technical Report TR-CTIT-06-38.

Jones, B. F., Wuchty, S., & Uzzi, B. (2008). Multi-university research teams: Shifting impact, geography, and stratification in science. *Science, 322*(5905), 1259–1262. doi:10.1126cience.1158357 PMID:18845711

Jonkers, H., Band, I., & Quartel, D. (2012). *ArchiSurance Case Study*. The Open Group.

Juric, M., & Weerasiri, D. (2014). *WS-BPEL 2.0 beginner's guide*. Birmingham, UK: Packt Publishing Ltd.

Kaitano, F. (2007). Change Control Audits – A Must for Critical System Functionality. *Internal Auditor*. Retrieved from http://www.theiia.org/intAuditor/itaudit/archives/2007/march/change-control-audits-a-must-for-

Kane, G. C. (2017). The evolutionary implications of social media for organizational knowledge management. *Information and Organization*, 2737–2746. doi:10.1016/j.infoandorg.2017.01.001

Kaplan, A. M., & Haenlein, M. (2010). Users of the world, unite! The challenges and opportunities of social media. *Business Horizons, 53*(1), 59–68. doi:10.1016/j.bushor.2009.09.003

Karlsson, F., & Ågerfalk, P. J. (2004). Method configuration: Adapting to situational characteristics while creating reusable assets. *Information and Software Technology, 46*(9), 619–633. doi:10.1016/j.infsof.2003.12.004

Käster, T., Heßler, A., & Albayrak, S. (2016). Process-oriented modelling, creation, and interpretation of multi-agent systems. *International Journal of Agent-Oriented Software Engineering, 5*(2-3), 108–133. doi:10.1504/IJAOSE.2016.080892

Keet, C. (2007). Prospects for and issues with mapping the Object-Role Modeling language into DLRifd. In *20th Int. Workshop on Description Logics (DL'07)* (pp. 331-338). CEUR-WS.

Kim, P. (2012). *The definition of social business*. Retrieved February 05, 2018, from http://dachisgroup.com/2012/06/the-definition-of-social-business/

Klotzbücher, M., & Bruyninckx, H. (2012). Coordinating Robotic Tasks and Systems with rFSM Statecharts. *Journal of Software Engineering for Robotics, 3*(1).

Kocbek, M., Jost, G., Hericko, M., & Polancic, G. (2015). Business process model and notation: The current state of affairs. *Computer Science and Information Systems, 1*(00), 1–35.

Koetsier, J. (2015). *KLM's 150 social media customer service agents generate $25M in annual revenue*. Retrieved November 05, 2015, from http://venturebeat.com/2015/05/21/klms-150-social-media-customer-service-agents-generate-25m-in-annual-revenue/

Kostoska, M., Gusev, M., & Ristov, S. (2016). An overview of cloud interoperability. In *Federated Conference on Computer Science and Information Systems* (pp. 873-876). Piscataway, NJ: IEEE Computer Society Press. 10.15439/2016F463

Kotter, J. P. (1995). Leading Change: Why Transformation Efforts Fail. *Harvard Business Review On Point*, 60-67.

Krötzsch, M., Simancik, F., & Horrocks, I. (2012). *A Description Logic Primer*. Retrieved from http://arxiv.org/abs/1201.4089

Krupitzer, C., Roth, F. M., VanSyckel, S., Schiele, G. & Becker, C. (2015). A survey on engineering approaches for self-adaptive systems. *Pervasive and Mobile Computing. 17*, 184-206. doi:10.1016/j.pmcj.2014.09.009

Kukreja, R., & Garg, N. (2014). Remote Procedure Call: Limitations and Drawbacks. *International Journal of Research, 1*(10), 914–917.

Kumari, S., & Rath, S. (2015). Performance comparison of SOAP and REST based Web Services for Enterprise Application Integration. In *International Conference on Advances in Computing, Communications and Informatics* (pp. 1656–1660). Piscataway, NJ: IEEE Computer Society Press. 10.1109/ICACCI.2015.7275851

Kunze, C. P. (2005). Demac: A distributed environment for mobility-aware computing. In *Adjunct Proc. of the Third International Conference on Pervasive Computing* (pp. 115-121). Academic Press.

La Rosa, M., van der Aalst, W.M.P., Dumas, M. & Milani, F.P. (2017). Business Process Variability Modeling: A survey. *ACM Computing Surveys, 50*(1), 2:1-2:45. Doi:10.1145/3041957

LanDesk. (2014). Resolving the Top Three Patch Management Challenges. Retrieved from http://info.landesk.com/NA-EN_LANDESKWeb_WhitePapersDynamic.html?wp=resolving-the-top-three-patch-management-challenges-LSI-1192&_ga=1.11167101.898317616.1445994114

Langley, G., Nolan, K. M., & Nolan, T. W. (1994, June). The Foundation of Improvement. *Quality Progress*, 81-86.

Langley, G. J., Moen, R., Nolan, K. M., Nolan, T. W., Norman, C. L., & Provost, L. P. (2009). *The Improvement Guide: A Practical Approach to Enhancing Organizational Performance* (2nd ed.). San Francisco, CA: Jossey-Bass.

Lankhorst, M., Iacob, M. E., Jonkers, H., Van Der Torre, L., Proper, H. A., & Arbab, F. … Janssen, W. P. M. (2013). Enterprise architecture at work: Modelling, communication, and analysis (3rd ed.). Springer-Verlag Berlin Heidelberg.

Lankhorst, M. M. (2004). Enterprise architecture modelling - The issue of integration. *Advanced Engineering Informatics, 18*(4), 205–216. doi:10.1016/j.aei.2005.01.005

Leal, C. A., Mazón, J. N., & Trujillo, J. (2013). A business-oriented approach to data warehouse development. *Ingenieria e Investigacion, 33*(1), 59–65.

Lee, E. (2010). *Disciplined Heterogeneous Modeling*. In MODELS 2010, Oslo, Norway.

Lemmen, K., & Punter, T. (1994). The Approach Model (2): Methodology Engineering with the MADIS framework. Informatie, 36(6), 368-374.

Lenz, R., & Reichert, M. (2007). IT Support for Healthcare Processes -Premises, Challenges, Perspectives. *Data & Knowledge Engineering, 61*(1), 39–58. doi:10.1016/j.datak.2006.04.007

Leshob, A. (2016). Towards a business-pattern approach for UML models derivation from business process models. *13th IEEE International Conference on e-Business Engineering*, 244-249. 10.1109/ICEBE.2016.049

Levy, P. (1999). *Collective Intelligence: Mankind's Emerging World in Cyberspace*. Perseus Books.

Lin, N. (2017). Building a network theory of social capital. In *Social capital* (pp. 3–28). Routledge.

Lipnack, J., & Stamps, J. (2008). *Virtual teams: People working across boundaries with technology*. John Wiley & Sons.

López, L., Behutiye, W., Karhapää, P., Ralyté, J., Franch, X., & Oivo, M. (2017). Agile Quality Requirements Management Best Practices Portfolio: A Situational Method Engineering Approach. *PROFES, 2017*, 548–555.

Lotz, A., Inglés-Romero, J. F., Vicente-Chicote, C., & Schlegel, C. (2013). Managing run-time variability in robotics software by modeling functional and non-functional behavior. In S. Nurcan, H. A. Proper, P. Soffer, J. Krogstie, R. Schmidt, T. Halpin, & I. Bider (Ed.), BPMDS and EMMSAD (pp. 441-455). Springer. doi:10.1007/978-3-642-38484-4_31

Lotz, A., Inglés-Romero, J. F., Vicente-Chicote, C., Stampfer, D., Lutz, M., Vicente-Chicote C., & Schlegel., C. (2014). Towards a Stepwise Variability Management Process for Complex Systems – A Robotics Perspective. *International Journal of Information System Modeling and Design, 5*(3), 55-74.

Lotz, A., Hamann, A., Lange, R., Heinzemann, C., Staschulat, J., Kesel, V., ... Schlegel, C. (2016). Combining Robotics Component-Based Model-Driven Development with a Model-Based Performance Analysis. *Proceedings of IEEE International Conference on Simulation, Modeling, and Programming for Autonomous Robots*. 10.1109/SIMPAR.2016.7862392

Loury, G. C. (1987). Why should we care about group inequality? *Social Philosophy & Policy, 5*(1), 249–271. doi:10.1017/S0265052500001345

Lowry, P. B., & Wilson, D. (2016). Creating agile organizations through IT: The influence of internal IT service perceptions on IT service quality and IT agility. *The Journal of Strategic Information Systems*, 25211–25226. doi:10.1016/j.jsis.2016.05.002

Lubbers, P., Albers, B., & Salim, F. (2010). *Pro HTML5 Programming: Powerful APIs for Richer Internet Application Development*. New York, NY: Apress. doi:10.1007/978-1-4302-2791-5

Lubke, D., Schneider, K., & Weidlich, M. (2008). Visualizing use case sets as BPMN processes. In *Requirements Engineering Visualization* (pp. 21–25). IEEE. doi:10.1109/REV.2008.8

Lutz, M., Verbeek, C., & Schlegel, C. (2016). Towards a Robot Fleet for Intra-Logistic Tasks: Combining Free Robot Navigation with Multi-Robot Coordination at Bottlenecks. *Proceedings of the 21th IEEE International Conference on Emerging Technologies and Factory Automation (ETFA)*. 10.1109/ETFA.2016.7733602

Machado, R., Fernandes, J. a., Monteiro, P., & Rodrigues, H. (2006). Refinement of software architectures by recursive model transformations. In Product-Focused Software Process Improvement (pp. 422-428). Springer Berlin Heidelberg. doi:10.1007/11767718_38

Madan, B. B., Goseva-Popstojanova, K., Vaidyanathan, K., & Trivedi, K. S. (2004). A Method for Modeling and Quantifying the Security Attributes of Intrusion Tolerant Systems. *Performance Evaluation, 56*, 167–186.

Magnani, M. & Montesi, D. (2009). *BPDMN: A conservative extension of BPMN with enhanced data representation capabilities*. arXiv preprintarXiv:0907.1978

Majchrzack, A., Cherbakov, L., & Ives, B. (2009). Harnessing the Power of the Crowds with Corporate Social Networking "How IBM does it". *MIS Quarterly Executive, 8*(2), 103–198.

Malone, T. W., Laubacher, R., & Dellarocas, C. N. (2009). *Harnessing Crowds: Mapping the Genome of Collective Intelligence.* MIT Sloan Research Paper No. 4732-09. Retrieved February 05, 2018, from http://ssrn.com/abstract=1381502

Malone, T. W., & Crowstone, K. (1994). The Interdisciplinary Study of Coordination. *ACM Computing Surveys, 26*(1), 87–119. doi:10.1145/174666.174668

Mangan, P., & Sadiq, S. (2002). *On Building Workflow Models for Flexible Processes. 13th Australasian Database Conference (ADC2002),* Melbourne, Australia.

Mantz, F., Taentzer, G., Lamo, Y., & Wolter, U. (2015). Co-evolving meta-models and their instance models: A formal approach based on graph transformation. *Science of Computer Programming, 104,* 2–43. doi:10.1016/j.scico.2015.01.002

Marinescu, A., Dusparic, I., Taylor, A., Cahill, V., & Clarke, S. (2015, May). P-marl: Prediction-based multi-agent reinforcement learning for non-stationary environments. In *Proceedings of the 2015 International Conference on Autonomous Agents and Multiagent Systems* (pp. 1897-1898). International Foundation for Autonomous Agents and Multiagent Systems.

Martin, A., & van Bavel, R. (2013). *Assessing the Benefits of Social Networks for Organizations.* Retrieved November 06, 2015, from http://ftp.jrc.es/EURdoc/JRC78641.pdf

Martin, D., Wutke, D., & Leymann, F. (2008, September). A novel approach to decentralized workflow enactment. In *Enterprise Distributed Object Computing Conference, 2008. EDOC'08. 12th International IEEE* (pp. 127-136). IEEE. 10.1109/EDOC.2008.22

Maskell, P. (2000). Social capital, innovation, and competitiveness. In *Social capital* (pp. 111–123). Oxford University Press.

Mathiassen, L., Ngwenyama, O., & Aaen, I. (2005, November). Managing Change in Software Process Improvement. *IEEE Software,* 84–91.

Mazón, J. N., Pardillo, J., & Trujillo, J. (2007). A model-driven goal-oriented requirement engineering approach for data warehouses. In *Advances in Conceptual Modeling–Foundations and Applications* (pp. 255–264). Springer Berlin Heidelberg. doi:10.1007/978-3-540-76292-8_31

McAfee, A. (2009). *Enterprise 2.0: New Collaborative Tools for Your Organization's Toughest Challenges.* Harvard Business Review Press.

McAfee, A. (2006). Enterprise 2.0: The Dawn of Emergent Collaboration'. *MIT Sloan Management Review, 47*(3), 21–28.

Mcculloch, A. (2015). *KLM: Putting Social Customer Care First.* Retrieved November 08, 2015, from http://www.socialbakers.com/blog/2374-klm-putting-social-customer-care-first

McKinsey & Company. (2015). *Transforming the business through social tools.* Retrieved February 05, 2018, from http://www.mckinsey.com/insights/high_tech_telecoms_internet/transforming_the_business_through_social_tools

McKinsey & Company. (2016). *How social tools can reshape the organization.* Retrieved from April 05, 2017 from https://www.mckinsey.com/business-functions/digital-mckinsey/our-insights/how-social-tools-can-reshape-the-organization

McKinsey & Company. (2017). *Advanced social technologies and the future of collaboration.* Retrieved April 05, 2017, from https://www.mckinsey.com/business-functions/digital-mckinsey/our-insights/advanced-social-technologies-and-the-future-of-collaboration

McPherson, M., Smith-Lovin, L., & Cook, J. M. (2001). Birds of a Feather: Homophily in Social Networks. *Annual Review of Sociology*, *27*(1), 415–444. doi:10.1146/annurev.soc.27.1.415

Meister, V.G. (2011). Geschäftsregelbasierte Ansteuerung betrieblicher Anwendungssysteme am Beispiel der Open Source Process Engine Activiti. *Betriebliche Anwendungssysteme*, 65.

Melancon, D. (2006). The Three Cs of IT Change Management. *Internal Auditor*. Retrieved from http://www.theiia.org/intAuditor/itaudit/archives/2006/april/the-three-cs-of-it-change-management/

Meyer, A., Smirnov, S., & Weske, M. (2011). *Data in business processes*. Universitatsverlag Potsdam.

Meyer, B. (2000). *Object-Oriented Software Construction*. Upper Saddle River, NJ: Prentice Hall.

Meyer, M. J., & Lambert, J. C. (2007, November). Patch Management: No Longer Just an IT Problem. *The CPA Journal*, 68–72.

Milanovic, M., Gasevic, D., & Rocha, L. (2011). Modeling Flexible Business Processes with Business Rule Patterns. *Distributed Object Computing Conference (EDOC) 15th IEEE International*, 65 – 74. 10.1109/EDOC.2011.25

Millen, D. R., Feinberg, J., Kerr, B., Rogers, O., & Cambridge, S. (2006). *Dogear : Social Bookmarking in the Enterprise*. Academic Press.

Millie, M. K., & Balasubramanian, P. R. (1997). Dynamic Workflow Management: A Framework for Modeling Workflows. In *Proceedings of 13th HICSS*. IEEE.

Monge, P. R., & Contractor, N. (2003). *Theories of communication networks*. Oxford University Press.

Mordonini, M., Poggi, A., & Tomaiuolo, M. (2016). Preserving Privacy in a P2P *Social Network. In International Conference on Smart Objects and Technologies for Social Good* (pp. 203-212). Springer.

Moreira, F., Seruca, I., & Ferreira, M. J. (2015). Towards a Framework for Classification and Adoption of Social Media Monitoring Tools. *Proceedings Of 2nd European Conference Social Media (ECSM 2015)*.

Motahari-Nezhad, H. R., & Swenson, K. D. (2013). *Adaptive Case Management: Overview and Research Challenges*. Conference on Business Informatics, Vienna, Austria.

Motahari-Nezhad, H. R., Spence, S., Bartolini, C., Graupner, S., Bess, C., Hickey, M., ... Rahmouni, M. (2013). Casebook: A cloud-based system of engagement for case management. *IEEE Internet Computing*, *17*(5), 30–38.

Motik, B., Horrocks, I., & Sattler, U. (2009). Bridging the Gap Between OWL and Relational Databases. *Journal of Web Semantics*, *7*(2), 74–89. doi:10.1016/j.websem.2009.02.001

Mowshowitz, A. (1994). Virtual organization: A vision of management in the information age. *The Information Society*, *10*(4), 267–288. doi:10.1080/01972243.1994.9960172

Müller, D., Reichert, M., & Herbst, J. (2006, September). Flexibility of data-driven process structures. In *International Conference on Business Process Management* (pp. 181-192). Berlin, Heidelberg: Springer.

Mundbrod, Kolb, & Reichert. (2012). Towards a System Support of Collaborative Knowledge Work. In *Business Process Management Workshops*. Springer-Verlag.

Murphy, J., Kim, A., Hagood, H., Richards, A., Augustine, C., Kroutil, L., & Sage, A. (2011). Twitter Feeds and Google Search Query Surveillance: Can They Supplement Survey Data Collection? *Shifting the Boundaries of Research*, 228.

Nahapiet, J., & Ghoshal, S. (1998). Social capital, intellectual capital, and the organizational advantage. *Academy of Management Review*, *23*(2), 242–266. doi:10.5465/amr.1998.533225

Nasiri, A., Wrembel, R., & Zimányi, E. (2015) Model-Based Requirements Engineering for Data Warehouses: From Multidimensional Modelling to KPI Monitoring. In *International Conference on Conceptual Modeling* (pp. 198-209). Springer. 10.1007/978-3-319-25747-1_20

Object Management Group. (2016). *Case Management Model and Notation v1.1*. Object Management Group. Retrieved from http://www.omg.org/spec/CMMN/1.1/CMMN

Object Management Group. (2017). *OMG Unified Modeling Language (OMG UML), version 2.5.1*. Retrieved from http://www.omg.org/spec/UML/2.5.1/

Okhravi, H., & Nicol, D. M. (2008). Evaulation of Patch Management Strategies. *International Journal of Computational Intelligence: Theory and Practice, 3*(2), 109–117.

OMG CMMN & the Object Management Group. (2014). *Object Management Group Web site*. Retrieved from http://www.omg.org/spec/CMMN/1.0/PDF/

OMG. (2011). *Business process model and notation (BPMN), version 2.0. Technical report*. Object Management Group.

Panetto, H., & Whitman, L. (2016). Knowledge engineering for enterprise integration, interoperability and networking: Theory and applications. *Data & Knowledge Engineering, 105*, 1–4. doi:10.1016/j.datak.2016.05.001

Park, G., Fellir, F., Hong, J.-E., Garrido, J. L., Noguera, M., & Chung, L. (2017). Deriving use cases from business processes: A goal-oriented transformational approach. *Proceedings of the Symposium on Applied Computing, SAC '17*, 1288–1295. 10.1145/3019612.3019789

Parkhe, A., Wasserman, S., & Ralston, D. A. (2006). New frontiers in network theory development. *Academy of Management Review, 31*(3), 560–568. doi:10.5465/amr.2006.21318917

Parr, T. (2013). *The Definitive ANTLR 4 Reference*. Raleigh, NC: Pragmatic Bookshelf.

Patel-Schneider, P., & Franconi, E. (2012). Ontology Constraints in Incomplete and Complete Data. *Proc. 11th International Semantic Web Conference*. 10.1007/978-3-642-35176-1_28

Paucar, L. H. G., Bencomo, N., & Yuen, K. K. F. (2017). Juggling Preferences in a World of Uncertainty. *IEEE 25th International Requirements Engineering Conference (RE)*, 430-435. 10.1109/RE.2017.12

Paunova, M. (2015). The emergence of individual and collective leadership in task groups: A matter of achievement and ascription. *The Leadership Quarterly, 26*(6), 935–957. doi:10.1016/j.leaqua.2015.10.002

Pautasso, C. (2014). RESTful web services: principles, patterns, emerging technologies. In Web Services Foundations (pp. 31-51). New York, NY: Springer. doi:10.1007/978-1-4614-7518-7_2

Pesic, M., Schonenberg, M. H., Sidorova, N., & van der Aalst, W. M. P. (2007). Constraint-Based Workflow Models: Change Made Easy. In *Proceedings of the OTM Conference on Cooperative Information Systems (CoopIS 2007) (vol. 4803, pp. 77-94)*. Springer-Verlag.

Philips, E., Van Der Straeten, R., & Jonckers, V. (2011). NOW: Orchestrating services in a nomadic network using a dedicated workflow language. *Science of Computer Programming*.

Pierce, R. (2008). Using Customer Input to Drive Change in User Assistance. In *Proceedings of the 26th annual ACM international conference on Design of communication*. ACM. 10.1145/1456536.1456541

Pollock, S. (2016). Change management: It is not a choice. *Talent Management Excellence Essentials*. Retrieved from http://lib-proxy.jsu.edu/login?url=https://search-proquest-com.lib-proxy.jsu.edu/docview/1955087691?accountid=11662

Popplewell, K. (2014). Enterprise interoperability science base structure. In K. Mertins, F. Bénaben, R. Poler, & J. Bour-rières (Eds.), *Enterprise Interoperability VI: Interoperability for Agility, Resilience and Plasticity of Collaborations* (pp. 417–427). Cham, Switzerland: Springer International Publishing. doi:10.1007/978-3-319-04948-9_35

Powell, A., Piccoli, G., & Ives, B. (2004). Virtual Teams: A Review of Current Literature and Directions for Future Research. *The Data Base for Advances in Information Systems*, *35*(1), 7. doi:10.1145/968464.968467

Prakash N. (1996). Domain Based Abstraction for Method Modelling, Ingénierie Des Systèmes d'Information. *AFCET/HERMES, 4*(6), 745-767.

Prakash, D., (2018). Direct Conversion of Early Information to Multi-dimensional model. *ENASE 2018*.

Prakash, N. (2018). Measuring Understandability of Organizational Policies: A Metric Based Approach. *International Journal of Cooperative Information Systems*, *27*(2).

Prakash, N., & Bhatia, M. P. S. (2003). Developing Application-Centric Methods. *CAiSE Short Paper Proceedings*, 225-228.

Prakash, N., Prakash, D., & Sharma, Y. K. (2009). Towards Better Fitting Data Warehouse Systems. In The Practice of Enterprise Modeling (pp. 130-144). Springer Berlin Heidelberg. doi:10.1007/978-3-642-05352-8_11

Prakash, D., & Gupta, D. (2014). Eliciting data warehouse contents for policy enforcement rules. *International Journal of Information System Modeling and Design*, *5*(2), 41–69. doi:10.4018/ijismd.2014040103

Prakash, D., & Prakash, N. (2015, November). Towards DW support for formulating policies. In *IFIP Working Conference on The Practice of Enterprise Modeling* (pp. 374-388). Springer. 10.1007/978-3-319-25897-3_24

Prakash, N. (1994). A process view of methodologies. *CAiSE*, *94*, 339–352.

Prakash, N. (1997). Towards a formal definition of a method. *Requirements Engineering Journal*, *2*(1), 23–50. doi:10.1007/BF02802896

Prakash, N. (2006). On generic method models. *Requir. Engg.*, *11*(4), 221–237.

Prakash, N., & Goyal, S. B. (2007). Towards a Life Cycle for Method Engineering, *Eleventh International Workshop on Exploring Modeling Methods in Systems Analysis and Design (EMMSAD'07)*, 27-36.

Prakash, N., & Goyal, S. B. (2008). Method Architecture for situational method engineering. *RCIS*, *2008*, 325–336.

Prakash, N., Prakash, D., & Gupta, D. (2010, June). Decisions and decision requirements for data warehouse systems. In *Forum at the Conference on Advanced Information Systems Engineering (CAiSE)* (pp. 92-107). Springer.

Prakash, N., Srivastava, M., Gupta, C., & Arora, V. (2007). An Intention Driven Method Engineering Approach. *RCIS*, *2007*, 281–288.

Preidel, C., & Borrmann, A. (2016). Towards code compliance checking on the basis of a visual programming language. *Journal of Information Technology in Construction*, *21*(25), 402–421.

Pryss, R., Reichert, M., Schickler, M., & Bauer, T. (2016). Context-Based Assignment and Execution of Human-centric Mobile Services. In *Mobile Services (MS), 2016 IEEE International Conference on* (pp. 119-126). IEEE. 10.1109/MobServ.2016.12

Pryss, R., Geiger, P., Schickler, M., Schobel, J., & Reichert, M. (2016). Advanced Algorithms for Location-Based Smart Mobile Augmented Reality Applications. *Procedia Computer Science*, *94*, 97–104. doi:10.1016/j.procs.2016.08.017

Pryss, R., Mundbrod, N., Langer, D., & Reichert, M. (2015). Supporting medical ward rounds through mobile task and process management. *Information Systems and e-Business Management*, *13*(1), 107–146. doi:10.100710257-014-0244-5

Pryss, R., Musiol, S., & Reichert, M. (2013). Collaboration Support Through Mobile Processes and Entailment Constraints. *Proc. 9th IEEE Int. Conf. on Collaborative Computing: Networking, Applications and Worksharing*. 10.4108/icst.collaboratecom.2013.254063

Pryss, R., & Reichert, M. (2016). Robust execution of mobile activities in process-aware information systems. *International Journal of Information System Modeling and Design*, *7*(4), 50–82. doi:10.4018/IJISMD.2016100104

Pryss, R., Tiedeken, J., Kreher, U., & Reichert, M. (2010). Towards Flexible Process Support on Mobile Devices. *Proc. CAiSE'10 Forum*, 150–165.

Pryss, R., Tiedeken, J., & Reichert, M. (2010). Managing Processes on Mobile Devices: The MARPLE Approach. *Proc. CAiSE'10 Demos*.

Putnam, R. D. (1995). Bowling alone: America's declining social capital. *Journal of Democracy*, *6*(1), 65–78. doi:10.1353/jod.1995.0002

Ralyté, J., Deneckere, R., & Rolland, C. (2003). Towards a Generic Model for Situational Method Engineering. *CAiSE*, *2003*, 95–110.

Ralyté, J., Rolland, C., & Deneckere, R. (2004). Towards a Meta-tool for Change-Centric Method Engineering: A Typology of Generic Operators. *CAiSE*, *2004*, 202–218.

Reichert, M., & Weber, B. (2013). Process Change Patterns: Recent Research, Use Cases, Research Directions. In Seminal Contributions to Information Systems Engineering - 25 Years of CAiSE (pp. 398–404). Academic Press.

Reichert, M., Bauer, T., & Dadam, P. (2009). *Flexibility for distributed workflows*. Academic Press.

Reichert, M., Dadam, P., Rinderle-Ma, S., Lanz, A., Pryss, R., Predeschly, M., ... Goeser, K. (2009). *Enabling Poka-Yoke workflows with the AristaFlow BPM Suite*. Academic Press.

Reichert, M., & Weber, B. (2012). *Enabling Flexibility in Process-Aware Information Systems: Challenges, Methods, Technologies*. Springer. doi:10.1007/978-3-642-30409-5

Reijers, H. A. (2006). Workflow flexibility: The forlorn promise. In 15th IEEE International Workshops on Enabling Technologies: Infrastructures for Collaborative Enterprises (WETICE 2006) (pp. 271–272). IEEE Computer Society.

Rezaei, R., Chiew, T., & Lee, S. (2014). A review on E-business interoperability frameworks. *Journal of Systems and Software*, *93*, 199–216. doi:10.1016/j.jss.2014.02.004

Rinderle, S., Reichert, M., & Dadam, P. (2004). *On Dealing with Structural Conflicts between Process Type and Instance Changes*. BPM. doi:10.1007/978-3-540-25970-1_18

Ritson, P. (1994). *Use of Conceptual Schemas for Relational Implementation* (Doctoral dissertation). University of Queensland.

Ritter, D., May, N., & Rinderle-Ma, S. (2017). Patterns for emerging application integration scenarios: A survey. *Information Systems*, *67*, 36–57. doi:10.1016/j.is.2017.03.003

Robkin, M., Weininger, S., Preciado, B., & Goldman, J. (2015). Levels of conceptual interoperability model for healthcare framework for safe medical device interoperability. In *Symposium on Product Compliance Engineering* (pp. 1–8). Piscataway, NJ: IEEE Computer Society Press. 10.1109/ISPCE.2015.7138703

RobMoSys Project. (2017-2020). *Composable Models and Software for Robtics Systems, towards an EU Digital Industrial Platform for Robotics*. Available at: http://robmosys.eu/wiki/

Rodríguez, A., Fernández-Medina, E., & Piattini, M. (2007). Towards CIM to PIM transformation: From secure business processes defined in BPMN to use-cases. Business Process Management, 408-415.

Rodríguez, A., Fernández-Medina, E., & Piattini, M. (2008). Towards obtaining analysis-level class and use case diagrams from business process models. In *Advances in Conceptual Modeling Challenges and Opportunities* (Vol. 5232, pp. 103–112). Springer Berlin Heidelberg.

Rolland, C., & Prakash, N. (1994). Guiding the Requirements Engineering Process. *APSEC*, 82-91.

Rolland, C., & Prakash, N. (1996). A proposal for context-specific method engineering. *Proceedings of the IFIP TC8, WG8.1/8.2 Working Conference on Method Engineering*, 191-208.

Romero, D., & Vernadat, F. (2016). Enterprise information systems state of the art: Past, present and future trends. *Computers in Industry, 79*, 3–13. doi:10.1016/j.compind.2016.03.001

Romero-Mujalli, D., Cappelletto, J., Herrera, E., & Tárano, Z. (2017). The effect of social learning in a small population facing environmental change: An agent-based simulation. *Journal of Ethology, 35*(1), 61–73. doi:10.100710164-016-0490-8

RoQME Integrated Technical Project. (2018-2019). *Dealing with non-functional properties through global Robot Quality-of- Service Metrics*. Available at: http://robmosys.eu/roqme/

Roth, S., & Matthes, F. (2014). Visualizing Differences of Enterprise Architecture Models. *International Workshop on Comparison and Versioning of Software Models (CVSM) at Software Engineering (SE)*.

Rouse, M. (2013). *Social media listening*. Retrieved February 05, 2018, from http://searchcrm.techtarget.com/definition/Social-media-monitoring

Rovida, F., Crosby, M., Holz, D., Polydoros, A. S., Großmann, B., Petrick, R. P. A., & Krüger, V. (2017a). SkiROS - A skill-based robot control platform on top of ROS. Robot Operating System (ROS): The Complete Reference (Volume 2). *Studies in Computational Intelligence, 707*, 121–160.

Rovida, F., Grossmann, B., & Krüger, V. (2017b). Extended behavior trees for quick definition of flexible robotic tasks. *Proceedings of 2017 IEEE/RSJ International Conference on Intelligent Robots and Systems (IROS)*, 6793-6800. 10.1109/IROS.2017.8206598

Roy, S. R. (2012). Digital Mastery: The Skills Needed for Effective Virtual Leadership. *International Journal of e-Collaboration, 8*(3), 56–66. doi:10.4018/jec.2012070104

Russell, B. (1905). On Denoting. *Mind, 14*(4), 479–493. doi:10.1093/mind/XIV.4.479

Russell, S., & Norvig, P. (2009). *Artificial Intelligence: A Modern Approach* (3rd ed.). Upper Saddle River, NJ: Prentice Hall Press.

Saeki, M., & Wenyin, K. (1994). Specifying Software Specification & Design Methods. *CAiSE, 1994*, 353–366.

Salinesi, C., & Gam, I. (2006, June). A requirement-driven approach for designing data warehouses. In Requirements Engineering: Foundations for Software Quality (REFSQ'06) (p. 1). Academic Press.

Sambamurthy, V., Bharadwaj, A., & Grover, V. (2003). Shaping Agility through Digital Options: Reconceptualizing the Role of Information Technology in Contemporary Firms. *Management Information Systems Quarterly, 27*(2), 237–263. doi:10.2307/30036530

Sandhu, R. S., Coyne, E. J., Feinstein, H. L., & Youman, C. E. (1996). Role-based access control models. *Computer, 29*(2), 38–47. doi:10.1109/2.485845

Saydjari, O. S. (2006). Is Risk a Good Security Metric? In *Proceedings of the 2nd ACM Workshop On Quality of Protection (QoP'06)* (pp. 59-60). New York, NY: ACM. 10.1145/1179494.1179508

Schaad, A. (2003). *A Framework for Organisational Control Principles* (PhD thesis). The University of York, York, UK.

Scheer, A. W. (1999). *ARIS-Business Process Modeling* (2nd ed.). Berlin: Springer. doi:10.1007/978-3-642-97998-9

Schippers, H. (2009). Towards an Actor-based Concurrent Machine Model. In I. Rogers (Ed.), *Proceedings of the 4th workshop on the Implementation, Compilation, Optimization of Object-Oriented Languages and Programming Systems* (4-9). New York, NY: ACM Press.

Schlegel, C., Lotz, A., Lutz, M., Stampfer, D., Inglés-Romero, J. F., & Vicente-Chicote, C. (2013). Model-Driven Software Systems Engineering in Robotics: Covering the Complete Life-Cycle of a Robot. In Workshop Roboter-Kontrollarchitekturen, Informatik 2013. Springer.

Schmidt, H., & Hauck, F. J. (2007). SAMPROC: middleware for self-adaptive mobile processes in heterogeneous ubiquitous environments. In *Proc. 4th Middleware Doctoral Symposium* (pp. 1-6). Academic Press. 10.1145/1377934.1377935

Schmidt, H., Kapitza, R., & Hauck, F. J. (2007). Mobile-process-based ubiquitous computing platform: a blueprint. In *Proc. 1st Workshop on Middleware-application interaction* (pp. 25-30). Academic Press.

Schmidt, D., & White, J. (2017). *Why don't big companies keep their computer systems up-to-date. The Conversation, September 26.* Vanderbilt University.

Schmiedel, T., & vom Brocke, J. (2015). Business process management: Potentials and challenges of driving innovation. In BPM - Driving Innovation in a Digital World, Management for Professionals (pp. 3-15). Springer International Publishing.

Schobel, J., Pryss, R., Schickler, M., & Reichert, M. (2016). A Lightweight Process Engine for Enabling Advanced Mobile Applications. In *OTM Confederated International Conferences On the Move to Meaningful Internet Systems* (pp. 552-569). Springer International Publishing. 10.1007/978-3-319-48472-3_33

Schobel, J., Schickler, M., Pryss, R., Nienhaus, H., & Reichert, M. (2013). Using Vital Sensors in Mobile Healthcare Business Applications: challenges, Examples, Lessons Learned. In *Proc. 9 Int'l Conference on Web Information Systems and Technologies* (pp. 509–518). Academic Press.

Schobel, J., Pryss, R., Schickler, M., Ruf-Leuschner, M., Elbert, T., & Reichert, M. (2016, June). End-user programming of mobile services: empowering domain experts to implement mobile data collection applications. In *IEEE 5th International Conference on Mobile Services* (pp. 1-8). IEEE. 10.1109/MobServ.2016.11

Schobel, J., Pryss, R., Wipp, W., Schickler, M., & Reichert, M. (2016). A Mobile Service Engine Enabling Complex Data Collection Applications. In *International Conference on Service-Oriented Computing* (pp. 626-633). Springer International Publishing. 10.1007/978-3-319-46295-0_42

Schultz, M. D., Koehler, J. W., Philippe, T. W., & Coronel, R. S. (2015). Managing the Effects of Social Media in Organizations. *SAM Advanced Management Journal, 80*(2), 42-47.

Securities and Exchange Commission (SEC). *SEC Charges Goldman Sachs With Violating Market Access Rule.* Retrieved from http://www.sec.gov/litigation/admin/2015/34-75331.pdf

Sharma, A., Kumar, M., & Agarwal, S. (2015). A Complete Survey on Software Architectural Styles and Patterns. *Procedia Computer Science, 70*, 16–28. doi:10.1016/j.procs.2015.10.019

Sharma, R., & Panigrahi, P. (2015). Developing a roadmap for planning and implementation of interoperability capability in e-government. *Transforming Government: People. Process and Policy, 9*(4), 426–447.

Shostack, A. (2003). Quantifying Patch Management, Secure. *Business Quarterly, 3*(2), 1–4.

ShuiGuang., D., Zhen, Y., ZhaoHui, W., & LiCan, H. (2004). Enhancement of Workflow Flexibility by Composing Activities at Run-time. *Proceedings of the ACM Symposium on Applied Computing, 667-673.*

Sideraworks. (2013). *What Is Social Business?* Retrieved November 11, 2015, from http://www.sideraworks.com/wp-content/uploads/2012/03/WhatIsSocialBusiness_SideraWorks.pdf

Sikos, L. (2017). The Semantic Gap. In *Description Logics in Multimedia Reasoning* (pp. 51–66). Cham, Switzerland: Springer. doi:10.1007/978-3-319-54066-5_3

Silva, A. R. (2015). Model-driven engineering: A survey supported by the unified conceptual model. *Computer Languages, Systems & Structures, 43*(October), 139–155. doi:10.1016/j.cl.2015.06.001

Silverman, R. E. (2011, Oct. 17). Managing & Careers: For Bright Ideas, Ask the Staff --- Companies, Striving to Cut Costs and Encourage Innovation, Seek Suggestions from Rank and File. *Wall Street Journal.* Retrieved from http://search.proquest.com/docview/898496273?accountid=11662

Skeels, M. M., & Grudin, J. (2009). When social networks cross boundaries: A case study of workplace use of Facebook and LinkedIn. In GROUP'09. Sanibel Island, FL: ACM. doi:10.1145/1531674.1531689

Slooten, K., & Brinkkemper, S. (1993). A Method Engineering Approach to Information Systems Development. *Information System Development Process, 30,* 167-186.

Slooten, V. (1995). *Situated Methods for Systems Development* (Dissertation). University of Twente.

Slooten, V., & Hodes, B. 1996). Characterizing IS Development Projects. *Proceedings of the IFIP TC8, WG8.1/8.2 Working Conference on Method Engineering,* 29-44.

Snowdon, R. A., Warboys, B. C., Greenwood, R. M., Holland, C. P., Kawalek, P. J., & Shaw, D. R. (2007). On the architecture and form of flexible process support. *Software Process Improvement and Practice, 12*(1), 21–34. doi:10.1002pip.307

SolarWinds Press Release. (2012). Results Of Patch Compliance Survey Reveal Increased Need For Automated Patch Management Tools. *Security Dark Reading (Online).* Retrieved from http://www.darkreading.com/vulnerability-management/167901026/security/news/240007602/results-of-patch-compliance-survey-reveal-increased-need-for-automated-patch-management-tools.html

Sousa, P., Lima, J., Sampaio, A., & Pereira, C. (2009). An approach for creating and managing enterprise blueprints: A case for IT blueprints. *Lecture Notes in Business Information Processing, 34,* 70–84. doi:10.1007/978-3-642-01915-9_6

Stampfer, D., Lotz, A., Lutz, M., & Schlegel, C. (2016). The SmartMDSD Toolchain: An Integrated MDSD Workflow and Integrated Development Environment (IDE) for Robotics Software. *Journal of Software Engineering for Robotics, 7*(1), 3-19.

Stavrakantonakis, I., Gagiu, A. E., Kasper, H., Toma, I., & Thalhammer, A. (2012). An approach for evaluation of social media monitoring tools. *Common Value Management, 52.*

Steck, A., & Schlegel, C. (2011). Managing execution variants in task coordination by exploiting design-time models at run-time. In *Proceedings of 2011 IEEE/RSJ International Conference on Intelligent Robots and Systems (IROS)* (pp. 2064–2069). IEEE. 10.1109/IROS.2011.6094732

Sterman, J. D. (1989). Modeling managerial behavior: Misperceptions of feedback in a dynamic decision making experiment. *Management Science, 35*(3), 321–339. doi:10.1287/mnsc.35.3.321

Stoddard, M. B. (2005). Process Control System Security Metrics–State of Practice. *I3P Institute for Information Infrastructure Protection Research Report.*

Streitz, N., Prante, T., Röcker, C., Alphen, D. V., Magerkurth, C., Stenzel, R., & Plewe, D. A. (2003). Ambient Displays and Mobile Devices for the Creation of Social Architectural Spaces. *The Kluwer International series on Computer Supported Cooperative Work, 2,* 387-409.

Stürmer, G., Mangler, J., & Schikuta, E. (2009). Building a modular service oriented workflow engine. In *Proc. Service-Oriented Computing and Applications (SOCA), 2009 IEEE International Conference on* (pp. 1-4). IEEE. 10.1109/SOCA.2009.5410270

StuzoGroup. (2013). *Doritos-Become The Doritos Guru.* Retrieved November 08, 2015, from http://www.stuzo.com/case-studies/Stuzo_CaseStudy_Doritos_BecometheDoritosGuru.pdf

Su, C., & Contractor, N. (2011). A multidimensional network approach to studying team members' information seeking from human and digital knowledge sources in consulting firms. *Journal of the American Society for Information Science and Technology, 62*(7), 1257–1275. doi:10.1002/asi.21526

Sungkur, R., & Daiboo, S. (2015). SOREST, A Novel Framework Combining SOAP and REST for Implementing Web Services. In *Proceedings of the Second International Conference on Data Mining, Internet Computing, and Big Data* (pp. 22-34). Red Hook, NY: Curran Associates, Inc.

Sungkur, R., & Daiboo, S. (2016). Combining the Best Features of SOAP and REST for the Implementation of Web Services. *International Journal of Digital Information and Wireless Communications, 6*(1), 21–33. doi:10.17781/P001923

Swede, V., & Vliet, H. (1994). Consistent Development: Results of a First Empirical Study on the Relation Between Project Scenario and Success. *CAiSE, 1994,* 80–93.

Swenson, K. D. (2012). Position: BPMN Is Incompatible with ACM. In Business Process Management Workshops. Springer-Verlag.

Swenson, K. D. (2014). Demo: Cognoscenti Open Source Software for Experimentation on Adaptive Case Management Approaches. *2014 IEEE 18th International Enterprise Distributed Object Computing Conference Workshops and Demonstrations,* 402-405. 10.1109/EDOCW.2014.67

Swenson, K. D. (2010). *Mastering the Unpredictable: How Adaptive Case Management Will Revolutionize the Way That Knowledge Workers Get Things Done.* Tampa, FL: Meghan-Kiffer Press.

Sykes, D., Corapi, D., Magee, J., Kramer, J., & Russoetal, A. (2013). Learning revised models for planning in adaptive systems. *Proceedings of the 2013 International Conference on Software Engineering,* 63-71. 10.1109/ICSE.2013.6606552

Tajudeen, F. P., Jaafar, N. I., & Ainin, S. (2018). Understanding the impact of social media usage among organizations. *Information & Management,* 55308–55321. doi:10.1016/j.im.2017.08.004

Tajvidi, R., & Karami, A. (2017). Full length article: The effect of social media on firm performance. *Computers in Human Behavior.* doi:10.1016/j.chb.2017.09.026

Teigland, R. (2004). Extending richness with reach: Participation and knowledge exchange in electronic networks of practice. In *Knowledge networks: Innovation through communities of practice* (pp. 230–242). IGI Global. doi:10.4018/978-1-59140-200-8.ch019

Thakar, U., Tiwari, A., & Varma, S. (2016). On Composition of SOAP Based and RESTful Services. In *Proceedings of the 6th International Conference on Advanced Computing* (pp. 500-505). Piscataway, NJ: IEEE Computer Society Press. 10.1109/IACC.2016.99

Thalheim, B. (1989). On Semantic Issues Connected with Keys in Relational Databases. *J. Inf. Process. Cybern.*, *1*(2), 11–20.

The Open Group. (2013). *ArchiMate® 2.1 Specification*. Retrieved from http://pubs.opengroup.org/architecture/archimate2-doc/

Tomaiuolo, M. (2013). dDelega: Trust Management for Web Services. *International Journal of Information Security and Privacy*, *7*(3), 53–67. doi:10.4018/jisp.2013070104

Tran, H., Zdun, U., Oberortner, E., Mulo, E., & Dustdar, S. (2012). Compliance in service-oriented architectures: A model-driven and view-based approach. *Information and Software Technology*, *54*(6), 531–552. doi:10.1016/j.infsof.2012.01.001

Tribolet, J., Sousa, P., & Caetano, A. (2014). The Role of Enterprise Governance and Cartography Enterprise Engineering. *Enterprise Modelling and Information Systems Architectures Journal*, *9*(1), 38–49.

Tuysuz, G., Avenoglu, B., & Eren, P. E. (2013, September). A Workflow-Based Mobile Guidance Framework for Managing Personal Activities. In *Next Generation Mobile Apps, Services and Technologies (NGMAST), 2013 Seventh International Conference on* (pp. 13-18). IEEE. 10.1109/NGMAST.2013.12

Uhl, A., & Gollenia, L. (2016). *Digital Enterprise Transformation: A Business-Driven Approach to Leveraging Innovative IT*. Routledge Taylor & Francis Group.

Valente, P., & Sampaio, P. N. M. (2012). Analysis of Interactive Information Systems Using Goals. In Innovative Information Systems Modelling Techniques. InTechOpen. doi:10.5772/36389

Valentin, B. A. (2017). Methods of Assessment and Training of a Company Towards the Enterprise 4.0. *Annals of DAAAM & Proceedings*, *28*, 1065-1073. doi:10.2507/28th.daaam.proceedings.148

Van Belleghem, S. (2012). *The Conversation Company, Boost your Business Through Culture. People & Social Media*. London, UK: Kogan Page.

Van de Ven, A., Delbecq, A., & Koenig, R. (1976). Determinants of coordination modes within organizations. *American Sociological Review*, *41*(2), 322–338. doi:10.2307/2094477

van der Aalst, W. (2015). Business process simulation survival guide. In Handbook on Business Process Management 1, International Handbooks on Information Systems (pp. 337-370). Springer Berlin Heidelberg. doi:10.1007/978-3-642-45100-3_15

van der Aalst, W. M., & Weske, M. (2001, January). The P2P approach to interorganizational workflows. In Advanced Information Systems Engineering (pp. 140-156). Springer Berlin Heidelberg.

Van der Aalst, W. M. P., Pesic, M., & Schonenberg, H. (2009). Declarative workflows: Balancing between flexibility and support. *Computer Science— Research for Development*, *23*(2), 99–113.

Van Oosterhout, M., Waarts, E., & van Hillegersberg, J. (2006). Change factors requiring agility and implications for IT. *European Journal of Information Systems*, *15*(2), 132–145. doi:10.1057/palgrave.ejis.3000601

Vannoy, S. A., & Palvia, P. (2010). The Social Influence Model of Technology Adoption. *Communications of the ACM*, *53*(8), 149–153. doi:10.1145/1743546.1743585

Verborgh, R., Harth, A., Maleshkova, M., Stadtmüller, S., Steiner, T., Taheriyan, M., & Van de Walle, R. (2014). Survey of semantic description of REST APIs. In C. Pautasso, E. Wilde, & R. Alarcon (Eds.), *REST: Advanced Research Topics and Practical Applications* (pp. 69–89). New York, NY: Springer. doi:10.1007/978-1-4614-9299-3_5

Verizon. (2015). *2015 Data Breach Investigations Report*. Retrieved from http://www.verizonenterprise.com/DBIR/2015/

Verjus, H., Cîmpan, S., & Alloui, I. (2012). An Architecture-Centric Approach for Information System Architecture Modeling, Enactement and Evolution. In *Innovative Information Systems Modelling Techniques*. InTechOpen. Doi:10.5772/36808

Vlaar, P. W., van Fenema, P. C., & Tiwari, V. (2008). Cocreating understanding and value in distributed work: How members of onsite and offshore vendor teams give, make, demand, and break sense. *Management Information Systems Quarterly*, *32*(2), 227–255. doi:10.2307/25148839

W3C. (2011). *Turtle – Terse RDF Triple Language*. Retrieved from http://www.w3.org/TeamSubmission/turtle/

W3C. (2012a). *OWL 2 Web Ontology Language: Primer* (2nd ed.). Retrieved from http://www.w3.org/TR/owl2-primer/

W3C. (2012b). *OWL 2 Web Ontology Language: Direct Semantics* (2nd ed.). Retrieved from http://www.w3.org/TR/owl2-direct-semantics/

W3C. (2012c). *OWL 2 Web Ontology Language Manchester Syntax* (2nd ed.). Retrieved from http://www.w3.org/TR/owl2-manchester-syntax/

W3C. (2012d). *OWL 2 Web Ontology Language Structural Specification and Functional-Style Syntax* (2nd ed.). Retrieved from http://www.w3.org/TR/owl2-syntax/

W3C. (2017). *OWL Web Ontology Language Current Status*. Retrieved from https://www.w3.org/standards/techs/owl#w3c_all

Wachsmuth, G. (2007). Metamodel adaptation and model co-adaptation. In *The European Conference on Object-Oriented Programming* (Vol. 4609, pp. 600–624). Academic Press.

Wakholi, P. K., & Chen, W. (2012). *Workflow Partitioning for Offline Distributed Execution on Mobile Devices. Process Aware Mobile Systems. Applied to mobile-phone based data collection*. Academic Press.

Want, R., Schilit, B., & Jenson, S. (2015). Enabling the Internet of Things. *IEEE Computer*, *48*(1), 28–35. doi:10.1109/MC.2015.12

Wasko, M. M., & Faraj, S. (2005). Why should i share? examining social capital and knowledge contribution in electronic networks of practice. *Management Information Systems Quarterly*, *29*(1), 35–57. doi:10.2307/25148667

Wasserman, S., & Faust, K. (1994). *Social network analysis: Methods and applications* (Vol. 8). Cambridge University Press. doi:10.1017/CBO9780511815478

Weeger, A., Wang, X., & Gewald, H. (2016). IT consumerization: BYOD-program acceptance and its impact on employer attractiveness. *Journal of Computer Information Systems*, *56*(1), 1–10. doi:10.1080/08874417.2015.11645795

Weske, M. (2007). *Business Process Management: Concepts, Languages, Architectures*. Springer-Verlag.

Weske, M. (2012). *Business Process Management Concepts, Languages, Architectures*. Springer Science & Business Media.

Wheatley, M., & Frieze, D. (2006). Using emergence to take social innovation to scale. The Berkana Institute.

Williamson, O. E. (1991). Comparative Economic Organization: The Analysis of Discrete Structural Alternatives. *Administrative Science Quarterly*, *36*(2), 219–244. doi:10.2307/2393356

Wintraecken, J. (1990). *The NIAM Information Analysis Method: Theory and Practice*. Deventer: Kluwer. doi:10.1007/978-94-009-0451-4

Wodtke, D., & Weikum, G. (1997). A formal foundation for distributed workflow execution based on state charts. In Database Theory—ICDT'97 (pp. 230-246). Springer Berlin Heidelberg. doi:10.1007/3-540-62222-5_48

Wood, J., & Khan, G. F. (2016). Social business adoption: An empirical analysis. *Business Information Review*, *33*(1), 28–39. doi:10.1177/0266382116631851

Workflow Management Coalition (WFMC). (2014). Retrieved from http://www.wfmc.org/

World Economic Forum. (2015). Deep Shift - Technology Tipping Points and Societal Impact. *Global Agenda Council on the Future of Software & Society*. Retrieved November 13, 2015, from http://www3.weforum.org/docs/WEF_GAC15_Technological_Tipping_Points_report_2015.pdf

Wuchty, S., Jones, B. F., & Uzzi, B. (2007). The increasing dominance of teams in production of knowledge. *Science*, *316*(5827), 1036–1039. doi:10.1126cience.1136099 PMID:17431139

Xavier, F., Jolita, R., Anna, P., Alberto, A., David, A., Jesús, G., ... Alberto Siena, A. S. (2018). A Situational Approach for the Definition and Tailoring of a Data-Driven Software Evolution Method. *CAiSE 2018*, 603-618.

Xtext. (2013). *Development of programming languages and Domain Specific Languages*. Available at: http://www.eclipse.org/Xtext/

Yang, H., Ma, K., Deng, C., Liao, H., Yan, J., & Zhang, J. (2013). Towards conformance testing of choreography based on scenario. In *Proceedings of the International Symposium on Theoretical Aspects of Software Engineering* (pp. 59-62). Piscataway, NJ: IEEE Computer Society Press. 10.1109/TASE.2013.23

Yin, R. (2009). *Case Study Research: Design and Methods*. London, UK: SAGE Publication, Inc.

Yunus, M. (2007). *Creating a World Without Poverty: Social Business and the Future of Capitalism*. New York: PublicAffairs.

Zakić, N., Jovanović, A., & Stamatović, M. (2008). External and Internal Factors Affecting the Product and Business Process Innovation. *Facta Universitatis Series: Economics and Organization*, *5*(1), 17–29.

Zanzig, J. S., Francia, G. A. III, & Francia, X. P. (2014). Internal Control Considerations for Information System Changes and Patches. In H. Rahman & R. de Sousa (Eds.), *Information Systems and Technology for Organizational Agility, Intelligence, and Resilience* (pp. 161–179). Hershey, PA: IGI Global; doi:10.4018/978-1-4666-5970-4.ch008

Zanzig, J. S., Francia, G. A. III, & Francia, X. P. (2015). A Consensus of Thought in Applying Change Management to Information System Environments. *International Journal of Information System Modeling and Design*, *6*(4), 24–41. doi:10.4018/IJISMD.2015100102

Zaplata, S., Dreiling, V., & Lamersdorf, W. (2009). Realizing mobile Web services for dynamic applications. In Proc. I3E'09 (pp. 240-254). Academic Press. doi:10.1007/978-3-642-04280-5_20

Zaplata, S., Hamann, K., Kottke, K., & Lamersdorf, W. (2010). Flexible execution of distributed business processes based on process instance migration. *Journal of Systems Integration*, *1*(3), 3–16.

Zaplata, S., Kottke, K., Meiners, M., & Lamersdorf, W. (2010). Towards run time migration of WS-BPEL processes. *Proc. WESOA'09*.

Zhang, Z., Wu, C., & Cheung, D. (2013). A survey on cloud interoperability: Taxonomies, standards, and practice. *Performance Evaluation Review*, *40*(4), 13–22. doi:10.1145/2479942.2479945

Zhao, F., & Kemp, L. (2012). Integrating Web 2.0-based informal learning with workplace training. *Educational Media International*, *49*(3), 231–245. doi:10.1080/09523987.2012.738015

Zimmermann, O., Tomlinson, M., & Peuser, S. (2012). *Perspectives on Web Services: Applying SOAP, WSDL and UDDI to Real-World Projects*. Berlin: Springer-Verlag.

About the Contributors

António Miguel Rosado da Cruz currently is Adjunct Professor in the Polytechnic Institute of Viana do Castelo, where he teaches since 2005. Previously he worked for 12 years in software industry companies. He is also integrated member of the ARC4DigiT Research Center – Polytechnic Institute of Viana do Castelo, and collaborator in the Software Engineering and Management Group of the ALGORITMI Research Center – University of Minho. He holds a PhD in Informatics Engineering, from the University of Porto in 2011, and is PMP – Project Management Professional certified by PMI since 2014. He has participated in several research projects and published several works in Conference Proceedings and book chapters, and has participated in several international scientific events. He has supervised MSc project works/dissertations in the areas of Computer Science, Informatics Engineering and Information and Communication Technologies.

Maria Estrela Ferreira da Cruz is an Adjunct Professor at the Higher School of Management and Technology, Polytechnic Institute of Viana do Castelo. PhD in Information Systems and Technologies from University of Minho in 2016. Researcher of the ALGORITMI Research Centre, University of Minho in Portugal and ARC4DigiT Research Centre, Polytechnic Institute of Viana do Castelo. She was a Software Engineer for 13 years in the next companies: Nokia, SIEMENS S.A. and Edinfor (Grupo EDP). Her research interests include business process modeling, software design and modeling, data warehousing and data models.

* * *

Nancy Alexopoulou completed her studies in Informatics (BSc and MSc) at University of Athens, Department of Informatics and Telecommunications. Subsequently, she did a Ph.D on Agile Business Process Modeling at the same department. During this period, she started working as a Research Associate and as a lecturer at Harokopio University of Athens, where she did research on modeling languages for Information Systems as well as on Enterprise Architectures. After the completion of her Ph.D, she moved to Austria, where she worked for three years as a Research Associate at Johannes Kepler University in Linz, Department of Communications Engineering, through a Marie Curie fellowship. Her research at Johannes Kepler University focused on Subject-oriented Business Process Modeling as well as on Adaptive Case Management. At the Department of Communications Engineering, she was also responsible for the organization and teaching of courses on Business Process Management. Then, she returned to Harokopio University of Athens, where she has been working as a Research Associate until today.

José C. Delgado is an Associate Professor at the Computer Science and Engineering Department of the Instituto Superior Técnico (University of Lisbon), in Lisbon, Portugal, where he earned the Ph.D. degree in 1988. He lectures courses in the areas of Computer Architecture, Information Technology and Service Management. He has performed several management roles in his faculty, namely Director of the Taguspark campus, near Lisbon, and Coordinator of the B.Sc. and M.Sc. in Computer Science and Engineering at that campus. He has been the coordinator of and researcher in several international research projects. As an author, his publications include one book, 25 book chapters and more than 50 papers in international refereed conferences and journals.

Maria João Ferreira is an Associate Professor and researcher of Information Systems at the Science and Technology Department at the Universidade Portucalense, Portugal. She received a M.Sc. (1993) and a Ph.D. (2003) degree both in Computation from the University of Manchester. Currently, she teaches subjects in the areas of IT in Organizations, Information Systems, Requirements Engineering and Information Systems Development at undergraduate and master level as well as supervises M.Sc. and Ph.D. students. She is both a researcher at REMIT Center, Universidade Portucalense and an invited researcher at Algoritmi Center, Universidade do Minho. Her research includes Information Systems, Digital Transformation in Organizations and ICT in High Education. She is a co-author of several scientific publications with peer-review on national and international conferences, book chapters and journals, and she has been involved in several conferences as a program committee member and organizer committee member and local-chair member and she is an Editorial Board Member of the IJADS and the IJAS.

Paolo Fornacciari obtained a laurea cum laude in Computer Engineering at the University of Parma, in 2015. During his career, he did different tutoring activities on Python and C++. He is currently a PhD student at the Department of Engineering and Architecture of University of Parma. His research activity is focused on Machine Learning Algorithms for Sentiment Analysis Problems.

Xavier P. Francia received his BS in Nuclear and Radiological Engineering from Georgia Tech and his MS in Systems and Software Design with Information Assurance concentration from Jacksonville State University. His professional career is mainly on the design and implementation of security architectures and controls for major power and utility companies in the Southern States and Northern California.

Guillermo A. Francia III received his BS in Mechanical Engineering degree from Mapua Tech. His Ph.D. in Computer Science is from New Mexico Tech. Before joining Jacksonville State University (JSU), he was the chairman of the Computer Science department at Kansas Wesleyan University. Dr. Francia is a recipient of numerous grants. His projects have been funded by prestigious institutions such as the National Science Foundation, Eisenhower Foundation, Department of Education, Department of Defense, and Microsoft Corporation. In 1996, Dr. Francia received one of the five national awards for Innovators in Higher Education from Microsoft Corporation. Dr. Francia served as a Fulbright scholar to Malta in 2007 and a Fulbright Cybersecurity research scholar to the United Kingdom in 2017. Currently, Dr. Francia is the Director of the Center for Information Security and Assurance at JSU.

S. B. Goyal has a special interest in the area of Information Systems Development Methods. His interest lies in ensuring that information/software systems are systematically developed through use of appropriate technological support and are well aligned to the business needs that they address. He has about 16 years experience in the area of Information Systems Development Method and working as a Dean-IT at City University, Malaysia. He is on the editorial board of IJITWE, IJWSC and AIRCC. He is an active member of IEEE Delhi section.

Terry Halpin, BSc, DipEd, BA, MLitStud, PhD, is a data modeling consultant, former professor in computer science and now adjunct research fellow at INTI International University, Malaysia. His industrial experience includes several years in data modeling technology at Asymetrix Corporation, InfoModelers Inc., Visio Corporation, and Microsoft Corporation, and his prior academic experience includes many years on the computer science faculty at The University of Queensland (Australia) and Neumont University (USA). His doctoral thesis formalized Object-Role Modeling (ORM/NIAM), and his current research focuses on conceptual modeling and rule-based technology. He has authored over 200 technical publications and nine books, including Information Modeling and Relational Databases and Object-Role Modeling Fundamentals, and has co-edited nine books on information systems modeling research. He is a member of IFIP WG 8.1 (Information Systems), is an editor or reviewer for several academic journals, is a regular columnist for the Business Rules Journal, and is a recipient of the DAMA International Achievement Award for Education and the IFIP Outstanding Service Award.

Juan F. Inglés-Romero is a researcher at Biometric Vox S.L. (Spain). He received a BSc in Telecommunication Engineering (2009) and a MSc in Information and Communication Technologies (2010) at the Technical University of Cartagena. His research interests focus on the application of design patterns, components and model-driven engineering techniques to develop (self-) adaptive software for different application domains, such as, robotics, middlewares or data visualizations. He is working on a PhD at the University of Extremadura.

Gianfranco Lombardo received a Bachelor's degree in Computer, Electronics, and Telecommunication Engineering in 2014 and a Master's degree in Computer Engineering in 2017, both from the University of Parma. He is currently a PhD student in Information Technologies at the Department of Engineering and Architecture of University of Parma. His research activity is focused on Machine Learning and Data Mining algorithms for the analysis of Big Data.

Alex Lotz is a Research Associate at the Service Robotics Research Center of the Ulm University of Applied Sciences, Germany. He is currently involved in the EU Horizon 2020 project RobMoSys (Composable Models and Software for Robotic Systems) and in the BMWi/PAiCE SeRoNet project (a platform for service robots). His research focus is on applying Model Driven Software Development methods to cope with the ever-increasing software complexity by managing nonfunctional properties in a component-based software development workflow. He has studied Computer Engineering and Information Systems in Ulm where he has received his Master's degree. He has completed his PhD in 2018 with the Technische Universität München (TUM).

Matthias Lutz is a Research Associate at the University of Applied Sciences Ulm, Germany. He is a member of the service robotics research center (www.servicerobotik-ulm.de) and involved in the LogiRob-Project. His research interests are in the area of system integration for service robotics as one of the challenges from laboratory towards real world. He has studied Computer Engineering and Information Systems in Ulm where he has received his Master's degree. He is working on a cooperative PhD with Technische Universit at München (TUM).

Ricardo J. Machado is a full professor of Information Systems Engineering and Technology in the Dept. of Information Systems at the University of Minho (UMinho), School of Engineering. Within the Information Systems Engineering domain, his primary research interests are in modelling and requirements for systems analysis and design and in process and project management life-cycles. He has supervised 50 completed PhD and MSc theses in these areas. He has published over 150 scientific publications and 4 industrial patents, and has acted as coordinator (PI) and senior researcher of over 50 R&D projects. Some of these projects are related to the Digital Transformation of the Society in the Industry 4.0 and Smart Cities contexts and other application domains.

Miguel Mira da Silva is an associate professor of Information Systems at the University of Lisbon, and coordinator of the Digital Transformation group in the INOV research institute. Miguel graduated in 1989 and received his MSc degree in 1993 in electrical and computer engineering from the University of Lisbon, received his PhD in 1997 in computing science from the University of Glasgow, and a "Sloan Fellowship" master in management in 2005 from the London Business School. Miguel has supervised 6 PhD and more than 130 MSc theses and published over 170 research papers in international conferences and journals, as well as four teaching books.

Monica Mordonini is a researcher at the Department of Engineering and Architecture of the University of Parma. She received a Laurea degree in Electronics Engineering in 1994 (defending a thesis on the "Compression of images using massively parallel algorithms") and a Ph.D. in Information Technologies in 1998 (defending a thesis on the "Navigation of autonomous vehicles in partially known environments"), both from the University of Parma. Her research was conducted mainly in the field of Artificial Intelligence and in particular, she has studied techniques of analysis and processing of signals and images, with particular emphasis on computational aspects related to these topics and their applications in the field of the classification of human activity and the assistive domotics. More recently, the research has focused on issues of information and knowledge extraction from complex systems, applications of semantic web, analysis of social networks, sentiment analysis and opinion mining.

Mara Nikolaidou is a Professor in Information Systems at the Department of Informatics and Telematics, Harokopio University of Athens.

Agostino Poggi is full professor of Computer Engineering at the Department of Engineering and Architecture of the University of Parma. His research focuses on agent, Web and object-oriented technologies and their use to develop distributed and complex systems. He is author of more than two hundreds of technical papers in international scientific journals, books and refereed conference proceedings, and his scientific contribution has been recognized through the "System Research Foundation Outstanding Scholarly Contribution Award" in 1988 and through the "Innovation System Award" in 2001. He is currently editor of Software Practice & Experience and in the editorial board of the following scientific journals:: International Journal of Agent-Oriented Software Engineering, International Journal of Hybrid Intelligent Systems, International Journal of Multiagent and Grid Systems and Open Software Engineering Journal.

Deepika Prakash obtained her Ph.D. from Delhi Technological University, Delhi in the area of Data Warehouse Requirements Engineering. She has co-authored a book entitled "Data Warehouse Requirements Engineering - A Decision Based Approach" published by Springer in 2018. She has also authored a number of papers in international journals/conferences. She has a total of about 5 years of experience, which includes two years of experience in industrial R&D, building data marts and in data mart integration. She has also delivered invited lectures at a number of Institutes. Her current research interests include Data Warehouse systems, NoSQL databases and Health Informatics.

Rüdiger Pryss studied at the Universities of Passau, Karlsruhe, and Ulm. He holds a Diploma in Computer Science. After graduating, he worked as a consultant and developer in a software company. Since 2008, he has been a research associate at Ulm University. In 2015, he received a PhD in Computer Science. In his doctoral thesis, Rüdiger Pryss focused on fundamental issues related to mobile process and task support. In particular, he investigated how mobile devices can be integrated with process management technology in a robust and reliable way, e.g., to allow for the autonomous execution of process fragments or single process tasks on mobile devices. Rüdiger Pryss was local organization chair of the BPM'09 and EDOC'14 conferences. Moreover, he is experienced with teaching courses on database management, programming, service-oriented computing, business process management, document management, and mobile application engineering. Currently, he is a senior researcher and lecturer with the Institute of Databases and Information Systems at Ulm University.

Manfred Reichert holds a PhD in Computer Science and a Diploma in Mathematics. Since 2008 he has been appointed as full professor at the University of Ulm, where he is director of the Institute of Databases and Information Systems. Before, he was working as associate professor at the University of Twente in the Netherlands. There, he was also a member of the management board of the Centre for Telematics and Information Technology, which is one of the largest academic ICT research institutes in Europe. Manfred's research interests include business process management (e.g., adaptive and flexible processes, process lifecycle management, data-driven and object-centric processes) and service-oriented computing (e.g., service interoperability, mobile services, service evolution). He has been PC Co-chair of the BPM'08, CoopIS'11, EMISA'13 and EDOC'13 conferences, and General Chair of the BPM'09 and EDOC'14 conferences.

Ioannis Routis is a Ph.D. Candidate at the Department of Informatics and Telematics, Harokopio University of Athens.

Maribel Yasmina Santos is an Associate Professor at the Department of Information Systems and Researcher of the ALGORITMI Research Centre, University of Minho (UMinho), in Portugal. She received the Aggregated title (Habilitation) in Information Systems and Technologies (IST) from UMinho in 2012 and a PhD in Information Systems and Technologies from UMinho in 2001. She was Secretary-General of the Association of Geographic Information Laboratories for Europe (AGILE) from May 2013 to June 2015. Her research interests include business intelligence and analytics, big data, (spatial) data warehousing and mining and (spatio-temporal) data models.

Christian Schlegel is the Technical Lead of the H2020 RobMoSys project and elected coordinator of the euRobotics Topic Group on Software Engineering, System Integration, System Engineering. He is also Co-Founder and Associate Editor of the open access journal JOSER – Journal of Software Engineering for Robotics and Co-Organizer of the series of International Workshop on Domain-Specific Languages and Models for Robotics Systems (DSLRob). Christian Schlegel is the Head of the service robotics research group at Hochschule Ulm, Professor for Real Time Systems and Autonomous Systems in the Computer Science Department of Hochschule Ulm since 2004 and is a co-opted member of the Faculty of Engineering, Computer Science and Psychology of the University of Ulm.

Nuno Silva is a PhD candidate in Information Systems and Computer Engineering at the University of Lisbon and a researcher at the INOV research institute. Nuno graduated in 2012 and received an MSc degree in 2014 in Information Systems and Computer Engineering from the University of Lisbon. His current research interests are focused on Enterprise Architecture and Business Process Management.

Pedro Sousa is an associate professor at the University of Lisbon and Principal Consultant at Link Consulting in the areas of Enterprise Architecture, in Portugal. He has a vast experience in Enterprise Architecture, both in private and public sectors, having worked over one hundred projects in different industries, from financial, health, telcos, retail, and public administration. At University he created several courses in the domain of Enterprise Architecture and Business Processes and has published over one hundred articles in international scientific forums.

Dennis Stampfer is a Research Associate at the Service Robotics Research Center of the Ulm University of Applied Sciences in Germany. His research interests include systematic engineering of software for service robotics by system composition in an ecosystem, applying separation of roles and model-driven software development. He is currently involved in the EU Horizon 2020 project RobMoSys (Composable Models and Software for Robotic Systems) and in the BMWi/PAiCE SeRoNet project (a platform for service robots). Dennis Stampfer is a member of the "Technical Committee on Software Engineering for Robotics and Automation" (IEEE RAS TC-SOFT) and the topic group on "Software Engineering, System Integration, System Engineering". He has studied Computer Engineering and Information Systems in Ulm where he has received his Master's degree. He has completed his PhD in 2018 with the Technische Universität München (TUM).

Michele Tomaiuolo received a M.Eng. in Computer Engineering and a PhD in Information Technologies from the University of Parma. Currently he is an assistant professor at the Department of Engineering and Architecture, University of Parma. He has given lessons on Foundations of Informatics, Object-Oriented Programming, Software Enigineering, Computer Networks, Mobile Code and Security. He participated in various research projects, including the EU funded @lis TechNet, Agentcities, Collaborator, Comma, and the national project Anemone. His current research activity is focused on social media analysis and peer-to-peer social networking, with attention to security and trust management, multi-agent systems, semantic web, rule-based systems, peer-to-peer networks.

Cristina Vicente-Chicote is an associate professor in the Department of Informatics and Telematic System Engineering at the University of Extremadura (Spain), where she belongs to the Quercus Software Engineering Group (QSEG). She received a BSc in Computer Science at the University of Murcia (Spain) in 1997, and a PhD degree (European Mention) at the Technical University of Cartagena (Spain) in 2005. Her current research interests are in the areas of Model-Driven Engineering, Component-Based Software Development, (Self-) Adaptive Systems, and Robotics. She is a member of the Technical Committee on Software Engineering for Robotics and Automation of the IEEE Robotics and Automation Society (IEEE RAS-TCSOFT), and member of the Spanish Research Networks on Model-Driven Engineering and on Software Architectures and Variability. She coordinates the RoQME Integrated Technical Project (2018-2019), funded by the H2020 EU RobMoSys Project.

Jeffrey S. Zanzig is a Professor of Accounting at Jacksonville State University in Jacksonville, Alabama. He holds a Ph.D. in Accounting from The University of Mississippi, a Master of Accounting from the University of Alabama at Birmingham, a Master of Business Administration from Jacksonville State University, and a Master of Science in the area of Computer Systems Software and Design from Jacksonville State University. His professional certifications include: Certified Internal Auditor, Certified Public Accountant, Certified Management Accountant, and Certified in Financial Management. He has authored a number of publications in the areas of information systems, internal auditing, and financial reporting.

Index

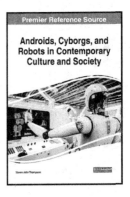

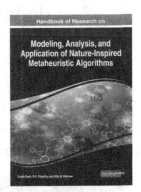

Ensure Quality Research is Introduced to the Academic Community

Become an IGI Global Reviewer for Authored Book Projects

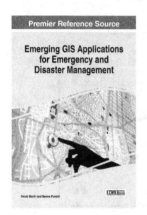
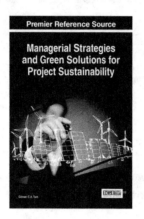

The overall success of an authored book project is dependent on quality and timely reviews.

In this competitive age of scholarly publishing, constructive and timely feedback significantly expedites the turnaround time of manuscripts from submission to acceptance, allowing the publication and discovery of forward-thinking research at a much more expeditious rate. Several IGI Global authored book projects are currently seeking highly qualified experts in the field to fill vacancies on their respective editorial review boards:

Applications may be sent to:
development@igi-global.com

Applicants must have a doctorate (or an equivalent degree) as well as publishing and reviewing experience. Reviewers are asked to write reviews in a timely, collegial, and constructive manner. All reviewers will begin their role on an ad-hoc basis for a period of one year, and upon successful completion of this term can be considered for full editorial review board status, with the potential for a subsequent promotion to Associate Editor.

If you have a colleague that may be interested in this opportunity,
we encourage you to share this information with them.

Printed in the United States
By Bookmasters